WORK AND FAMILY LIFE

LAMBROS COMITAS is Professor of Anthropology and Education, Director of both the Center for Education in Latin America and the Center for Urban Studies and Programs, and Associate Director of the Division of Philosophy and Social Sciences at Teachers College, Columbia University. He is also Associate Director of the Research Institute for the Study of Man, an institution for research and scholarship of the Caribbean. Awarded a Fulbright Graduate Study Grant (1957–58) and a Guggenheim Fellowship (1971–72), Mr. Comitas' field research was done in Barbados, Jamaica, Bolivia, and the Dominican Republic. He has written numerous articles, he serves as consultant or editor for several publishing projects including *Caribbeana 1900–1965: A Topical Bibliography.*

DAVID LOWENTHAL, a geographer and historian, has devoted twenty years to research on the West Indies. He has taught at Vassar College and has been visiting professor at a number of universities in the United States and at the University of the West Indies, where he was Fulbright Research Fellow at the Institute of Social and Economic Research (1956–57). During 1961–62 he worked in the Lesser Antilles with the assistance of a Rockefeller Foundation research grant and later received a Guggenheim Fellowship. Until 1972, he was Secretary and Research Associate at the American Geographical Society, and he is currently Professor of Geography at University College, London. His most recent book is *West Indian Societies,* a comprehensive study of the non-Hispanic Caribbean.

Four books, edited and introduced by Lambros Comitas and David Lowenthal, provide a broad variety of material for the West Indies as a whole; each has the subtitle *West Indian Perspectives:*

SLAVES, FREE MEN, CITIZENS
WORK AND FAMILY LIFE
CONSEQUENCES OF CLASS AND COLOR
THE AFTERMATH OF SOVEREIGNTY

WORK AND FAMILY LIFE

West Indian Perspectives

Edited and Introduced by
Lambros Comitas and David Lowenthal

Anchor Books
Anchor Press/Doubleday
Garden City, New York, 1973

The Anchor Books edition is the first
publication of *Work and Family Life:*
West Indian Perspectives.

Anchor Books edition: 1973

ISBN: 0-385-04365-1
Library of Congress Catalog Card Number 72–84900

Printed in the United States of America

CONTENTS

EDITORS' NOTE

The West Indies, the earliest and one of the most important prizes of Europe's New World and the first to experience the full impact of the black diaspora from Africa, were also the most enduringly colonized territories in the history of the Western Hemisphere. Here more than anywhere else masters and slaves constituted the basic ingredients of the social order; here more than anywhere else class and status were based on distinctions of color and race. Yet out of that past, here more than anywhere else societies with black majorities have emerged as self-governing, multiracial states.

This collection of four volumes—*Slaves, Free Men, Citizens; Work and Family Life; Consequences of Class and Color;* and *The Aftermath of Sovereignty*—chronicles the remarkable story, played out on the doorstep of the North American continent, of transitions from slavery to freedom, from colonialism to self-government, and from self-rejection to prideful identity.

The West Indies face a host of continuing problems—foreign economic domination and population pressure, ethnic stress and black-power revolts, the petty tyranny of local rulers, and an agonizing dependence on expatriate culture. For these very reasons, the West Indies constitute an exceptional setting for the study of complex social relations. The archipelago is a set of mirrors in which the lives of black, brown, and white, of American Indian and East Indian, and of a score of other minorities continually interact. Constrained by local circumstance, these interactions also contain a wealth of possibilities for a kind of creative harmony of which North Americans and Europeans are scarcely yet aware. Consequently, while these volumes deal specifically with the Caribbean in all its aspects, many dimensions of life and many problems West Indians confront have analogues in other regions of the world: most clearly in race relations, economic development, colonial and post-colonial politics and government, and the need to find and express group identity.

It can be argued that the West Indies is a distinctive and unique culture area in that the societies within it display profound similarities: their inhabitants, notwithstanding linguistic barriers and local or parochial loyalties, see themselves as closely linked. These resemblances and recognitions, originally the product of similar economic and social forces based on North European settlement, plantation agriculture, and African slavery, have subsequently been reinforced by a widespread community of interest, along with interregional migration for commerce, employment, marriage, and education. These volumes focus mainly on these underlying uniformities. Within the Caribbean itself, however, one is more conscious of differences than of resemblances. While each Caribbean land is in part a microcosm of the entire archipelago, local conditions–size, resources, social structure, political status–also make it in some significant fashion unique.

The range of these essays is the entire non-Hispanic Caribbean, but most of the material that is not general in character deals with the Commonwealth Caribbean, a preponderant share of this specifically with Jamaica and Trinidad. This reflects neither a bias in favor of these territories nor a belief that they are typical, but rather the fact that most recent scholarly attention has concentrated on, and literary expression has emanated from, the Commonwealth Caribbean. Close understanding of, and expression in, the smaller French and Netherlands Caribbean and larger but less well-known Haiti lie in the future.

In the Caribbean, a real understanding of any problem requires a broad familiarity with all aspects of culture and society. Thus the study of economic development relates intimately to that of family organization, and both of these interlink with aspects of political thought, systems of education, and patterns of speech. Consequently, the subject matter of this collection lies in the domains of history, geography, anthropology, sociology, economics, politics, polemics, and the arts. For example, essays on work and family life by economists and anthropologists are complemented by other studies tracing the historical background and sociological interplay of these with other themes. Throughout these volumes economists and geographers indicate how social structure bears on and is influenced by economy and land use, and linguists, littérateurs, lawyers, and local journalists provide insights on the impact of these patterns in everyday life.

The reader will find here not a complete delineation of the Caribbean realm but rather a sketch in breadth, with fuller discussion of significant themes, given depth and personality by picaresque flavor. He may gain a sense of what West Indians were and are like, how they live, and what problems they confront; he can see how their own view of themselves differs from that of outsiders; he will know where to look for general studies and for more detailed information. And if there is such a thing as a regional personality, this collection may enable him to acquire a sense of it.

What is currently available to most students of Caribbean affairs is woefully inadequate by comparison with most other regions of the world. A few general histories, technical analyses on particular aspects of Caribbean society or culture, and detailed studies of one or two individual territories comprise the holdings of all but the best-equipped libraries. Moreover, no book has yet been published that includes a broad variety of material for the area as a whole, and few studies transcend national or linguistic boundaries. We therefore aim to make available a wide range of literature on the Caribbean that is not readily accessible anywhere else.

Most of this collection is the work of West Indians themselves, for they contribute forty-five of the seventy-two selections. Seventeen of these are by Trinidadians, fifteen by Jamaicans, four by Guyanese, three each by Vincentians and St. Lucians, two by Martiniquans, and one by a Barbadian. Non-West Indian writers contribute twenty-seven selections: fourteen by Americans, ten by British, two by Canadians, and one by a French author. Many of the North American and European contributors either have been permanent residents in the West Indies or have worked there for long periods of time.

Editorial comment has been held to a minimum, but readers will find three levels of guidance. An introduction to each of the four volumes summarizes the general implications of the issues therein surveyed. A paragraph of topical commentary together with a few lines identifying the author introduces each selection. Finally, a selected West Indian reading list appears at the end of each volume, and a general comprehensive bibliography is appended to *The Aftermath of Sovereignty*.

The papers and documents included here have been altered only for minimal editorial consistency and ease of reference. All original titles of articles have been retained, but where none appear or where book chapter headings do not identify the contents of excerpted material, we have added descriptive titles, identified by single asterisks in the text. Series of asterisks also indicate the few instances where material is omitted. When required in such cases, we have completed some footnote references. Otherwise, only obvious typographical and other errors have been corrected. Our own two translations from French sources adhere to the originals as closely as possible, within the limits of comprehensibility.

The editors are grateful to those who have assisted them in this enterprise, both in and out of the Caribbean. We owe special thanks to Marquita Riel and Claire Angela Hendricks, who helped with the original selections and styled the references. Miss Riel also made the original translations from the French. We are indebted to the Research Institute for the Study of Man, and its Director, Dr. Vera Rubin, to the American Geographical Society, and to Teachers College of Columbia University, and notably to their library staffs, for many facilities.

Our main gratitude goes to the contributors represented in these pages and to their original publishers, who have in most cases freely and uncomplainingly made available their work and have helped to correct errors. We are particularly obliged for cooperation from the Institute of Social and Economic Studies and its Director, Alister McIntyre, and to the Department of Extra-Mural Studies, both at the University of the West Indies, under whose auspices a large number of these studies were originally done. We are also obligated to M. G. Smith for encouragement throughout the course of selection and composition.

Lambros Comitas
David Lowenthal
March 1972

Introduction
Work and Family Life

This volume focuses both on West Indian economic life and on domestic organization among the black laboring classes. The first of these themes falls generally within the purview of economics, the second of anthropology and sociology; as subjects of study each has its own distinctive perspectives. Nevertheless, these two aspects of behavior, which together exert more influence in daily life than any other social institutions, are closely and systematically linked. And in the context of slavery and forced labor, of continuing economic exploitation, and of chronic overpopulation, the two related themes take on critical importance for understanding the West Indies.

The first section deals with problems of making a living in an impoverished environment with a sharply disjunctive economic system. One side of this system geared to the mass production of such export commodities as bauxite, oil, and sugar, is dominated by metropolitan markets and by heavily capitalized, technologically advanced multinational corporations. The other side, producing for subsistence and for local markets, depends on small farmers and artisans working with rudimentary tools and limited capital, with expectably low yields and small profits. This dualism exacerbates the chronic instability of a region which has a surplus of available manpower but is woefully short of arable land, energy supplies, and other natural resources.

Macroeconomic analysis of the Caribbean has made rapid headway since the onset of self-government in much of the region. West Indian economists, often combining academic inquiry with governmental assignments, have assessed the socioeconomic effects of out-migration, weighed the benefits and costs of industrialization and tourism, debated the consequences of regional and hemispheric economic cooperation, and drafted national development plans. A growing literature details the influence of multinational corporations exploiting bauxite in Guyana and Jamaica, oil in Trinidad and the Netherlands Antilles, and sugar throughout the Caribbean. All these powerful foreign-owned enterprises contribute substantially to local government revenues, but the bulk of their profits is siphoned off to Europe and North America.

The internal economy of the West Indian folk, the other face of the dual production system, is less well understood. Plantations, oil refineries, alumina processing plants, and tourist hotels provide jobs for only a small fraction of the local working force. Most West Indians still have to wrest their living from the land or from occupations closely tied to "peasant" agriculture. Unpaid family help, work partners, and other cooperative arrangements must satisfy the labor needs of most small farmers growing essential food staples on scattered, economically marginal lands. Small surpluses are sold in local markets by women vendors. Limited farm earnings are frequently supplemented by fishing, masonry, carpentry, and wage labor. The folk economy operates on deep-rooted understandings of reciprocal obligations more than on classic market economy principles and remains poorly integrated with the more conspicuous export sector. And for most rural people, life remains hard. The majority of those who move to towns and cities swell the ranks of the unemployed; relatively few manage to migrate abroad.

The "peasant" sector of West Indian life has largely been studied by anthropologists, geographers, sociologists, and a few agricultural economists. "Making a Living," the first section of this volume, is primarily concerned with the social and cultural parameters of rural economic life. A vivid account of a higgler's weekly round is followed by an assessment of the relationship of small farming to

Jamaican agriculture as a whole. Next comes an exploration in depth of the factors impinging on small farming in a hill community; then an inquiry into allegations of labor shortage in rural Jamaica, in the context of the differences between the cooperative labor patterns of the peasant and the "rational" labor requirements of commercial farmers.

The next two selections deal with labor organization and conditions on sugar estates: one is a description of work arrangements on small estates in Barbados, the other an account of cane reaping, labor recruitment, and social factors affecting labor supply and productivity on large Jamaican plantations. Then comes an article on multiple occupation patterns found among the rural poor; a description of how the urban poor eke out a livelihood in Kingston, Jamaica's capital; and a detailed critique of the local impact of massive emigration to the United Kingdom. The final selection presents a comprehensive overview of Caribbean economies, with special emphasis on those distinctive characteristics that differentiate the West Indies from other countries in the developing world.

The second section of the volume, "Interpretations of Domestic Organization," focuses on mating, marriage, household, and family among African descendants in the West Indies. References to slave domestic patterns date back to the earliest plantation settlements, and European chroniclers and travelers characteristically dwelt on the bizarre and exotic in the life of the transplanted African slave. The systematic study of family and household organization in the Caribbean and elsewhere has generated valuable insights bearing on mating and on domestic grouping. Among other matters, these are of major consequence for policy and legislation in the United States and Great Britain, where black patterns of mating and cohabitation are subjects of public concern and controversy. Much of the debate has been singularly uninformed and ethnocentric. Some observers, for example, view the high illegitimacy rates of Afro-Americans, the brittle and serial nature of their conjugal unions, and the reported matrifocal emphasis of many of their households as aberrant deviations from normative standards and "pathological" in their community and personality impacts. Most scholars, on the other hand, now consider these traits—which are by no means confined to ethnic minorities—functional adaptations to a hostile social environment.

Modern inquiry into West Indian family forms, the primary concern of the selections presented here, stems from a preoccupation with the origins of black folkways. Afro-American studies by Melville Herskovits, in particular, sought to link ancestral West African culture traits with patterns found among a majority of present-day West Indians. But while this approach launched the systematic study of domestic life in the region, its methodology and hypotheses were called into serious question, and alternative historical explanations were propounded and explored. Some scholars argued that slavery had had an overwhelming impact on domestic organization; others held that the plantation system *qua* system was the primary determinant; and still others maintained that the roots of present-day Caribbean domestic forms lay in medieval European society.

Interest in origins and historical roots gave way to synchronic and comparative research after World War II, owing to emergent local concern with welfare and development and to increased sophistication in the social sciences. The functional links between domestic patterns and other aspects of culture and society became a major focus of attention. This perspective generated typologies of mating and family organization, analyses of variations in domestic forms, and studies relating household and family types to socioeconomic status and to the nature of the social order. The dominant thrust in these efforts was generated by British social anthropology, with its stress on structure, function, and institutional relationships.

The past forty years have given rise to a diversified corpus of data on Caribbean domestic organization. But this body of research suffers at least one serious deficiency: the concentration on the black, rural majority entails almost complete neglect of the domestic patterns of the influential urban middle and upper classes. A better balance of future research should reveal a fuller picture of West Indian domestic organization in its complex totality.

The second section opens with an influential essay by Melville Herskovits, who sets forth a program of proposed Afro-American research. Herskovits' scientific approach is critically examined and evaluated in the next selection. The following five articles provide specific case material on domestic organization and disclose the major perspectives on the origins and context of West Indian family forms. The first, by the Herskovitses, describes marriage and family among rural Trinidadian blacks and posits the continuity of these patterns from a West African source. A Trinidadian clergyman and social scientist then emphasizes the impact of slavery on contemporary domestic patterns. This hypothesis is reinforced in the next selection, by a Jamaican sociologist who finds precedents in the slave system for contemporary domestic groupings; in addition, he offers a typology of family forms, based on variations in cohabitation. The following essay, by a Jamaican civil servant turned anthropologist, argues that the diversity of cohabitation and household patterns in rural Jamaican communities primarily reflects socioeconomic factors. The penultimate selection deals with variations in household structure as they develop over the course of a lifetime; the author, an English anthropologist, postulates a developmental cycle for Guyanese Negro households and shows how this cycle fits into the larger social system. Finally, an essay by a leading West Indian scholar summarizes the various positions social scientists have taken on West Indian domestic forms and provides the reader with a thorough critical review of the topic.

I MAKING A LIVING

1.

Problems of making a living are paramount in the lives of most black West Indians. Adverse environmental and social circumstances—high population densities, preponderance of monocultivation for export, insufficient land for subsistence, and a dearth of industrial opportunity—severely limit the economic prospects of many West Indians, men and women alike, who find making a living a harsh daily struggle. Necessity requires most country women to work, some in the cane fields, others in their kitchen gardens or on small subsistence plots, and still others in domestic and other employment in towns and urban centers. Many thousands are involved in petty trading, typically for small returns. The daily routine of one type of petty trader, a Jamaican higgler on her weekly round from countryside to city and back, is detailed here by an American. This description would fit almost any territory in the Caribbean with only minor modifications.

MARGARET FISHER KATZIN received a doctorate in anthropology from Northwestern University, where she later served as lecturer. She has also been associated with the Research Center for Economic Development and Cultural Change at the University of Chicago.

The Jamaican Country Higgler[1]

Margaret Fisher Katzin

Jamaica is primarily an agricultural country in which a large part of the population lives by the cultivation of small, relatively inaccessible farms. Because the economy is not self-sufficient, each household must have cash to buy necessities that are imported, such as food, clothing, tools and household articles. Most farms grow crops that enter into all three levels of the distribution system—subsistence, internal exchange and export. The larger cash payments for the rural household come from the sale of crops for export, but for small recurrent necessities each household depends on cash income derived from the local sale of produce. To ensure subsistence and some surplus for sale against the hazards of weather, plant disease and a glut of one crop, most farmers diversify their planting by putting in small plots of several short-term crops in addition to those for export.

It is customary for a woman of the household to take the goods produced for local sale to market and sell it. However, this practice is followed regularly only by

From *Social and Economic Studies,* Vol. 8, No. 4, December 1959, pp. 421–40. Reprinted with permission of the author and the Institute of Social and Economic Research, University of the West Indies.

[1] This paper is a part of the writer's doctoral dissertation, entitled "Higglers of Jamaica," for which data were collected during a nine-month field study in the fall of 1956 and the spring of 1957. Many persons in Jamaica, in addition to a number of higglers, gave valuable assistance to the writer, particularly Dr. H. D. Huggins, Dr. M. G. Smith, Mr. Russell LeWars, and Mr. W. D. Burrowes. Dr. Sidney Mintz, of Yale University, also made helpful suggestions.

women of the comparatively few households that have sufficient land under cultivation to produce enough goods each week to justify the cost of the market trip.[2] *Most rural women go to urban centres only on rare occasions to sell farm produce and make household purchases. The majority of small farms have goods for sale in the internal market only in very small quantities such as a few bunches of carrots, escallion, beets or a few hundred grapefruit or oranges. It would not be economic to undertake a trip to market to sell the small quantities of produce that can be harvested at any one time, yet the goods must be sold when they are ready and the households are always in need of cash to buy imported necessities.*

The link between the isolated, small farmer and the market is the country higgler,[3] *usually a woman of the neighbourhood or a nearby area, who walks and buys produce to take to the market. Some country higglers spread their goods in the markets and sell directly to house buyers, and others sell to town higglers, town residents who rent stalls in the markets where they buy at wholesale and sell at retail. The following is an account of the weekly routine of a typical country higgler of Jamaica.*

The eastern sky showed only faint traces of light when Miss A rose from her bed in her tiny, three-room cottage in an upland valley in Eastern St. Andrew. Without disturbing her sleeping husband, she put on a denim dress

[2] These women are not middlemen, since they sell only produce that is grown by their own household personnel. They are distinguished from higglers in this paper by being designated as "country people".

[3] According to Webster, to "higgle" means "to hawk or peddle provisions" and a higgler is "one who higgles". Yet, while logically the trade should be called "higgling", the term "higglering" is preferable for both ethnographic and contextual reasons. As concerns the first, there is the fact that it is used by Jamaicans; and from the second point of view, most English-speaking readers interpret "higgle" as a synonym for "haggle", which means something other than the carrying on of a particular trade.

and heavy men's work shoes. She pulled on an old blue sweater against the morning chill and crossed the yard to the mud and wattle shed that was her kitchen. She piled a few twigs under the crossed iron pieces on the fireplace and struck a match to light a fire. As it began to burn, she added a few lengths of small branches. With a battered enamel cup, she dipped some water from a kerosene tin into the *yabba*[4] teapot and set the pot over the fire.

As her sixteen-year-old daughter came into the kitchen, Miss A said: "Lillie, feed the chickens! Dem is off the roost." But Lillie was already filling a tin can with feed to put in the chicken trough. Another daughter, thirteen-year-old Mamie, was sweeping the hard, dirt surface of the yard.

By the time "tea"[5] of boiled green bananas and coffee was ready, Miss A's husband appeared and went to the crude bench in the yard where an enamel wash bowl stood beside a large water pitcher. He washed his face in the cold water and returned to the house to sit beside a small table. Lillie took a plate of green bananas, a slice of bread and a cup of coffee to her father, who ate alone at the table. Miss A took her tea standing in the kitchen while the girls ate sitting in the yard.

When they were finished, Mr. X, who was too old and ill to work hard, took his hoe from the shed next to the kitchen and went out of the yard to work in the field behind the house. Mamie washed the dishes in cold water at the bench in the yard while Miss A and Lillie filled two washtubs with soiled clothes. They went down the path toward the river in single file, Miss A in the lead, each with a filled washtub on her head. Since this was the usual weekly washing, they would be finished and back at the yard soon after twelve o'clock.[6]

[4] *Yabba* is a crude type of earthenware made locally in Jamaica.

[5] Breakfast is called "tea". Preparing breakfast is termed "boiling tea".

[6] Laundry of a few small pieces is done in the yard. The weekly household washing is done in the nearest running stream, and the big laundry of all the large household articles —bedspreads, blankets, curtains—is done communally in a river

While banana and yam peelings boiled in a pot on the fire, Mamie put an empty, sixteen-quart kerosene tin on her head and went down the narrow, tortuous path a quarter of a mile to the spring. She filled the can with drinking water at the spot where a stream flowed from between the rocks and carried the full can back to the kitchen on her head. After the boiled peelings had cooled, she poured the mixture in the trough behind the shed for the pig and goat. The dog and cat were fed the remains of the breakfast.

Mamie made the beds and then changed from her rough work clothes to fresh, clean school clothes. She put on a while cotton blouse, a dark skirt and polished oxfords, took her school books and called to her father that she was leaving the yard. She went down to the road to walk the three miles to the district elementary school.

Miss A and Lillie washed the clothes, towels, and sheets in tubs filled from the running river and spread them to dry. By the time they were finished, nearly all of the pieces that they had spread in the sun earlier had dried. They rested for a short time, sitting in the shade of a tree, before they gathered everything in the tubs and returned to the yard. Lillie put the laundry down in a basket for ironing while Miss A fried some fritters of salt-fish and flour in coconut oil for their lunch. Mr. X came in from the field to eat his lunch and then returned to his work.

Before she left the kitchen, Miss A started the soup for dinner by putting some dried "gungo peas"[7] in a pot with escallion and some slices of yam. Lillie washed the dishes and helped her mother clean the house. Soon after two o'clock Lillie changed from her work clothes into a clean, white blouse, skirt and neat oxfords. She took her school books from a shelf and started down the path to the school.

Lillie had finished primary school and had passed the

---

as a social occasion as a prelude to the two most important holidays, Easter and Christmas.

[7] "Gungo peas" are a lima-bean-like vegetable that grows on bushes in the St. Andrew hills. The proper name is Congo beans.

first Jamaica Local Examination, but she had failed the second examination the previous June and was then "taking lessons" after school hours with one of the elementary teachers to prepare for the third examination. Four days each week, from Monday to Thursday, she and three other girls went to the school for the special instruction, for which each girl's family paid tuition because free education ends in Jamaica at fifteen years of age. If Lillie passed the third examination, she could teach in a primary school or get a job in Kingston as a salesgirl or a clerk in an office. Without it she could only stay and help her mother or work as a domestic servant or a higgler.

After Lillie had gone, Miss A added some carrots and Irish potatoes to the simmering soup and then busied herself nearby where she could stir it often. She parched some coffee beans that had been drying in the sun since they had been picked a few days before. Soon Mamie returned from school, changed from her school clothes and went for drinking water.

Mr. X came in from the field soon after four o'clock and Miss A served everyone a plate of the gungo soup, leaving some in the pot for Lillie. After the dishes were washed, Miss A washed her face and hands and sat down beside Mamie in the "hall"[8] to mend one of her work dresses while Mamie did her homework. Lillie came home just before dark, took her dinner and then brought a lighted kerosene lamp into the hall where she, too, sat down to study. Mr. X had walked down the road to the shop[9] after dinner, but soon after dark he returned and everyone went to bed.

Tuesday's routine was very like Monday's, except that Miss A and Lillie went to the field near the house in the

[8] In Jamaican farmers' houses that are larger than one room, the room on which the front door opens is usually furnished with a table, chairs, a china cabinet with glass doors and, often, a bed. Guests are received in this room which is called the "hall".

[9] A shop is a small store selling household necessities, primarily foods, that is owned and operated by a resident of the district, almost always a person of African descent.

morning to weed "red peas"[10] and in the afternoon they ironed the clothes that had been washed on the previous day. The clothes were ironed on a board by the alternate use of four tiny irons that were heated over red hot charcoal.

On Wednesday, Miss A left her yard at dawn to buy "load".[11] She wore a heavy denim "bib"[12] over her dress, a sweater, a headtie and heavy men's work shoes. On her head she carried her two-bushel market basket with a water bottle and some biscuits. She was easy in her mind about the home, for she had assigned each of her daughters her tasks for the day and had given instructions about the meals. Mr. X always worked near the yard when she was away.

That Wednesday, as on every other Wednesday, Miss A took the rough, precipitous path that led upwards from her yard. She climbed for two hours before she came to the gate of her first supplier.[13] She called out; and an immediate response revealed that she was expected. Her supplier came to the gate to say that some carrots, beets and escallion were ready to be taken from the field and that Miss A might accompany her while she did the reaping.[14] They chatted while the supplier selected and reaped the vegetables. Miss A always kept her suppliers informed about the latest news in her own neighbourhood and in Kingston. Their discussion of the price of the vegetables was short because all were selling at the usual prices, since there had been no abnormal conditions to alter demand or supply for some time. After examining each of the three bunches of carrots, two of beets and three of

[10] Jamaica's "red peas" are known as red kidney beans in the United States.

[11] The goods a higgler takes to market are termed her "load".

[12] A bib is a coverall apron worn by higglers. Its most conspicuous feature is two deep pockets that extend from the waist almost to the hem, designed to foil pickpockets.

[13] A higgler refers to her suppliers as her "customers".

[14] To guard against spoilage, farmers do not take the vegetables from the ground until the higgler is at the gate. On occasion higglers help with the reaping to save time, but some farmers do not allow any one else to take their crops from the ground.

escallion to see that they were all in good condition, Miss A paid 1/- for each bundle of carrots and beets and 2/- for each bundle of escallion. The other said that she expected to have about the same quantity to sell the following week and Miss A packed the vegetables in her basket, said good-bye and went on up the trail.

Although each of her suppliers expected her, it was noon before Miss A had bought from four of them because the yards were far apart on the rough path and reaping consumed time. Her progress was slow because she stopped at the yard of everyone who had ever sold to her, even though she knew that some of them had nothing to offer at the moment, for she wanted to remind them that she would buy from them whenever they did have anything. Along the way she stopped to greet and chat with everyone she met.[15]

By noon her basket was getting heavy for she had bought 19 bundles of carrots, 2 of beets and 11 of escallion and, as was her custom, she stopped for a rest and to eat at the yard of a distant relative where she was always welcome. Miss A took out her water bottle and biscuits, but her hostess offered her a cup of soup as she always did. They sat, eating and talking for nearly an hour, the two exchanging gossip. Miss A gave the news from Kingston and Mavis Bank and the other contributed an account of neighbourhood happenings. After a time, Miss A filled her water bottle, took her leave and went off down the path to continue buying.

By four o'clock she had made several more stops and had gone on to a nearby community where she had four more suppliers: her basket was heavy as she began the long trip home. Until a month before, it had been easier for her because she had had a mule to carry the load, but the beast had died. Long years of climbing the steep trails with heavy loads had made Miss A's muscles as firm and bulging as those of an athlete, but she had foreseen that

[15] Jamaican canons of politeness dictate that a person greet everyone he meets. But, in the case of a higgler, this is not merely etiquette or idle chatter, for the size of her load is likely to be directly correlated with her reputation for friendliness, helpfulness and reliability.

her load would be too heavy for her to carry alone and had arranged with Lillie and Mamie to meet her. From her farthest point to the automobile road[16] was a two-hour walk and her yard was three miles farther down the road. Not long after she left there she met the girls, each of whom took part of her load.

They reached their yard as night was falling and stored the load in the shed for the night. From six different suppliers Miss A had bought 19 bundles of carrots, 12 of escallion, 5 of beets and 5 of turnips, for a total outlay of £2.11.9.

On Thursday morning, Miss A again left her yard at daybreak to buy load, but this time she went in another direction where the rest of her regular suppliers lived. The road was so difficult and the customers' yards so far apart that she did not return until six o'clock, though only three customers had anything to sell to her. They did not argue about price, but all initially asked for threepence more for each bundle. However, Miss A assured them of what they already knew, that she could pay only the usual price because the prices she could expect to get at the market would yield only her recognized margin, and all agreed to the regular price.

The Thursday buying trip would not have been justified by the small load that she was able to buy, except that these suppliers, being at a higher altitude than those from whom she bought on Wednesday, grew thyme, a commodity that was nearly always in short supply in the market. On that trip she bought 10 bundles of escallion at 2/- per bundle and 30 of thyme at 1/- per bundle, for a total outlay of £2.10.0.

Along the automobile road, Miss A saw many country people and country higglers waiting at the truck stops to take the truck into town. At every stop, women were taking their loads from mules and packing them into market baskets and bailings.[17] Each woman, who had

[16] Rural Jamaicans refer to precipitous paths hacked out of steep hillsides as roads. They distinguish paths from roads passable for vehicles by terming the latter "drivin' roads".

[17] Squares of gunny of varying sizes, called "bailin's" or

brought her load down packed in panniers slung from the back of a mule, had been accompanied by at least one member of her household, who helped her prepare her load for the truck and then took the beast back.

At one stop near a shop, country people were selling vegetables to higglers of the neighbourhood. They were regular suppliers of the local country higglers who brought their loads down to the road to save the higgler the trip to the hills. Only a few country higglers were among those who had come down from the hills, the remainder being country people. Among the scores of women was an occasional man, more than likely substituting for a woman who had no other woman in her household to replace her.

Since it was Miss A's custom not to go to market until Friday, she continued on to her yard, where she found that Mamie and Lillie had prepared for market the vegetables that she had bought the day before. They had taken them down to the river, untied the bundles, washed them clean and retied them in bundles of almost exactly equal weight.

On Friday Miss A worked about the house and prepared for the market trip by washing and ironing the clothes which she intended to wear and carefully packing the entire load for the truck. Neighbours came with messages and packages for her to deliver to relatives and friends in town. Some asked her to make purchases for them.

Miss A regularly goes to the market on the truck that leaves her gate at about eight o'clock on Friday evenings. A few country people go to Kingston on the daily trip from Monday through Wednesday, but most of them sell at retail and do not like the crowding and confusion on the truck and in the market on the big market days of Friday and Saturday. The truck makes three trips on Thursdays and Fridays and two on Saturdays. Most higglers and country people go on Thursdays, but the truck is almost as crowded on Friday. Few people take the truck to town on Saturdays, but the return trips are crowded

---

"load sheets", are used by higglers to hold vegetables on the market trip.

with passengers who went down on Thursday and Friday. The particular day chosen by a higgler depends on her home situation, her personal preferences and the kind of town higgler and retail customer contacts that she has in town.

The containers used by higglers are a large round basket with a small opening at the top, usually called a market basket; bailings and crocus bags made of gunny. Produce, easily crushed, such as mangoes, grapefruit or oranges, is packed in the basket; yams and cabbage in crocus bags and root vegetables in bailings. Carrots and escallion are laid in the bailing with the bunches alternating, so that the tops of one bunch are next to the roots of the next to prevent them from rubbing against each other. ("Me lay dem head to tail.") *Then the bailing is drawn together by the corners and tied very tightly to prevent movement and crushing in transit.*

Every woman carries her own water bottle and a small stool to sit on while she sells. All take precautions about money because of the constant fear of being robbed. They tie a small cloth bag to the shoulder strap of an undergarment and keep the bag always hidden at the breast. Cloves of garlic, small limes, small dry onions and grains of guinea pepper or corn are put in the bag and in the pockets of the bib as a charm against thieves or people who can "draw" money.[18] *Women who can afford to do so take an older child with them to help guard the load, run errands and help with the selling. Those who cannot afford the extra passenger fare stay near friends during the*

[18] Higglers believe that some persons have the power to draw money from their pockets magically; the power may be conferred by obeah or by a lodestone. The thief contrives to get a coin of his own, which he has previously treated with a magical potion, into the pocket of his victim. He does so by asking the victim to give him change for a 2/- piece or by buying something for a few pennies and giving the victim a 2/- piece in payment. Once his treated coin is among the victim's money, the magical power works to draw all of the victim's money into the pocket of the thief. The belief is so widespread that most higglers look askance at any 2/- piece and nearly all refuse to give change to a stranger. This last is also a defence against counterfeit money.

trip and all co-operate with each other in guarding the loads.

Even though the truck driver is required to keep a precise schedule, he rarely is exactly on time at any stop. The drivers admit that they always tell their passengers that they expect to leave at least an hour before they actually intend to do so because Jamaicans are notoriously lax about time. To be certain of catching the truck, those at a distance from the road leave their homes well ahead of time and always arrive early. Those near the road pack their loads, take them down to the road and then go about their preparations in the yard until they hear the truck. In the hills there is so little motor traffic and it is so quiet that everyone hears and can identify all the vehicles that regularly use the road. Since the mountain road is full of curves, the direct distance is much less than the road distance.

Thus Miss A, standing in her own yard, had plenty of time to get down to the road after she heard the truck leave the last stop before her gate, because the road runs next to her yard. The rest of the family was there to see Miss A and Mamie off when the driver climbed down to set the charge for her load. He lifted the bailing slightly with one hand to gauge the weight, then asked Miss A about the contents. *The passenger fare is fixed by a government agency, the Transport Board, but the driver sets the charge for the load. Weight and bulk are important factors in the charge, but not the determining ones because drivers charge more for goods of small bulk and greater value, such as red peas. As a result, country higglers and country people try to hide these items from the driver, but they are seldom able to do so because the drivers are adept at finding them. There is a customary charge for each market basket, hand basket, crocus bag and bailing of a certain size.*

When the driver told Miss A the charge for her load, she protested mildly, but soon agreed to it because it was very near his usual charge for a load of that size. After the driver had written the amount of the charge beside her name in a small book, the sidemen lifted the load to the truck while Miss A and Mamie climbed over the wheel and the stakes to find a seat on the boards placed across the body of the back of the truck. The boards were less than four inches wide and little more than six inches apart, so that each row of passengers sat almost in the laps of the row behind. Miss A always tried to find a seat at the side where she could hold onto the side and minimize the effect of the jolting and bouncing. She was usually successful because she boarded the truck near the beginning of its run.

There was a long stop at Church Corner where many country people from the farm communities atop the foothills waited with their loads. At Mavis Bank, the largest community in the area, so many country higglers came aboard that almost an hour had elapsed before the driver had set the charges for all of their loads and the sidemen had put them in the truck. Miss A was not idle during the long waits, but inquired for news of the state of the market in town and of the prices of vegetables. As was usually the case, the prices in the market for the crops of the area were the principal subject of conversation among the crowds. Since farmers and higglers, in addition to drivers and sidemen, had been coming and going on every trip since the previous day, the prices being brought by local produce were known in the home district within a few hours.

The truck finally left Mavis Bank at ten o'clock and made no further stops to take on passengers. As the night was dry and clear with little wind, the passengers sat in the open all the way. *In case of rain or high winds, a tarpaulin is stretched over the back of the truck. It gives some protection, but not enough to keep the passengers from getting wet and cold. Each truck is assigned a maximum load limit of freight and passengers, but few, if any drivers adhere to it all the time. At peak seasons they remove the boards and force the passengers to stand during the whole trip. Passengers could report the driver to the transport authorities, but they prefer to avoid antagonizing him, since he sets the charge for their loads. When the truck is very crowded, arguments are likely to develop because one passenger may be thrown hard against another, or one person might crush the basket of another. At times the arguments develop into fights that put the entire truck into such an uproar that the driver is compelled to stop and calm the passengers. Often he can restore peace only by taking one of the disputants to ride in the cab with him for the remainder of the trip.*

When good weather and little crowding prevailed, as on this trip, the sidemen, riding at the tailgate, led the passengers in singing familiar songs. Often, as the truck rounded curves in the mountain road, the rear of the body hung in space, giving the passengers a breathtaking view of the drops along-side in the bright moonlight. Most of the passengers rode with complete confidence; some slept all the way to the market because there had been no fatal accidents on that hazardous road in the twenty-five years since it had been built. The truck drivers knew the road well and the drivers of all other vehicles knew the schedules of the trucks and avoided meeting them at curves.

Near the bottom of the mountain road the truck went through Gordon Town without stopping, for other trucks and taxis provided transportation from that point to town. A few miles farther on, the driver pulled up for a short stop at Papine Corner. No passengers boarded or left the truck, but it was immediately surrounded by friends or relatives of the passengers who had come to receive or deliver messages or packages. Miss A's eldest daughter, who was attending secondary school in Kingston and boarding at Papine, met her mother, chatted with her and received a basket of produce. Miss A regularly paid a part of her daughter's boarding charge with food.

The first unloading stop was made at Cross Roads Market, which is in the middle of the largest outlying centre of business and population. Most of those who left the truck at Cross Roads were country people, but some were country higglers who had been selling at that market for many years and had a clientèle on whom they could rely to take most of their loads. They preferred to sell there rather than at Coronation, the largest market in

Jamaica located in downtown Kingston, because Cross Roads is a peaceful, quiet market where violence need not be so much feared. The market is much smaller than Coronation and well supervised; most of the customers are middle-class housewives or their maids.

A short while later, the truck drove through the business section of Kingston and into the front compound of Coronation Market, where all of the passengers disembarked and waited beside the truck for the sidemen to toss down the loads. Miss A was met by her regular cart man and two of her weekend town higgler customers, who gave her news of prices.

The cart man put Miss A's load on his cart and, with her walking beside him, pushed it to the first assessing clerk, who wrote the amount of the fee on a slip of paper which he gave to her. She handed the slip, together with the amount of money written on it, through a window to a cashier sitting at a cash register, and received a cash register receipt in exchange. The boy then pushed the load through the gate where another assessing clerk asked about the contents, checked the amount on the receipt and waved them through.[19]

As she walked toward her stall, Miss A looked for indications of scarcity or glut in her lines, such as the quantities on display and the number of potential buyers waiting for her.[20] Ten higglers, an average number, greeted her with requests for carrots, escallion and thyme, and she knew that the usual prices that had prevailed for some weeks were still in effect. She decided to ask 1/6 per bundle of carrots, beets and thyme and 2/6 per bundle of escallion, which would yield her a gross profit of sixpence per bundle, to meet her expenses and pay for her time. She had hoped for a sixpence rise in at least one

[19] The double check of the market fee is designed to prevent collusion between a higgler and any particular clerk.

[20] Wholesale country higglers, who are accompanied by a helper, often leave the load with the helper to see it through the entrance gate and themselves go at once into the market to walk through the sections where their type of goods is being sold to check on the prices before they begin to sell.

of her lines, but she was relieved to find that she would get her usual margin.

As soon as her load was put down, Miss A was surrounded by town higglers, all talking at once and all trying to grab at her load. She calmly and deliberately opened the bailing and took out two bunches of carrots, while she told Mamie to go and tell two other higglers that she had arrived. The higglers surrounded her, pressing in upon her, calling out requests for goods, calling her by name, all the while trying to snatch a bundle of vegetables. Miss A kept her load behind her with one hand holding the top tightly closed as she began to deal with the higglers. She gave her full attention to the one nearest her. She handed the town higgler the bundles that she had asked for, telling her the price. The town higgler protested, saying that she could not pay it because the retail price was too low, but Miss A stood firm, keeping her attention riveted on the one higgler with whom she was dealing until she either agreed to the price or returned the carrots. She dealt with each one individually, while she guarded her load against the constant attacks on it by the other assembled higglers. Ignoring their constant shouts and jostling, she spoke only to the one with whom she was treating.[21]

Miss A handled the difficult situation masterfully, but, though her regular customers knew that she was not an easy mark, they still tried their usual technique. A higgler in a red dress bought one bundle of thyme for 1/6 and wanted to buy another, but argued about the price of the second bundle. "No, it's not worth 1/6! It too small!" and she handed Miss A one shilling. Miss A said: "No! Not *one* shilling–one and six!" Miss A held the two shil-

[21] Unless a country higgler has mastered the technique of selling her load while guarding it, she will be robbed by the town higglers. Their technique is to descend on her in a pushing, shouting group. All of them grab bundles from her load at the same time and either go away without paying or insist that they have already paid her in the confusion. One may have paid her, but five more will insist that each of them was the one who paid, or one may pay for a single bundle when she has actually taken several.

lings and the sixpence in her hand while the argument was going on. Another higgler, seeing that Miss A's attention was diverted, reached into the load and took a bunch of thyme. When Miss A asked her for the money, she insisted that she had already paid. Miss A showed her the money in her hand, saying that the girl in the red dress had given it to her and she had not put any in her pocket. The other insisted loudly that she had already paid her and either she had put the money in her pocket or it was still in her hand. Miss A was certain that she had not put any money in her pocket, so she turned to the girl in the red dress to ask the amount that she had paid. The girl in the red dress took offense and screamed her story of paying Miss A in detail four times over to all the higglers within reach. Miss A became agitated and tried to pin them both down but each only repeated her original story.

Miss A resigned herself and, after getting the additional sixpence from the first higgler, she let them both go with the thyme, knowing that she had been cheated. She reasoned aloud: "I don't know that girl (the one in the red dress) for a tief. That's the second time that woman from Chiggerfoot[22] do that to me. When you lose your character for a shilling, that bad!" She resolved to avoid such losses in the future by concluding each transaction before she looked at anyone else and taking out only enough of her goods to complete that one transaction. As she sold to each of the higglers in turn, they agreed upon the price, but she only took the money from those whom she did not know well, did not trust or who sold in other markets. All the rest took the goods on credit with the understanding that payment would be made by ten o'clock Saturday morning. As each higgler walked away with goods taken on credit, Miss A checked the quantity and then called out to Mamie: "Remember, Miss Addie take three bundles carrot and five bundles thyme!" No written record was kept.

Within an hour after she had arrived at her place, Miss

[22] "Chiggerfoot" is the nickname for a nearby market whose official name is Queen's Market.

A's load was sold except for a few bundles that she had kept for regular customers who would come in later. As soon as the town higglers were all gone, she sent Mamie for a broom to sweep the floor around the stall and carefully packed her bailing, the crocus bag and her remaining goods in the big market basket. Another higgler approached and asked for thyme. "It's finished." The higgler complained: "You sold me last week, why not today?" Miss A replied: "Why you not come before? It finished."

As the town higgler walked away a country higgler from St. Thomas approached and asked Miss A to sell her load for her because she could not manage the town higglers, but Miss A declined. She explained: "I don't want the higglers vex with me. They will tief her, but I can't help her."

Although it was then only one o'clock, Miss A had nothing more to do until time to collect her money, so she and Mamie looked around for a bench or chair. Miss A sat down on a bench on which a heavy, barefooted woman was stretched asleep. The sleeping woman, who was a friend of hers, roused herself and seeing that it was Miss A made no objection. A woman approached asking Miss A to change a two-shilling piece, but she replied: "I don't get any money as yet."[23]

Wholesale trading continued all through the night, but soon after five o'clock the pace of activity quickened and the noise became a continuous loud roar. Miss A and Mamie awakened and sat up when the woman arrived who occupied the stall that Miss A used as a selling place. To make room for the pots and pans filled with coffee and cooked food that the stall holder had brought, Miss A removed her basket to the storage space under the stall of another town higgler.

It became apparent that the higglers for whom she had saved two bundles of carrots were not coming, so Miss A asked Mamie to break up the bundles and retie them into three-penny bunches and take them to the main centre aisle to sell to retail buyers. Mamie obeyed her mother,

[23] As stated above, this is a defence against counterfeit money or magical practices.

but did so reluctantly because the town higglers in "King Street"[24] resented such competition and might complain to the market police. She could be arrested because walking about and selling is a breach of the market regulations, but at her mother's urgent insistence, she kept at it until all the carrots were sold. In open violation of the regulations men and women in a steady stream walked through the aisles selling all kinds of novelties, rope, brassières, undershirts, home-cooked foods and soft drinks.

During the morning while Miss A and Mamie waited, higglers and friends living in town stopped to visit and exchange news about mutual acquaintances. A daughter of one of Miss A's neighbours came to collect vegetables that her mother had sent by Miss A. A granddaughter of another gave Miss A a message to take to her relatives in the country. Miss A's half sister, who lived in town and sold citrus on the street, came to visit. During all this time, Miss A kept a sharp lookout for market boors, keeping her right hand deep in the long pocket where she kept her money. She almost never took her eyes from her basket and its contents; when she was forced to leave to speak to someone, to buy something or to go to the toilet, she called to Mamie and told her to keep watch until her return.

Around eight o'clock she left Mamie watching the basket while she went to buy yams to take back to the country and to buy coconuts from the higgler who allowed her to store her basket under the stall. At ten o'clock she sent Mamie to collect from the town higglers to whom she had given credit and, upon Mamie's return, Miss A counted the money. Mamie reported that one of the higglers was a sixpence short and had said that she could not pay the entire amount. Immediately, Miss A went to that higgler's place and told her, in a friendly manner, that she had to have her money. The higgler showed her the vegetables still at her stall and said that she did not believe that she could get her price for them. Miss A assured her that she would because it was still early and asked again for

[24] The main centre aisle of the market is called "King Street" after the principal thoroughfare of downtown Kingston.

the sixpence. The town higgler still demurred, so after a few minutes of bargaining, Miss A accepted a three-pence and they parted with a smile.[25]

Miss A returned to her place to find awaiting her the cart man, who had changed his dirty khaki clothes for a clean white sport shirt and dark slacks. When he trucked Miss A's load he had agreed to wait for his fee until she had sold her load. He asked for two shillings, but Miss A insisted that the fee was only 1/6,[26] and took her market entry ticket from her pocket to show him. When he saw that the amount was indeed 1/6, he accepted payment and walked away. Then Miss A and Mamie took leave of their friends and left the market for the first time since their arrival the evening before. They carried their baskets to a Chinese-owned grocery store on Heywood Street near the truck stop, where they put them down. Mamie was left to guard them while Miss A went to the counter to buy her groceries for the week. The store, sidewalks and lanes were thronged with country people buying and waiting for trucks. Miss A bought sugar, flour, rice, cornmeal, salt mackerel, salt codfish, condensed milk, Ovaltine, coconut oil, bread, butter and cheese. She also purchased groceries for neighbours. Since school was in session she bought supplies for the school kitchen as a favour to the head teacher.

Returning to Mamie, Miss A sent her around the corner to a bakery on Orange Street where she had heard bread was selling for a penny under the usual price, but Mamie soon returned, saying: "The bread is finished." Mamie again guarded the baskets while Miss A went to the dry goods stores along the lane to look for dress material for one of her suppliers. She compared the material from several stores with the sample that she had brought before

[25] In such cases, Miss A does not believe that it is in her interest to insist upon the agreed price, if she is convinced that the town higgler genuinely believes that she will not be able to get a price that will yield the usual margin. Miss A is willing to cut her own margin a little to keep the town higgler as a customer.

[26] Many cart men have adopted the practice of charging higglers the same price that is assessed by the market clerks.

she found just the right thing at the right price. She rejected a print with large, red flowers, saying: "Him a big, ripe woman. It wouldn't suit him."

Miss A and Mamie did not go to the section of Kingston where one finds the government buildings, better stores, banks and hotels, but remained in the crowded slum area surrounding the markets. There all the lanes and streets are lined with shops, stores and pushcarts catering to poor city dwellers and country people. On rare occasions a country woman went to King Street to buy a needed book or to clear a package from overseas at the custom office. Most country women feel very uncomfortable in the main business area because they know that they are recognizable as country people by their clothes and manners. Miss A's eldest daughter, who was much more sophisticated than the rest of the family, always did any family errands in that part of the city.

While Mamie guarded the baskets, country higglers passed on their way into a small side room of the grocery store, which the proprietor reserved for storage of market clothes and groceries for his customers. All the women who went in were higglers who knew their way about the city or had friends living in town. After their market and buying transactions were completed, they changed into dress clothes and went off to enjoy the sights and entertainments. Some country women spent the night with friends or relatives living in town, if their loads were sold early or if they had a safe place to leave them. However, the vast majority of country women, like Miss A, were afraid to leave the comparative safety of the market where they were surrounded by friends and acquaintances. No country women or country higglers were encountered who would be willing to pay for a night's lodging; they preferred to sleep in the market to save the money. Hardly any of them would venture on the streets at night unless accompanied by trusted friends. They express their fear of thieves: "Dem would lick you down."

While they waited for the truck Miss A and Mamie, like the rest of the crowd about them, visited with friends and relatives who were also in town from other country districts. Everyone knew where to find everyone else. If one came to the truck stop to find that the particular person she wanted was absent, she could always find someone else who knew where the one she sought had gone and when she would return. Messages were taken and delivered with remarkable efficiency.

In order to be certain of the seat she preferred, Miss A, together with other regular passengers, tried to meet the truck when it arrived at the loading station, even though that was usually more than an hour before departure time. Boarding it as soon as it arrived, they sat patiently in the hot sun for more than an hour until all the passengers were aboard and the truck finally left for the country at three o'clock. Miss A had more freedom in this respect than most of the women because she could put her baskets on with Mamie to guard them and hold her place.

At a particular spot just outside the city, the driver stopped the truck to collect fares[27] for both the trip down and the return. His regular riders made the trip to market on credit because they left their homes with only enough cash to pay the market gate fee. Collection time, as always, was a tense moment because some passengers always argued about the charges, while others did not have enough money to pay. One woman had spent all of her money; another had had bad luck in selling; still another disputed the charges because her load had been damaged and she insisted that the driver should pay for it. Another pleaded that her money had been stolen.

The driver was unsympathetic, looking upon all arguments as invented excuses to deprive him of his just due. To the higgler who disputed the amount of the charge, he showed the entry in his notebook to which she had agreed when she boarded the truck, and insisted upon payment of the full amount. To the one who cried: "Me load mash!" he listened not at all, and she finally paid him. The one who had said that her money had been stolen took out the proper amount and paid him when she saw that he

[27] If the driver does not trust a passenger or is not certain that she will ride back on his truck, he goes or sends a sideman to her place in the market to collect his fee.

would not relent. He refused to reduce the price for the one who pleaded "bad market" because he knew that goods were selling at the usual prices. He told the woman who had spent all of her money that he would keep her basket with her town purchases at his yard until she came with the money, and refused to modify his stand even when she told him that her family would have nothing to eat if he kept her basket.[28]

After a short stop at Papine Corner where, again, a small knot of people spoke to passengers, the truck began to climb. At each of the stops, friends and family members were waiting to greet the returning higglers and help them carry their purchases home. Each stop was a happy scene of conviviality. Most stops were near rum shops where those who waited could have a drink with friends and possibly a game of dominoes. Farmers from the neighbourhood swelled the groups, even though they were not meeting anyone, to hear all the gossip and news about conditions and prices in city markets.

When Miss A climbed down from the truck at her own gate she was greeted by her family and some of the neighbours who had given her errands to do in town. All of them went up the steep path to Miss A's yard, where she unpacked her basket and gave each one her package. She delivered all of the messages together with news of former neighbours now living in town and the general news of local interest.

After the neighbours had gone, she unpacked her own purchases and gave each member of her family a little present. When her children were small she had never failed to bring them some tidbit from town and, now that they

[28] Arguments are settled in different ways depending upon the driver, the passenger and the relationship between them. Some drivers are far more sympathetic and liberal than others, but all of them are aware of the wiles used by some higglers to avoid payment. The record book is kept to minimize disputes about the original charge, but some drivers will make reductions if they believe the higgler has a case. Every driver knows the state of the market and can evaluate the "bad market" excuse. Passengers must continue to ride with unreasonable drivers because there is seldom another truck going into town at a time that is convenient for them.

were almost grown, she continued the practice. If she did not buy each of them a needed article of clothing, a tool or a book, she bought tobacco for her husband and a bit of ribbon for Lillie and Mamie. At intervals she also bought a yard or two of rope tobacco to cut into smaller lengths and give, as gifts, to her farmer suppliers. As she went wearily to bed, she was satisfied with the results of the week's hard work, because she had made enough net profit to pay for her household purchases for the next week.

Though Miss A and her family were members of the Wesleyan Church in the nearby village, she was usually too tired to attend services on Sunday morning. This Sunday was spent, as were most Sundays, doing the chores that her husband and children had been unable to do in her absence. She also took the opportunity to rest more than was possible during the week. Both daughters dressed in their best clothes after the morning chores were done and went off to attend church. Just before one o'clock they returned to a typical Sunday dinner of pork cooked in coconut oil and a dish of rice and red peas.

If there had been any activity at either the Wesleyan or Anglican churches in the afternoon, Miss A and the girls would have attended, but as none was planned, they stayed in their own yard. Local community organizations, the Jamaica Agricultural Society and the People's National Party local branch, hold their meetings on Sunday evenings, but Miss A seldom attended because she was usually occupied at home. Moving pictures were shown on Sunday evenings in the basement of the Chinese-owned grocery store in the village, but Miss A never attended and would not permit her daughters to do so. She never allowed her daughters to leave the yard except for necessary purposes, and then they were allowed to stay away only long enough to perform the specified errand. Her two younger daughters were not permitted to go to any social or recreational gatherings unless they were accompanied by Miss A or her eldest daughter, whom she trusts to keep them away from contacts with men.

The family spent Sunday evening quietly in the yard.

2.

Small farming is a Jamaican way of life that is rooted in the provision grounds kept by slaves. After emancipation, many newly freed slaves abandoned the estates to farm for themselves on land in the mountainous interiors. Since plantations traditionally have produced little for local consumption, foodstuffs are either imported at considerable cost or grown by local farmers on minuscule plots. Thousands of small peasant producers supply the root crops, vegetables, and fruits basic to the Jamaican diet. This article by an agricultural economist places small farming in the perspective of Jamaican agriculture in general. The author argues that the small farmer's cultivation techniques, often stereotyped as wasteful and inefficient, may in fact reflect the best available adjustment to the limitations of local environmental and economic opportunity.

DAVID T. EDWARDS, a Welshman long resident in the West Indies, received his doctorate from the University of London. Author of *Report on an Economic Study of Small Farming in Jamaica,* he is currently Professor and Head of the Department of Agricultural Economics and Farm Management at the University of the West Indies, Trinidad.

Small Farming in Jamaica: A Social Scientist's View

D. T. Edwards

Before discussing small farming,[1] as it exists in Jamaica today, and what it might become, it will be useful to consider briefly how it emerged and developed.

It is commonly said that small farming in Jamaica was born when the slaves working on the large estates and plantations were freed, about 120 years ago. Despite considerable efforts on the part of most of the estate managers to retain the services of the freed man—by combining high charges for the rental of living accommodation and provision grounds, with low rates of wages, and by declining to sell them land—the former slaves left the estates in large numbers. They squatted on abandoned land and managed, often with the help of the Non-Conformist Missionaries who negotiated on their behalf, to buy land in the hills—away from the flat land under sugar cane and other plantation crops.

The large scale purchase of land by the former slaves is at first sight surprising. How could slaves have acquired sufficient funds to buy land? Mainly by selling the surplus of crops produced on their provision grounds, and by the sale of handicrafts. The slaves were encouraged to produce much of their own food because this was a more certain source than importation, and a cheaper means than buying imported food or producing food as

From *Proceedings of the American Society for Horticultural Science: Caribbean Region,* Vol. 9, 1965, pp. 192–205. Courtesy of the author and the American Society for Horticultural Science: Tropical Region.

[1] For the purpose of this paper a small farm is regarded as one under 25 acres in area.

part of the estate system. Substantial sums were saved out of the income from selling produce, and these were devoted to buying land after emancipation.

The existence of these provision grounds cultivated by the slaves raises the question of whether it may not be more accurate to think of the establishment of small farming as having preceded emancipation. Were not these provision grounds small farms cultivated by tenants at will whose main employment was enforced work on the sugar cane?

In addition to providing the means of financing the purchase of land the provision grounds also allowed the slaves to keep alive their knowledge and skills of cultivation, and sustained their inclination for independent action. These qualities were invaluable to the freed men who had to farm under difficult conditions with little encouragement, and even in the face of opposition from the plantocracy.

At first, attention was given almost exclusively to producing crops for local consumption and rearing small stock, but later export crops were also introduced.

The area of land under small farms has risen, up to the present time, as a result of the small farmers' initiative and, particularly in the last 35 years, through Government Land Settlement Schemes which have made available approximately 200,000 acres of land to small farmers.

THE IMPORTANCE OF SMALL FARMING

There can be no question of the present importance of small farming in Jamaica. Farms of less than 25 acres occupied, in 1961, about one-third of the land in farms, and one-half of the cultivated area in the island. They produce a considerable proportion of total agricultural output. Root crops and vegetables for local consumption largely come from these farms, as do the lesser export crops such as coffee, cocoa and ginger. Their production of many other crops and livestock is also far from being negligible.

Politically too, the small farms are important. They

contain a significant part of the total vote in many rural constituencies. Recognition of this political fact of life is reinforced by faith in the contribution that the small farm sector can make to the country's economic development and by a sympathy for small farming rather than for the large estates, some of them owned and operated by foreign companies.

Finally, in referring to the importance of small farming, it is to be realized that the small farms are a source of a substantial number of Jamaicans whether they have migrated to urban areas or remained on the farms. (At a conservative estimate, of only four persons per small farm family, the *resident* small farm population in 1961 would have numbered over 600,000, or more than one third of the total population.)

EFFICIENCY OF SMALL FARMING

There is no lack of opinions about the standard of small farming in Jamaica. Many observers would not hesitate to describe it as 'poor' or 'bad'. As evidence they would point to low yields, backward practices, soil erosion, poor incomes, and fragmented holdings. There can be no question that there is tremendous scope for improvement, whether a comparison is made between small farming and the better large farms in Jamaica, or between poorer and better small farms in the island.

It is equally true that the growth of the small farming sector in Jamaica has been very impressive for an 'inefficient' system operating under difficult conditions. It may even be thought inappropriate to describe as 'inefficient' a system which has survived and grown in the face of considerable hardships and without, until the last few years, any appreciable help.

Rather than to debate this issue at any length it will be more constructive to consider the response of the small farmer, as revealed in his farming.

The total amount of resources used by individual small farmers in their farming is very limited. However the combinations of individual resources are juggled, the total output and income which could be produced would still be small. The basic limitation, then, lies with the small amount of resources employed. Why is the amount small? One answer is that in as far as the small farmer's resources are his own, it should be a matter of no surprise that coming as he does from a poor family which had to support several children, and himself pursuing a profession which provides a low income with which to sustain his own family, he owns few resources. His opportunity of inheriting and acquiring land and capital in various forms is obviously strictly limited. At first sight the supply of family labour may seem considerable, but this is somewhat reduced by the need to earn income outside the farm, and the domestic demand of the family on the wife's time, while the use of hand tools (which is widespread) allows only a small area to be cultivated per man. Two to three acres of bananas and tree crops is a commonly quoted figure for a strong man to cultivate alone, using hand tools in the hills.

A further question has to be asked. Why should the farmer restrict himself to his own resources? Why not borrow?

There are in the world people who are apparently indifferent to their economic welfare, who are without ambition for material improvement or the possibilities which follow from it. The mass of Jamaican small farmers cannot be grouped with such people. They have a real desire to improve the lot of themselves and their families. The reason for not using loans, to an extent sufficient to escape from their smallness, lies elsewhere. Either the persons with capital will not or cannot lend it, or the small farmers themselves cannot or will not borrow.

It is, of course, very difficult for lending institutions to lend to small farmers. Frequently the farmers are without adequate and suitable capital assets to serve as security for a loan, while the man's personal security is difficult to assess under small farming conditions.

Even when loans are offered, the conditions are sometimes regarded as unacceptable: there may be a reluctance to hand over as security the title to a piece of land—especially when a farmer's home stands on it; the terms of repayment may be considered too onerous; or, again, the interest may be considered too high. But much more widespread than these particular considerations is the thought that the uncertainty of farming may make it impossible to repay the loan on time—with disastrous consequences. Thus, borrowing to finance substantial productive projects is unpopular, in contrast to a willingness to borrow to meet family needs (such as purchase of food or burial of a relative), or to purchase land—where the worst that can happen is that the much prized land is not obtained.

Aversion to borrowing is, then, a reaction to the high uncertainty under which a family with pressing needs and limited reserves operates. Further, the farmers do have something to lose: they have a modest status which is envied by those below them.

The causes of the high uncertainty are several: the natural conditions (including droughts, floods, and the occasional hurricane); illness and accidents to family and animals; theft from fields; and great ignorance of the effects of improved practices.

It is not surprising that, in addition to avoiding the use of borrowed money, another reaction of the farmer is to reject a whole range of unfamiliar, improved practices (except on a small, trial scale) in favour of familiar practices which cannot be practised on as large a scale as the farmer would wish, because his resources are too limited.

Reserves are built up (in the form of cash and kind, land and animals) so that misfortune may be guarded against. Opportunities for more productive investment are sacrificed so as to be protected against the consequences of heavy and unforeseen losses.

Small farms grow many crops and most of them actually grow many of them mixed up together in the same fields, for diversification of products (and particularly of crops) produced is employed very widely as an informal means of insurance; avoiding 'putting all your eggs in one basket'.

Taken together these reactions add up to 'bad farming'

but looked at from the farmers' point of view they make sense even if they are not entirely justified. One writer summed up his assessment in these words: Jamaican small farming was "technically bad, but economically it appears to represent a reasonable response to the conditions under which farming is practised."

It is not feasible to adduce in detail the evidence on which such a judgment is based. It is necessary to observe, however, that there is inadequate information to prove to the small farmer that he would in his circumstances undoubtedly be better off if he used the array of improved practices recommended to him. (This problem must be reserved for discussion in connection with agricultural research.)

THE PROSPECTS FOR SMALL FARMING

It may seem that not too much can be hoped for from the small farm sector. Real efforts have been made over the last ten years to improve small farming without achieving conspicuous success. An examination of statistics shows that the production of crops produced on small farms has not been increased in most cases and has even fallen in some.

In addition there are forces at work which could prejudice small farm development. (a) The rapid increase in population pressure threatens further the viability of small farms. (b) The gloomy prospects for many products of tropical agriculture are particularly alarming for high-cost producers, who may also lose some of the protection hitherto enjoyed. (c) And thirdly the growing power of the demonstration effect whereby rural dwellers are becoming increasingly aware of being 'left behind' by their urban compatriots is hardly likely to encourage the enterprising farmers to continue their laborious and poorly paid labour.

But against these discouraging features there are real opportunities which can be exploited.

There is a huge untapped market for agricultural produce in Jamaica itself, as shown by the 20,000,000 pounds sterling value of food imported during 1964. This is equivalent to an appreciable proportion of the total value of agricultural output produced in Jamaica. Markets for Jamaican products are also available abroad if Jamaican products are produced in sufficient quantities and at competitive prices.

One of the crucial problems in improving small farming is to reduce uncertainty in farming. Several measures could be used to reduce the uncertainty. These include: giving a formal undertaking that the period allowed for loan repayment would be extended when farm income is reduced by natural hazards; replacing landed security by other forms of security more acceptable to the farmers; granting subsidies for the introduction of unfamiliar practices; establishing guaranteed minimum prices for agricultural products whose prices are most unstable; and introducing greater security of land tenure and compensation for permanent improvements. Some of these measures are, indeed, already practised in Jamaica, and their adoption on a far greater scale–*if understood and accepted by the farmers–together with the provision of an increased flow of knowledge to the farmers,* would encourage them to invest more than token amounts of resources in unfamiliar practices, and would promote borrowing to secure funds for both familiar and unfamiliar forms of investment. The farmers' informal experiments would be extended and successful trials would, by increasing the farmers' knowledge, accelerate the adoption of improved farm practices.

Until farmers are much better informed, acceptance of much of the advice given will involve too great a strain on their faith. One drastic way of increasing knowledge and skill is to train farmers (as is being done for the establishment of new dairy farms) just as persons are prepared for other professions. The mass of existing farmers will have to depend on 'in-service' training, which should be more effectively undertaken following the recent separation of 'development' and 'extension' functions in the Ministry of Agriculture, so that the extension staff can devote all their efforts to extension work. The problem of 'what to extend' is still, however, a very real one.

When the farmers are prepared to invest seriously in new practices their requirement of grants and loans is likely to be insatiable and beyond the capacity of the Government. But in such circumstances the commercial banks may well find themselves able to lend substantial funds, possibly through intermediaries, to the farmers.

It would seem that there are grounds for cautious optimism about the possibilities of improving small farming in Jamaica. Clearly, however, a sustained and co-ordinated effort will be necessary. All the links in the chain of production must be made sufficiently strong.

AGRICULTURAL RESEARCH AND THE SMALL FARMER

Even if Jamaica grew only a small number of crops under its strikingly varied and extremely variable natural conditions, and employed the same methods of cultivation for all of a particular crop, the task of conducting adequate agricultural research, with the volume of resources that could be expected from such a small not too rich country, would be an extremely formidable one. But Jamaica produces many crops. And when the problem is further complicated by the presence of marked differences between farming systems producing the same crops, so that large scale monoculture on good, flat land using numerous improved methods exists alongside very small (one might almost say microscopic scale) production of the crop mixed with other crops, on hilly eroded land, using few modern techniques, a Director of Research might be pardoned if he thought the situation impossible.

It is not surprising that for these and other reasons the state of knowledge for many of the problems connected with small farming is highly deficient. It may be of interest to give examples of subjects for which little work has been done under Jamaican conditions. Possibly the most obvious is food crops, especially staple ground provisions like yam and sweet potatoes, and tree crops such as the ackee, star apple and naseberry. The list is almost endless. (An authority on tropical agriculture, writing at the end of the last century, observed: "Jamaica possesses possibly the most varied and valuable collections of economic or industrial plants of any tropical country. These have nearly all been introduced from other countries by the Botanic Gardens, and their distribution throughout every part of the island, begun in 1777, has been continued uninterruptedly to the present day.")

It should, however, be said that in recent years the Jamaican Ministry of Agriculture and the University of the West Indies have turned their attention to such crops, and particularly to the staples. The School of Agriculture of the University of the West Indies, which has its headquarters in Trinidad but has responsibility for work throughout the area, is concentrating a considerable part of its resources on these staples. Thus there is a Food Crops Breeding Unit (engaged mainly in work on sweet potatoes, gungo peas, tomatoes, yams and tannias) while the Department of Crop Production and the Department of Agricultural Economics and Farm Management are co-operating in assessing the returns from food crops grown under commercial conditions. Other related work, in fertilizer application and entomology for instance, is envisaged. The Department of Botany at this branch of the University has also undertaken work in this field.

Another example is provided by intercropping. Most crops on small farms are grown mixed together. Only a small part of this mixed cultivation is considered desirable (to provide necessary shade for example) by technical officers of the Ministry of Agriculture. It is certainly obvious on general grounds that mixed cropping imposes limitations on the introduction of improvements, such as sprays which, while benefiting one crop, may damage others. But it is equally clear that small farmers think that mixed cropping suits their circumstances better than growing most crops by themselves. Some of them have pointed out how although they may get a lower yield per crop grown mixed than pure, the *combined yield* is higher (under their conditions, of course). It would certainly be of interest to determine under what conditions it would be worth growing crops pure rather than mixed.

A third example relates to soil erosion and conservation. Much of the hill land of Jamaica occupied by small farmers is badly eroded and there can be no question that the erosion is allowed by the methods of cultivation practised, but there is little *precise* information about the process of erosion under Jamaican conditions and how it may be satisfactorily and economically reduced to an acceptable rate.

Turning now to the experimental work that has been conducted, it is observed that much of it has been carried out under conditions which approximate much more closely to the conditions which obtain on the well-managed estate than to small farm conditions. The implication for small farmers who wished to apply this work would seem to be: change your system drastically until it becomes close to those of experimental conditions and then the findings of research will be more relevant to you. In the absence of such a change the result may be at least largely irrelevant, and at most, if applied, economically harmful. The difficulty, of course, is that the small farmer cannot be expected to change his system so radically in a short time.

It would seem that the only feasible alternative is to study much more thoroughly, than has been done in the past, the small farm systems in an attempt to see what changes can usefully be introduced. In short an operations research approach is needed. It would involve the method of a survey rather than of a classic field experiment, although simple trials would need to be included and evaluated. The agricultural economist and rural sociologist would have their contribution to make in co-operation with the agronomist.

An essential question is, of course: How can changes be effected which will make the farmer better off, rather than: What improved practices should the farmer be persuaded to use? Obviously more attention needs to be devoted than hitherto to the system (and the man) which it is hoped to change: preoccupation with the changes themselves is not adequate. This may not be what the agricultural scientist calls 'research' but it does seem to be a necessary stage in bringing about the development of small farming in Jamaica, and has already been widely proved in some of the economically advanced countries.

3.

This detailed study of a farming community in the foothills of the Blue Mountains of Jamaica supplements the preceding overview of small farming. A team of geographers and anthropologists here explores factors bearing on soil erosion, a major West Indian problem. The history of land-use, local farming practices, patterns of cooperative labor, household organization, marketing arrangements and their interrelation with production, community institutions, and political attitudes are shown to affect local beliefs about and behavior toward soils, soil erosion, and conservation.

JAMES M. BLAUT, the principal author, was on the staff of the Department of Geography at Yale University at the time of the study. Subsequently with the College of the Virgin Islands, St. Thomas, and at Clark University, he is currently Professor of Geography at the University of Illinois, Chicago Circle. Nan Harman was a graduate of the Yale Conservation Program, and Ruth P. Blaut and Michael Moerman were trained in anthropology.

A Study of Cultural Determinants of Soil Erosion and Conservation in the Blue Mountains of Jamaica

James M. Blaut; Ruth P. Blaut; Nan Harman; Michael Moerman[1]

BACKGROUND OF THE RESEARCH

Soil erosion and depletion are generally recognized as being among the most formidable obstacles to socio-economic development among groups practising slopeland agriculture in the humid tropics. This holds true equally for systems of shifting agriculture in which population pressure has forced a shortening of the rotation, and for most sedentary dry-field (non-irrigated) systems in areas of moderately dense population. In the absence of measures designed to slow erosion and maintain soil nutrient levels, most cultivated slopeland soils are highly erosive and subject to rapid depletion, in consequence of the high and intense rainfall, high rate of decay of organic matter, and often steeper slopes which characterize cultivated areas in the tropics.

In spite of the ease with which tropical slopeland soils erode and the rapidity with which their nutrients tend to

From *Social and Economic Studies,* Vol. 8, No. 4, December 1959, pp. 403–20. Reprinted with permission of the authors and the Institute of Social and Economic Research, University of the West Indies.

[1] The present paper was written principally by James M. Blaut, who directed the research. The assistance of the Conservation Foundation, Inc., and the Program of Research and Training for the Study of Man in the Tropics (Columbia University) in providing financial support for the research is gratefully acknowledged.

be depleted after clearing has taken place, it is by no means inevitable that these processes will occur at such a rate as either to preclude the maintenance of sedentary dry-field systems or depress their yields to an extremely low level. Erosion and depletion are, of course, serious problems in most of the tropical areas where peasant farmers practise sedentary dry-field agriculture. Yields have generally failed to keep up with population growth, and in some instances have actually declined. However, in some few tropical areas sedentary dry-field agriculture effectively maintains soil fertility, while sustaining dense farming populations. These areas occur on poor as well as good soils.

It seems clear that a combination of cultural factors is responsible, in most cases at least, for failure to maintain tropical farming systems in ecological equilibrium at high output levels. These cultural factors are related to social, economic, and political patterns in the farming communities, to indigenous technology, and to the apperception of soil resources and soil loss. Soil conservation efforts which merely evaluate the resource potential in a given area and attempt to persuade farmers to apply advanced technology to the problem, and which fail to take into account these underlying cultural factors, can have little hope of success.

PURPOSES

The research described here took place between June and September of 1957 and during September of 1958. The work dealt with a community in the Blue Mountains of Jamaica, an area known to include some of the most erosive, and highly eroded, farming land in the world. The general purpose of the investigation was to explore the cultural mechanisms which determine erosion-inducing soil management behaviour and which inhibit the acceptance of conservation measures in this community. The research had three principal aims, one substantive, one methodological, and one theoretical.

The substantive aim of the study was to undertake a thorough ecological, economic, and social analysis of the community, with a view toward discovering the causes for erosion-inducing soil management behaviour, the reasons for lack of acceptance of extension efforts in soil conservation, and possibilities for removing these obstacles. An investigation of this sort should assist in interpreting some of the economic problems of peasant farmers in Jamaica and other portions of the West Indies possessing similar cultural attributes, and should assist also in soil conservation efforts.

The methodological aim was to work out a set of techniques for interdisciplinary study of this type of problem, which, by its nature, requires the efforts of a variety of specialists in social and agricultural sciences. The research thus aimed in part at serving as a pilot study in the analysis of erosion-inducing soil management behaviour and its cultural determinants.

The theoretical aim of the study was to attempt to work toward cross-cultural regularities in the economic and ecological patterns of sedentary peasant farming systems in tropical slopelands. In particular, the research sought data tying together cultural and physical phenomena in a non-environmentalistic manner, and thus sought to add to our meagre store of knowledge on man-environment relations in the tropics.

PROCEDURES

Selection of a field site. The first choice for a field site was the Yallahs Valley, a portion of the Blue Mountains which has received a certain amount of notoriety for the extremely advanced soil loss on its farms. On arriving in Jamaica, however, we discovered that complicating factors ruled the area out: the Yallahs Valley Land Authority had succeeded in persuading most farmers in the valley to take up soil conservation measures, in part through a system of subsidies whose effects might or might not be permanent. Our second choice was an area adjoining the valley, where some of the anti-erosion practices used in the valley had been taken up by some farmers, without benefit of subsidy.

Unfortunately, no community could be found of a size or degree of agglomeration suited to the practical requirements of our field study. (These included a settlement pattern and community size such that, by living in the community, we could become thoroughly acquainted with, and fully observe, all farm families.) Having rejected both localities, we explored other portions of the mountains.

The area finally chosen possessed a number of highly desirable features for our purposes. Slopes averaging over 30° were being worked, with erosion so serious as virtually to have eliminated topsoil from all cultivated areas. The community had recently been selected as a development area, and a few of the farms had begun to respond to extension in matters of soil conservation, thus allowing comparisons to be made between "progressive" farmers and others. It showed a broad spectrum in tenure relations, including various tenancy arrangements and significantly high ownership. While possessing certain community integrative mechanisms, thus allowing us in some respects to deal with it as a social "community," it showed significant cleavages, based on religion, status, politics, etc., and attendant multiple leadership patterns, providing possibilities for internal correlations between land use and certain cultural elements. Farming systems included elements from both the northern, wetter, slopes of the mountains and the southern, drier, slopes. And finally, it proved possible to rent a dwelling from one of the farm families. This community, which for purposes of publication we have given the fictitious name of *Mt. Chester,* proved to be an excellent site.

Field procedures. An initial period of perhaps two weeks in the community was spent largely in getting to know, and be known by, Mt. Chester farm families, and in studying on an exploratory basis a single farm, that of the family which cooked our meals and owned the house we occupied. Toward the end of this period a map was made of the locations of farm dwellings (52 in all), entering and numbering the dwellings on air photos after a ground survey. A simple random sample of 17 farms to be investigated was then drawn. (Stratification proved unworkable, because it would have required prior mapping and interviewing of all farms, to derive a basis for stratifying the population, and this procedure would have been unwise since careful groundwork had to be laid with each family before full-scale interviewing, mapping, and soil analysis took place on each farm. We felt it best to accept the limitations of a one-in-three simple random sample rather than begin intensive work with farm families before we achieved *rapport.*) A subsample of eight farms was drawn, also at random, for intensive analysis. Sampling as a whole provided at least a fairly representative segment of the farms; in particular, it countered a tendency we noted toward bias in favour of those families who were friends of our landlord, and therefore belonged to one fairly distinct, wealthier-than-average, segment of the community.

A continuing series of interviews with both male and female adults on the eight farms was carried out. We sought here to learn as fully as possible the economic and social characteristics of each family, the farming patterns, and the attitudes toward soil management and erosion. Simultaneously, land-use, soil, and slope maps were prepared for most of their fields. Towards the end of the field period, our work with the eight farms made it possible for us to draw up a minimal questionnaire covering essential items of information, which we administered to the remaining farmers in our sample.

In addition to the preceding, general community-wide data, dealing particularly with social relationships, political attitudes, leadership patterns, impact of extension efforts etc., were obtained. Historical research was also carried out in the West Indian Reference Library in Kingston and in the island archives at Spanish Town.

RESULTS

The following discussion of data obtained in the study is strictly preliminary. It consists of a brief description, largely non-quantitative, of salient facts about Mt. Chester. We shall deal in order with the following topics: (i) location and environment; (ii) history of land use; (iii) the farms; (iv) the community; and (v) soil erosion and conservation.

Location and environment. Mt. Chester, Jamaica, lies in foothill country to the west of the western ridges of the Blue Mountains. The elevation of the community ranges between 1,200 feet and 1,700 feet above sea level, including the land worked by its farms. Mt. Chester is 12 miles by highway and unimproved road from Kingston, its market and supply focus. It lies off the main Kingston-Annotto Bay road, two miles and roughly 500 feet above it. The community is perhaps as accessible to Kingston as is any farming area in the island.

The terrain in this region is distinctly rugged, more so than in most farming areas of the Blue Mountains, or of Jamaica as a whole. There is virtually no flat land, except for occasional broadenings of the usually narrow (knife-edge) ridge-crests and a few small hollows along the slopes of hills. Valleys are universally gorge-like, with narrow bottoms, sometimes occupied by permanent or intermittent streams. Slopes appear to average between 30° and 40°, and rarely are less steep than 20°. Occasionally they may attain 63°. (One such slope, cultivated with bananas and clean-weeded, occurred in our sample.) Differences in elevation between the gorges and knife-edge ridges may be as much as 300 feet.

The climate of this area must, in the present stage of analysis, be inferred from records for stations located some distance away, and values to be given are therefore not accurate. It is clear, however, that Mt. Chester receives in the neighbourhood of 100 inches of rainfall annually; and that its rainfall régime, resembling that of the north-eastern portion of Jamaica, involves no dry season (i.e., has no month with less than 2.5 inches of rain in a normal year). Rain tends to be concentrated in the period from October to December, with a secondary maximum in May. February, March, and July are the driest months, each receiving perhaps 4–5 inches.

Mean annual temperature for Mt. Chester may average about 76°F., with little seasonal change: the warmest-month average is about 78°, the coolest about 74°. The mean daily maximum temperature for the warmest month (August) is about 89°; the mean daily minimum for the coldest months (January and February) may be about 64°.

The rainfall régime is thus distinctly equatorial. While the temperature régime cannot be described as equatorial, it is within the range of climates which are distinctly lowland-tropical; neither elevation nor altitude have markedly altered its climate from an inter-tropical norm.

Two sorts of rock underlie Mt. Chester, and help to form its soil types. One is a purplish conglomerate, rather soft, and generally deeply weathered. The second is a variable, usually yellowish-brown, shale formation, also soft and deeply weathered. Neither sort yields plant nutrients in abundance, and both are subject to serious erosion. However, the softness and degree of weathering of the rocks is such as to permit rapid rejuvenation after erosion; the removal of top layers reveals well-weathered C-horizon material which, in most cases, does not resist root penetration seriously and releases its nutrient content readily.

The overall picture of the environment of Mt. Chester may be summed up briefly. The area is distinctly tropical, sub-equatorial in temperature and equatorial in rainfall. The quantity of rainfall, the frequency of heavy, brief showers, the steep slopes, the easily-eroded parent material, all combine to provide a soil-slope-drainage complex in which soil erosion is extremely active when vegetative cover is removed. Since, as we shall see, the soil is not adequately protected on most fields, either with ground cover or surface irregularities, there can be no question but that the Mt. Chester area is subject to some of the most intensive man-induced soil erosion to be found anywhere in the tropics. One result of this is the almost total absence of topsoil (A-horizon) throughout the entire region, and thus the prevalence of "sub-soil farming" on nutrient-poor soils.

History of land use. During the latter half of the eighteenth century the Mt. Chester area included portions of several coffee estates. A few of the old estate maps have been recovered, and show the land to have been divided, roughly equally, between coffee fields and "slaves' provision grounds," i.e., ground-crop fields. Unfortunately it has not yet proven possible to tie these old maps to the present-day landscape so that we can judge which portions of present-day Mt. Chester were under coffee in 1800 and which were not. Doing so, we should be able to determine the approximate length of time various parts of the farms have been under ground-crop cultivation. All we can say on this point at the moment is that, in all probability, the bulk of the land now under cultivation has been growing ground crops continuously (except for grass fallow and short-term "ruinate") for at least 100 years. There is no evidence that true shifting agriculture occurred here during this period.

About the middle of the nineteenth century a process of break-up of estates began. There is some evidence that the estates stopped growing coffee in the area shortly after emancipation, and that the use of land during the fourth decade of the nineteenth century was largely (though not entirely) limited to smallholders' fields, probably of ground crops, under tenancy arrangements with the landlords. One estate listed, in its crop returns for 1845, rent received from farm tenants in the form of labour on coffee fields, the fields probably lying in an area adjoining Mt. Chester which continued to grow coffee until late in the century and was owned by the same party.

During the latter half of the nineteenth century, and continuing to the present, estates were subdivided into successively smaller ownership plots; few, if any, large properties remain in the area today. This process of break-up may or may not have reflected change in land use, probably not: most likely the lands had been worked as small-holder farms, growing ground crops (with some derelict coffee in a few spots), long before actual transfer took place.

We might observe at this point that all the evidence points away from the conclusion that soil erosion forced the abandonment of coffee culture in the area—a conclusion apparently held by most authorities with regard to the coffee industry of the Blue Mountains.[2] It seems, rather, that,

[2] See, for example, Great Britain, Colonial Office, *Agriculture in the West Indies* (London: H.M.S.O., 1942), p. 31: "The

so far as Mt. Chester is concerned, changing economic conditions in the industry, and particularly the economic and social effects of emancipation, resulted in a change from coffee production to smallholder ground-crop production.

The Farms. The principal food crop of the area is yams, of which numerous varieties are grown. (The preferred, and probably most widespread variety is yellow yam. Others include Lucea yam, St. Vincent yam, and Negro yam.) Other root-and-tuber crops include dasheen, tannia, sweet potatoes, and cassava, with many varieties of the first two being grown. These underground crops constitute the important food staples, as well as an important source of cash, for the area.

Bananas, primarily a cash crop, are also used for food. The Lacatan and Gros Michel varieties are grown for sale, but small or imperfect bunches are consumed. Other varieties, such as the Chinese banana and frog banana, as well as the varieties of plantain, are largely consumed on farms; these, however, form only a small part of total production.

Many other varieties of ground crops are grown. Several beans and peas, tomatoes, calaloo (a spinach), and cucumber may be mentioned. In addition, the mixed gardens found on most houseplots include innumerable varieties of spice and herb plants. For all of these crops, the bulk of production is sold; calaloo, spices (other than ginger, an important cash crop), and herbs may possibly be exceptions.

Tree crops, with the partial exception of fruit trees, are grown primarily for sale. The principal varieties of cash tree crops are cacao and coffee; a relatively small amount of citrus of various types is also grown. The most widely grown fruits, in addition to citrus, are breadfruit, mango (of which 24 varieties are grown), star apple, and guava. Coconut, ackee, pimento, and many other fruits are present though not abundant.

In terms of both acreage and value, yams and bananas are the chief crops of the area. Their combined value (both

---

decrease in acreage is entirely attributable to the devastating effects of soil erosion."

for sale and farm consumption), and probably acreage as well, exceeds that of all other crops combined. Tree crops are quite secondary on most farms.

Animal production in the area is not great, although the larger farms usually have one or more cows and pigs. (Some of the smaller farmers raise a cow or pig purchased by a wealthier member of the community; the income from the animal is split evenly between owner and fattener.) Beef cattle are usually found only on the larger farms, whereas pigs are also found on medium-sized farms. Most farms have a few chickens, and goats are present on a few farms. The relative lack of importance of beef cattle, and the lack of use of pig manure by most farmers, indicate that the area as a whole does not practise true mixed farming.

The medium number of acres owned or rented by farmers is perhaps two. Some farmers operate as many as 15 acres; some, on the other hand, operate only one acre. (Most of these latter, however, are part-time farmers.) Few of the farmers own all the land operated. This holds true both for small and medium-sized farms. Rental of farming land is primarily from two sources, either from a wealthier resident of Mt. Chester (or a neighbouring community), or from a larger estate nearby. The typical rental basis involves cash rent. Family land (a system of tenure whereby siblings inherit land which may not be sold outside the family without permission of all) was present but not as widespread as individually-owned land. By agreement, fields within a plot of family land are operated individually. Nearly all farms operate between two and five separate plots.

The typical farming system, applicable to all ground crops except bananas, involves a rotation with a periodicity varying with soil quality, between one-half and two-thirds of the period being devoted to cropping and the remainder to a grass fallow. Bananas are rotated also, but on a long-term basis, with several years of cropping followed by a relatively short fallow. Tree crops such as coffee and cacao are of course relatively permanent. Each plot is divided up into a number of separate fields, growing different crops and combinations of crops. Intercropping, with as many as five or six varieties grown in combination in the same field, prevails on all fields except those devoted to tree crops and bananas. (Young bananas, however, are intercropped with food crops.)

The seasonal rhythm of farming activities centres on the yam crop. Digging of yams takes place between October and May, the period of greatest harvest lying between November and perhaps March. During these months there is a severe shortage of labour; during the "summer" months, by contrast, there is under-employment in the region (and also a shortage of subsistence crops). Short-term crops, such as tomatoes and peas, take up part of the slack during the "summer." Bananas are harvested and planted throughout most of the year.

Operations associated with the yam crop include the following: digging out, with a crowbar, the previous year's crop, followed by further working of the soil in preparation for the new crop; building the soil into convex terraces (rows of connected "hills," roughly contoured); planting; and weeding. More commonly, the yam heads are either removed from a worked-out plot to another, in which grass has been billed down (cut with the machete) and the soil worked with a hoe or spade; or a minimum of re-working is given the old yam plot, a ratoon crop being taken off the field without replanting.

Bananas are either planted between the yam hills or planted out in newly billed and cultivated, i.e., relatively virgin, land. In the former instance the yam vines (supported on stakes) provide early shade. After harvest of a bunch of bananas the old stem is cut back, and one of the suckers allowed to grow. Sometimes the suckers are moved to a new location (either to a new plot or to replace a dead stem). During the growing period of the banana (from 12 to 18 months, depending in part on soil quality) the only important operation carried out on most farms is weeding, although some few farmers apply fertilizer (urine or artificials) during this period.

In the case of coffee and cacao, a complex of operations surrounds harvesting and preparation for sale, although the period between harvest sees only minor tasks carried out in the field. Both coffee and cacao have to be worked over before sale. In the former case the extraction of beans from pods is sometimes done by others after the crop is sold. In the case of cacao, however, all farmers themselves remove the beans from the pods, dry the beans, and usually ferment them.

One of the key farming operations is, of course, marketing. The technique of marketing varies as among three groups of crops, although all methods involve trucking the produce to Kingston. Food crops are sold in Kingston markets by the farm women. Bananas are sold at a collecting point in Constant Spring by the men, and coffee and cacao are taken, also by the men, to wholesalers in Kingston and elsewhere. Citrus is purchased in the area and carried away by truck.

Field labour is largely carried out by the men, although women assist, and some crops (the catch crops for market—peas, tomatoes, etc.) are largely grown by the women. In the case of yams, men carry out the heavy labour of digging (harvesting) and soil preparation, while women assist in planting and weeding. Most operations associated with banana-growing, except perhaps weeding, are undertaken by the men. Marketing is a woman's task, with the exception of banana, cacao, coffee, and citrus marketing. Sometimes bananas are sold in Kingston markets by the women, usually when the quality (size of the bunch) is below export standards; small amounts of cacao and citrus are likewise sold in the markets. Field labour begins for men at the age of about 15.

Hiring labour and participating in co-operative labour groups ("partnerships") are the two methods of supplementing farm-family labour during periods of high labour need, as during the yam-digging season. Hired labour is used principally on the larger farms and farms in which adult males are employed elsewhere, either as specialists (e.g., carpenters) or unskilled labourers. Wages for unskilled labour, e.g., on the local roads, are somewhat greater than for farm labour, and are thought by some farmers to justify hiring labour while they themselves work elsewhere. In general, however, only the wealthier farmers and part-time carpenters or masons consistently employ hired farm labour, and the total quantity of hired labour employed at any one time is slight.

Co-operative field labour groups, or "partnerships," are present in the area but are not, it appears, as important as elsewhere in Jamaica. They consist of groupings of farmers, sometimes stable over long periods of time and sometimes transitory, which work as units on the farm of each member in turn, the recipient furnishing food to his helpers. Their economic function is to obtain for each member the required amount of field labour at times of maximum need without obligating the member to lay out cash for this labour. Three types of farmers generally do not participate: part-time farmers whose outside work provides adequate capital for hiring labour, and whose trade does not permit advance commitment as to days when the farmer will be available for work on his own or partners' farms; the more well-to-do, who appear to prefer to hire labour; and the older farmers who find themselves unable to keep the pace. Among the wealthier group, some do participate, but frequently they contribute a sum of money to the recipient of a given day's labour in place of working on his farm themselves. The partnership system is strongest among the poor and middle group of farmers and here serves an important function. It should be stressed, however, that the convening of "partner days" is not frequent, and tends to occur mostly during the yam-digging season. Larger co-operative-labour groupings, in which large numbers of farmers are invited to a single man's farm for a special occasion (house-building, yam-digging), occur very infrequently. Two additional types of partnerships were encountered, neither as important as the above. Marketing partnerships consist of informal groupings of farm women who take one another's produce to market. The groups are small, usually comprising two, three or four women, and have a relatively stable membership based, it appears, on friendship—considerable mutual trust is involved. However, the occasions on which women market for their partners are not very frequent; usually, all farm women go to market when they have a load to sell. Further, the partnerships are not directly reciprocal (as is the case with field partnerships): some take other women's loads more frequently than theirs are taken by the others.

A third type of partnership, only one instance of which was encountered, involved group sessions for ginger-peeling by women from farms raising ginger. These peeling "bees" take place in the evening, the recipient providing food and drink. Women with larger ginger harvests benefit at the expense of those with smaller harvests, since the "bee" continues until each member's ginger is finished.

In contrast to the women's marketing partnership, the men have no such partnership in their major marketing effort, the sale of bananas. In some instances farmers with few bananas give them to others to market for them, but in such cases the one who does the marketing (a bigger banana producer in all cases) receives credit for the bananas marketed, thus receiving a small remuneration in the form of All-Island Banana Growers Association benefits which in part depend on the long-term amount sold, while the smaller grower receives only the cash payment for sale.

An analysis of the pattern of farm income and expenses on Mt. Chester farms cannot be given as yet. At this point we can merely indicate the major categories of costs and returns. To begin with, it is clear that non-cash expenses far outweigh cash expenses. Most of the former consist of unpaid family labour; the latter, livestock and planting materials. From the standpoint of expenses, these farms are far closer to subsistence than commercial farming. On the other hand, cash returns, except on the smallest farms, appear to outweigh non-cash returns; most production, in other words, is sold. There is no clear-cut distinction between farm products used for home consumption as against sale, except in the case of coffee, cacao, ginger, and citrus fruits, which are sold. Generally, yams are sold and consumed in about equal proportions; bananas, sugar cane, beans, peas, tomatoes, and cucumbers are mostly sold; and secondary root and tuber crops (tannia, eddoe, cassava, etc.) are mostly consumed.

Farms in Mt. Chester seem to be somewhat more prosperous than the average for Jamaica. This can be attributed in part to the accessibility of Kingston markets—close enough, incidentally, to virtually eliminate one link in the normal Jamaican marketing chain, the "higgler," who buys from farmers and sells in urban markets. In part, also, it reflects the fact that rainfall is adequate for the production of Jamaica's principal export crops, and soils, while poor, are relatively deep, and are capable of growing three important export tree crops (cacao, coffee, citrus). Other factors undoubtedly enter in, also.

The modal farm-dwelling unit consists of perhaps four household members. Generally, Mt. Chester farm households include a single cohabiting couple, their unmarried children, and outside children where such exist. Frequently, especially on more wealthy farms, dependent godchildren and aged parents are also in the household. Stable cohabiting unions and formal marriages seem to be somewhat more frequent in Mt. Chester than is typical for rural Jamaica, partly due to the relatively strong influence of the Roman Catholic church and partly to the relative prosperity of farms here. The former encourages formal marriage directly; the latter permits it—in Jamaica formal marriage tends to replace informal cohabitation when a couple has achieved some measure of economic security. Wealthier community members are usually Roman Catholic and formally married.

Patterns of descent, inheritance, kin terminology, and residence in Mt. Chester are much the same as those found in England and the United States.[3] The ideal pattern of residence is neolocal, i.e., young couples prefer to establish their own households away from those of their parents. Two frequently encountered alternatives are: ambilocality (residence with either set of parents) on inherited land; and a pattern which involves the man visiting the woman at her parents' home. Children tend to remain with the mother if parents separate.

Income distribution tends to be rather clearly differentiated within the household, some income going to the male

[3] Descent and inheritance are bilateral; kin terms are lineal avuncular in parents' generation and Eskimo in ego's generation.

farm operator, some going to the adult female. This, we think, relates to the instability of the household unit, and, since it leads to different emphases in crop production by men and women, relates to problems in soil conservation. "Man's load," generally the crops over which males have full control in production, includes bananas and citrus varieties (when sold to the export collecting centre), cacao, and coffee. "Woman's load" includes crops sold in the local retail markets–where women do the marketing–except for yams, the income from which, ideally, is divided. The foregoing actually describes control, rather than distribution, of income: in practice, women contribute market money to the farm's upkeep, although they prefer to use it for their retail purchases, while men contribute the cash obtained from the sale of export crops to the household budget, although preferring to use it for production expenses. We might note that livestock tend not only to be selectively owned as between sexes, but also to be owned individually by household members.

The community. A number of economic and social forces tend to divide the community into parts, although not into strictly separate subcommunities or classes. The most important stratifying mechanism is income, which reflects size of farm (both value and area) for full-time farmers. A number of other important characteristics tend to vary with income and size of farm: (1) size of the farm as a whole increases with the amount of land owned (as against the amount rented); (2) emphasis on tree crops reflects the amount of land owned, since tree crops are rarely grown on rented land; (3) emphasis on livestock, especially beef cattle, increases with size of farm; (4) partnerships decline with increasing income level, as does part-time non-farm work except for specialist craftsmen; (5) consumption level, quality of the farm house, and education increase with size of farm; (6) larger farms are owned by Roman Catholics, on the whole; (7) status in the community generally reflects income; (8) participation in agricultural societies and government-sponsored projects and organizations, including those relating to soil conservation, is greater for the larger and wealthier farms; and (9) the few supporters of the Administration Party, as against the Opposition Party, are owners of the larger farms. It was also observed that informal organization (visiting groups, friendships, etc.) tended more often to reflect income-level than any other differentiating factor.

Among the formal community organizations present in Mt. Chester, the most significant are religious. Three religious organizations claim Mt. Chester families as members. The most influential is the Roman Catholic church, which is also the only church actually within the community, and the oldest of the three. The other two include a Church of England and a Baptist group. As indicated above, wealthier community members are, on the whole, members of the Roman Catholic church. Baptismal and marital godparents are required by both the Anglican and Roman Catholic churches. Generally prosperous, respected and—certainly among Catholics—legally married individuals are chosen. Godparenthood relations appear to have an effect on leadership, but this question is still under study.

Education, although church-related, does not entirely mirror the religious breakdown of the community, because the only school within the community—the others are three miles away—is connected with the Roman Catholic church, and a number of community children of non-Catholic families attend the local school.

Politics would be an important divisive force in Mt. Chester were it not for the fact that few community members support the Administration Party. An undercurrent of ill-feeling toward these few individuals was detected; some of the latter, in fact, are hidden rather than acknowledged supporters of this party. Part of the resistance to government-sponsored soil conservation and agricultural improvement measures reflects an identification of "government" with "Administration Party," and a transferred dislike for the former. Political beliefs are in a sense an integrator of most of the community. Strong feelings against the Administration Party are one of the avowed common values and seemed to constitute the main permitted expression for feelings of hostility toward authority.

The remaining group of formal community organizations includes the several agricultural societies and government-sponsored organizations. Foremost among these is the Jamaica Agricultural Society, an independent, though government-connected, organization. Membership in this group is almost universal in Mt. Chester, but degree of activity in it—holding of office, acceptance of its recommendations for agricultural improvement, etc.—tends to be limited to the wealthier farmers (and Catholics). This, of course, has implications for soil conservation.

A second agricultural group, the All-Island Banana Growers Association, claims as members nearly all community farmers who grow significant amounts of bananas, its ubiquity reflecting the tangible benefits of membership (crop insurance, etc.). Here, also, the larger farms are the most active. Government-sponsored coffee-, citrus-, and cacao-producing organizations are important among the few who grow these crops in significant amounts; these farmers, also, are among the more prosperous, possessing enough land to permit some of it to be devoted to crops of this sort, and having the resources to wait several years for a return on investment. The Savings Union, as might be expected, draws its membership, and particularly its officers, from the wealthier (and, again, Catholic) segment of the community. A branch of the Jamaica Women's Federation (newly begun) draws its membership principally from those active in other organizations, such as the Savings Union.

Informal groupings within the community include, in addition to partnerships (field, marketing, and ginger-peeling), informal visiting groups, games groups, drinking groups, and dances. Several factors seem to prevail in determining the membership of visiting groups. Among these are: friendship, length of residence in the community, kinship, economic status, generation, and proximity, with the last-named far less important than might be expected. The games groups centre on the game of dominoes, which claims the attention of nearly all adult males in the community. Mt. Chester boasts a winning domino team, and is quite proud of the community's showing in intercommunity matches. Indeed, the matches draw large numbers of spectators who, with the team, hire a truck and proceed to the place where the match is to take place with great spirit and much singing. More frequent are the evening domino sessions in front of farm houses or in local shops. Checkers is a less important game for the community, also played by the males in evening sessions. Dominoes, or at least the occasional tournament, appears to be the one entirely community-wide integrative mechanism. The evening domino sessions, however, mirror visiting group patterns. The Saturday-night dances generally attract only the youth of the community.

Soil erosion and conservation. The principal function of the research reported here was to determine the physical and cultural causes of soil erosion in Mt. Chester, the mechanisms introduced by the community or government to combat it, and the degree of acceptance of these mechanisms. Since these facts can only be established after thorough analysis of the data obtained–they are in every sense the "conclusions" to be reached–only preliminary findings can be presented in this progress report. A summary of these findings follows.

We may begin with a description of the extent and seriousness of erosion in farm lands cultivated by Mt. Chester families. It was stated previously that erosion here is extremely serious: little if any topsoil remains, and active erosion exists on all fields surveyed except those under full-grown tree crops or grass. This conclusion may be amplified here. Sample borings were taken on 16 cultivated and grass-fallowed fields, and in the great majority of cases it was found that (below the litter layer) soil pH did not significantly change with depth, and that nutrient status actually improved with depth. This indicates that no nutrient-rich topsoil exists. Further, it suggests that the nutrient level of the soil corresponds at best to that of the rotten rock itself; at worst, plants are subsisting on an even lower supply in the upper few inches of soil. This suggests that, where the soil is deep enough, further erosion can actually improve yields, since it bares lower, less depleted, levels of subsoil. The hypothesis that the increase in nutrient status with depth implies that the surface soil has only been eroded down to the A_2 horizon, i.e., horizon of eluviation, and that successive layers are B horizon (horizon of accumulation), was rejected, in part because of the evidence provided by particles of rotting rock in the soil: Mt. Chester "soil" is largely C horizon (parent material) to the surface.

A further indicator of the seriousness of erosion is stoniness. The more heavily eroded soils have a wash of gravel on the surface, rotting rock subsequently hardened by exposure.

One locally important variety of erosion deserves special mention. A combination of climate, slope, and depth of weathering–cultivation practices may or may not contribute–has led to the frequent occurrence of "breakaways," landslips covering a surface area of perhaps 200 to 3,000 square feet or more.

That soils which have been eroded to this degree are still in cultivation seems due to one important characteristic of Mt. Chester soils (both conglomerate- and shale-derived). These soils, as indicated previously, are weathered to unusual depths, even for the humid tropics. Thus the removal of the upper horizons exposes subsoil which is neither too hard for roots to penetrate nor too coarse-grained to release its nutrients. By providing frequent grass fallows and some rudimentary soil conservation measures, Mt. Chester farmers have achieved a rather unstable equilibrium, with a low but reasonably sustained yield obtained from the soil.

To what extent do Mt. Chester farmers perceive soil erosion and its effects? The answer to this question, to which a great deal of attention was paid in farm interviews, can only be sketched in the most general terms here; clearly, it is a key element in the larger question of erosion causes and cures.

The typical belief-systems appear to be roughly as follows. Soil is either "strong" (sometimes called "fat") or "weak." It is "strongest" after a period under grass fallow, during which the grass has been periodically cut back with a cutlass. The "strength" of the soil lies in the "juices" which are the remains of decayed grass. These "juices" are lost either by rain washing down the slope or by crops making use of them. There are no "juices" released from the mineral content of the soil itself, nor does this mineral content wash away in any appreciable degree. (Most farmers dismissed the evidence of muddy water coming off a field as unimportant, or else attributed the muddy colour to the "juices" being washed away.) Some farmers believed that the terrace-like rows of yam hills slowed the wash of "juices,"–and a few agreed that "contours"–grass lines planted on the contour–and ditches dug on the contour also slowed the removal of juices, and thus let the soil remain "fat" longer. Others, however, felt that nothing could slow the loss of the "juices." ("Why we plant grass contour? Government pay us to put in contour. It a grass government!") All agreed, however, that the rather dramatic "breakaways" (landslips) were a serious problem, and that tree crops held the soil in place through their deep rooting systems. Opinion was divided as to whether tree crops slow the washing away of "juices." Some farmers recognized the fact that grass or weeds in a banana field slowed the loss of "juices"; others did not accept this; and the majority felt that a banana field (no matter what the slope) should be clean weeded, since both bananas and grass are surface-rooting, and grass competes with the bananas for the soil's "juices." And finally, the prevailing practice of multiple cropping (growing several crops together in the same field) was not believed by most to have the function of providing better ground cover. Rather, it was justified on the basis of providing harvests, and thus income, at different times of the year from the same piece of land, providing shade, simplifying planting (several varieties are sometimes planted in the same hole, and minor crops are planted in the already-tilled soil of the yam fields), and allowing different crops with different rooting depths ("friends") to utilize the soil "juices" more fully.

The foregoing represents what we feel to be the typical beliefs regarding soil erosion and its effects. It should be pointed out that some farmers were well aware of what might be termed the scientific attitude toward soil erosion, and others were prepared to recite this attitude (having heard about it from agricultural agents or others) while still, we feel, holding to the traditional beliefs. In view of the brief time during which agricultural extension work has been underway in Mt. Chester, it is no criticism of the extension agents (whose work impressed us highly) to say that most farmers have yet to give up their traditional beliefs regarding soil erosion or the lack thereof, particularly in view of the elements of resistance to "government men" which will be discussed below.

Space does not permit us to review in detail the many cultivation practices which tend to encourage erosion. The most important, however, should be mentioned. Among them are the following: (1) clean-weeding of banana and certain other fields; (2) exposure of the soil in yam fields (and fallow fields preparatory to planting yams) during the wettest time of the year; (3) consistent downslope movement of soil as a result of hoeing; (4) lack of tree crops; and (5) absence of most conservation measures.

A number of traditional conservation measures are practised. These may be placed in two groups: the unconscious measures, felt to achieve a purpose other than soil conservation; and the conscious measures. The former include the following: (1) planting of tree crops; (2) planting of mixed tree- and ground-crop gardens adjoining the house plot; (3) achieving the effects of broad-based terracing by building yam hills along the contour; (4) inter-cropping several varieties in the same plot; (5) in some cases leaving a cultivated field (e.g., one taken out of grass) in the half-tilled stage of large clods, only broken down into finer tilth immediately before planting; and (6) throwing clods back uphill after digging yams–i.e., refilling the holes from below. The conscious measures which, it should be emphasized, are by no means common, include the following: (1) using tree crops to prevent "breakaways;" and (2) digging ditches roughly on the contour. Formerly logs were laid along the contour, but this is no longer done, perhaps because wood is quite scarce.

The government and the Jamaica Agricultural Society recommend certain specific practices to prevent erosion. The more important may be listed here. One is the planting of grass lines along the contour. A second (recommended only for certain soil-slope conditions) is ditching. A third is greater emphasis on tree crops. A fourth is greater emphasis on animal husbandry. A fifth is the preparation of a farm plan for each farm, one which will keep the steeper land in tree crops, maximize grass fallow or grazing land, and generally suit the crop to soil-slope conditions. Obviously, there are other reasons as well as those pertaining to soil conservation for recommending the third, fourth, and fifth. The degree of adoption of these measures is, as we have seen, limited.

There is no single answer to the question why conservation measures are not more widely adopted. There appear, in fact, to be a large number of perceptual, social, economic, and even political factors involved, and—pending further analysis of the data—we can only touch on the more important of these factors in the present report. We shall present them in the order mentioned above—first social, then economic, then political factors—without attempting to weigh any one factor.

Mt. Chester is not what might be termed a well-integrated community. Physical separation of houses (the pattern is one of semi-dispersed settlement) contributes to this, but more important are religious and economic cleavages. While there are recognized community leaders —e.g., the Catholic priest and a Catholic lay teacher who, though he works elsewhere, resides in the community—their influence is limited as regards farming. The fact that the two leaders mentioned are not farmers contributes to the absence of one universally-important element in acceptance of development programmes: active farm leaders whose farming practices are imitated by others. The local extension agents, although they attempt mightily to influence farmers, have not been in the area long enough to have acquired the prestige or "reputation for success" necessary for widespread adoption of their recommendations. The natural breakdown of the community into informal and formal groupings, e.g., visiting groups, is in a sense a cause for resistance to recommended conservation measures, since the groupings (with the exception of the Catholic church-related and JAS-related ones) do not centre around individuals who may be expected to lead in the direction of improved methods; indeed, the opposite is often the case. There are, however, instances of progressive farmers influencing others to adopt improved methods. These progressive farmers are generally also leaders in such organizations as the Jamaica Agricultural Society, and tend to be wealthier than average. Discussions among friends concerning the recommended practices seem to be the chief means by which the recommended measures are spread from the progressive farmers to others.

A rather subtle but nevertheless important social factor relates to the family structure of the community, and particularly to the sex division of labour. It was noticed that women, whose principal economic function is marketing, tend to exert some measure of influence in favour of planting those crops which they can take to market, as against crops which are marketed by men. The former are ground crops; the latter, tree crops and bananas. There appear to be two elements involved. One is the pleasure which marketing gives the farm women; this usually weekly event gives the women a measure of excitement, a chance to get together with their friends (in the trucks, and at the market stalls), and the satisfaction of contributing to the always-precarious income of the family. The second factor relates to the instability of common-law family unions in Mt. Chester. In common-law unions, particularly the sort found in Jamaica, where the children stay with the mother, it is to be expected that the farm women will want to maximize their economic role, specifically, their control of family income. The greater the emphasis on crops which women, rather than men, market, the larger portion of family income is under the control of women. We do not insist that this factor of insecure unions necessarily results in strong pressure by the women of such families to plant ground crops, but we suspect greater pressure in this direction in common-law, as against formally married, families. Our results here must, however, be treated as inconclusive. In any event, women did exert some measure of pressure in the direction of planting ground crops, although both the degree of effort and the results were highly variable.

Among the economic factors, an important one is related to land tenure. Mt. Chester farmers simply will not plant trees on rented land, even if the same plot of land has been rented from the same landlord (local or non-community) for 30 years or more. The universal feeling is that the man who plants trees on another man's land will not reap the benefit of his labour, which appears in any case only after several years. Since much of the land in Mt. Chester is rented, this factor obviously holds back what appears to be the most valuable anti-erosion measure of all, tree-crop planting.

A second economic factor relates to capital scarcity, and to lack of time on the part of Mt. Chester farmers to overcome with labour what they cannot purchase with capital. Direct anti-erosion measures–ditches, grass lines, etc.–require considerable input of labour, which must be contributed by the farmer or paid for in the form of hired labour. Among those farmers who would be willing to put in such measures, most point out that they cannot spare the labour and do not have the capital to hire labour for it. Even where, as under the Farm Development Scheme, the government pays a portion of the cost, farmers claim that the time they must put in, i.e., the portion of the cost which they must bear, is prohibitive. (This may or may not be a rationalization, since, as we shall see, farmers have other reservations about the "scheme.") There proved to be a strong relationship between capital availability and acceptance of capital-requiring soil conservation measures: generally, only those with more than the average amount of capital responded. (Several of the farmers who accepted such measures were among those who had worked on contract labour in the United States. The capital this gave them may well have been an important factor in their response, although one can infer also that some selection factor operates so as to put both the progressive farmers and contract labourers in the same "innovating" group. The contract labourers, in addition, may have seen conservation practices at work in the U.S.)

The Farm Development Scheme, under which generous subsidies are paid farmers for various practices having to do directly or indirectly with soil conservation, had only just been instituted in Mt. Chester at the time of our study, and it is probable that the farmers' reservations about joining the "scheme" will diminish with time. (Note: this has not been the case in a nearby community where the F.D.S. has been operative since 1955, but there is a strong possibility that other factors are at work in the latter area.) These reservations are both economic and political. Farmers possessing valid title to at least a portion of their land (others are not admitted to the scheme) are unwilling to surrender their title as security on loans provided under the scheme, and there is a general lack of awareness of the fact that a farmer can join the scheme, and obtain some of its benefits, without taking out a loan. In a situation of acute land hunger, such as prevails in Jamaica, it is understandable that farmers are quite anxious about jeopardizing the title to their land. An even more serious problem is the lack of valid titles to owned land, preventing many of the farmers who might wish to join the scheme from doing so. Unregistered titles are, of course, an island-wide problem, and Mt. Chester is no exception to the rule that land ownership is based more commonly on unregistered documents (will, "paper," etc.) or no documents at all than on valid, registered titles. Finally, and perhaps most important, is the problem of distrust of government. Most farmers in Mt. Chester are strong supporters of the Opposition Party, rather than the majority Administration Party. Most do not fully separate in their minds the activities of the government from those of the Administration Party: this applies specifically to the Agriculture Department, and even, for a few farmers, to the Jamaica Agricultural Society.

Thus, distrust of the Administration Party is transferred to the government and, occasionally, the JAS. Some few farmers, for example, believe that the Administration Party wishes to socialize the land, which to them means taking title away from them, and suspect that the agricultural people may have this in mind in the surrender of titles under the FDS. Added to this is the almost universal latent distrust of peasant farmers for a government with which, in the past, they have had little contact.

The most fundamental factor of all appeared to us to be the lack of perception of erosion, its causes, consequences, and control. This point has been discussed in a preceding section, where an attempt was made to portray the typical set of beliefs regarding soil erosion. It is clear that the chief hindrance to soil conservation is lack of awareness on the part of farmers that serious erosion exists, or alternatively, that anything can be done about it.

4.

Allegations of labor shortages in parts of rural Jamaica, notwithstanding acute unemployment and underemployment, led the Jamaican government in 1955 to commission an inquiry by a local social scientist, from whose report the following extract is taken. In many areas with alleged labor shortages, the author found that owners of small and medium-sized farms had no difficulty in getting as many temporary workers as they needed and often had to discourage job seekers. The "labor shortage" issue was not one of labor scarcity but of how estates recruited and treated workers and how well the traditional expectations of the rural laborer were fulfilled. Such traditional cooperative arrangements as "partners," "lend-day," "day-for-day," "morning sport," and "digging" are shown here to conflict with the "rational" labor requirements of the large estates.

M. G. SMITH, a social anthropologist born in Jamaica, was the recipient of an Island Scholarship; he took an undergraduate degree at McGill University and received his doctorate at University College, London. He has done extensive field research in Jamaica, Grenada, and Carriacou and also in Nigeria. Smith has been Research Fellow and Acting Director of the Institute of Social and Economic Research at the University of the West Indies, Jamaica, and Professor of Anthropology at the University of California, Los Angeles. Currently, he is Professor of Anthropology at University College, London.

Patterns of Rural Labour

M. G. Smith

Jamaican farms can be divided for present purposes into three categories: (1) Large estates which operate as industrial or quasi-industrial concerns under an impersonal employed management, are controlled mainly by syndicates, and on which the labour is unionized directly; (2) Middle or large sized properties lacking this overtly industrial character, lacking direct union representation for their labour, administered under individual or family ownership, and personal, often paternalistic, control; (3) Small farms proper which are purely individual in their administration, focussed on production for household subsistence as well as exchange in local and overseas markets, and on which no element of trade unionism has yet appeared. The historical foundations and development of these three different categories of Jamaican farming are too well known to need elaboration here. What is important for our purpose is the difference in labour recruitment and relations characteristic of the two extreme types, the small farm and the large estate.

ESTATE LABOUR. The large estate employs a trained agricultural and administrative staff, themselves subject to dismissal or transfer, promotion and the like, and these people operate the estate within the framework of ultimate responsibility to their directors, and under conditions acceptable to the trade unions. The worker on such estates knows the efficacy of his complaint in the union room, and feels a degree of assured protection or support from

From *A Report on Labour Supply in Rural Jamaica,* Kingston, Jamaica, The Government Printer, pp. 9–23. Reprinted with permission of the author.

external organizations when conflicts arise with management. The impersonal nature of management itself on such estates to some extent facilitates the type of labour recruitment and administration most suited to the agricultural needs of these concerns.

The problems of labour administration on estates themselves consist ultimately in the simultaneous deployment of labour at a variety of tasks in a manner reducing the load of supervision to the minimum on the less technical operations, and also permitting rapid switches of the estate labour-force from one set of completed tasks to another as the estate requires. Such conditions are fulfilled by a combination of task, day, and weekly or monthly employment, the monthly employees being predominantly administrative in function, the weekly and some monthly employees being mainly technicians or personnel necessary for the performance of routine tasks such as cattle-care, while the task workers are primarily employed in the field as agricultural operations make necessary. These task workers are recruited by the estate headmen who are charged with supervision and allocation of work under the control of the estate overseer or manager himself, who directs the strategy of field operations, makes payment after inspecting the completed task, and deals with the estate owners. Simultaneous performance of a variety of operations by a relatively large number of workers in the field in the most rapid and efficient manner with the minimum of supervision *during* the period of work is achieved by reliance on task, job or piece work as the standard pattern, and the use of task, job or piece work on this scale enjoins a mode of recruitment for such units which in turn treats all field workers of this category as casual employees.

When new canes are six weeks old or thereabouts, the weeding is performed by women. When the canes are a little older, women tend to avoid the weeding and men have to be called in. The headmen on such estates recruit for the task to be discharged by visiting or sending messages to areas from which labour has commonly been drawn for the estate, to the effect that one or two hundred persons of this or that sex will be required on Monday morning. The "casual" who has worked regularly on this estate and turns up on Tuesday may very well find himself out of luck. The jobs once allocated are the responsibility of the worker. The task-rates are known to all concerned, as they have been the subject of union activity and discussion and are well publicized. Measurement on Thursdays is followed by payment on Fridays. Even if the entire area allocated to a worker has not been completed by the weekly measuring-time, he can receive payment for the work done that week; and clearly, the presence of other people in the field pushing ahead with their tasks presents a stimulus to increased output.

WAGE-LABOUR ON SMALLER UNITS. Employment on a small and medium-sized farm differs in many ways from the pattern of task work by casual labour which has been adapted so successfully by the estates in Jamaica. The small farmer is frequently a native of the community in which his home is situated, and his labour relations are very much mixed up with his social relations as a member of that community. Bad social relations, a reputation for vindictiveness, hostility, meanness or the like can go a long way towards depriving a person of local labour supply. A good reputation, even if undeserved, may do the opposite. Some illustrations of this point may be given: (1) In one "shortage" area, a man who found himself unable to recruit labour to weed his corn crop last year—which he consequently lost—asked another to recruit on his behalf. This the man asked failed to do, although he himself received many applications from people looking for work with him. When he suggested to such workers that he could find them employment on his friend's place they went elsewhere. Interestingly enough, the farmer who in 1955 faced such a shortage of labour as involved the loss of his corn crop, two years ago used to find six or seven people in his yard at 6 or 7 o'clock in the morning begging him for work.

(2) In an area of "good supply" which happens also to be one of the intense under-employment and unemployment, the man with the heaviest demand for farm labour

found it difficult to get workers. I asked his headman about this, and got the following answer:—"If you handle me to any dimension, you cuss me, you rush me, you abuse me, I not going to work for you, I not going to work for you. If this man wanted one man and there were a hundred, he couldn't get the one because he cuss them all broadside". The people in this district occupy themselves as best they can breaking stones for Government.

(3) In another area of reported shortage the greatest demand for local farm-labour comes from a property adjoining the district. The political allegiance of the small man of this area is to one political party and that of the property owner to another. The estate overseer complained extensively about the local supply and quality of labour and asked me to recommend that Government make labour on properties compulsory for 5 days a week, that is to say, something like the apprenticeship system. Over the past 12 years various workers have left this property and taken up land on a new Government settlement or elsewhere in the area, partly out of dissatisfaction with the owner's political activity. Apparently these issues between property owner and local labour came to a head after the last general election, and resulted in the withdrawal of most of the local labour from this estate. The property now recruits its labour from villages in the hill country five or six miles distant, and finds the local labour supply extremely difficult. But it appears that local people are under the impression that the property owner personally ordered his rangers to turn them off the estate. The net result has been to provide small farmers in this area with a temporary windfall as regards labour supply, and though it is possible that these small men experienced "labour shortages" previously, on the whole they did not in 1955.

Labour recruited for small farms is known as "local labour", and is distinguished from labour on properties or sugar estates by rural folk. Local labour is wage-labour normally recruited from the associates or children of the associates of the employer, or from his partners or kinsfolk. The rates are prevailingly low, in areas of abundant supply averaging 3/- to 3/6d. per man-day plus lunch, and possibly as in South St. Elizabeth, a snack or two.

A small farmer, 40 years old, will normally recruit local labour from young men of 20 or thereabouts, who are his juniors in the community age status system, or from his age-peers of similar economic and social standing who are well disposed towards him. Typically the equals whom he recruits will be kinsfolk or partners. The juniors may be affinal kin, migrant labourers from other areas, or relatively destitute young men of the district.

The employer whose kinsfolk in the area also use wage-labour to help them may sometimes share workers with them. In this way all parties enjoy a more stable relationship. When the worker completes his assignment for employer A, the latter's cousin or brother has work ready for him; and when employer C who is also linked in with this group wants a worker, he "borrows" the man known to A, and adds him to the man with whom he deals. Employers in such positions do not complain of "shortage". That is to say, they have solved their labour recruitment problem. Such people generally work "partners" among themselves, and this further consolidates the group structure.

Other employers may not have sufficient work or contacts which can provide sufficient work for their people, and consequently are not in a position to keep labourers attached to them for any length of time, since they cannot provide sufficiently frequent employment. Such men tend to meet their labour requirements by the institution of "partners" or "lend-day", "day-match" or "day-for-day"; and to discharge emergency tasks of a large nature by calling free work, which is of two types, "morning sport" and "digging". These institutions are historically the basic foundations and forms of labour-exchange among small-settlers, and the viability of innovations in labour relations, that is to say, the successful adaptation of new patterns of employment, depends on the consistency which these developments have with the traditional forms of distributing labour within such communities. It is therefore necessary to discuss these patterns in more detail.

MORNING SPORT: DIGGING. Free work by a large group on another's farm is known as "morning sport" or "digging". In some areas, as near Morant Bay, St. Thomas, morning work ceases at noon and takes place only on Saturdays. In areas of good labour supply it normally continues till 5 p.m. and may happen on week days also. In Portland, diggings sometimes attract 60 people; and groups of 15 to 20 were commonly observed doing morning work. The idea of some urban folk that these working-bees are now a thing of the past in rural Jamaica, is therefore simply a measure of their ignorance. Both sexes attend a "digging", the women being responsible for planting the yam or potato hills, and for preparation of the food. One digging attended by about 60 persons involved an outlay of 10 quarts of rum and £7 food-stuffs, which works out at something like the local cost of the total assistance derived. But the social value of a "digging" to all concerned is greater than the immediate return of work measured solely in economic terms. The farmer finds his reputation for generosity and community spirit greatly enhanced, and has no difficulty in securing such supplies of local labour as he thereafter needs. The community through this institution expresses the values of farm labour and co-operation. I have observed in Portland persons telling others whom they expect to hold a digging soon not to fail of inviting them. The same sort of thing holds true for morning sport when called by a popular farmer.

There is of course an implied reciprocity in these two institutions. When A does morning sport on B's place he reckons that B will reciprocate if called on his own. But this is a very indirect and hypothetical balance or exchange of work.

PARTNERS, LEND-DAY. Direct reciprocity obtains in the institutions of partners and lend-day. Lend-day may be exchange of work between two men limited to one day each; or it may be a local term used to denote "partner" or "day-for-day" work. Partner work is a continuous reciprocal exchange of work between two or more individuals who take it in turn to cultivate one another's holdings. There is no definite rule that B should pay back A's day before A does another for B, but this is largely understood although handled elastically. Partners may work with one another throughout the year, or, as in Upper Clarendon, mainly at certain seasons, such as March to June. Since farming is predominantly a male pursuit, partners are normally male, but in certain areas women too may exchange labour on a time-limited and strictly reciprocal basis for certain farming operations such as harvesting, planting and the like. The partners' women folk may also assist in the co-work, both by preparing the food and by farming themselves.

Sometimes a man has only one partner, but normally three or four and sometimes more individuals work partnership together. In this way the group feels able to handle relatively large areas of work in a single day and also to spread their social contacts more widely. The assistance which partners give one another is not of course limited to the farm. It may extend to the rearing of children, may be based on kinship, or may develop into something rather like substitute kinship if the partnership is maintained harmoniously for several years. Men whose distant holdings lie close to one another tend to work these holdings together by partnership, and in this way to halve the opportunities for praedial larceny therefrom. The long walk to faraway plots is passed pleasantly, and the partnership ensures that assistance is at hand on the distant holding should any accident or illness suddenly develop.

PARTNERSHIP AND WAGE-WORK. Partnership is free and voluntary co-work. When A works on B's place, B feeds A and the two start and stop work together. B expects similar treatment in his turn. The partners are not fully on the local labour-market to the extent that their partnership obligations remain to be discharged. That is to say, if A owes B, C and D one day's work each, he is not really available for wage-employment by local small farmers should B, C or D wish for his services. Often enough he will accept the offered employment and fail to turn up when consultation with his partners makes it clear that they expect his attendance first.

A common arrangement is to perform wage-employment on farms by means of the partnership system. This complex is so important that it deserves direct discussion and illustration. Where the circulation of money is low, wage-rates are low, 3/- to 4/- per man-day plus lunch; the only hope of small farmers to realize 15/- or 20/- as a lump sum during off-crop seasons in such areas, is by local farm employment together with their partners. This is how it works. Five men, A to E, work partners. A wants one pound for some purpose. He does a day's work for each of the other four and then approaches a small farmer whom he feels has work to be done. He offers to do five days work at the standard rate, and after ascertaining that payment will be immediate, tells his employer that he will bring his partners to clear it off in one day. The employer is normally pleased, as this ensures rapid performance of the task. Moreover, it is often cheaper to provide food for five men at one time than for one man on five days. A then brings his partners and they work for him on his employer's farm. They expect to be treated and fed in the manner typical of their partnership; that is to say, the agreement about hours of work and food are identical when partners work freely together or in a wage context. So too, the rule about cessation of work if rain falls, an important source of contention in day-work for wages, remains in the wage as in the partnership situation. The employer deals directly with A and pays him the pound when the day is over. All the partners are aware that they may be called on to do this type of work by one another.

It is impossible to illustrate the significance of this partnership relation for wage-work more clearly than from a case which occurred in the field. Two small farmers whose holdings are in bound, one with 60 acres, and the other with 17, both under fair cultivation, declared themselves to be employers of labour, and were interviewed as such, the larger man first. He purchases bananas on commission and has a relatively steady and sizeable weekly cash income. He said that he took up his family holding in 1954 from his ageing parent and started to cultivate it intensively himself. He now has several acres of bananas and is seeking to expand. To secure regular and sufficient labour in the area for a holding of this size, in 1954 he offered to pay 4/- a day plus food, for a day of 8 a.m. to 4 p.m., working on the average 7 to 9 people including 2 women for 4 days a week. This day-wage was one shilling higher than the prevailing local rate, so that he was able to attract labour and held it quite easily. His neighbour, the 17-acre man, like everybody else in the immediate vicinity, also pushed up his rate to 4/- to keep his work-team.

Asked whether he had experienced any labour shortage, the 60-acre man hesitated, denied such experience, and then gave an instance of irrationality on the part of one of his workers who had been with him for 18 months. This worker had refused to continue working for the interviewee two weeks before our interview. The ground for refusal given is revealing in itself. The worker complained that he did not want the lunch, as his employer's mother was not cooking it. The employer said that none the less he himself was eating it. The worker said that this didn't matter, and so broke off the relationship. The employer instanced this as an example of the over-weening demands and "ignorance" of the local labourer. This employer is himself very kindly disposed towards the local people, and a native of the district. The worker having left this employer has been doing day work for other people in the area quite frequently, at 3/6 per day plus lunch.

As the interview continued the employer revealed that he had switched from day work to task work in June 1955, and was "training" his people to get the task-habit so that he could reduce his load of supervision. During this transitional period he has been giving out work by day and task alternately to his team of regulars. The day-worker is provided with lunch, but the task worker provides his own. Normally this employer bought bananas on the Monday and had been present with his workers in the field for the rest of the week, but now he wants to cultivate two patches at some distance from each other and would be unable to give this close personal supervision himself.

The 17-acre man stated that people in this area do not want task work *"since they want to bring lots of men, their partners, and get lunch same time, and this can't happen on task"*. He also said that until June 1955 he had to pay 4/- a day plus food, following the bigger man's rates, but since then had been paying 3/6 a day, getting all the people he wants, besides having a steady gang of five who come and tell him in advance when they will be able to come and how many persons they can bring. Really then, the worker who protested about food was simply trying to draw his employer's attention to the implications of task-work for partnership. Far from being "ignorant" or "overweening", he was too polite and indirect. In other words, the task system breaks down in that area because it does not permit the partners to discharge their obligation of feeding one another at the work. In consequence people prefer day work at 3/6 to task giving an equivalent of 4/- to 4/6 a day.

PARTNER, DAY, AND TASK WORK. This conflict of partnership and the task system obtains wherever they concur, and is an important background factor giving the effect of shortage. In some areas, some employers object to task-workers who bring their partners to assist them on other grounds also. Firstly, they say that partners, being responsible only for the allocation of time and only to the hired task worker, do not do satisfactory wage work. Secondly, they say that the partners should bring their own tools for the job. By convention the task worker normally provides his own tools for the job. But often enough when partners do task work together there is a shortage of tools and a run on the employer's stock. Finally the provision of food is not reckoned part of the obligation of the employer in the situation of task work. Some men may give food to one or two task-workers who are cultivating the home-patch; sometimes also employers grant permission to task-workers to dig up coco, or pick breadfruits and the like which are in the area of their work. But since the task-worker's partners are not responsible to his employer, the latter has no control directly over the amount which they use on the premises, and often suspects that some provisions are taken away. Meanwhile, the man short of ready cash and seeking it by farm-work, whether by day or task, can only hope to secure a fair sum quickly by using his partners to assist him.

Due to this discordance of partnership and the strict task system, small farmers who practice employment principally by the task system often find themselves facing problems of labour supply. Sometimes such employers attempt to solve their problems by leaping out of the frying pan into the fire. They do this by abandoning the attempt to cultivate a "regular" set of workers, "my customers" as one man puts it, and by recruiting casuals whenever they need. This adjustment sometimes leads to the self-defeating situation, as near Linstead, in which certain employers refuse to employ people who come looking for work on the ground that these casual employees are so short of money, and the wage-rate is so low, that praedial larceny is almost certain and on a scale greater than normal. Again, casuals who approach the man and fail to secure work will tend to look elsewhere and also to tell their fellows.

Day work and partnership fit easily together. Partners discharging their obligations by wage work on the day basis for a particular farmer receive the same "treatment" as that to which they are accustomed, come at the same times, leave at the same time, get the same meals, have the same understandings about the provision of tools and about the cessation of work when rain falls. Moreover, the "smallest" men, who only need to hire occasionally either due to a seasonal rush of work, or to loss of time through sickness, ceremonial, family engagements and the like, can ask their partners to "favour" them with a day's work for wages, that is to say, to give them a day which will not be repaid in time, but at nominal rate of 2/- to 3/- plus lunch. Men of this sort normally have two or more partners; hence they are usually able to obtain assistance from one partner or another. In fact such associations produce interesting situations in which one man will work for another at 2/- or 3/- a day rather than for a third at 4/- or 5/- or more. The economic assumption of higher rates attracting workers fails here because of the social obligations and securities of the partnership relation. But the partnership relation, because of these very securities, helps to keep the local wage-rate at a lower level than it may well need to be.

Partners tend to be approximate age-mates. When a man of 26 or so has for partner another of 45 or more there is always some specific factor which compensates for this age-distance and makes them roughly of equal status within the district or neighbourhood.

Young men in areas which offer no significant alternatives to own-account farming strive to develop their holdings and group relationships by working in partnership, but as they grow older and have families and holdings of their own their ability to participate in these multiple partnerships declines, and by the time they are 45 to 50, they tend to do so marginally. Their sons have been taken into the institution, and the partners of these sons work on the old men's farms occasionally. This, in point of fact, means that the young men are drawn by the partnership bond to work more for their own account, whether on holdings of their own or on plots of their family land, or for wage, than to work for their parents. The net result is that the older men are more prone to experience difficulties of labour supply than the younger ones, especially since the majority of the cultivation is in the hands of these middle-aged and senior males. This means that the older men rely for assistance on hired hands more than do their juniors, but the juniors are obliged by the partnership bonds to assist one another, and this obligation often takes precedence over individual wage arrangements by partners.

In Africa, as among the Hausa or Mende, this type of situation does not normally arise because the father is responsible for the maintenance of the entire family, including his sons, for providing their marriage-payments, and ultimately, for building a separate compound for them. To discharge these obligations the father controls the total family labour force, and while allotting individual plots to his sons, uses their labour on the family farm for a specific time each week.[1]

In Jamaica, family instability is probably lower among rural small farmers than is generally supposed, but so too is access to land and to alternative employment. Provision of necessary cash is an individual obligation, and young men are forced to seek this for themselves as best they can. From the age at which they "get sense," 6 to 7 years, they are made to feel inferior to their parents purely on grounds of age. It is common to hear a man of 38 or so addressed by his adolescent son as "Mass Papa"; and the youth who called his father from a distance of thirty-five yards was given a severe lecture for this misdemeanour. That is to say, generation differences between father and son are emphasized heavily and become status differences to which no obvious social or economic function attaches; but this emphasis, which prevents closer association of parents and their juniors, pushes the young men into a group of their own away from home and the group of their fathers. The net result is to reduce the ease with which these older men can recruit labour from the junior generation. Complaints about youth which have this basis are common in all districts.

COMPOUND FORMATIONS. So far we have been looking at the fit between partner and day work on the one hand, and partner and task work on the other. Often enough the nexus of employment relations set up by small farmers is far more complex than this. Kinship or affinity of the parties is frequently involved, but these can be ignored as largely stabilizing factors.

In South St. Elizabeth the notion of "day-task" obtains. The employer shows the worker a task which is reckoned by both to form a fair day's work, and leaves him to work unsupervised, but provides the expected meals. The worker leaves when he is finished with the task, which may be later than the normal hour at which day work ceases, or

[1] M. G. Smith, *The Economy of Hausa Communities of Zaria* (London: H.M.S.O., 1955); see also K. Little, *The Mende of Sierra Leone* (London: Routledge and Kegan Paul, 1952).

sometimes earlier. If the work is to be performed by partners as a team, then the "day-task" is multiplied by the number of men involved. Here the day pattern, the task pattern, and the partnership pattern produce a compound formation.

Often also, as in Upper Clarendon and other areas of good supply, A works for B one day for hire, and gives a day free, solo, or in a morning sport. Sometimes a man combines morning sport with hired workers. Sometimes the same team gathers for a morning sport, completing the day's work on the farm of a second man. Often, where share-cropping is prevalent, a small farmer gives out land on share and pays the croppers to work for him on his own holding also when they are not available to give free work. In some share-cropping arrangements too, the land-owner provides such food, tools, fertiliser, and seed as are necessary to the cultivation, and is responsible for certain operations, such as planting, taking a larger proportion of the share than in other conditions. Under such circumstances the share-cropper will often bring his partners at wages to work on the share-land for the land-owner, when the latter is obliged to discharge certain tasks and is responsible for certain parts of the cultivation. Here share-cropping, partnership and wage-work by the day or task system run together in a single relation.

All these compound relations can only flourish to the extent that they harmonise the varying elements of which they are composed, particularly partner and wage work. Cases of breakdown occur in the system of day-work particularly where the employer does not belong to the same social class as his worker, and consequently emphasizes the economic aspect of the work relation more exclusively than do the folk. This type of friction develops sometimes about the hours of work, the amount of rest ("cotching") during the day's work, or the rate of pay, but principally about the payment due when work is interrupted by rain. Clearly, if day workers use partners to assist them, and under partnership norms, the day's work is defined in one way with regard to work interruptions by weather, but differently in regard to day work for wage, conflicts may be expected to develop which can set employer and workers at logger-heads.

Partnership norms about this matter are relatively simple. If rain falls before 12 o'clock the work can be reckoned at half a day. If rain falls after lunch it is reckoned as a full day. This often does not suit employers with large cultivations and little capital, and many instances have been met in which interruptions of work by rain led to calculations of three-quarters or seven-eighths of a day, with pay proportionate. This means that the worker whose partners have assisted him loses by the deal, as he has received a day's work from each of the partners and is only paid by his employer for the work done until the time rain fell. Consequently, employers who practise this particular form of economy, sometimes find themselves facing a certain amount of labour difficulty. This follows inevitably, since only those persons who are not dependent on partnership are free to accept such employment without loss to themselves. In wage-work by the day as by the task system, a man with partners can only participate freely if the two sets of norms and expectations are consistent.

Lack of cash among small-settlers leads sometimes to direct barter of labour. The carpenter may do a day's work for X to be paid for by two days' work on his farm. X may bring in his partners to assist him. Sometimes an elderly bachelor does day-work for the woman who washes his clothes as payment. Solitary labourers work off their rent for one family and the cost of cooking for another. Weekly attached workers are relatively scarce; in one case a man was retained at a pound a week, allowed to farm on some 8½ acres, provided with food and a small two-room house for himself, and worked not merely for his employer, but for the employer's kinsmen on different holdings as required. Often a man hires his daughter's lover if the latter is living at home with him, and on occasion a man may hire his own wife. The "caretaker" relationship, one in which a "foster" child performs menial household or farm labour for the "foster" parent, and sometimes for the latter's kin as well, is also significant.

These and certain other patterns are devices by which the

small farmer secures fairly constant labour supply at extremely low cost to himself, and unwittingly creates a condition in which he is unable to sell his labour at any higher cost to others. Share-cropping is matched by share-shopping, an arrangement in which one man keeps shop for another for a share in the profits. Disputes develop here mainly over the taking of stock. "Apprenticeship" may be somewhat similar. The apprentice is normally unpaid for a long period, and thereafter receives about 2/6d. a week. But when his skill is just beginning to mature, he may find that his master has secured other apprentices, and no longer needs his services. Somehow there are large numbers of "assistant" masons, "assistant" carpenters and the like, thrown back on to the farm-labour market for every one skilled craftsman in rural areas.

Doubling-up is another device. The classic instance met with in the field is of a domestic servant who was also shop-keeper, working roughly 70 hours a week for 6/- a month. Clearly such combinations defeat the aims of minimum wage laws. Another case observed involved a woman hired at 7/- a week, as domestic for a family who lived by themselves in one house only to find herself working for two households for the same wage, because the family of her employer ate and spent the day in the second household some distance away. Caretaking arrangements on holdings, "yard-work" which includes farm labour and cattle-care, in one case studied for a wage of 7/- a week—these are some other devices for keeping wage-rates low. As a rule such patterns multiply bonds between employer and employee which are extraneous to the strict task-situation, and are linked with relatively low payments made once only for several quite distinct tasks.

Middle-sized properties, that is, units of 50 to 500 or 600 acres, vary to some extent in the success with which they handle the task-system according to their capital resources. The property with large available capital tends to be run along estate lines, relying on task work by casual labour as far as its actual farming practice permits. Its management is typically the function of an employed overseer, and, though personal in character, may be unexpectedly amenable to workers simply because of the class distinction involved between labour and management. The trouble with insufficiently capitalized holdings of medium size develops when attempts to expand or maintain their cultivation are made which involve substituting kind for cash payments. These kind-payments consist mainly in permission to local folk to use and cultivate small plots free for one year or more, and thereafter at a gradually increasing rental; or in various share-cropping arrangements, for instance, the cultivator keeping ground provisions but being obliged to put in bananas or some other cash crop. Here the landowner hopes to tie workers by share-cropping arrangements, and tenancies, free or otherwise. In point of fact this device often boomerangs, and the sudden demand for rental may prompt a withdrawal of workers who feel that their efforts in clearing and tilling the bush have been taken advantage of by the landowner. Sometimes too, the landowner wishes to terminate these relationships because of the relatively unrestricted access to the property which they permit, and his fears or experiences of praedial larceny.

TASK-WORK. The historical foundations of task-work in the British West Indies are well known. On Emancipation, systems of task work were developed by those responsible for administering estates, which were then faced with problems of relative labour shortage. Newspapers of the period contain complete lists and specifications of these tasks and rates of pay. Prior to this, farm-labour in the West Indies had not relied heavily on task patterns, although "jobbing" or contract-work was of some importance.

Continuation of task-work on estates up to the present has depended on its utility for estate management and its relative convenience to the workers. The great convenience of task-work to Jamaican farm-workers lies in the freedom which it gives them to distribute their labour-time in wage-work or own-account occupations, especially on their own farms, but also at home. The ability of own-account farmers to accept wage-work is limited, as has already been observed; and is mainly effective in short-term employment on the one hand, or in the flexible time-disposals of the task system on the other.

Initially the task system involved scales standardized for each estate separately, but nowadays, it involves scales standardized for estates which are graded and grouped under union-management bargaining of an annual character. Variations in payment rates between estates of different grades and types are for this reason far less impressive than are differences associated with different task descriptions, both off and on estates. For example, comparisons of particular task-rates listed in the summary schedules of various sugar-cane estates reveal a difference which can only be explained in terms of the content of the task. Similarly in St. James, digging yam hills by piece work averages 25/- a hundred; in some other areas the rate is as little as 8/-; but the depth of the hill and the type of the soil are important in this context. A similar sort of thing applies to output and wage-rates for work under varying conditions. In Upper Clarendon there are some places planted with yam in which a strong man is not expected to dig more than 6 to 8 hills a day, while in other parts moderate work outputs run at about 30 hills per day, the hills in both soils being of the same depth. A further variation is introduced on small holdings according to the quality of work expected from different people; thus the same task will be given to one man for 10/- and to another for £1, the work of the latter being regarded as twice that of the former in quality and value. These points are worth bearing in mind throughout the following discussion.

It is commonly stated by small farmers that they pay task-rates equivalent to or higher than those of the estates closest to them; but there is all the difference in the world between weeding one patch of banana-walk which receives 6 or 8 weedings per year and a patch of equal size last cut 8 months ago. There is also a great deal of difference in the amount of available work which estates and small holders offer to the labour that they recruit. Thus in St. Thomas some properties were paying 2/3 a hundred to pick and husk coconuts while adjoining small settlers were paying 2/6 to 3/-; but in fact a man could make as much as or more per day's work on the property at this task than on any of the small-settlers' holdings. The same point applies to cane-cutting rates by weight. There is great difference between cutting canes which yield 25 to 40 tons and other fields yielding 14 tons per acre or thereabouts. Even so, in some districts studied, cane-cutting is carried out by free local labour and so constitutes no problem, the workers rewarding themselves by taking trash as stock feed.

TASK-STANDARDS. Another important difference between use of task-work by estates and small-settlers, lies in the standardization of the task. Task-work properly connotes work measured in certain standard units, as for instance the weeding, forking or reforking of one square chain or more. It also involves an agreed and accepted standard of performance between the parties, based on ultimate comparisons of an individual worker's effort with that of his colleagues. If a man's work is poor in quality, improvements have to be made in order to warrant pay. This system is used by Government on Parochial and Public Works road maintenance as well as on estates, the headmen, whether of road or property, being responsible for the quality of the work and/or its measurement under the overseer's or foreman's direction. Now if harvesting is excluded, the task worker on any small-holding generally finds himself to be the only person engaged in that particular type of job, apart from his employer, unless the worker himself brings his partners to assist him. Consequently the only direct comparison possible is between the employer's performance and the worker's. Indirect comparisons of present work with performances by other men in the same task or spot at past times are sometimes made by the employers vocally, and may understandably lead to friction. Thus there is little chance of developing or improving standards of task-performance on the plots of individual small holders. What does happen is that the farmer who finds that work of a particular type done by a certain man suits him, tries to maintain contact with that worker and to recruit him whenever that particular type of task becomes available again. This in turn leads to a certain amount of recruitment difficulty and fosters occupational immobility. Farm-labour is a highly diversified affair indeed, and a forkman may well be able to make twice as much per day's work at his specialty as he can at any other farm task, as for instance trench-cutting or banana-spraying, weeding or the like. The net result is that the forkman tends to stick to forking work and to be called on principally for this, at one time finding that many farmers want his services simultaneously, at another that he is unemployed.

SUPERVISION. All employers were asked about their modes of supervising workers. Those men who used day-work normally worked alongside of their hired help in the field, and in some areas day-tasks were allocated. Those who used task-work were sometimes present in the field with their worker, either by accident, or when they suspected that malpractices were likely to develop. The general idea is that the task-worker functions on his own; having taken up the task he is free to attend to it or to draw off from it as he pleases, without constant supervision by the employer. This is its great attraction for workers with other commitments. When the employer finds that a task is unsatisfactorily performed there is not a great deal that he can do, other than direct withholding of payment, if such has not already been made, until the work has come up to the expected quality. This type of thing once done normally breaks up casual worker-employer relationships. The worker won't return, the employer won't want him back. Other employers will make the payment without protest, or after discovering that mild protests are ineffective, partly in order to maintain a liberal reputation; but they also take care thereafter to look for other workers when next they need them. This in turn may lead an employer to depend increasingly on casual recruitment. Still other employers cultivate regular associations with workers whose output and quality please them and in this way seek to avoid the problems of unsatisfactory standards as well as unstable labour supply, today's work being judged in such cases against the last performance of the same worker.

MEASUREMENT. Measurement itself raises another series of problems. On the whole small farmers do not normally measure work given out, but they still rate their tasks in terms of square chains, acres and the like, or in hundreds of yam hills, potato hills and so forth. Where the work-unit is constant, problems of measurement hardly arise, as in the matter of digging yam hills, picking coconuts, harvesting pimento, coffee and so forth. Consequently, employers find the recruitment to these types of tasks relatively easy. But when the task forms an area of work, and measurement is imprecise, delayed or otherwise unsatisfactory, disputes frequently develop, and labour may withdraw.

On one occasion a farmer pointed out a common on which the grass had been cut at a rate working out at about 3/4 a square, taking his estimate of five acres to be correct. The rate on a nearby government farm for cutting grass of the same height and type was then 7/6 per square, so that the complaint of high wage rates rang hollow; but, in point of fact, the common shown to me could not have been less than seven acres in extent. When I mentioned this, the farmer's mother and family observed that they had said the same thing several times themselves. In other words, underpayment sometimes obtains by allocating tasks of a greater extent than that for which agreement is made.

A worker may be told that when last this field was measured it was so many squares in extent and that it has not grown since. In point of fact it may never have been measured or may have been measured inaccurately, or the true measurement may have been reduced or forgotten. On one property run by an overseer and regular staff, a worker contested in my presence the area for which payment was proposed as being less than the whole extent. Measurement proved him to be correct; but often it seems that workers cannot easily secure such measurement promptly; the chain is missing, and the rope, commonly suspected by workers to be more than one chain's length, is substituted.

Consequently, measurement of certain tasks, especially weeding and general cultivation, provides a great many grounds of possible friction which do not arise in systems of day-labour. Workers who feel dissatisfied with the employer's assessment of the work done tend to withdraw and go elsewhere. Property owners who leave measurement purely to headmen, or who refuse to satisfy their workers for one reason or another when the latter demand measurement of their completed tasks, invite the withdrawal of labour. Insufficiently supervised headmen may be expected to remunerate themselves by understating to the worker the amount of work done and by keeping what differences they can. The worker not directly protected by a union is hardly in a position to carry his protest beyond strong language and withdrawal. I was present at a discussion in which a small farmer asked a friend to check his calculation of an area, work on which had been completed by the task system in less than the expected time. No complaints were made about the quality of the completed work, but when his friend's calculation agreed with his and my own, this employer took the line that the rate of performance had been so rapid that it was advisable to understate the area involved. Presumably this was intended to keep the rate of payment at something like the current day-rates for moderate outputs. Thus, even when measurement does proceed by chain, the calculation may not be by rule.

PAYMENT. Payment for task-work is also a problem. In this respect some employers may suffer as much as workers, sometimes more so. The normal technique when a young man wants to leave a district seems to be as follows: he approaches somebody for a task, does a half day's work, asks for a sizeable advance, and disappears overnight. But other workers who remain in the district may also take advances, and then hold up the work. Female employers suffer more from this sort of treatment than men. Moreover, workers sometimes take so much of the complete payment in the form of advance that it is impossible for the employer to withhold a great deal to ensure an adequate standard of work.

On the other hand the worker may frequently fail to collect a payment due to him for the task which he has completed. An employer may nevertheless explain that he is a man of the greatest integrity and always pays promptly. In one case, which was being checked on by daily interviews for a week, a worker sought on three occasions to collect a payment of a few shillings due to him from an employer who, when interviewed, stated blandly that he had never owed a worker any payment in his life, but always paid promptly.

The problem of payment is sometimes complicated by the dependence of farmers on their women folk, wives or other, for the marketing of goods on Saturdays. The farm women take these goods and produce to market and return with the proceeds. The farmer often has to ask his workers to wait until the wife comes back from the market when he will have the money to pay them. But the woman often has other ideas about the outlay of this money and traditionally understates her market returns. This is simply a form of female self-protection. However, even when quite untrue, a small farmer may declare that his wife has had a "bad market", and on this ground ask his creditors to wait until next week. This waiting may go on for two or three months.

Some property headmen abuse their position in a comparable fashion. When I asked one unoccupied young man to accompany me in a car to the overseer of a particular property, he said he was sorry he could not go there, but was willing to go anywhere else. A local of some importance pressed him on this point, and it turned out that the worker had been so violently irritated with the headman of that property for withholding payments due to him that he dared not trust himself on the place again. This type of thing does not affect the two people concerned only, but spreads by talk throughout the area, and can lead to a general disinclination of workers to accept employment from particular people.

Similarly, workers with a reputation for holding up jobs

or for seeking advances and the like beyond what is regarded as the norm will find employers unwilling to accept their services. Again, when a man has been found committing praedial larceny, he normally has to leave the area of his discovery for a long period if he depends on employment, as none will normally risk employing him.

When an employer delays payment or leaves a task-worker dissatisfied with the payment, he frequently finds a quite specific form of praedial larceny developing on his remoter holdings. This consists of the cutting of yams from the hills and covering up with the mould. The vines are broken but are not pulled away, and for some days the farmer visiting the holding may think that his yams are still in the ground. Normally the yam-heads are left in the ground in this style of thieving. Small settlers are quite clear that this type of yam removal is either done by their family, the women whose children they do not support by cash, or by people familiar with their fields and habits, and who thus can go about this leisurely form of thieving. The "real" thief, they say, has little time in which to cover his tracks, and always empties the yam-hills he visits. It appears that the form of thieving just described may be simply a self-help by disappointed task-workers. If so, it may be compared with the larceny of low-grade bananas on banana properties, which operates to subsidise the prevailing wage-rates. Thus praedial larceny is itself to some extent bound up with the task system of labour relations. As such praedial larceny is notably more common in areas depending on task work than in those areas which recruit farm-labour for day work.

Another payment problem which faces the people in some areas is due to the low circulation of money. As one man stated, "you can always get people here to work for you whenever you want them. The problem is money. After two or three days at job-work a man has to call for an advance, if you can't give it to him he has to go elsewhere to find it. This is because he has to feed his family. This is called the 'custom'." This custom can lead to inordinate delays in the completion of tasks on particular holdings. It is simply a product of low levels of cash circulation.

Men who do task work for small-settlers most commonly are single and under 30 years of age. When a man has a woman living with him and has to feed a family, he has to get pay on Fridays to cover the weekend expenses of marketing and shop-goods. Because of the uncertainties about payment on small farms for task work, such men prefer to work for their neighbours by day-rates; but since they are sure of bringing home money as needed from task work on estates, they will take task work on any such unit which has a regular pay-day, simply for the regularity with which they will be paid. On these large units the man gets pay on Friday for the task as far as it has been completed at the time of measurement.

Small holders may say and with reason that their workers will receive no further advance until the tasks have been finished; but in such a case the worker may have little option but to look elsewhere for the ready money that his home needs.

JOB-WORK. An attempt to get around some of the problems presented by measurement and the like is made in job or piece work. Here employer and worker clearly understand that the arrangement is a bargain. No measurement will be attempted or enters into the issue. The two men look at an area of work to be done and each side states a price he considers especially profitable to himself. The job is given out as a bargain and advances may very well be refused until it is completed. This type of arrangement invites the dissatisfaction of both parties by the invidious comparisons which it stimulates. Thus a job-worker who has realised 8/- or 9/- per day for A will not take up a job offered by B after an initial experience that returns from B's work are lower than he had elsewhere obtained. Likewise an employer whose job was performed by one worker for a certain amount is unlikely to offer the next man more, even if wages have risen generally.

In day-work areas especially, many small farmers eschew this system of job-work completely. The worker who has to feed himself until the task or job is finished needs money with which to buy his provisions, unless he is permitted to take root-crops and the like from the field where he works. If he is not so permitted and receives insufficient advance, then he is completely unable to invite his partners to assist him in this work, and may find himself quite unable to complete the task at a profitable rate.

CASUAL AND REGULAR RECRUITMENT

Both day and task patterns lend themselves to the employment of labour on a casual or recurrent basis. But the day-work system seems more in accord with use of regular workers in that it fits more closely with the reciprocity norms of partnership and the communal standards of rural society. This particularly develops over the issue of "treatment". Good treatment consists in food, company on the job, equable and pleasant social relationships. These social relations precede and continue beyond the specific task-situation, and can hardly be created within it immediately or alone.

As mentioned above, task-work is traditionally unsupervised and does not entitle the worker to any food, cooked or otherwise at the employer's expense. Hence good treatment is not normally possible within the strict task system, though there are scores of employers who modify the task relation in one way or another to "facilitate" their workers, and give them "privileges" to help themselves from the non-commercial crops at hand. Such farmers may be able to keep task-workers attached to them over a period of months or years.

The issues of measurement, quality of work, payment, cash advance, debts, use of food, provision of tools, all loom as sources of friction to greater extent when casual labour is recruited than in regular or recurrent relationships. Clearly, two men, previously ignorant of one another except possibly by hearsay, are liable to be a great deal more suspicious in their dealings with one another, than are a couple already familiar with each other's habits and standards. For this reason an employer will normally make more liberal advances of cash to his regular task-workers than to his casual recruits. Problems of measurement are also much less important when dealing with regular workers than with casual recruits.

Frequently, such is the low level of cash availability in some areas that young men who deal regularly with a small farmer as their employer, will ask him to credit clothes from a shop on their behalf against work not even contemplated at the moment. In this way they are able to clothe themselves and make the relatively larger outlays needed at holiday seasons. Sometimes too, an employer is asked by his regular team to withhold their pay until it becomes sufficient for some specific purpose, such as the purchase of a pig. When regularly employed by a particular farmer, men frequently turn up, point out that certain jobs had better be done soon, and undertake to clear them off. When they expect payment and the small farmer is unable to meet this expectation, the regular team do not desert him, but seek temporary advances from others.

Thus the entire nature of employer-employee relations in casual and regular associations are different. For this reason too, recruitment problems which face an employer who relies predominantly on casual labour do not obtain for his peer who uses a regular work team, so long as this regular team is sufficient for his needs. As pointed out above, this regular work team itself quite often develops on or around a basis of partnership.

5.

Sugar reigned in the British West Indies for more than two centuries, with overwhelming economic and social consequences. In the nineteenth and twentieth centuries, its dominance declined with rising production costs and increasing competition from the much larger enterprises of Hawaii, Puerto Rico, Cuba, and the Dominican Republic and from the European sugar beet. Commonwealth Caribbean sugar remains marginally profitable only because of the United Kingdom's preferential prices. Even so, sugar is still the mainstay of many Caribbean economies; most West Indians are affected by fluctuations in sugar price, and many depend directly on the industry for a livelihood. The following article describes working arrangements on small estates in Barbados. Tasks of estate employees and earning and employment profiles constitute a labor system wholly unlike that of the West Indian small farmer.

JEROME HANDLER received his doctorate in anthropology from Brandeis University. He is presently Associate Professor of Anthropology at Southern Illinois University.

Some Aspects of Work Organization on Sugar Plantations in Barbados[1]

Jerome Handler

Although sugar plantations have been the concern of a number of students of Caribbean societies,[2] there still appears to be a relative dearth of descriptive materials which deal with the kinds of tasks plantation laborers perform and the ways in which laborers are organized in the performance of these tasks. When such discussions have taken place they have usually centered upon large "field-and-factory combines"[3] which grow cane on relatively flat lands and whose physical size and facilities, corporate and sometimes absentee ownership, etc., involve large-scale organization and role complexes. In addition, these descriptions have usually been embedded within, and often incidental to, a larger discussion of such topics as cultural change or the historical development of specific plantation types, the plantation as a social system or as an "economic institution,"[4] the culture of communities formed by plantation workers or aspects of the culture of such communities.[5] From studies such as these it is apparent that

From *Ethnology,* Vol. 4, No. 1, pp. 16–38. Reprinted with permission of *Ethnology,* University of Pittsburgh, Pittsburgh, Pennsylvania, and the author.

[1] I would like to thank Lambros Comitas and Charles Lange for their assistance in preparing various drafts of this paper.

[2] Vera Rubin, ed., *Plantation Systems of the New World* (Washington, D.C.: Pan American Union, 1959).

[3] J. H. Steward, "Perspectives on Plantations," in Rubin, *op. cit.,* p. 10.

[4] I. Greaves, "Plantations in World Economy," in Rubin, *op. cit.,* p. 14.

[5] C. Jayawardena, *Conflict and Solidarity in a Guianese Plantation* (Monographs on Social Anthropology, No. 25, Lon-

there are sufficient differences in production techniques and work organization between various plantation areas to warrant presentation of data along these lines.

This paper is specifically concerned with the more salient features of work organization on several small-scale sugar plantations in the Scotland or highland district of Barbados. Emphasis is less upon the plantation as a productive enterprise or social system than upon the organization of work activities and the statuses which workers fill as they perform these activities. It is the workers, the kinds of jobs they perform, and the organization involved in the performance of these jobs which form the subject matter of this presentation.

The southern Caribbean island of Barbados lies about 100 miles east of the arc of volcanic islands which constitute the Lesser Antilles. Its 166 square miles include several physical regions. One of these is the Scotland District—the sole highland area in Barbados—which is separated from other regions of the island by a semicircular limestone escarpment fourteen or fifteen miles long. In contrast to the rest of the island, which consists of a series of gently undulating plateaus of varying elevations, the landscape of the Scotland District is fairly rugged and is free of the limestone cap which covers the other six-sevenths of Barbados' surface. According to Buie:[6]

> The topography is generally steep . . . slopes of 75 per cent or more are not uncommon. . . . The area is characterized by deeply dissected, narrow valleys.

---

don School of Economics, 1963), pp. 1–159; S. Mintz, "Cañamelar: The Subculture of a Rural Sugar Plantation Proletariat," in J. H. Steward, ed., *The People of Puerto Rico* (Urbana, Ill., 1956), pp. 314–17; E. Padilla, "Nocara: The Subculture of Workers on a Government owned Sugar Plantation," in Steward, *People of Puerto Rico,* pp. 265–313; G. E. Cumper, "A Modern Jamaican Sugar Estate," *Social and Economic Studies,* Vol. 3 (1954), pp. 119–60; G. Lasserre, "Une Plantation de Canne aux Antilles: La Sucrerie Beauport," *Cahiers d'Outre-Mer,* Vol. 5 (1952), pp. 297–329.

[6] T. S. Buie, "Report of a Study of the Scotland District, Barbados, B.W.I. with Recommendations for a Soil Conservation Program," *Barbados Official Gazette,* Supplement (Jan. 31, 1955), p. 1.

Since the middle of the seventeenth century Barbados has been a sugar island. Sugar continues to dominate its economy, and various agreements with the British Government, especially since the Second World War, have minimized the vicissitudes of marketing which plagued the industry for many years. As in former times, sugar today is largely a plantation crop. Of the island's total cane production in 1961 and 1962, for instance, plantations accounted for 84.2 and 84.8 per cent, respectively, the remainder being grown by small farmers on parcels of about an acre.

The materials for this paper are drawn from the plantations for which the villagers of Chalky Mount work.[7] Their village is a small one, located in the heart of the Scotland District. Although it is not entirely an agrarian community, much of the villagers' cash income is derived from pursuits associated with one form or another of land use. Chalky Mount has an adult population of about 215 persons. Some 70 to 75 of these, including persons of both sexes representing 63 of the village's 117 households, are regular plantation workers. However, more individuals and households become involved in plantation wage labor during the cane reaping season when regular laborer contingents are augmented as work demands increase. Close to 70 per cent of the laborers are also actively engaged in small-scale cane farming, 63 per cent of them renting their "working lands" from the plantations for which they work. It is not unusual to find a worker growing cane on his own small freehold land parcel as well. Virtually all of the workers are members of households which own their own houses, although about half of the households to which they belong rent their house sites from plantations.

Aside from small-scale cane farming, many people are likewise engaged in other cash-producing activities, in-

[7] Field work was carried out in Chalky Mount and its environs during the summer of 1960 and from August, 1961, to July, 1962. Financial support from Brandeis University and a grant-in-aid from the Research Institute for the Study of Man made my stay in Barbados possible.

cluding the raising of income-producing livestock such as cows, sheep, and goats, the cultivation of minor cash crops, wage labor on the lands of other small farmers, and even occasional employment in the village's small pottery industry.[8] People also follow a number of other occupational pursuits, some of which are not directly associated with land use. Not only are a variety of income-producing activities characteristic of the village's economy, but adults normally combine several such activities throughout the year. Approximately 80 per cent of the plantation working males, for instance, and 35 per cent of the households with regular plantation workers combine at least three income-producing activities such as those mentioned above. A number of households have four major sources of income, and a handful regularly combine five income-producing activities.

Chalky Mount is a community consisting neither of a landless rural proletariat nor of a peasantry. In general, its inhabitants, including those who are not regularly engaged in plantation work, seem to exemplify what Comitas[9] has called occupational multiplicity—"a situation wherein the modal adult is systematically engaged in a number of gainful activities which form for him an integrated economic complex." In terms of the villagers' extreme dependency upon cash (virtually all of the goods and services they regard as essential can be acquired only with cash) occupational multiplicity has distinctive adaptive advantages in the social and economic environments of Barbados. This paper, as suggested above, is concerned with only one aspect of Chalky Mount's occupational multiplicity, that of plantation wage-labor.

Since this presentation is focused upon the plantations for which Chalky Mount villagers work, the sample is a small one; it is composed of four plantations, though better than 90 per cent of the village's regular laborers work for

[8] J. Handler, "Pottery Making in Rural Barbados," *Southwestern Journal of Anthropology*, Vol. 19 (1963), pp. 314–34.

[9] L. Comitas, "Occupational Multiplicity in Rural Jamaica," *Proceedings of the American Ethnological Society, 1963* (Seattle, 1964), pp. 41–56.

but two of these. All plantation fields are within relatively short walking distances from the workers' homes. None of the sample plantations has its own factory (each contracts with one or more of the island's factories for the selling of its cane); many of their fields are located on hillsides, some of which are quite steep; the plantations are totally dependent upon rainfall for their water supply; there is a moderate amount of mechanization (primarily in certain phases of cultivation and the hauling of cane to factories); and the average land unit upon which sugar cane is grown is about 154 acres. Furthermore, the owners and managers of these plantations are all Barbadians, and, in general, the plantations' organization and role complexes are relatively simple. In many of these characteristics the plantations for which most Chalky Mount people work contrast rather sharply with the "field-and-factory combines" which have been described, for example, for British Guiana,[10] Puerto Rico,[11] Jamaica,[12] and Guadeloupe.[13]

PLANTATION STAFF AND THE WORKERS

Although owners are the ultimate sources of authority, the person who is largely responsible for the day-to-day operation of the plantation, and consequently the one with whom the workers have the greatest contact, is the manager. The dual role of owner-manager is not uncommon in Barbados, but no owner in the sample also functioned as a manager. The manager's role demands that he makes virtually all operational decisions on production activities in addition to functioning as director of field activities, bookkeeper, and paymaster.

The manager is often assisted by a "superintendent" (or foreman) in the supervision of certain kinds of field labor. Overseers or submanagers immediately subordinate to the managers, though present in the hierarchies of larger plan-

[10] Jayawardena, *op. cit.*
[11] Mintz, *op. cit.*
[12] Cumper, *op. cit.*
[13] Lasserre, *op. cit.*

tations elsewhere, are absent in Chalky Mount. Superintendents come from the ranks of the laborers and live in the local villages, toward which their lives are oriented. One occasionally hears the word "driver" in reference to this position—a survival from slave days when favored field hands were placed in positions of relative authority over other field hands—but the term superintendent is generally preferred today.

The superintendent is paid a fixed weekly salary, whether there is work in the fields or not, is exempt from manual labor, and is eligible for a number of benefits which vary according to the personal relationship between himself and the manager. He is often allowed a fairly wide latitude in his authority over the laborers, and it is rare for a manager to contradict a superintendent's labor decision. In an altercation with a laborer, for example, the manager will invariably support the superintendent even before the "facts of the case" are known to him.

The superintendent functions primarily in the supervision of labor crews that are paid on a "day work" basis. People working at piece, or "task," rates usually receive periodic inspections from the manager. In jobs paid at day rates, however, the superintendent is normally in constant attendance over labor crews, insuring that work proceeds according to the manager's standards. His work demands are consequently heaviest during the out-of-crop season, or "hard times," when proportionately more day work is done. Nevertheless, he exercises nominal supervision over some cane-cutting crews (who are paid at "task" rates) during the reaping season to insure that "things is done right." The superintendent, then, functions as a foreman. His authority, though limited, may be increased to the extent that the manager, in the absence of overseers and other supervisory staff, has to depend upon him in everyday plantation work. His official authority, however, is largely confined to the field laborers and does not extend to other plantation workers, e.g., truck and tractor drivers, most of whom come under the direct authority of the manager.

Other statuses on a plantation's staff, i.e., those which are paid weekly salaries, include house servants, yard men or grooms, and the watchman. Persons who perform these roles, though considered "staff members," do not, of necessity, enjoy any higher status or prerogatives than many of the field laborers or truck and tractor drivers.

The field laboring segment of the plantation's labor force —its largest contingent—can be classified into five categories on the basis of age, sex, and task performance: Class A males, Class A females, Class B males, Class B females, and Class C, composed of children of both sexes under eighteen years of age. These categories are recognized in discussions between the Barbados Workers' Union and the Sugar Producers' Association when, for example, wage rates are negotiated. Class A males are defined as those who perform at least two of the following jobs: cutting cane, digging cane holes, and digging drainage ditches in the fields. Class B males consist of those who do not meet these criteria. Class A females are defined as those who, during "crop," i.e., the harvest, carry and/or load cane and during hard times carry baskets of dung. Class B females perform other tasks. Class C includes boys and girls under eighteen years of age and, according to the law, not less than twelve. Each class receives a corresponding wage for day labor, ranging from Class A males at the top, through Class B males, Class A females, and Class B females in order, to Class C members at the bottom.

Class A males are among the younger men, averaging about 40 years of age. They work primarily as cane cutters and truck-crew members during the crop season and as cane-hole diggers during the out-of-crop season, and they average the highest earnings among the field groups. Since most of the jobs they perform are paid for on a task basis, differences in work output are largely reflected in earnings, even though mechanized equipment used in cultivation has made their services unnecessary for extended periods during the out-of-crop season (see below).

One Class A man is known as the "first row man." Though not a staff member, he assumes this status as a management appointee and is usually considered a faster and more responsible worker. The first row man can be viewed as a subforeman. He works with the groups of Class

A males who perform such task-paid jobs as digging cane holes, doing the same kind of work and being paid at the same rates, but he is responsible for noting the amount of work each man does and reporting this to the manager at the end of the day. His privileges are limited, though he does receive some extra money for his duties, and his authority is indeterminate and poorly defined, so that conflicts are more likely to arise between him and other laborers than between the latter and the superintendent. If the superintendent cannot work, the first row man usually substitutes for him. Superintendents have usually been first row men themselves, and the position can be viewed as an apprenticeship to the job of superintendent.

Class B men are the older men, their average age being 61, and they are largely employed in the clearing and weeding of drainage ditches and other assorted and minor jobs. They are employed in smaller numbers and receive proportionately less work than any other adult labor class. Much of the work they could do, e.g., weeding fields and cutting potato slips, is more commonly performed by Class A women, who receive less daily pay and who can perform these tasks just as effectively and probably faster.

Females find, on the average, more employment during the year than either of the male groups (see Tables 1 and 2). Mechanized equipment has diminished the need for male labor during the out-of-crop season, whereas the kinds of jobs that females perform, such as weeding and distributing fertilizer, are in fairly continuous demand. Moreover, the plantations of the Scotland District normally employ two female "headers"—people who collect and tie the cut cane and carry it on their heads to a road—per cutter during the crop season, and most out-of-crop chores can be effectively performed by females who receive less pay on a daily basis.

In terms of actual plantation operations, the foregoing classification of workers requires some qualification in the case of Class B females. As defined above, these include women who do not "head" during the crop nor carry dung baskets during "hard times." Yet there is one group of female workers, known as "farmers," who, though technically Class B workers, are nevertheless paid at Class A female rates. The system of "farming," i.e., the practice of jobbing out fields to be weeded by particular individuals, dates back to the early 1840s.[14] The "farmers" are actually specialized weeders who are kept occupied, regardless of the season, weeding fields of newly planted cane with hoes. They are paid on a task basis by the fields they hoe, which are assigned to them as individuals. Hence their work, contrary to most other major plantation labor, is not performed in the context of a group environment. As compared with workers of other classes, "farmers" find relatively full employment throughout the year. Like other Class B women, who are engaged more sporadically in such chores as picking cattle fodder and carrying drinking water to field laborers, "farmers" are older women. While the average age of Class A women is 37, that of Class B women is about 61.

Whereas membership in the A and B classes is determined by sex and task as well as by age, membership in Class C is determined primarily by age. Class C laborers—the "third gang"[15] or simply the "children"—are used only

[14] O. P. Starkey, *The Economic Geography of Barbados* (New York, 1939), p. 120.

[15] One often hears the three major field groups referred to as the first, second, and third gangs—terms which survive from the days of slavery when field slaves were thus divided, each gang having a complex of task responsibilities in many respects comparable to the tasks performed by the several classes of today (cf. F. Pitman, "Slavery on the British West India Plantations," *Journal of Negro History,* II (1926), pp. 599–602). The discussion of an eighteenth-century Barbados plantation by J. H. Bennett, Jr., *Bondsmen and Bishops: Slavery and Apprenticeship on the Codrington Plantation of Barbados, 1715–1838* (University of California Publications in History, Vol. 62, 1958), pp. 11, 15, is relevant here: Of the 276 Negroes at Codrington in February, 1781, some 162 were organized into three field gangs. Drummer and Johnny Sharry, the black drivers, led the first or great gang of 35 men and 49 women in their tasks of holing the ground for canes, planting, and cutting, and carrying the canes to the mills. Quawcoe Adjoe, a boy, and two women, Sue and Sarah Bob, directed ten boys and thirteen girls in the lighter duties of the second gang, such as planting corn, carrying dry trash to the boiling house for fuel, turning manure, and weeding the fields. Old Dinah drove the little "meat pickers"—23 boys and 26 girls—of the third . . . gang

occasionally on some plantations; during 1961–62 only one of the Chalky Mount plantations employed child labor regularly, and even this group of about ten children did not find employment throughout the year.

Children work as a group, usually in hand weeding and the distribution of fertilizers. Each child is paid on a daily wage basis, at a rate considerably lower than that of any adult class. When working, the children's group is supervised by a Class A woman. She is, for the time being, a quasi-superintendent, although there is no special term to designate her status. At other times she is engaged in the usual Class A female work of the particular season, under the direction of the superintendent, but when the children are working she is assigned to supervise their labor, being paid her normal Class A daily wage.

Plantations usually have a regular labor contingent which they augment during the reaping season. There is no large-scale migration of workers from other parts of the island; most of the added laboring force comes from the village or other adjacent villages. Although some laborers work for one plantation during "hard times" and for another during "crop," or for one plantation one year and a different one the next year, the majority of the regular employees, barring severe altercations with managers, continue with one plantation and are not inclined to change. In fact, since wage rates are similar throughout the area, the choice of the employer is generally based upon the proximity of the plantation's fields to the worker's residence. This is a matter of convenience for the worker not only in reaching his job but commonly also in visiting the small "farmer" fields when plantation work ceases for the day.

Although most major plantation jobs except "farming" are performed by groups, tasks are for the most part assigned to individuals (with important exceptions occurring during "crop," to be noted below). In general, although a worker may be part of a labor group engaged in the per-

---

to their work of shovelling manure into cane holes before the cane was planted, helping to weed young canes, and gathering fodder, called hogsmeat, for the livestock. . . . A few declining men and women were members of the second gang.

formance of one job, he is paid not on the basis of the group's performance but of his own, regardless of whether payment is on a day or task basis.

The majority of jobs most fundamental to a plantation's productive activities are today performed on a task basis. Laborers overwhelmingly prefer this manner of payment, for they can often make as much or more money by "breakfast time" (early afternoon) doing task work as they could make during the entire day working at day rates. It is also both usually admitted and clearly observable that performance is slower in day work and not necessarily better. In fact, the speed and earnestness with which task work is performed differs in an often remarkable way from the performance observed on day-work jobs. The contrast is even more dramatic when one has an opportunity to observe the same individuals working under the different systems, especially if the day work is not under managerial supervision. Managers, well aware of this, make every effort to subject day-work crews, regardless of the job they are performing, to as much supervision as possible. Task work is supervised to a considerably lesser extent, and primarily to insure that the work is conducted according to the manager's standards.

There are other general differences, regardless of the particular job involved, between task and day work. Day workers take off an hour for lunch around noon, while task workers normally quit for the day in the early afternoon and then go home for their midday meal. In some cases, task workers can work longer hours if they so desire–provided there is still work to be done on the assigned job and the manager does not limit the amount of work that may be done in a day. Usually, however, task workers prefer to quit after they have done what they consider a "fair day's work," i.e., have made a satisfactory wage for the day. They like to quit early not only because of the rapid pace of the work and the concomitant fatigue–a reason managers sometimes give–but also because they are then free to work for the remainder of the day on their own parcels of land or at other unpaid or cash-producing chores. During "hard times," consequently, it is not unusual to see male workers returning home from the fields about 1:30 P.M. and soon after taking their hoes and forks to their own land parcels to "work on de ground" for the remainder of the afternoon.

TASKS AND THE AGRICULTURAL CYCLE

This section will outline the major tasks performed by the several work classes and will attempt to correlate them and the organization involved in their performance with the two major phases in the agricultural year. The same individuals usually perform a number of different tasks at different periods of the agricultural year. Aside from the customary assignment of tasks along sexual lines, few workers are considered so specialized that they cannot perform a variety of jobs. There are, to be sure, individual differences in abilities, and managers attempt to allocate the more specialized jobs in terms of these differences.

During the months from February to May, when the cane is reaped, the majority of the laborers are occupied with cutting and heading the cane and transporting it to factories. We turn first, then, to the cutters, headers, and truck workers and to the particular characteristics of their roles within the plantation environment.

The procedure involved in cutting cane is relatively simple. Wielding their "bills,"[16] the cutters move through a field, each one taking two or three rows, while the headers move behind them tying the cane stalks into bundles and

[16] The cane "bill" is a short, wide, cast-steel knife about ten inches long and seven inches wide. The blade tapers from its widest point at the top to its base, where it is forged into the handle. The latter is about an inch in diameter and six inches long. The "bill" has two cutting edges. One edge is fairly straight and is used in the actual severing of the cane stalk from its base. The other edge has a more convex blade with a two-inch sharpened hook projecting from it at the top. By injecting the hook between the cane trash and stalk and slicing downwards the trash can be quickly stripped from the stalk. Cane "knives" or cutlasses, which resemble machetes, are not employed in cutting cane but are used by truck crews to chop the bindings from the cane bundles and to trim the stalks ejecting from the truck's sides.

then heading these to the nearest road, whence they are loaded onto trucks and transported to the factories to be sold. Ideally, cutters can cut as much cane as they wish, and all are paid task rates, but limits are set to the amount of cane a plantation will cut during the day by the daily quotas that factories assign to the plantations which have agreed to send them their cane. These quotas are established in order to insure the operation of the factories at maximum efficiency. If a plantation's daily quota has been met the cutters must cease their activities for the remainder of the working day. Cutting activities can also come to a stop during the day, especially during the initial phases of the crop season, as a result of mechanical failures at the factories. The latter commonly accept no more cane when they have accumulated what they consider a sufficient amount for immediate grinding, and the plantations must then perforce stop cutting to avoid loss through drying at the roadsides or in the fields. Cutters are then freed, as they are at the end of the week, to work their own cane fields or on the holdings of other small farmers.

Most Chalky Mount workers who cut plantation cane during 1961 and 1962 worked alone and not as members of cutting "gangs." Though cutters usually work in groups, "gang" refers specifically to a formally organized group whose members pool their labor resources in a co-operative effort and divide equally each week the total amount received for their collective tonnage. Only one-fourth of the Chalky Mount males who cut plantation cane for most or all of the 1962 crop, for instance, did so as gang members. The rest, for the most part, worked alone. It is noteworthy, however, that about 63 per cent of them started out as gang members at the beginning of the crop season, most of them discontinuing their membership after a week or so. In fact, only three or four gangs in the plantation sample persisted throughout the season. Whatever their duration, gangs rarely include more than three men, and most are formed by only a pair of cutters.

A cutting gang is a voluntary association; membership is left to the choice of the cutters, and a manager seldom interferes with its composition. Laborers who wish to form a gang have two primary considerations: equal work capacity and personal compatibility. The former is a necessary precondition to association, the latter a necessary condition for the group's survival. Regardless of personal compatibility, fast cutters refuse to work with slow cutters. Although slow cutters may be willing to join a gang, they may not be able to find anyone willing to accept them. Some workers insist upon cutting alone. In general, there seems to be no correlation between a man's cutting ability and his proclivity to work in a gang. Among the faster cutters observed, some work singly and others as gang members.

Because gangs are voluntarily formed, they can easily be dissolved. Their fragility is attested by the impermanence of most of those which started the 1962 crop season. Here the issue of personal compatibility is essential. Fundamental to the gang's output is not only the speed at which its members cut cane but also the necessity that all put in an equal amount of work. If one member rests too often, quits early, or does not keep pace with the others, the effectiveness of the group is lessened and antagonism among its members can easily erupt. Personal compatibility and previous strong friendship among the members minimize instances of this kind, but gangs formed solely on the basis of equal work capacity, unleavened by concessions to friendship, readily dissolve under undue stress. Because gang members are capable of fairly equal performance, it is unlikely that a man who rests too often, for instance, will be able to catch up and cut as much cane as his peers, yet he shares equally in the proceeds with those who have worked harder. It is not a question of the other members resting to let the recalcitrant one catch up and produce an equal share; since it is task work, all try to work at top speed to cut as much cane as possible. Gang members usually start work at the same time, take time off for lunch together, stop for cigarette breaks together, and so on. Unless they are extremely good friends it is unusual for one person to continue cutting cane while the others are resting, and quite often the gang will not work at all if, for some reason, one of its members is not present for the day.

Men who form a gang justify their behavior in terms of

their feeling that they can cut more cane as members of a group than they could as individuals. This is presumably the reason why so many individuals start a crop season as gang members. Although some of the fastest cutters observed worked in gangs and felt that this increased their output, I have no evidence that their work output would have been significantly less had they cut as individuals nor that gang membership, in and of itself, results in greater cutting speeds.

On Scotland District plantations a pair of headers normally works behind each cutter. This pattern reflects the topography of the area, which frequently prevents trucks from entering the fields to be loaded, as occurs in the more level parts of the island. Since there is no mechanization of loading, the cane must usually be carried from the fields to the closest accessible road, and it is the headers who perform this important activity.

The alignment of headers with cutters is effected by the workers themselves. The faster cutters and headers consequently make an effort to associate with one another. Managers sometimes influence the composition of a cutting unit, especially when cutters and headers are added to the labor force during the course of the crop season, but even then the choice of association is commonly left to the workers themselves. Because the selection of a work group is voluntary, headers can change their membership–provided, of course, that work is available with another group. Since headers work as a co-operative unit, and payment is determined by their combined tonnage, it is essential that both members contribute an equal amount of work. If one header does less work than the other, for whatever reason, she nevertheless receives the same payment. Arguments can arise as a result, especially with headers who do not form part of the normal working contingent of the plantation. Regular plantation workers commonly base their association on friendship whereas others, who join later, have less chance to do so and may have to accept any opening offered. Headers and cutters together form an integrated working unit whose earning capacity is dependent not only upon the ability of the cutter but also upon the speed with which the headers can move his cane out of the field to a road.

Transporting the cane to a factory is the third major task performed during the crop season. Since all transportation is by trucks, their drivers and crews have major roles to play in the production cycle. Truck drivers occupy one of the most prestigeful positions in the plantation's labor force. They are absolved from agricultural labor, they enjoy relative freedom from constant supervision, and their earnings exceed those of most other workers.

During the crop season the plantations, especially the larger ones, augment their truck contingent by pressing more trucks into service along with additional laborers to man them. Most members of truck crews are male workers in their twenties and early thirties, many of whom do not normally work on the plantation during the out-of-crop season. A truck crew is usually composed of five men plus the driver, who is the formal leader. He is responsible for the operation of the truck and is held accountable by the manager if anything goes wrong. Although he does not have the power to hire and fire the members of his crew, he exerts a great deal of influence in choosing them, and under normal circumstances the manager does not interfere with his choice.

Because of the nature of the work it is important that the truck crew operate as a well co-ordinated unit, and physical qualifications and personal compatibility are again relevant here. Since all trucking personnel, drivers included, are paid according to the tonnage delivered at the factory it is of utmost importance to carry as much tonnage (within the five-ton maximum prescribed by law) as possible in each load and to transport it quickly so as to be able to maximize the number of daily round trips. Hence, when a truck returns from a factory, it is immediately reloaded for a return trip. The men work rapidly and strenuously in lifting the cane bundles from the road into the truck. Unless each member of the crew performs his share of the physical labor, arguments can arise and the rate of work may be slowed. For this reason drivers are concerned to have men who are not only physically qualified but also relatively compatible. Trouble can easily develop among crew members who are chosen at random when a new truck is quickly pressed into service, and younger men are often reluctant to work with older men who they feel cannot meet the physical demands of the task.

While the work required of a crew member is physically demanding, it is confined to relatively short spurts–the 30 minutes or so at a time needed fully to load a truck. Other things being equal, e.g., the cutters are working and cane is waiting to be shipped, the payment received by the driver and crew is contingent upon their functioning harmoniously and at maximum speed. Although crew memberships shift throughout the reaping season, it is interesting to note that those crews and drivers which remained together for the entire duration of the 1962 crop were precisely those whose circumstances permitted the greatest latitude in the exercise of free choice in association.

Since truck crews and drivers are paid by the cane tonnage they haul, it is generally to their advantage to haul this cane to the nearest factory to which the plantation's cane has been committed. Furthermore, since truck drivers strive to make as many round trips per day as possible, they tend, if left alone, to exceed the plantation's quotas to particular factories while short hauling to others. Hence, as cutting proceeds during the day, the manager is forced to increase his supervision of truck movements. The only regular altercations witnessed between truck drivers and managers revolved around this issue. If, as sometimes happens, all of a plantation's cane is committed to one factory, this problem naturally does not arise.

Some other jobs are performed during the crop season; for example, women farm fields, older men clear drainage ditches, and children pick cane trash for animal fodder. Nevertheless, most of the plantation's labor force is focused upon the performance of the three basic tasks of cutting, heading, and transporting the cane. Each cane-cutting group of cutter and headers and associated trucking group of driver and crew are economically dependent upon one another though socially autonomous. Within each group, however, the interdependency of the members is so great that the group is likely to be extremely fragile unless its members have similar work capacity and are personally compatible.

After the last canes have been cut, plantation work all but ceases for the following two weeks except for minor jobs like cleaning the roads of trash. This is the beginning of "hard times," which today spans the period from June to January. Not only is there proportionately less work on the plantations, but weekly earnings are also commensurately less. The work demands placed upon the labor force are different in kind, the labor force loses part of its augmented contingent, and activities relate to the demands of cane growing and preparations for the next crop season.

After reaping, the fields are mulched by crews of women, who spread trash around the cane holes. As the rains commence, fertilizer is spread on the fields, and bulldozers or tractors begin plowing the fields that are to be planted to new cane and those which are to remain fallow during the coming year. Throughout June and July crews are kept fairly busy planting food crops, such as yams, sweet potatoes, and corn, which are grown in alternate rows between the cane holes in some fields. Although some of the steeper fields are still cultivated by hand, most plantation land is cultivated today by mechanized equipment, mainly bulldozers.

Soon after the preparation of the non-ratoon fields by this equipment the cane holes are dug by hand. The practice of planting cane in holes dates from the earliest days of the Barbadian sugar industry, and cane-hole digging is today the chief task performed by Class A male workers during the out-of-crop season. Before the holes are dug, the field is laid out in grids five feet square by a man who is considered a specialist in "lining." Cane-trash markers are set up at the corners of every square to serve as reference points.

The field is now ready for the hole diggers. Each man, working with a pitchfork, takes a different row in the field and, following the markers, digs the holes in two-foot squares, leaving three feet of "bank" between each one. Cane-hole digging is task work. Each worker is paid solely on the basis of the number of holes dug, and each man works at his own pace. A fast and experienced worker can dig as many as four or five hundred holes per day, although informants estimated the normal rate at around 250. Daily work output is recorded by the first row man, who transmits this information to the manager. Cane-hole diggers normally start work at about eight o'clock in the morning and work steadily until one or two o'clock in the afternoon, when they quit for the day even though the field may not be completed, for they consider they have done a "fair day's work."

By late summer or early autumn all fields to be planted in cane and/or food crops have been "holed." During November and December the new "plant canes"—those to be reaped the year after next—are set out by Class A men who are especially proficient at this task. The "plant canes" are cut from the fields planted the year before. Plant cutting is done during a very limited period in the fall and involves, at best, not more than two or three men per plantation. Other men then plant the cane, placing two stumps in each hole, and later replace those which have not taken root.

Though Class A men also work on trucks, dig drainage ditches, etc., their major job during the out-of-crop season is digging cane holes. When this is completed, there is little other work for most of them.

Not more than a handful of Class B males find relatively continuous employment, mainly in weeding gutters in the ratoon fields and planting food crops. A few younger men, paid at B rates, are kept busy spraying weeds growing along the roadsides and on other assorted jobs.

Weeding is a primary female task which continues throughout the agricultural year. During the crop season "farmers" weed the fields of "plant cane," and after the crop, with other Class A women, they clear trash from the newly cut fields, piling it around the holes while weeding. "Weeding and clearing" are usually paid for at task rates, and it is during this process that the fields are mulched. Later, as the cane grows and other demands (see below) have been met, female crews return to the fields of growing cane, and the "farmers" revert to weeding the new "plant cane." Weeding of the fields to be reaped continues through December or until the growing cane has so congested the fields that they can no longer be conveniently worked upon. Hoe weeding is primarily a female job, although labor crews of children are sometimes engaged in the removal of weeds that are most effectively pulled by hand.

The distribution of fertilizer is another primary responsibility of Class A females. Both animal and chemical fertilizers are used, although plantations rely less upon pen manure or dung than they did in former times, and some plantations do not use it at all. The plantations that use pen manure normally distribute it on the new "plant canes" from about November to January. Although this task is normally performed by Class A women, the children's group can be involved as well. Since the organizational procedure in the distribution of animal and chemical fertilizers is essentially the same, both will be discussed together.

Regardless of the kind of fertilizer used, it is conveyed to the fields in trucks. In the case of dung, the load is dumped at the side of a road, and two men with pitchforks load basketfuls which are "headed" out to the fields, where each cane hole receives one basketful. In the case of chemical fertilizer, members of the truck crews slit the bags and fill the pails which certain laborers carry. These are "headed" into the fields, and from them are filled the smaller containers carried by other women. These women then proceed down the rows scooping out handfuls of fertilizer for each cane hole. Meanwhile, the pail carriers return to the truck for another load and should be back in the fields when the distributors have emptied their containers.

Fertilization of the fields is best accomplished by relatively large groups and is paid for at day rates. Because of the size of the groups and the need for rapid and effective distribution, the workers are kept under constant surveillance and receive active verbal direction from the manager, superintendent, and, if the children's labor crew is working as well, their female superintendent. The degree of direction, e.g., by verbal prodding to carry heavier loads, varies with the personality of the manager and the time limits set for the completion of the task. Although the distribution of fertilizer is always done in large groups, the people work as individuals. If there is slacking, the pressure to proceed at a more rapid pace comes not from within the group, as in the cane-cutting and trucking units, but from the superintendent or, more usually, the manager himself.

Women also engage in other work during the out-of-crop season, e.g., cutting grass for animal fodder and planting food crops, but their two major tasks are weeding and fertilizing.

By December little work remains to be done. The cane to be reaped in February is high, and it is difficult for females to move through the fields weeding them. Class A men, unless odd jobs are found for them, are generally unemployed. Most fertilizing has already been completed, and in the last two weeks of December work all but ceases (see below). There may be a spurt in work demands during the first weeks of January, mainly to complete the fertilization of the fields, but by the end of that month the plantation is ready, and the laborers are eagerly looking forward to the new crop season.

EARNINGS AND EMPLOYMENT

Prior to World War II, before the days of effective collective bargaining and the growth of the Barbados Workers' Union, wage scales were more arbitrary than they are now. Wages were much lower, and they varied from plantation to plantation. Today this situation has been considerably altered as the negotiating power of the Barbados Workers' Union has increased, and wages on both task and day jobs, though subject to periodic renegotiation, are more or less standardized. Plantation workers have received steady wage increases over the past decade, and various other benefits have helped considerably in augmenting their annual earnings.

One of these innovations, the Holiday with Pay, provides for a two-week paid vacation for plantation workers. The amount of money received is roughly 4 per cent of the earnings for the previous year (exclusive of the production bonus). The Holiday with Pay was enacted as a national law in 1951 and is but one manifestation of the relatively liberal social legislation passed over the years as popularly supported political parties have increased their control in the island's legislative assembly.

The sugar production bonus—often called by the laborers "back pay"—is subject to periodic renegotiation between the Barbados Workers' Union and the Sugar Producers' Association, neither of which is a governmental agency. Unlike the Holiday with Pay, the production bonus is not written into law, but it is nevertheless normally paid to all plantation workers who have worked during the crop season. It is based upon the amount of money earned during the season in relation to the island's total sugar production. The production bonus agreement, first negotiated in 1951, provides that each worker receive a bonus of 2.5 per cent of his earnings whenever island production reaches 131,906 tons of sugar. For each 5,000 tons in excess of this amount an additional 1.5 per cent is added.

Both the production bonus and the Holiday with Pay are important factors in a worker's total earnings. They are, however, based upon the individual worker's capacity to earn money during the year, and this is contingent not only upon the number of days when employment is available but also upon the physical ability of the worker, the season of the year, the type of work done, and the work class to which the worker belongs. These differences in earning capacities make it difficult to discuss wages meaningfully in blanket terms. It can be misleading, if not in many cases positively erroneous, to discuss the earnings and employment of plantation laborers as a single generalized occupational category. This will become clear from an examination of Tables 1 and 2.

Table 1 presents data on the earnings received and days worked during 1961 by laborers of the four adult classes who were employed during both the crop and out-of-crop seasons and worked for 120 days or more. Superintendents, other staff personnel, and truck and tractor drivers, as well as children under eighteen, are excluded. Monetary figures

TABLE 1

Average Earnings and Days Worked of Plantation Laborers Who Worked at Least 120 Days During 1961

Workers		Days Worked and Wages Received												Additional Earnings		Total Earnings
		Crop Season					Out-of-Crop Season			Total for Year						
Sex and Class	Number	Days worked	% of total days worked	Wages received	% of total wages	Average daily wage	Days worked	Wages received	Average daily wage	Wages received	Days worked	Average daily wage		Production Bonus	Holiday with Pay	
Male																
Class A	18	72	44	$404.66	60	$5.62	91	$271.76	$2.99	$676.21	163	$4.15		$40.46	$27.21	$743.88
Class B	2	50	36	137.60	38	2.75	87	221.01	2.54	358.61	137	2.62		—	14.35	372.96
Female																
Class A	16	66	38	248.28	54	3.76	110	211.41	1.92	459.69	176	2.61		24.82	18.25	502.76
Class B	14	74	44	145.28	46	1.96	93	173.33	1.86	318.61	167	1.90		14.52	12.81	345.94
TOTAL	50	66	41	233.96	50	3.52	95	219.38	2.33	453.28	161	2.82		26.60	18.16	491.39

are given in British West Indian dollars ($1.00 B. W. I. = $0.58 U. S.). The production bonus amounted to 10 per cent of the wages received during the crop season, except for Class B males. The Holiday with Pay earnings amounted to approximately 4 per cent of the total wages exclusive of the production bonus.

Table 2 presents similar, though not strictly comparable, data on laborers who worked fewer than 120 days during 1961. Two Class A males, three Class B males, and nine Class A females worked during both seasons; four Class A males and three Class A females worked only during the crop season; three Class A males, one Class B male, and one Class A female worked only during the out-of-crop season; no Class B females worked fewer than 120 days. Table 2 largely comprises such people as women in the later stages of pregnancy, males going to the United States on contract farm-labor programs, and males who supplemented the regular plantation contingents during the crop season only. The total number of days these persons worked and their total earnings are thus not properly comparable with the similar data in Table 1.

Reference to Tables 1 and 2 reveals that the majority of Chalky Mount's plantation workers (50 out of 71) were employed for at least 120 days during the year, that females outnumbered males among both the regularly and irregularly employed, and that females were employed on the average more days during the year. That Class A males found slightly more employment during the crop season reflects the inclusion of truck-crew members, who normally work a longer week than do either headers or cutters. Mechanization has affected male more than female employment. It has reduced the number of males employed on a major out-of-crop task, and the surplus has not been absorbed in such jobs as weeding and fertilizing because these can be performed just as adequately by females and at less cost to the plantations.

Despite the fact that males worked fewer days over the year, both their average wage and total earnings were substantially higher than for females, the contrast being

TABLE 2

Average Earnings and Days Worked of Plantation Laborers Who Worked Less Than 120 Days During 1961

Workers by Sex and Class	*Days Worked and Wages Received*												*Additional Earnings*				*Total Earnings*	
	Crop Season				Out-of-Crop Season				Total for Year				Production Bonus		Holiday with Pay			
	No. workers	Days worked	Wages received	Average daily wage	No. workers	Days worked	Wages received	Average daily wage	No. workers	Days worked	Wages received	Average daily wage	No. workers	Amount received	No. workers	Amount received	No. workers	Amount received
Male																		
Class A	6	63	$317.16	$5.01	5	44	$120.57	$2.74	9	67	$275.09	$4.11	6	$31.71	9	$10.95	9	$307.18
Class B	3	26	83.54	3.14	4	75	211.19	2.82	4	94	273.84	2.91	4	—	4	10.95	4	284.80
Female																		
Class A	12	54	209.86	3.87	10	38	66.52	1.75	13	78	244.88	3.14	12	20.98	13	9.47	13	273.72
TOTAL	21	48	203.52	4.00	19	52	132.76	2.44	26	80	264.60	3.39	22	26.35	26	10.46	26	288.57

most striking during the crop season. For regularly employed workers of Class A, for example, males averaged $241 more than females in total earnings, although they worked on the average thirteen fewer days during the year.

In his comprehensive survey of the sugar industry of Barbados, McKenzie[17] states that "field workers earn the major part of their yearly earnings out of crop and this proportion does not carry the increase due from the production bonus." Our Chalky Mount data, though admittedly based on a limited sample, suggest a trend toward greater dependency upon crop earnings. Table 1 reveals that regular workers of all classes earned about 50 per cent of their total wages during the crop season, and this despite the fact that Class B workers of both sexes are in considerably less demand during this season. Although the crop season covers only about 30 per cent of the working weeks of the year, Class A male workers earned approximately 60 per cent of their total wages during this period. That a worker can earn proportionately more during the crop season on a daily or even weekly basis is, of course, not new information. It is of interest to note, however, that, with the changing demands for labor, Class A males in particular are coming to depend increasingly on their crop earnings. Should automatic loaders be introduced, this could drastically affect the already precarious earning potential, not only of Class A male truck crews but of Class A female headers as well.

The earning capacity of a worker also depends, of course, on the kind of work he does. Table 3 shows the average weekly wages (exclusive of the production bonus) for the four major roles during the crop seasons of 1961 and 1962, which lasted fifteen and fourteen weeks respectively. Truck drivers, who were omitted in Tables 1 and 2, are included here for purposes of comparison. In level of earnings the roles range from truck drivers at the top, through cane cutters and truck crew members, to headers, some of whom are males. The three lower posi-

[17] A. F. McKenzie, *Report of an Inquiry into the Sugar Industry of Barbados* (Barbados, 1958), p. 27.

TABLE 3

Average Weekly Earnings During Crop Season of Plantation Workers Who Worked Ten Weeks or More in 1961 and 1962

	Average Weekly Wage	
Roles	1961	1962
Truck driver	$34.65	$39.57
Cane cutter	26.47	26.91
Truck crew	21.69	22.57
Header	18.74	20.00

tions may overlap. Some of the slower cutters average about the same as some truck crew members. The faster cutters average more than the highest paid truck crew members and for this reason often prefer to cut cane. Headers, too, can average more than truck crew members, especially those who work behind the faster cutters.

THE UNION AND LABOR SHORTAGES

The Barbados Workers' Union, the primary bargaining agent for the island's workers, has played an active role in bringing about the wage increases and improved working conditions which have characterized the sugar industry of Barbados over the past ten or fifteen years. Yet the Union has no members among Chalky Mount's regular plantation laborers nor among the laborers from other villages who work for the same plantations being considered in this paper. The collective bargaining power of the Union nevertheless extends even to those who are not its members. The workers of Chalky Mount, for example, profit by its agreements with the Sugar Producers' Association, and this seems to be one of the key factors in the difficulties the Union has experienced in organizing the workers of the area. So long as the workers derive benefits from wage increases and improvements in working conditions, they are not motivated to join the Union, even though they are well aware of its role in securing these benefits for them. It is important to note also that the local plantation owners do not belong to the Sugar Producers' Association, yet for the most part they comply voluntarily with whatever settlements it reaches with the Union. It is suggested that this compliance reflects their need to maintain a consistent and reliable labor supply.

There seems to be a growing recognition that labor shortages, particularly of cutters during the crop season, are growing more imminent as the years go by. The older managers and officials of the Sugar Producers' Association confess that recently it has become increasingly difficult to be assured of having enough cane cutters to reap the crop effectively. Among the more common alleged reasons for this are the recent large-scale emigration to England, which has drained some areas of Barbados of many younger people, and the increased availability of government jobs for unskilled workers. There is also a decreasing willingness to engage in certain kinds of plantation work —to "work with the hoe," as one manager put it—on the part of younger people, including even those without a secondary school education. That this situation has existed for several decades is attested by the observations of Starkey:[18]

> The availability of education has been both an advantage and a disadvantage to the island's economic system . . . many of the laboring classes have become dissatisfied with field labor and, at times, there has been a shortage of field laborers and a considerable surplus of clerks and artisans.

Although no plantation manager in the Chalky Mount area complained of any acute labor shortage, they all admitted that they could have used more cutters, and in some cases headers and truck crews as well. It is not uncommon for planters in certain locales to be forced to

[18] Starkey, *op. cit.*, p. 197.

rely upon labor contingents from other plantations during the closing days of the crop in order to finish reaping their fields before the factories close for the season. It would merit further investigation to ascertain whether the pessimistic attitude of managers reflects a genuine scarcity of labor at certain times or simply an occasional difficulty in acquiring labor which is exaggerated by assumptions traditional to plantation operations, e.g., that labor should be "plentiful and cheap."[19]

DISCUSSION

The plantations for which most Chalky Mount laborers work are small in terms of their cultivated acreages, labor forces, and lack of factories. Mechanization is limited to certain aspects of field cultivation and to the transportation of cane. Moreover, the hierarchical organization and major role complexes are relatively simple.

The major work classes were created in the days of slavery and have persisted through time with some alterations in the recent past as a result of the influence of modern labor unions. The fact that work groups are often referred to as "gangs" further suggests the continuity with the past in formal plantation organization. Females continue to play a vital role in plantation operations, which is sustained by the customary sexual division of labor in field jobs, a double standard in wage rates, and ecological conditions which favor the use of females as headers. The plantations are not owned by large foreign corporations but by Barbadians operating in simple partnerships or as individual proprietors.

Although there are pronounced status differences between owners and managers on the one hand and laborers on the other, they reveal numerous cultural similarities, and both operate in terms of many shared values and an awareness of reciprocal expectations. Proximity of living

[19] E. Wolf and S. Mintz, "Haciendas and Plantations in Middle America and the Antilles," *Social and Economic Studies*, Vol. 6 (1957), p. 400.

and common life experiences affect the working of the plantations in a number of ways. Although the plantations are fundamentally profit-seeking enterprises geared to the production of a monocrop for a large-scale external market, a personal quality nonetheless enters into their everyday operations and creates an atmosphere different from that of the large field-and-factory combines described elsewhere in the Caribbean. In a number of respects, then, the plantations for which most Chalky Mount laborers work have some of the characteristics of the "old style plantation" of Wolf[20] or even of the hacienda.[21]

The Chalky Mount area does not present a situation wherein there is a great deal of competition for a few jobs. Its plantations do not operate with an oversupply of labor. Their laboring contingents are composed of persons who come from the immediately surrounding communities, and one does not find the labor migrations and extended absences from natal villages that are recorded for such larger sugar-producing areas as Jamaica[22] and British Guiana.[23] Labor—especially male labor on the more skilled field jobs—is not as expendable as might be expected in so densely populated an island.[24]

Conflict is infrequent, and workers are rarely fired. Two cases of firings were reported during 1961 and 1962, and in both instances they resulted from altercations between workers, and the managers thought it best to remove the "trouble makers," who found no difficulty in acquiring jobs on other plantations. The loss of job need not pose a "serious problem of biological survival."[25] Not only is

[20] E. Wolf, "Specific Aspects of Plantation Systems in the New World: Community Sub-cultures and Social Class," in Rubin, *op. cit.*, pp. 136–46.

[21] Wolf and Mintz, *op. cit.*

[22] Comitas, *op. cit.*

[23] R. T. Smith, *The Negro Family in British Guiana* (London, 1956).

[24] In 1960, Barbados had a population density of close to 1,400 persons per square mile. The two parishes of St. Andrew and St. Joseph, which comprise most of the land area of the Scotland District, had 570 and 913 persons per square mile, respectively.

[25] Wolf and Mintz, *op. cit.*, p. 400.

work usually available on other plantations, but workers often fall back on other sources of income. It is not intended to underestimate the limited alternatives available to workers, but nonetheless there are alternatives. During the crop season no one need be without work. In "hard times," though cash resources are limited, the presence of other opportunities to earn money, albeit limited in number, still make it inappropriate to view the problem in terms of biological survival. In fact, plantation managers, rather than paring their labor crews to a minimal core of workers during the latter phases of "hard times," generally try to provide two or three days of work per week for all or most of their regular workers. The sugar production bonus is paid during the early fall, and the Holiday with Pay also injects modest sums of cash into households during the latter phases of the out-of-crop season. During this time, too, sugar factories are making terminal payments to small cane farmers on the cane received during the previous crop, and this adds cash to the village's households and provides money for small farmers to hire workers on their small holdings.

Regular plantation workers have some notion of their occupational unity and commonality of interest, but this does not promote unique bonds of solidarity among them within the village.[26] In Chalky Mount plantation workers do not form a distinctive subcultural unit, nor do they feel that their problems, economic or otherwise, are unique to themselves as plantation workers. Their consciousness of kind is that of "poor people," and as such they align themselves with most other villagers regardless of occupational pursuits. This sentiment is further promoted by the frequent overlapping of the cash-oriented activities of individuals and the multiple economic activities or sources of income of most households. Only 54 per cent of Chalky Mount's households include regular plantation workers, and few of these households are totally dependent upon the plantations for their income. Most households have other means of support as well, and some are highly de-

[26] Mintz, *op. cit.;* Jayawardena, *op. cit.*

pendent upon remittances from abroad. Plantation wage labor, then, is only one means by which the people of Chalky Mount adapt to their social and physical environments. It is beyond the scope of this paper to consider other means of support such as small-scale cane farming, livestock raising, pottery-making, cultivation of minor cash and subsistence crops, or the various other wage-labor and income-producing activities, and the ways in which these are integrated in the total economic life of the community.[27]

[27] J. Handler, *Land Exploitative Activities and Economic Patterns in a Barbados Village* (Unpublished Ph.D. dissertation, Brandeis University, 1964).

6.

In 1965 the Sugar Manufacturers Association of Jamaica commissioned a study of the sugar-industry labor force. Three sections have been extracted from the ensuing report. The first categorizes workers and their responsibilities, describes the general pattern of cane reaping on large estates, and details one company's attempts to mechanize and modernize production. The second section considers recruitment patterns and the seeming paradox of labor shortages "side by side with people clamouring for work." The final passage focuses on social factors affecting labor supply and productivity, such as commissary and housing facilities, the use of ganja, gambling and drinking, and, above all, the growing reluctance of young Jamaicans to take what is considered socially degrading work in the cane fields.

R. B. DAVISON has a doctorate in economics from the University of London. He is presently Senior Lecturer in the Department of Economics, University of the West Indies, Jamaica.

The Labour Force in the Jamaican Sugar Industry*

R. B. Davison

LABOUR ORGANISATION ON A SUGAR ESTATE

Work on a sugar estate follows a marked seasonal pattern. The crop year begins about Christmas time, in January or possibly February and continues until June or July. As the canes are cut and removed for grinding to the central factory, next year's crop is planted either by "ratooning" (cultivating new shoots growing from the old stools) or by a complete replanting of the field. The crop year lasts approximately 20 weeks and throughout the year the normal agricultural operations—weeding, ditching, irrigating, fertilising, etc. continue. The managerial organisation of the estate tends to follow this functional pattern, although each estate differs from the other in the precise allocation of duties and the terminology used to describe the different managers. At Innswood, for example, there are three assistant field managers, one in charge of land preparation (planting, weeding), another responsible for irrigation, drainage, fertiliser and roads whilst the third is in control of the reaping operations, compound maintenance and dealing with cane farmers. The field staff are usually demarcated from the factory engineers, office accountants or chemists, all being responsible to the general

* [Editors' title]

From *Labour Shortage and Productivity in the Jamaican Sugar Industry,* Institute of Social and Economic Research, 1966, pp. 1–10; 22–31. Reprinted courtesy of the Institute of Social and Economic Research, University of the West Indies, Jamaica.

manager. In the boom years following the Cuban crisis the Jamaican sugar industry has expanded greatly. This is a fact of considerable significance and highly relevant to the present labour situation—these boom years are already passing and the workers in the industry, or at least the more thoughtful leaders amongst them, are well aware of the transient nature of the present prosperity and high demand for labour.

Associated with every estate there is a galaxy of cane farmers, large and small, many of whom rent the land from the estates and are quite large operators in their own right. They supply canes to the factory on a pre-allocated quota basis. Each estate varies in the number of cane farmers attached to it—Gray's Inn has about 450, Trelawny has 2,000 (50% of their cane comes from farmers). United Estates rely on farmers for 60% of their cane and the produce of their own fields is, as they put it, a "buffer stock". This is another factor of great significance in considering the supply and productivity of labour on the estate itself. The estates are not entirely free agents in the question of cane farmers—Government regulations control the proportion of cane cultivation to be allocated to cane farmers—but that aspect of the industry is outside the scope of this enquiry, which is exclusively concentrated on the reaping operations of the estates themselves, specifically the performance of the cutting and loading gangs. The existence of the cane farmers was simply taken as an uncontrolled variable in the system, as was the technical production process in the factory and the cultivation labour force. The cultivation workers, although usually paid by task, resemble the factory labour force in that their numbers are usually fairly stable throughout the year.

The fluctuation in the labour force, which is marked seasonally, arises mainly from variations in the number of cutters and loaders employed for the crop time. Discussion of cutters and loaders must be kept sharply distinct. Cutters are usually highly individualistic and will rarely cut with more than one partner,[1] because a serious prob-

[1] The Monymusk system differs so fundamentally that it requires separate treatment.

lem would arise at the end of the day in determining the individual output with larger numbers. Sometimes a cutting team will be a family affair in which case there may be more than two in the team. In this case by mutual agreement they may carry an absentee or allow say, the father to have his full share of the pay although he cuts less than the rest. Groups[2] of four were found on one estate but this was unusual. The estate is expected to carry on its payroll the names of all workers engaged in a particular operation. There are several reasons for this, including coverage under the Workmen's Compensation Law, the calculation of bonuses, grants of sick and vacation leave etc. Loaders, on the other hand, work in groups of four to six: no problem of allocation arises here for the internal discipline of the group ensures that each man carries his fair share of the work. Typically, an operative group consists of a headman, who usually picks his own assistants, one man on the truck itself stacking and two or three men throwing up the cane in bundles from the ground on to the truck. Variations in the type of loading group vary to some extent according to the method used for conveying the cane from the field to the weighing scale. On the different estates the author saw moveable narrow gauge railways, fixed railways, road vehicles of different kinds such as horse drawn drays, tractors with trailers, lorries which go into the cut cane field and are there loaded. On one estate, Appleton, where the soil is a heavy clay and the rainfall averages 70 inches per year, a lot of drainage is necessary. The field drains make tractor haulage difficult and here the cutters are required to head load the cut canes to the interval (roadway) where they dump them on the ground. Loaders then pick them up from there. The cutters are paid extra for this work and were the nearest example to a combined cutting/loading opera-

[2] The word "group" is used here in preference to the word "gang" which appears to carry some ambiguity in current usage in the industry. In some cases a "cutting gang" is regarded as a large unit of workers under some supervisor. A large estate may thus have, say, 3 cutting "gangs" to harvest the entire crop, with no standardised name for the smaller operative unit within the gang.

tion observed in this enquiry. Even so, the loads are deposited on the ground–the cutters will not dump them in trucks which would presumably be just as easy for them once the load has been lifted from the ground. The work of the cutter varies according to the distance he has to throw the cane. On one estate where a moveable railway is used, the cutters have to throw the cane up to 50 feet–with a mechanical loader the maximum distance would be 17 feet. Such differences in techniques clearly affect the nature of the job and the output per man that can be expected.

On all the estates except Monymusk, the organisation of the work is broadly similar. The headman is told the amount of cane to be cut for the day by the appropriate supervisor who makes his decision on the basis of the cane stock at the factory and the anticipated delivery of farmers' canes. The headman then allocates, say, 5 or 6 rows of cane to a cutting gang. The men may, or may not, cut the cane that day–a usual procedure is for them to mark it (and no-one else will then touch it) and go home. Next morning–perhaps at 4.30 a.m. in the cool of the morning the men will start work and cut until their task is completed. The cane is left in a heap on the ground and tagged. The headman always seems to know who cut which pile, although it was not possible to investigate what sort of disputes, if any, this procedure leads to in the field itself. Usually the work of one cutting gang is loaded on to one trailer, lorry, dray or waggon and then taken to the scale to be weighed. The scales are automatic in the majority of cases–the gross weight of vehicle and load is printed on to a document known as a "waybill" issued by the headman in the field. The scale clerk knows the unladen weight of each vehicle (the tare weight) and then calculates manually the net weight of each load, recording this figure on the waybill. Several points of relevance to the present enquiry arise here. In the first place it became clear on every estate that it is virtually impossible, given the present organisation of the industry, to keep any kind of accurate check on the number of hours spent by a cutter in the field. The work may be half finished by the time the overseer arrives, a system of time clocks would be quite impractical and serve no useful purpose anyway. The fact is that hours are not homogeneous–the amount that a man can cut between 4.30 and 6.00 a.m. is quite different from his potentiality between 11.00 a.m. and 12.00 noon when the sun is blazing into the cane field. A measure of hours spent without reference to the period of the day would be of little use, even if the information could be obtained, which it cannot at present. At an early stage, therefore, all effort to find the number of hours worked was abandoned. A sample survey could be organised which would yield approximate information but it would be expensive and unreliable. It would be possible to arrive at a better estimate of the hours worked by the loading teams by recording the hours their vehicles are in the fields. But there is no close connection between hours spent by a vehicle in the field and hours spent loading cane into the vehicle. Even for loaders, therefore, this part of the enquiry was dropped at a very early stage.

Of even greater significance, perhaps, is the fact that the task is set by the management, not usually chosen by the worker. The cane harvesting is not directly machine paced but it is so indirectly, being related to the factories' capacity to grind, the supply of farmers' cane and the fluctuations in the cane stock. This is important for any study of productivity in the industry–we may be able to discover the actual output per man-day but we must not assume that variations in that output from estate to estate or from time to time are necessarily the sole responsibility of the individual worker. There is clearly an upper limit somewhere to the amount of cane a man can cut in a day, although the figure varies enormously according to circumstances. The proportion he actually cuts, in relation to what he could cut also varies enormously partly from his own volition and partly in accordance with restraints imposed upon him by the management. The output of the loading gangs also varies considerably–they clearly can load only what has been cut and ideally then should remove it as quickly as possible to the factory, but practice varies considerably between the estates in handling this part of the process. Many estates do not engage the loaders on their payroll at all, but subcontract the job out to a truck driver who hires his own loading gang. At United Estates, for instance, 25% of the cane is loaded by subcontractors. The difficulty of servicing mechanical transport, and its unreliability, is one of the problems of estate management.

Under no circumstances will cutters load cane or vice versa. In some countries, for example Australia, cutting and loading may be performed by the same group of people. Not so in Jamaica, for here cutters will leave the cane to rot on the ground (and thereby lose their hard earned cash) rather than load it into carts. This phenomenon which seems to be yet another manifestation of the work-spreading philosophy so deeply ingrained in this industry, not without cause, would be worth examining more carefully. One wondered how long it would be before a combine harvester made its appearance in the Jamaican cane fields, mechanically cutting and loading the cane. It appears that the technical difficulties of such an innovation are considerable: no doubt the sociological difficulties are no less formidable.

The moment cane is cut it begins to depreciate. A series of trials conducted in 1963 by the Sugar Research Department on the Monymusk estate showed the following results:—

Sugar Weight of Burnt and Unburnt Cane Relative to Fresh Cane

	Fresh Cane	*Relative result after:*			
		1 day	2 days	4 days	8 days
Unburnt	100	99.1	95.9	85.0	69.4
Burnt	100	97.5	94.1	89.5	66.8

These figures (if they may be taken as typical) indicate the degree of deterioration in the cane, measured by the end product of sugar weight, and bring out the fact that there is no very great difference between burnt and unburnt cane. Indeed, after 4 days, burnt cane appears to produce better results than unburnt, according to this analysis. There is no doubt that the main object of estate management is to get the cane to the factory as soon as possible after it is cut in the field. At Monymusk every effort is made to get the cane from field to factory in 48 hours, using radio instructions to regulate and synchronise the cutting/loading operations to reduce estate cane stock at the factory to a minimum. A stockpile must still be retained of farmers' canes. On other estates the performance tends to be less efficient than this–men may cut for three days and only deliver on one. A tagged bundle may be on the ground for four days. It appears that this is a field for an Operations Research study team to enquire into the methods of cutting, loading and grinding, relating size of stockpile, variation in cutting requirements and capital stock tied up in road vehicles one to the other. An increase in radio equipment and a rationalisation of farmers' delivery may well reduce costs considerably, both the costs involved in the queues of waiting loaded carts at the factory scales and the costs of inefficient labour in the cutting operation. There is a choice to be made here. At the moment the choices are made by managements on every estate by rule of thumb and traditional practices–it may well be that great cost reductions could be achieved if this subject were to be given a closer scrutiny. Apart from the capital costs involved this relationship between factory performance, cane stockpile and farmers' delivery is germane to the labour performance of the reaping gangs. If the stockpile is large, or the factory breaks down, the word will spread quickly through the "grapevine" and affect the willingness of workers to report for work.[3] Their regular-

[3] According to the S.M.A. understanding of the position, insofar as daily paid workers are concerned, if they are not advised in advance of the Estate's inability to employ them on a particular day and they report for work they must be paid at least for half a day. If they have worked the morning period and cannot be employed during the afternoon because of factory breakdown or similar causes, they must then be paid for the full day. It is also stated that in recent years, during crop, cane cutters, loaders, and other workers engaged in reaping opera-

ity is a function, in part, of their expectation of regular employment. Furthermore their output is affected by the same factors–a large stockpile on Thursday may mean a smaller task on Sunday, a day paid at premium rates. It is logical, therefore, to reduce attendance and output on Thursday to maximise employer demands for labour on premium days.[4] Estates have various expectations as to the performance they expect from an individual cutter. Monymusk, with its particular system, requires a minimum of 5 tons per cutter per day and discharges a cutter who consistently fails to measure up to this standard. Most estates take what they can get and on different estates 3 tons, 1¼ tons and 2 tons are expected norms of output. As far as is known–W.I.S.Co. excepted–only one estate, Barnett, has made a systematic analysis of its records to try to determine the output and attendance of cutters. The author cannot vouch for the figures as he had no hand in their collation but they are interesting enough for comment. It appears that Barnett took the records for the 1963 crop and counted the output per cutter according to the waybills with the following result:

Output per Cutter–Barnett Estate, 1963 Crop

Tons cut average per week	*Number of cutters*	%
2 – 4	28	10
5 – 7	87	31
8 – 10	103	37
11 – 13	49	17
14 – 16	12	4
17 – 19	3	1
	282	100

tions are invariably in short supply. Provided they are willing to work, therefore, it is believed they can almost always get employment for 7 days a week for the duration of the crop.

[4] On some estates the amount a worker is *permitted* to cut on Sunday is related to the amount actually cut on the previous Thursday (or Friday).

This table suggests that it is physically possible to cut up to 19 tons of fresh cane a week–and certainly in excess of 10 tons. Yet most cutters produced between 8–10 tons. These figures are puzzling in many ways and really raise more questions than they answer–nevertheless they are interesting. On the same estate the number of weeks actually worked per cutter were counted and the following table produced.

Number of Weeks Worked per Cutter
Barnett Estate, 1963 Crop

Number of weeks on payroll	*Number of cutters*	*%*
1 – 5	50	18
6 – 10	42	15
11 – 15	48	17
16 – 20	85	30
21 or 22 (full crop)	57	20
	282	100

This table does not show a regular pattern, rising to a peak and falling away. It is at least bi-modal in statistical terms which suggests that the population is not homogeneous. Closer examination would probably reveal that the numbers working 1–5 weeks were a different group from those working 16 weeks or more. But one can only speculate what the differences are. The Barnett figures cannot help us with an explanation.

Mention has been made of the fact that on one estate, Monymusk, owned by The West Indies Sugar Company, there has been a complete break with tradition in the organisation of the reaping operation, and also in the system of record keeping. It is claimed that the system of harvesting adopted on this estate has enabled the operation to be rationalised, whilst the introduction of a data processing system using an electronic digital computer (the first to be used commercially in the island of Jamaica) has revolutionised not only the accountancy procedures, but opened the way to an integral managerial control of the entire system which is only possible when information can be analysed quickly and fed back to the management decision making centre in usable form. Under the new harvesting system which was introduced in 1961, the management decides the amount of cane to be cut and then the cane field is burnt. The following day the reaping gang, numbering about 100 cutters, goes to the field where each man is allocated a number of chains which he is expected to cut, working on an estimated yield for the field as a whole and assuming a minimum of five tons of cane per man per day. No effort is made to record the amount of cane cut per man in the field–he is paid at the end of the week on the distance actually cut at a rate per chain resulting from a provisional estimate of the cane collected from the whole field, adjusted later when the actual yield of the field is known. All cutters are paid at the same average rate per chain. The loading is then handled by mechanical loaders. A typical loading gang consists of:

(a) Loader operator.
(b) In-field haulage operator.
(c) Six "scrappers" (Gleaners).
(d) One wheeled tractor from field to factory.
(e) Two sidemen for wheeled tractor.
(f) One sideman for in-field tractor.
(g) Loading supervisor.

In the factory the cane is processed through a washing plant to clean the cane (mechanically loaded cane is much heavier than hand-loaded as a good deal of earth is collected by the grabber), but there is much less trash carried to the factory due to the preliminary burning. The effect of this system is that both cutting and loading gangs can expect relatively high earnings, easier work and regular employment. On the other hand they are expected to operate under a much tighter supervision than is normal and irregular attendance results in dismissal–there is always a surplus of cutters and loaders seeking employment at

Monymusk. Consequently a more highly developed personnel selection procedure can be used than on other estates. The fact that the payroll is produced on an electronic computer means that detailed reports on each worker can be produced quickly. Operating on the principle of management by exception, each quarter the computer produces a list of workers who have failed to put in a required minimum of attendances and they are investigated by the management. From the estate vehicles the cane is loaded directly into the mill, thus minimising the costly handling of large piles of cut canes. The cane usually arrives at the factory on the average about 48 hours after being cut in the field, with consequential improvements in the sugar yield. There is no problem of absenteeism or output restriction on this estate. A man can cut twice as much burnt cane as green cane and there is no incentive to limit production.

It is interesting to ask why this Monymusk system is not generally adopted throughout all the other estates. A number of arguments are used, all of which seem, in face of the actual performance at Monymusk, singularly unconvincing. It is claimed that burning cane increases cost of weed control, that insect pests (particularly the cane fly and the borer) increase, that burning cane is impractical unless it is allied to mechanical loading. It is stated that mechanically loaded burnt cane gives more trouble in the factory than unburnt cane and that burnt cane is always more trouble in the factory than unburnt cane. Opinions differ as to whether the loss of humus arising from the burning of the cane is a serious factor. Humus has a mulching effect on the soil and its importance depends upon whether the estate needs to be irrigated or drained. On the other hand cane trash is a problem, particularly on irrigated estates, where drains and canals are more expensive to maintain, inter-row cultivation is hindered and a lot of trash tends to delay the effect of fertilisers. If one takes as an example a field yielding 60 tons of cane per acre one would expect to get about 10 tons of trash, which would yield a maximum humus of about 10 hundredweights. This is not much in two million pounds of soil.

The author cannot make any final judgement on the relative merits and demerits of these arguments from the point of view of agricultural practice, entomology and soil science, but the weight of the argument seems to be strongly on the side of the Monymusk system so far as labour organisation and productivity is concerned—provided it is allied to mechanical loading, suitable modifications to the factory and radical changes in personnel procedure.

The estates might well face a problem in the transitional stage if workers refused to cut cane once it had been burnt in order to extract a higher price for their labour, in the knowledge that burnt cane deteriorates quickly if not removed to the factory within two or three days.

The question of the type, degree and implications of mechanisation is vital. The factory is, of course, already almost completely mechanised and slowly machines are appearing in the offices. There are still donkey drays to be seen conveying cane to the factory but these are rapidly disappearing before the tractor and the lorry. The weeding, drain digging and cane planting process is already fairly well mechanised at least on some estates. On one estate the author was told that 80 per cent of these processes are now handled by machines; no workers had been dismissed, employment was given to any able-bodied person who applied (and was willing to cut or load cane) and the estate is still short of workers. Mechanical loaders, introduced only a year or two ago are also spreading—cane farmers are increasingly using them and as we have seen the Monymusk system depends on them. In the attitude of workers to the mechanical loaders there appears to be a strange ambivalence. On one estate the author was told of cutters in the field who would tell the headman to "get the grabber", but if the machine appeared in the field great resentment was shown. In another case a farm had no loading gang, and a group of cutters wanted their cane lifted. The estate offered to bring a mechanical loader but the cutters objected. They were then told to provide their own loaders and the estate would employ them. They failed and finally asked for the machine. Apparently on at least one estate one of the unions operating in the industry has officially requested the use of mechanical cane loaders.

It is in cane cutting that the last bastion of resistance to mechanisation is being held. Estate managers told the author that there were technical difficulties involved in the use of cutting machines and that there was considerable political opposition to the use of cutting and loading machines to the point where the importation of such machines was prohibited. It was nevertheless clear to the author that mechanisation of both cutting and loading is the prerequisite to any further progress in the industry, perhaps a condition for its survival in the competitive modern world. There appears to be no reason to believe that the phased introduction of machines should prevent people from working who want to work nor does it appear that the workers on the estates have anything to fear from further mechanisation, in fact it appears that they have much to gain. At the same time it must be recognised that in this survey the author talked only to managers. There was no opportunity to talk to the workers themselves because time on each estate was so limited, nor has the author discussed the question with union or political leaders from whom he might well have heard a very different story.

POSTSCRIPT

The author's attention was drawn to the apparently unfavourable performance in the field output of sugar in Jamaica as compared with other countries. In a report by Dr. C. Y. Shepherd on cane cutting in Barbados, published in 1947, he reported that in 1944 the quantity of cane cut averaged almost 5 (4.9) tons per man per day. He further found that in 1945 the disturbed nature of the 1945 crop season was reflected in a slight fall off in the average amount of cane cut per man per day (4.8 tons) and in the smaller average number of days the cutter worked on any particular plantation. During the 1964 cropping season in Australia in the State of Queensland a worker was reported (in Sugar and Azucar June 1965) on the average to have hand cut, hand topped and hand loaded 8.92 tons of cane during an 8 hour day throughout the entire crop. It is clear that inter-territorial comparisons of this kind are possibly misleading, but they suggest that productivity in Jamaica leaves considerable room for improvement.

SUPPLY OF LABOUR

On most estates the recruitment of labour is a fairly casual process. Each estate has a large group of regulars who return for each crop season and who are known personally to the headmen or overseers. The normal procedure is for the estate to advertise by one means or the other that the crop is commencing and invite the workers to return. Under present conditions of expanded output no question of selection arises. Provided there is no very strong reason for refusing to engage a particular man, he will be engaged by the overseer or headman in the pay station or field as the case may be. Formally he should usually report to one of the farm offices or pay stations but in practice he is likely to be met by the headman in the road and told to report to a particular field the following morning. Some estates, Monymusk, Frome, Innswood and Bernard Lodge, for instance, for the last year or two have introduced more rigorous selection and registration procedures but only at Monymusk can it be said that any form of selection of workers takes place. Everywhere else, the estates are short of cutters and loaders at the present time. The introduction of the sugar workers' pension scheme has enforced a certain amount of system into the proceedings, for each worker must be registered with the pension authority. It appears that there must be a degree of multiple registration of workers in this scheme which may create difficulty in sorting out the pension claims when they arise in the future.

The policy of most estates is to take on more cutters

and loaders than are strictly required because of the likely wastage over the crop period.[5] A 100 men will be started, 30 just stop work or do not turn up at all leaving 70 to do the work that 60 could do comfortably. In consequence the work must be spread out at the start of the crop and productivity and earnings are low. Today, on most estates the cutters select the days they will work and they do so on a perfectly rational basis which happens to exasperate the management. Everywhere the author heard the words "labour shortage" and at the same time was constantly told that there were 10 men wanting every factory job. It may be said that a labour shortage exists *when management does not have enough men to do the jobs that are required to be done when they need to be done*. Accepting that definition, there is clear evidence of labour shortage in the sugar industry, side by side with people clamouring for work.

There are a number of factors which influence the supply of labour at a particular estate. The geographical location of the estate is important. The Caymanas Estate lies almost in the suburbs of Kingston and engages a lot of transit labour particularly from the St. Thomas district. The men are attracted by the bright city lights, the prospect of change and activity. Men drift to Kingston hoping to find industrial work and when they fail to do so they gravitate out to Caymanas which is then used as a springboard from which to leap into the first urban job that materialises. The Barnett Estate is almost part of Montego Bay, the town has grown up to the factory and will probably shortly engulf it. Ten years ago there was no labour shortage at Barnett but in the last decade the tourist boom has hit Montego Bay, new hotels and industries have appeared and a swamp reclamation scheme has pulled away most of the ambitious local workers. To complicate matters, a banana loading wharf nearby has the effect of reducing the estate's cutting group by 30 to 40 workers whenever a banana boat has to be loaded. The reaction of this estate has been to build new barracks or dormitories for the use of migrant workers some 200 of whom in the present crop

[5] Monymusk was the exception to the rule.

came from outside the immediate vicinity. At the other end of the island the Jamaica Sugar Estates faces no particular problem of alternative employment, the banana and coconut industries at present pay less than sugar, with the result that the estate cannot get its coconuts picked; the crop has been a dead loss. In the centre of the island the Serge Island factory is the only manufacturing business in the whole area, there are a number of towns and villages nearby which supply all the labour required. Workers leave this area to go to work at Caymanas or Bernard Lodge and the estate sometimes runs into difficulties if its own crop commences late. Gray's Inn on the north-east coast lies in a banana district centred on Port Antonio, here there is a decided oscillation of labour from bananas to sugar and back again. Each estate is different and has its peculiarities, thus generalisation is difficult, but the case studies are interesting.

The experience of the estates varies from year to year. At the Jamaica Sugar Estates, for instance, the pattern for the 1965 crop has been quite different from, say, three years ago. Then there was no problem of getting cutters. This year the estate had to begin with only 75 per cent of its labour requirement. For the first time in 35 years they were short of labour. The shortage was felt primarily amongst the cutters. As cutters on this estate aspire to be loaders there is continual "poaching" of labour by the loading groups at the expense of the cutters. At the Gray's Inn estate the experience has been quite different. The labour supply alternates between plenty and shortage. In the 1965 crop the labour supply has been adequate for the estate lands (as distinct from the cane farmers), but in 1963 the estate experienced a very bad year. They were chronically short of labour at the start of the crop. The position eased as the crop progressed, although continuous difficulties were experienced in trying to get jobs done by hand cultivation. The estate advertised in the press and appealed to the Ministry of Labour. Two groups of workers were sent down by the Ministry, but the majority never started to work at all and the rest departed very quickly. In 1964 the position had completely changed, and the labour supply was adequate throughout the entire crop. It is difficult to explain these variations with confidence but the Flora floods were a contributory factor. Those floods washed out many of the small cultivations in the hills and the men needed cash badly. Large bonuses, a direct result of the high price following the sugar shortage created by the Cuban crisis, had been paid in 1963 and proved an attraction. On the other hand this was one of the few areas where the migration of people to Britain was mentioned as a specific factor in the labour supply situation, although its significance is difficult to assess.

At Barnett estate in 1965 there has been no shortage of jobs, but imported labour is disinclined to do any task except cutting. The substantial bonuses paid in October apparently reduced the eagerness to work. "We have no worry now about people tearing down the place for lack of work" was one local comment. At Serge Island the cane cutter shortage widened during the crop to the point where the estate was 30 per cent short of its stated requirements. Holland reported a serious labour shortage three or four weeks after the start of the crop and they never have a surplus of cutters: work is always available. At Bernard Lodge they cannot get enough workers to do the work and find it difficult to understand the meaning of the word "unemployment" in these circumstances. The fact is that at the rates and conditions of work the estates are prepared to offer the workers are not coming forward at present in sufficient numbers to meet the demand for their labour. Furthermore the cane farmers are a variable factor over which the estates, as such, have little control. Cane farmers may hold back their canes at the start of the crop waiting until the sucrose content has increased (cane farmers are paid on the actual sugar produced from their canes), thus leaving labour for the estates who use their own canes to keep the factory going. Later, when the cane farmers want to increase their deliveries, competition forces up the price paid to cutters. Friend helps friend to the detriment of the more impersonal sugar estate.

On every estate visited the managements agreed that there is a marked seasonal pattern in the labour supply.

From a fairly plentiful supply of labour at the start of the crop the labour available dwindles slowly until Easter when the supply plunges downwards. Everyone also seems to be fairly agreed about the causes of this variation–at the beginning of the crop last year's bonus is spent, the men may be in debt, they are rested and fresh and ready to work. As the weeks pass the money position eases, they become tired and general physical as well as social fatigue sets in. The crucial factor, however, is the fact that the great majority of the workers have a small holding somewhere in the hills and this is their first love and loyalty. When rain comes around April, the planting time has arrived and at Appleton estate, for instance, the author was told that after a shower of rain as many as 60 per cent of the field workers will depart. "Gone ground" as the saying goes. The pattern of absenteeism varies according to the district of origin of the worker and its relationship to the estate. The transient workers will vanish for days on end, then return. The local people are more likely to take a day or two off during the week–on any day except Sunday. The author was told on one estate that the result of higher earnings is that the maintenance of a separate small holding is on the decline but he found no evidence to support that view. On the contrary it seems that at Frome a fairly high proportion of the regular workers in the factory are also cane farmers and small cultivators in their own right. In turn they employ labour in the villages where they live, on a task basis, whilst they themselves remain constantly on the job. Some of the field workers at Frome are also cane farmers, but not on the same scale.

Two other factors influencing the seasonal fluctuation in the labour supply may be mentioned, though neither of them is of much significance by comparison with the factors outlined above. One is the fact that government money for public works tends to dry up after Christmas, but becomes available again around April. In their eagerness to start road and other engineering jobs before the rainy season sets in public departments and municipalities may suddenly appear as competitors for manual labour. This point was mentioned to the author once or twice during his visits and seems to suggest that a closer liaison between the public and private sectors on both national and local level might be of mutual advantage. Neither the government nor the sugar industry can benefit from uncoordinated action which simply disrupts production when synchronised planning would enable a more even flow of work to be provided. Admittedly it is easier to state the problem than to find a practical solution to it, although a mutual recognition that a problem exists and at least informal discussions to seek a solution would be a useful start towards finding a satisfactory rational solution. Finally the author had expected to find that migration to the U.K. and to the U.S.A., particularly under the Farm Labour Scheme, would be mentioned as the cause of labour shortages. Far from it. If these migratory movements do have any effect on the labour supply position, the estate managements seem to be virtually unconscious of it. This may be because the casual worker on a sugar estate found it difficult to raise the passage money to the U.K. In any event the possibility of migrating to the U.K. is now so restricted, that the question is of academic interest only.

SOCIAL FACTORS AFFECTING SUPPLY OF LABOUR AND PRODUCTIVITY

There has been a noticeable change in the cane fields over the last twenty years. Even 15 years ago, children would come barefooted with their parents to the cane fields to help with "the task." Today, those children are going in shoes and socks to school where they quickly learn to believe the lesson taught at home that they want nothing to do with agricultural work. On being chided for the educational backwardness of his rural school the school teacher replied "You should be grateful for that. If we educate them they will not cut cane." He spoke the plain truth—but he should have added "with present methods." The educational advance in the schools is an essential prerequisite to the rapid mechanisation of the cane fields upon which the future of this industry may well depend, and the educational advance makes the spread of mechanisation quite inevitable. Women are still to be seen working in the fields, usually gleaning cane after the men have loaded the bulk. But the women, too, are disappearing from the cane fields. As the earnings rise, the men are better able to maintain the women at home.

Not a day passes on most estates but a man asks for a job in the factory. For any vacancy in the factory most estates could quickly find 10 applicants from which to choose: there is a hierarchy of occupations with cutting at the base of the pyramid, loading is a superior occupation, then there is field cultivation, ditching, draining and so to the factory. Somewhere the tractor drivers and handlers of mechanical loaders fit into the picture. Work in the field is subject to the vagaries of nature such as heat, rain, whilst physical bending and strain is involved in all reaping operations. Hence the universal desire to escape from the field into the factory. These physical conditions are sufficient to explain the unpopularity of cutting and loading as compared with other occupations on the estate but there are other factors going deep into history, to the dark days of slavery when attitudes were hardened which persist in the myth and folklore of the people to this day. The author could not begin to touch the fringe of this fascinating and perhaps highly significant field of study but it would be well worthwhile pursuing by patient enquiry amongst the people themselves. On one estate the manager reported that a man had turned down a job as a cutter because "I can't go home and tell my woman I do cane cutting." Cutting is regarded as socially degrading, the last resort when all else has failed. In consequence it appears that the average age of the cutter is increasing. The younger men refuse point blank to take it up. It seemed to be generally believed that the typical cutter would be in the 35–55 age range, and the typical loader in the 18–25 age group. These figures could be checked without too much difficulty, and it might be worthwhile to try to establish the facts in this direction.[6]

[6] The author's attention was later drawn to an enquiry conducted by the S.M.A. in 1962 which suggested that 17% of the male cane cutters employed in the industry were aged 50 and

Managers were also generally agreed that the older men were more steady and reliable workers than the younger generation. Perhaps this is universally true and not just a feature of Jamaican labour.

The social differences between cutting and loading are very real but not easy to define. On the Trelawny estate the transient workers are only cutters—they have no prospect of getting a job in a loading group, and on the Hampden estate it seems that cutters are always trying to become loaders. On the Sevens estate the author was told that loading is harder than cutting and the young men do the cutting; on the Hampden estate he was told that cutting is more difficult than loading. Twenty years ago much of the loading was done by women and boys; these days are over but in some areas at least loading is still regarded by the men as essentially women's and boys' work. Habit and tradition play a great part in the way jobs are done. On the Hampden estate men insist on putting canes together in large bundles before they heave the loads into the vehicle. When outsiders come in they show the local people how to load cane just as quickly but with much less effort by handling smaller bundles. But the old method still persists.

It should need no lengthy argument to establish the proposition that one of the factors affecting labour productivity is the quantity and quality of the food supply. On one estate the author was told categorically that the amount of cane cut and loaded is affected by the availability of the food vendors in the fields. If, for any reason, they do not appear, the overseer will go and find them. One of the reasons delaying an immediate start of full scale operations after a strike is that the food selling women are reluctant to come out. They refuse to give credit beyond the end of the week and as, after a strike, the first pay day is a fortnight away the men are often left to go the whole day without food or sustenance with consequential lowering of production. On some estates the women will not bring food out on Fri-

---

over, whilst 13% were under 25. In the case of loaders 4.5% were over 50 and 23% were under 25. These figures tend to support the general view that on the whole there are more loaders than cutters, proportionately, in the younger age groups.

days or Saturdays. On Friday they are in attendance at the pay stations, collecting money owed to them for meals supplied in the previous week. On Saturday they go to market. None of the estates have made any systematic effort to provide an adequate food supply, or to see that it is available. The catering is left to private women caterers, vendors or higglers who usually cook the food in the village and carry it, with one or two assistants, to the fields. There the estate may, or may not, have rigged up some rough shelter of thatch or even a tent in which the food is served and eaten, being sold by the plate, usually on credit. The cutters normally come to work very early in the morning and return home for the midday meal (unless they are migratory or must travel long distances). The loaders are most urgently in need of victuals for they usually work through the day. The problem of the food supply is not confined to the fields for few workers have the facility for storing any quantity of food at home. Refrigerators are rare or nonexistent and a large stock of food would be raided in the absence of the owner: food must therefore be bought almost for a day at a time. Most of the estates are extremely vague about the catering arrangements which apply to their workers: "there are about six cook shops on the estate" was the typical sort of reply to questions. At Trelawny the company pays the cooks for the loader groups, but the men buy their own food and a similar arrangement primarily for cultivation workers operates at Hampden. On Sevens estate the company built a special kitchen on the largest farm (Parnassus) but not on the others and left it to be operated by a private caterer. At Appleton the estate provided a building for catering purposes which is run by a person elected by the factory workers with the help of a committee of seven. The Jamaica Sugar Estates some years ago put up a building and proposed to lease a concession for catering in the factory to a group of women. There were numerous complaints from workers who wanted their own cooks, not the ones selected by the factory, and in consequence the scheme never went into operation.

One or two estates are becoming conscious not only of the welfare responsibilities involved in this question of catering, but are beginning to realise that the provision of good food at reasonable prices may pay off in the way of higher output, even if the service has to be subsidised. So far, however, these ideas have not been translated into practice. One estate is investigating the possibility of using mobile field kitchens, giving some private individual the right to operate a concession under supervision. Another idea is that the estate should institute a system of food tokens and issue them daily to be exchanged for food provided by registered food vendors. The estate would deduct the value of the food token from earnings, possibly allowing for a subsidy on each token and thus gain some control over the prices and quality of food supplied by the registered caterers. This is a subject which would merit more investigation. Clearly an industrial canteen would be inappropriate for field workers, but it would probably be to the advantage of each estate to establish a properly run industrial canteen in association with the factory and office with a mobile meal service out to the fields. Already drinking water is systematically supplied by most if not all the estates by means of tanks and drums. On at least one estate permission has been given for a vendor of soft drinks to open his business.

Whilst few people would disagree with the basic principle that adequate feeding arrangements should be available for workers–whether provided by the estate or by private enterprise, or whether subsidised or not are separate questions–it cannot be emphasised too strongly that *before* positive action is taken detailed consideration of the local situation should first be made, preferably in close contact with the trade unions, supervisors and other interested parties on each individual estate.

On the whole the estates have set their faces against providing housing for workers. Some of them must provide dormitories (or "barracks" as they are still called) for transient and migratory workers. On the Trelawny estate dormitories with beds and mattresses are provided for about 180 migrant workers. At Barnett they have six "barracks," four for temporary cane cutters and two for permanent residents. They also have about 30 "welfare cottages" of two rooms built with the aid of funds provided by the Sugar

Industry Labour Welfare Board which is financed from a levy on the sugar industry. Housing, where available, is usually allocated at the discretion of the overseer who thus controls both home and job, a most powerful position in relation to the individual worker. One could not help but wonder what degree of extortion and "kick-back" arises from this situation.[7] The effect of housing provision on labour supply and productivity is marked and immediate. There was general agreement on the estates that the worker who lives in the village, dealing with a private landlord, forced to produce the rent on pay day is more likely to be "responsible" (i.e. more regular in attendance) than a worker who is housed by the estate itself. The estate is always in difficulties when it comes to collecting rents, for private landlords have fewer scruples, it seems, about eviction. The example was quoted to the author of a farm on one estate where 90 per cent of the workers lived in privately owned houses off the estate. This was the only farm where women could be found to weed on Saturday. Problems created by squatters were not often mentioned, but where they are present it is clear that a regiment of police would be necessary to clear them off estate land and this would create great social resentment. Whenever possible estates appear to prefer to enter into tenancy agreements. The provision of adequate housing is undoubtedly an urgent social need in Jamaica but it is easy to see why sugar estates are not anxious to involve themselves in meeting the need. Any proposals for an extension of estate provided housing is likely to meet with strong resistance from estate managements, but one could not help but feel that a closer concern with the community efforts to solve the problem should be urged.

Ganja, gambling and drink are three of the ways in which some workers like to spend their money once the basic essentials of life have been met. Experience of ganja smoking seems to vary according to the part of the island. Estates

[7] The question of "kick-back" in relation to labour recruitment generally was hardly ever mentioned. Whether this is because it is rare, or because managements are unaware of the practice, is not clear.

lying to the east of Kingston reported little or no ganja smoking, whereas estates to the north and west reported considerably more. One estate manager gave it as his opinion that 75 per cent of the labour force on that estate smoke ganja regularly with noticeable effect on the performance of workers in such occupations as tractor driving. On another estate the manager explained that he would never discuss a grievance on a Friday or Saturday (pay day and ganja day) because only under the influence of "the weed" was a man likely to become violent. Few managers appeared to be unduly worried by ganja smoking. Indeed some of them pointed out that workers claim that it increases their productivity. On premium pay days, on some estates the author was told that the workers are "steeped in ganja" to increase their output. Whether or not this is a problem for the estates, it is clearly a social problem.

The social pattern of the Friday night spree is universally accepted. Rum flows freely, the week's work is done, it is market day tomorrow and extra premium time on Sunday. As a result of Friday night, when a significant proportion of the labour force may be drinking heavily, the turnout of labour on Saturday is usually very meagre. On the other hand it seems that there are few cases of drunkenness brought to the courts. Whether this proves more sobriety than might be expected or is an indication of police discretion on Friday night, the author does not know.

As with ganja, so with gambling, the incidence varies from estate to estate. One case was quoted of a man who collected £14 as his week's earnings. He began to gamble with 4 other men and came away penniless to return to his wife and four children at home. But the general impression the author gained was that gambling of the traditional kind (dice, crown and anchor, cards, dominoes) amongst the workers themselves was no more than a diversion and no real social problem. It has little or no effect on productivity. Yet there are traces of a new development, the advent of professional gamblers (sometimes accompanied by "strange ladies" who arrive in busloads to ply a different trade on Friday evening) and betting shops in the towns. These are still not used too much by the field workers but they are there, and growing in number. Gambling accompanies the drinking and general festivity of Friday night and is perhaps no more than a release of tension, a momentary hope of finding a quick way out of the cane field.

7.

The realities of West Indian rural life include acute shortages of arable land and severely limited opportunities for employment. The following article describes a Jamaican milieu in which sheer survival obliges those on the lowest economic levels to pursue several occupations at one time. A comparative study of fishing communities shows that the great majority of fishermen combine fishing with farming and wage employment. People in rural Jamaica keep up multiple and often intertwined pursuits as a necessary adaptation to a meager environment.

LAMBROS COMITAS has a doctorate in anthropology from Columbia University. An American, he has carried out field research in Barbados, Jamaica, the Dominican Republic, and Bolivia. At present he is Professor of Anthropology and Education at Teachers College, Columbia University, and Associate Director of the Research Institute for the Study of Man.

Occupational Multiplicity in Rural Jamaica

Lambros Comitas

Although it has not been completely neglected, an entire socio-economic stratum of rural Jamaican society is not easily accounted for in any of the taxonomic formulations presently available for the Caribbean area. Characteristic of this population segment is occupational multiplicity or plurality, wherein the modal adult is systematically engaged in a number of gainful activities, which for him form an integrated economic complex. This occupational multiplicity is the nexus of a socio-economic type significantly different from that of either the peasant, farmer, or plantation types in the West Indies.

Anthropology in the Caribbean during the past three decades has developed with at least five major concerns: a) ethnohistory and Afro-American studies, b) culture and personality, c) social anthropology, d) cultural ecology, and e) the community study. These have not been mutually exclusive categories, but they do delineate the principal theoretical and methodological orientations. However, for the description of the non-localized socio-economic type which follows, only the research of the cultural ecological school is generally applicable and comparable.

The work of this school is represented by Julian Steward and his associates, in an analysis of contemporary Puerto

Adapted from a paper given at the 1963 Annual Spring Meeting of the American Ethnological Society and printed in the Proceedings of the meeting, *Symposium on Community Studies in Anthropology,* Edited by Viola E. Garfield and Ernestine Friedl, 1964, pp. 41–50.

Rico[1] which concentrated on several of the main variants of the island's culture.

> . . . Each rural region has a distinctive environment and therefore particular crop potentials. In each region the productive arrangement—the kind of crop, mechanization in field production or in processing, land tenure, capitalization and credit, and the nature of labor and of owner–worker relations—has created distinctive subcultures among the people involved.[2]

Initial field research in Puerto Rico yielded descriptions and analyses; later study, by several in the group, led to broader statements which were based more on structural arrangements than on cultural content and which were not limited to a particular island. For the Caribbean as a whole, Padilla isolated three such contemporary social-rural types:

> . . . In terms of a typology of rural subcultures, the most important groups in the Caribbean today, from a numerical and sociological point of view, are peasants, farmers, and plantation workers involved within the corporate system.[3]

Wolf has written extensively on the peasant and Mintz has contributed to our knowledge of both plantation and peasant organizations. Each of these types can be defined as follows: the term plantation worker is applied to a landless wage employee who is attached to a large-scale agricultural organization geared to the production and marketing of an export crop for profit;[4] that of farmer is applied to an agricultural entrepreneur who owns land, hires wage labor or depends on sharecroppers or tenants for the cul-

[1] Julian H. Steward, et al., *The People of Puerto Rico* (Urbana: University of Illinois Press, 1956).

[2] Julian H. Steward, *Theory of Culture Change* (Urbana: University of Illinois Press, 1955), p. 212.

[3] Elena Padilla, "Contemporary Social-Rural Types in the Caribbean Region," in Vera Rubin, ed., *Caribbean Studies: A Symposium* (2nd ed.; Seattle: University of Washington Press, 1960), p. 28.

[4] *Ibid.*, pp. 23–24.

tivation of commercial crops;[5] a peasant is designated as an agricultural producer, distinct from fishermen, strip miners, rubber gatherers and livestock keepers, who retains effective control of land and who aims at subsistence not at reinvestment.[6] Each of these three economic types is accompanied by different social structural arrangements.[7] The issue raised here is—to what extent do these types cover the socio-economic realities of rural Jamaica?

Approximately a quarter of the island's population of about 1,600,000 live in the rapidly growing urban areas such as Kingston and Montego Bay; another quarter either reside in the sugar belt parishes of Westmoreland, Clarendon or St. Catherine or depend economically on these areas; and almost all of the remaining half eke out an existence in the mountainous interior or in circumscribed pockets of land along the coastlines. All are significantly different ecological areas.[8] It is not very difficult to perceive structural homologies between plantation workers and systems in rural Jamaica and those in Puerto Rico, and in other parts of the West Indies. The 25 per cent of the Jamaican population which lives in areas dominated by plantations exhibits social characteristics markedly similar to those found among parallel groups throughout the Caribbean region. Moreover, the historical and synchronic influence of the plantation on the total Jamaican society is of major significance, as it is in much of the general area. Difficulties arise, however, when the concepts of farmer and peasant, as defined are used to categorize

[5] *Ibid.*, pp. 25–26.

[6] Eric R. Wolf, "Types of Latin American Peasantry: A Preliminary Discussion," *American Anthropologist*, Vol. 57, No. 3, Part 1 (June, 1955), pp. 453–54.

[7] Padilla (*op. cit.*, p. 25), specifying the three types, puts it this way: "Thus, with particular reference to the Caribbean, the following types of local subcultures can be formulated at this moment. These types represent structural arrangements, not cultural content—they are likely to be modified in the light of further conceptual refinements and more empirical knowledge."

[8] M. G. Smith, "The Plural Framework of Jamaican Society," *British Journal of Sociology*, Vol. 12, No. 3 (1961), p. 249.

that half of the Jamaican population which is rural, but not directly involved in a plantation economy. Most members of this rural population segment fit into neither the farmer nor the peasant category.

To begin with, they do not own or control sufficient land to earn a living solely through agriculture. For example, 21.5 per cent of all farms in Jamaica are less than one acre; 48.2 per cent are between 1 and 5 acres; 17.5 per cent are 5 to 10 acres in size; and 9.3 per cent are between 10 and 25 acres. Only 3.5 per cent are over 25 acres, and these few farms and estates control 60.7 per cent of all productive acreage.[9] We can conservatively estimate that over half the farms in Jamaica average less than three acres, are composed of several fragmented pieces of marginal land,[10] and comprise somewhat less than one-tenth of the total available acreage. Often, the various fragments of a farm are held under different forms of land tenure thus complicating both the legal position and the efficient utilization of land.[11]

It is the rare landholder, therefore, who can depend only on cultivation, either for subsistence or for profit, without exerting additional economic effort in other directions. In an extensive survey of labor supply in the country districts of the island, M. G. Smith had this to say:

[9] David Edwards, *An Economic Study of Small Farming in Jamaica* (Kingston, Jamaica: University College of the West Indies, 1961), p. 30.

[10] Jamaican small farms are very often composed of more than one land fragment: ". . . only one third of the small farms each consist of one piece of land, just over one third consist of two pieces and the remainder consist of more than two pieces" (D. Edwards, *op. cit.,* pp. 29–30). As for the quality of land utilized by small farmers: "Typically, the large farm is situated on fairly flat naturally fertile land which is little eroded; but most of the small farms are to be found on hillside land where the soils of moderate natural fertility have been badly eroded" (*ibid.,* p. 27).

[11] For a discussion of land tenure and land use, see Edith Clarke, "Land Tenure and the Family in Four Communities in Jamaica," *Social and Economic Studies,* Vol. 1, No. 4 (August, 1953); *My Mother Who Fathered Me* (London: George Allen and Unwin, 1957).

> . . . the occupational classifications of the population of the various districts studied over the past 12 months . . . show quite clearly that except among the senior male age groups, farming is an occupation which is rarely carried out independently of other pursuits. Pure wage work is also relatively rare. The typical employment status and occupational combination for Jamaican small-farming populations involve own-account farming and ad hoc wage work.[12]

An agricultural economist, in an intensive study of eighty-seven farms in eight areas of Jamaica, makes the following observations about the non-farm activities of the individuals in his sample:

> . . . Work outside the farm was responsible for depriving the farm of labour by the older as well as the younger adults living in the household. In some few cases the farmers' wives engaged in off-farm employment so that the income earned would encourage the farmers to retain them, or if they were ejected they would be able to live without support for at least a short time. But much of the work off the farms by the wives and all such work by the farmers was prompted by different motives. The farm people worked off their farms to supplement their farm incomes; usually they worked to meet their day to day living and farm expenses but occasionally the income was reserved for unusual expenditures such as buying a bed or a piece of land. Some of the off-farm work was undertaken in slack periods and so did not compete with farm work, but there were exceptional instances when the pressing need for cash forced the people to neglect their farms at critical times. Under those circumstances outside work was done because the people 'can't do better.' There were also situations intermediate between those where no farm work was required on the home farm and those where the need for immediate cash income was so great that the tasks on the home farms had to be left undone. These were situations where, although there was work to be done at home, the outside work (which appeared

[12] M. G. Smith, *A Report on Labour Supply in Rural Jamaica* (Kingston, Jamaica: Government Printer, 1956), p. 5.

more remunerative) was undertaken; either labour was hired to replace the farmer's own or the farm was simply given that much less labour.[13]

We can deduce from the previous statistics and descriptions that own-account agriculture is rarely the sole economic activity of poor, rural Jamaicans. Since these people cannot hope to maintain a subsistence level through agricultural production even with effective control of their limited land, they do not easily fit into the peasant definition. Also, since they constitute the largest single element in the island's population, those who can be classified as peasants are few, if not altogether non-existent. It follows, then, that no viable peasant subculture exists in Jamaica. Nevertheless, in their general formulations on working people in the Caribbean, Wolf, Padilla, and Mintz have applied the term peasant to Jamaica, but in so doing have had to force or drastically adapt the concept. Wolf,[14] for instance, in discussing adaptations to life on "new-style plantations,"[15] presumes the existence of a peasantry and then hypothesizes the forms and directions of peasant change.

> . . . The first kind of double adaptation–involves the possession of at least two sets of cultural forms and thus two fields of manoeuver for a better balance of chances and risks: this is discernible in areas where peasants work on plantations, and step with one foot into the plantation way of life, while keeping the other foot on the peasant holding. Jamaica seems to be an example of an area where this occurs.

[13] Edwards, *op. cit.,* p. 75.

[14] Eric R. Wolf, "Specific Aspects of Plantation Systems in the New World: Community Sub-cultures and Social Classes," in *Plantation Systems of the New World,* Pan American Union, Social Science Monographs VII (Washington, D.C.: 1959), p. 143.

[15] ". . . Increasingly in the New World, systems using external coercion to exact performance have tended to give way to systems utilizing the worker's own drive for subsistence. It is thus possible to refer to plantations using bound labor as old-style plantations, to plantations using free labor as new-style plantations" (*ibid.,* p. 137).

While Wolf conceptualizes these individuals as peasants who do plantation work in order to broaden their economic base, Padilla includes in her taxonomy of social-rural types in the Caribbean a variant form of peasantry which depends on cash and wage employment and not necessarily within a plantation context. Pushing any standard definition of peasant to the extreme she characterizes this variety as,

> . . . landholders who cultivate special food crops for local markets or plantations, who depend on cash to supplement their own food and other needs, and who also may sell their labour. . . . They are likely to migrate for casual employment, or they may be tenants or sharecroppers. Examples can be found in St. Vincent, Jamaica, Puerto Rico.[16]

Mintz, specifying Jamaica among other cases, comes closest to reaching beyond the confines of the peasant-plantation worker-farmer triad by speculating that

> . . . the plantation worker who is also a peasant appears to be straddling two kinds of socio-cultural adaptations and may represent a cultural type which is not necessarily transitional but in a kind of flux equilibrium.[17]

All three writers utilize the peasant and plantation constructs as the taxonomic point of departure for defining rural social types in the Caribbean. In categorizing Jamaica, their undue emphasis on the peasant concept, based perhaps on insufficient data, appears to be misleading and possibly counterproductive for research. As already indicated, a functioning peasantry, in any rigorous sense of the term, does not exist in contemporary Jamaica and perhaps never existed in the past. Over the years, following Emancipation, large numbers of poor, rural Jamaicans found it necessary to combine several economic activities in order to subsist. Affected by the insecurities of own-account cul-

[16] Padilla, *op. cit.*, p. 25.
[17] Sidney W. Mintz, "The Plantation as a Socio-cultural Type," in *Plantation Systems of the New World*, p. 43.

tivation on minuscule, sub-standard fields, by the labor demands of plantations and large farms, and by the irregularity of other wage employment, these people developed a way of life based on a system of occupational multiplicity which maximizes as well as protects their limited economic opportunities and which in turn influences the nature of their social alignments and organization. They constitute a type qualitatively different from that of the peasant and plantation worker, which is characterized by its own set of structural arrangements and its own cultural distinctiveness, and as such, requires separate classification and analysis. What follows is an attempt to exemplify some limited dimensions of these occupational pluralists.

In 1958, the writer completed a study of five coastal settlements in rural Jamaica whose inhabitants were ostensibly fishermen.[18] At least they were so considered by those branches or agencies of the Jamaican government most concerned with the fishing industry.[19] The objectives of the study were to determine the effects of a government sponsored action program for the introduction of fishing cooperatives and to isolate the factors contributing to their success or failure in specific localities. Methodologically, the study took the form of a survey in depth[20] which, aside from the stipulated objectives, established the following: that the groups did not warrant blanket categoriza-

[18] Lambros Comitas, *Fishermen and Cooperation in Rural Jamaica* (Ph.D. dissertation, Columbia University, N.Y., 1962). This study was made possible by a fellowship from the Research Institute for the Study of Man and by a Fulbright Grant from the United States Government.

[19] The Jamaica Social Welfare Commission; Fisheries Division of the Ministry of Agriculture and Lands; the Beach Control Authority; etc.

[20] A two-pronged approach, quantitative and qualitative, was employed in each of five settlements studied. Utilizing the first, I collected data on kinship, marital status, internal migration, schooling, literacy, house types, land tenure, cultivation, livestock, occupations, type of fishing, etc. Employing the second approach, I gathered material on fishing, agricultural and handicraft technology, conducted depth interviews and studied the cooperatives in detail, etc.

tion as fishermen; nor, in spite of the fact that they cultivated some land, could these rural Jamaicans be classified as peasants, farmers, or plantation workers.

Detailed occupational statistics collected indicate that, except for one specialized settlement,[21] from 63 to 79 per cent of all males gainfully occupied are engaged in more than one economic activity. For the most part, these individuals do not specialize in fishing but combine it with own-account work such as cultivation, or various forms of wage employment, or some combination of the three. Concentration on fishing varies primarily with the availability of land and sea resources, the possibilities for wage employment, the regional demand for skills, and such factors as age and familial responsibilities. Although each settlement exists within its own micro-ecological niche, the three settlements to be discussed share in common economic possibilities or alternatives which are extremely limited. In most cases, no one alternative is sufficiently lucrative for individual full-time specialization, and therefore occupational multiplicity can become a necessity.

Because the available alternatives in each area are not the same, a somewhat distinctive modal form of vocational combination exists at each settlement. For example, in Long Hill the typical pattern is mixed cash and subsistence agriculture, night fishing, and occasional wage employment. In Whitehouse, the emphasis is on intensive day fishing, subsistence agriculture, and occasional wage employment. In Duncans, wage-employment, the primary economic activity, is interlocked with a particular form of early hour fishing and with little dependence on agriculture. For all three settlements, despite the dominance of one alternative, it is the obtained occupational balance which maximizes the possibility of individual and household security and from

[21] Only one settlement in the study had a male population most of whom practiced only a single occupation. Special conditions account for this situation: contiguity to large markets related to one of the most extensive sugar areas of the island together with excellent fishing resources attract large numbers of migrants who come to fish. Since there is no available agricultural land they are limited to this pursuit, even if their financial situation should improve.

which significant structural relationships develop. Unlike the variations of "peasantry" in Jamaica, suggested by Wolf and Padilla, agriculture in this vocational complex need not be the principal element.

Long Hill is a small open country district on the south-western coast of the island. The entire surrounding region is a zone of low labor demand. Large agricultural properties in the vicinity are committed to cattle rearing or to the cultivation of pimento, neither of which requires a large, steady labor force. Other lands nearby, in particular, one property of over 2000 acres, are not put to any economic use by their absentee landlords. Frome and similar great corporate sugar estates which require large labor forces during crop time are over 20 miles away and therefore of limited availability to the people of Long Hill.

This low level of labor demand is offset in part by the relatively large size of the average "fishing" household farm, which is three and a half acres, the highest figure for all settlements included in the study.[22] Legal land tenure forms predominate here so that each household owns its house and house plot, each keeps a quantity of livestock, cultivates subsistence crops such as cassava, yams, and corn and produces cash crops of bananas, limes, pimento and coconuts. The economic advantage of such agricultural diversification is substantial.[23] Nevertheless, two-thirds of all males gainfully occupied are engaged in more than one occupation. Modally, the Long Hill landowner combines cultivation with a particular form of night fishing[24] which requires little capital investment and a

[22] Since the study was concerned with fishing cooperatives, all households included in the five settlement samples and censuses contained at least one male or female member who either practiced fishing of some sort or was a fish vendor. Consequently, the study dealt only with a segment of any given locality. The size of this segment varied with the extent and number of alternative economic activities.

[23] Sidney W. Mintz, "The Role of the Middleman in the Internal Distribution System of a Caribbean Peasant Economy," *Human Organization,* Vol. 15, No. 2 (Summer, 1956), pp. 18–19.

[24] This takes the form of hook and line fishing in small canoes during the very dark hours of the night. Fish are at-

minimal consumption of valuable daylight time necessary for agricultural and wagework pursuits. Furthermore, since only two men are required for this type of fishing, the demands of an established crew relationship are not confining. Though night fishing might be secondary at Long Hill, it provides protein for the household's diet and a cash profit when a part of the catch is sold.

Agricultural and fishing activities are combined with other part-time wage work such as carpentry, occasional wage labor on adjoining properties and shopkeeping. This mixed vocational pattern is clearly accepted by the local folk. An individual must "look lines all about," as one Long Hill male put it to mean that a person cannot depend on one occupation to make a living.

Occupational multiplicity and age have a high correlation for all three settlements. The older the male, the greater the probability that he will have multiple occupations. In Long Hill, for example, only 33 per cent of men between the ages of 15 and 24 have more than one occupation; for those between 25 and 39 the percentage is 78; while for those over 40, it is 88 per cent. This progression is even more pronounced for the other two settlements. Some knowledge of Jamaican culture helps to understand these statistics. Young men in rural Jamaica ordinarily do not maintain separate households. Consequently, their responsibilities are few and their financial requirements low. These factors–combined with generally unrealistic vocational aspirations,[25] inspired by the mass communication media, the schools and even the parents–keep the young in hope of high paying and prestigious wage employment. Compounding the situation are ambivalent-to-negative attitudes towards the land itself and towards manual labor, both heritages from slavery.

---

tracted by use of a strong light thrown by a lantern. Return to the beach is usually by dawn. On moonlit nights there is no fishing at all. Consequently, only about half the month is utilized for maritime activity.

[25] M. G. Smith, "Education and Occupational Choice in Rural Jamaica," *Social and Economic Studies,* Vol. 9, No. 3 (September, 1960).

Young adults, then, often find themselves unemployed or underemployed. When they are employed, it is in a single occupation, and in these three settlements, that occupation is most likely to be fishing. Given the low technological level of fishing in Jamaica, this pursuit calls for little formal commitment or capital investment on the part of the casual practitioner. However, when the young adult begins gradually to perceive the socio-economic realities around him, and he begins to assume the responsibility for supporting a new household, he finds he must turn to cultivation on his own, rented or "family" land.[26] If he has no access to land, he must seek additional wage labor in order to meet the new demands upon him. As his years, responsibilities and commitments increase, his involvement in and dependence on multiple activities become complete.

Contiguous to Long Hill is the small market town of Whitehouse. Its physical environment is almost identical with that of Long Hill, its sea resources are the same, social interaction between the two settlements is extensive, and the cultural inventories of both are quite similar. Land holdings, however, are severely limited for the majority of Whitehouse residents. Most of these people can only rent or squat on half-acre parcels of government land of marginal quality; the relatively more affluent may rent an additional quarter or half-acre plot for subsistence cultivation at some distance from Whitehouse.

With the agricultural sector of the local economy thus restricted, Whitehouse males have developed fishing patterns of intensity and specialization in marked contrast to those of their neighbors at Long Hill. Long established, three- and four-man crews operate large, well constructed cottonwood dugout canoes and employ a variety of gear and techniques. More significantly, their fishing schedule is radically different from that of Long Hill. Fishing is pursued from the early morning hours until the afternoon. Allocation of daylight hours to agricultural pursuits is much less necessary here than it is a mere two miles away.

However, Whitehouse men also combine fishing with other activities wherever possible. Almost all are involved,

[26] Clarke, *My Mother Who Fathered Me,* pp. 33–72.

to some degree, with subsistence or kitchen garden cultivation. Many actively seek wage employment at distances farther from home than do their Long Hill neighbors. Others, with less commitment to the land and with little investment in fishing equipment, travel to the sugar belts at harvest time or apply for contract labor overseas. The fewer the occupational commitments, the greater the individual mobility.

The general vocational pattern of Whitehouse can be substantially modified by individuals should their basic economic resources shift, although this is a rare occurrence in rural Jamaica. A Whitehouse fisherman, for example, who acquires additional cultivatable land through inheritance, purchase or affinal connection, will turn from intensive daylight fishing to night fishing similar to that practiced by neighbors in Long Hill.[27] Such a person, generally, has insufficient capital to hire laborers to assist him; consequently, he must adjust his own work pattern to meet the new situation. Very rarely does he accumulate enough land to be able to concentrate completely on agriculture. Since fishing is more flexible than agriculture with regard to time and labor allocation, the changes necessary for a new economic equilibrium are made in that occupation.

In Duncans, a market town on the north coast of the island, wage employment is the dominant form of gainful labor for a group of occupational pluralists, for several reasons. Land is expensive and, given the narrowness of the coastal shelf in this region, fishing is not as productive as on the south coast. The town, however, has a key geographical position on the main coastal road, which is heavily plied by both tourist and commercial traffic. This has meant the development of facilities for repair work and ancillary services. Besides a relatively wide range of general and specialty stores, a market area and government offices, all of which provide opportunities for employment, Duncans is a regional administrative hub for parochial as well as national roadwork. In addition, the plateau above Duncans is partially occupied by two medium-size sugar estates. So, while the labor demand in Duncans is not

[27] Comitas, *op. cit.*, p. 67.

unmet, there is a wider range of possibilities for the average workman than at any of the other settlements studied.

Over a third of the heads of "fishing" households in Duncans come from different parts of Jamaica. This is indirectly reflected in the fact that over half of these households rent both their houses and their house plots. Consequently, this migrant group does almost no agriculture. Some agriculture is carried on by the non-migrant group, usually among older men who are more likely to control small portions of land. Fishing at Duncans, usually of a mixed cash and subsistence variety, is conducted in a highly individualistic manner, with almost no development of partnerships or crews. Fishermen utilize small, crude canoes and rudimentary gear, depending almost entirely on their own efforts. The schedule of fishing is significantly similar for all these men. Most put out along the coast just before daybreak and return by early morning in time to fulfill their other obligations. Several fishermen are employed by the island or parochial governments as Public Works personnel–one road headman must keep his fishing activities secret from his superiors. Some combine fishing with such semi-skilled work as shoe-repairing, masonry and carpentry, while others are employed as estate laborers or service station attendants. Several men combine fishing with two specific wage activities, such as tinsmithing and masonry. While fishing and cultivation are necessary pursuits, they must be practiced so as to cause the least interference with wage employment.

The social organizational implications of occupational multiplicity have intrinsic significance. Complexity of individual economic activity leads to complexity of ordered relationships. A worker in one of these settlements, theoretically, can be involved in as many as six different economic statuses: subsistence cultivator, commercial agriculturalist, wage laborer, own-account artisan or tradesman, subsistence fisherman and commercial fisherman. In each status, he is interlocked with a distinct set of individuals who perform requisite roles in production, distribution and consumption. If, for example, a man is occupied with mixed farming and mixed fishing, he may well be structurally linked with neighbors for the exchange of free labor in the fields[28] and with a finite number of "higglers"[29] who distribute any surplus subsistence crops within the Jamaican market; and he will most likely be organizationally tied to the local branches of the all-island crop association which markets his cash produce. For his fishing operation, he requires a clearly defined relationship with one or more members of a fishing crew, as well as with one or more fish vendors who, in turn, will be linked to a complex market system. In many cases, more than one role is performed by a single individual. This requires decisions as to work priorities and work schedules and ties individuals to a convoluted set of social obligations. Such structural links or patterned relationships, established for economic gain, are essentially lateral ones connecting members of the same stratum into horizontal socio-economic segments. Partially for this reason, interaction between these segments and the superordinate strata of the total Jamaican society tends to remain minimal and fragmentary. This contrasts with Wolf's description of the "open" peasant community in other parts of the world in which peasants maintain vertical ties or "informal alliances" with urban elements.[30]

The internal rationality of such a confined system is self-evident to its participants. A socio-economic balance is achieved which offers maximum security with minimum risk, in a basically limited environment. As the advantages are clear, so are the disadvantages: competition for scarce strategic resources within a finite area engenders tension and an emotionally disruptive atmosphere; social mobility is structurally hindered; capital accumulation is difficult; technological levels tend to remain rudimentary

[28] In "A Report on Labour Supply in Rural Jamaica," M. G. Smith describes a variety of Jamaican exchange labor patterns and their functional interconnections.

[29] A Jamaican expression for itinerant food vendors, generally women.

[30] Wolf, "Types of Latin American Peasantry," p. 465.

and communication with other segments in the society is incomplete and imprecise.

Certainly, from the perspective of the total society, such a vocationally heterogeneous and inwardly turned population segment creates problems in administration and development. Action programs, aimed at the socio-economic amelioration of such people but based on uni-occupational models developed in modern Western countries, start with limited chances for success. Occupational pluralists in Jamaica will not reject the material aid that often accompanies such schemes but they do reject, as evidenced by their behavior, the objectives and the intent of these programs. By their own logic, they find it impractical to develop fully one aspect of their economic life to the detriment of the others. The results of the action program, designed to improve the Jamaican fishing industry through technological and organizational assistance, are significant. In settlements such as Duncans, where fishing is balanced with or subordinated to other pursuits, newly introduced fishermen's cooperatives—one element in the development program—failed to provide economic cohesion and stimulus and, therefore, died stillborn. In settlements such as Whitehouse, where fishing is more important because of land scarcity, new cooperatives when adapted to local conditions proved more viable and performed relatively substantial services for its membership. The error made by the central authorities was that they introduced one cooperative model designed for full-time fishermen in other parts of the world to all varieties of Jamaican "fishermen." Agricultural development programs on a national scale sometimes suffer similar results for a very similar reason—an incorrect assessment of the pertinent conditions of rural life.

To sum up, taxonomic classifications of socio-economic types in the Caribbean region are not completely adequate for Jamaica. Stressing ecological and economic factors, the writer has attempted to delineate and define an additional type indicating particularly its multi-occupational basis and several of the structural ramifications that ensue. Clearly much more work and analysis is needed before a reasonable level of comprehension is reached. For purposes of social scientific research in the Caribbean, however, the identification and understanding of such population segments in an area noted for a lack of extensive kin networks and relatively weak community organization is especially pertinent and should prove of heuristic value.

8.

The drift from countryside to city is a fact of life in the West Indies, as in other parts of the world, but its effects have only begun to be systematically explored. This selection focuses on aspects of life among the poor—especially migrant newcomers—in Kingston, capital of Jamaica and reservoir of a quarter of that nation's two million population. These excerpts from *Social Structure and Social Change in Kingston, Jamaica* depict the city's high unemployment rates, overcrowded housing, swollen slums, and shanty towns—the most notorious of which have been bulldozed by the Jamaican government. The poorest Kingston residents adapt by "cotching" and "squatting" for a place to sleep and by "scuffling" or scraping for a living through handicrafts, pimping and prostitution, begging, stealing, and selling the scraps gleaned from garbage dumps.

COLIN G. CLARKE, an English geographer who received his doctorate at Oxford University, has done field research in Jamaica, Trinidad, and Anguilla. He is currently Lecturer in the Department of Geography and the Centre for Latin American Studies, University of Liverpool.

The Slums of Kingston*

Colin G. Clarke

UNEMPLOYMENT

. . . The problem of economic development in Kingston was compounded by the rapid growth of population; as a result of natural increase and in-migration the annual increment to the labour force approached 10,000 persons. The task of finding additional employment on this scale was made almost impossible by the large numbers in Kingston who were already out of work. According to material published by the 1960 census, 18.4 per cent of the city's potential labour force of 179,000 was either voluntarily or involuntarily unemployed.[1] Part-time employment, also, was widespread in Kingston, and 30 per cent of the classified labour force of 169,000 received employment for less than five days during the week preceding the census. Over ten thousand people in Kingston were looking for their first job, and they accounted for almost one-third of the total number of unemployed.[2] Approximately 70 per cent of this group was under 21 years of age,[3] and unemployment was chronic among school-leavers. These conditions were primarily the result of secular and not seasonal, frictional, technological or

* [Editors' title]

From *A Social and Geographical Study of Kingston,* Berkeley and Los Angeles, University of California Press, in press.

[1] The statistics relating to unemployment have been taken from the *Report of the 1960 Census of Jamaica,* Vol. 1, 1964.

[2] O. C. Francis, *The People of Modern Jamaica* (Kingston, Jamaica: 1963), 8.2–8.3.

[3] *Ibid.,* 8.5.

cyclical unemployment; they had existed in Kingston for almost thirty years, and were associated with 'an economy in equilibrium so that there is always a reservoir of involuntarily unemployed.'[4] Unemployment which had been originally cyclical, or associated with trade cycles, had been transformed during the 1940s and 1950s into a permanent feature of the socio-economic structure of the city.

Unemployment in Kingston increased from 15.5 per cent of the potential labour force in 1946, to 18.4 per cent in 1960. In the latter year the figure for the island as a whole was 12.6 per cent. The population of Jamaica was slowly concentrating in the capital, and so was unemployment. By 1960, more than half the unemployed Jamaicans were residing in the corporate area.[5] Opportunities for work in Kingston failed completely to meet the expectations of rural migrants, and it is significant that 36 per cent of the males and 51 per cent of the females who were looking for their first job in 1960 had been born in the rural parishes of the island. Manufacturing industry could not absorb the rapid growth of the population, and no system of social security existed to cushion the effects of unemployment. In these circumstances the personal service industry was important as an employer of domestic servants, gardeners, yard-boys and odd-job men, but at wages which barely exceeded subsistence rates.

Using full-time unemployment as the first criterion, it can be seen that conditions of population pressure had persisted in Kingston throughout the period 1944 to 1960; at the latter date 33,000 members of the potential labour force were affected. Since the potential labour force comprised almost 50 per cent of the population of the city, the total number of workers and dependants who were directly affected by unemployment may be estimated as at least 60,000.

* * * *

[4] W. F. Maunder, *Employment in an Underdeveloped Area, A Sample Survey of Kingston, Jamaica* (New Haven: Yale University Press, 1960), p. 8.

[5] O. C. Francis, *op. cit.*, 7.11.

OVERCROWDING

The overcrowding of dwellings in Kingston was one of the clearest indices of the persistence and growth of population pressure. Following standard procedure, the Town Planning Department defined as overcrowded dwellings in which there were more than two persons per habitable room or more than eight people to each hygienic water closet. Applying these criteria to data supplied by the 1960 sanitary survey and the 1960 census, areas were demarcated in which overcrowding existed. The sections which were badly affected were confined to the single-storey tenements and yards of West Kingston, and, in lesser degree, to those of Central and East Kingston. In contrast, the northern suburbs enjoyed better conditions, the notable exceptions being the pockets of dense population on the banks of the storm-water gulleys. Although overcrowding was widely associated with poor housing, especially in West Kingston, its incidence was more logically explained by the distribution and density of population. Some overcrowding was experienced wherever densities exceeded ten persons per acre, and severe overcrowding occurred wherever densities surpassed 100 persons per acre. However, while there was a cartographic relationship between high densities of population and overcrowding, some areas which recorded low densities of population also suffered from this condition. This blanket effect occurred because most areas in West Kingston lay beyond the zone served by the public sewage system. The absence or inadequacy of facilities, such as cess pits, in certain of the sparsely populated parts was simultaneously a product and an index of population pressure.

A further contributor to the problem of overcrowding must be taken into account; namely, house tenure. By far the greater proportion of housing was rented in the form of tenements, rooms, and flats, and in the yard districts of West Kingston shacks had been constructed on rented lots. Throughout those sections of the city which had been built prior to 1920, less than one-third of the dwellings were owned by their occupiers, and only in the central and northern suburbs did the percentage exceed 50. As at previous periods, there was a marked tendency for overcrowding to be associated with letting, and for the availability of rented accommodation to encourage overcrowding. Furthermore, suburbs in which rented accommodation was relatively scarce tended to record low densities of population; and where less than half the households were living in rented dwellings, overcrowding was slight or nonexistent.

While overcrowding was associated with various types of unemployment and with tenancy, much of the rented accommodation in West Kingston and inner East Kingston was dilapidated, and some of it lacking in sewage facilities. Conditions in these areas were exacerbated by the inadequate water supply. Throughout the greater part of the city, including the tenements, over 75 per cent of the households received public supplies of water which were piped into their dwellings. However, the proportion dropped to below 25 per cent in some of the densely populated sections of West Kingston and the overcrowded 'pockets' of population in St. Andrew. Yards were served by public supplies of water on a communal basis; in many instances groups of yards shared a stand-pipe. The availability of water for irrigating the lawns and gardens of the northern suburbs emphasized the deprivation of some of the overcrowded sections of the city.

In 1960 the Central Planning Unit of the government of Jamaica estimated that 80,000 people were living in overcrowded accommodation in Kingston. Most were living in West Kingston or inner East Kingston, and many were confined to areas which suffered from unemployment. According to the census half the household heads who were looking for work were tenement dwellers. The number of persons directly affected by both unemployment and overcrowding was remarkably similar and suggests that these phenomena were closely connected. Overcrowding, in a socio-economic sense, affected between one-fifth and one-sixth of the inhabitants of Kingston in 1960.

Conditions in the overcrowded districts are summarised in the following short description of a tenement in Jones Town. Comprising nine rooms which accommodated 41 people in 1961, this tenement possessed only 4 water closets, all of which were defective, four shower baths and two kitchen sinks. Two outdoor stand-pipes provided the sole supply of water. The monthly rent for each room was £4. 10. 0., a high sum when compared with the low wages of the inhabitants and their susceptibility to part-time unemployment. Pressure on the amenities was very great, but the high rent encouraged sharing of accommodation and thus increased the overcrowding. One room in this tenement housed eight people, while the remainder were occupied by three or four. In view of the revenue from this overcrowded accommodation, it is hardly surprising that many of the tenements on the periphery of the commercial area recorded high unimproved land values. Although values dwindled along the Spanish Town Road, the slums, contrary to popular opinion, generated a considerable income for their owners, most of whom resided in the better residential areas.

Between 1943 and 1960 the percentage of households in the corporate area relying upon pit latrines had decreased from 54 to 39, while the proportion inhabiting dwellings constructed of concrete had increased from 13 to 53 per cent.[6] Nevertheless, the general improvement in housing revealed by these figures was more than off-set by the rapid growth of the population. By 1960 more than half the households in the capital still occupied no more than one room and approximately one-third of the inhabitants were living in substandard accommodation. The combination of poor housing and overcrowding created slums in West Kingston and part of inner East Kingston which were virtually coterminous with the derelict areas recognized in 1935. Although some rehousing had been effected in these areas, in general they were characterised by population increase and social stagna-

[6] *Ibid.,* 6.17.

tion; the high rates of secular unemployment exemplify this condition. By 1960, therefore, the distinction between the slums and the better areas was as marked as, if not more marked than, it had been in 1943; gross population densities at the two dates certainly support this contention.

ADAPTATIONS TO POVERTY AND OVERCROWDING

In West Kingston population pressure affected even the most elementary human requirements, outstanding among which were housing, work and food. The solution to these basic needs was found within the context of a sub-culture which had been developed for decades among persons living at the level of subsistence. This sub-culture is suitably described by the Jamaican terms 'cotching' and 'scuffling.'

Between 1946 and 1959 only 40,000 people were housed in government schemes in the whole of Jamaica. Private, speculative building for rental at low rates was virtually non-existent in Kingston, and high rents were charged even for overcrowded accommodation. Permanently unemployed persons who were unable to obtain subsidised, government housing had either to 'cotch' (to put up for the night as best they could), or to adapt to conditions of enduring poverty by becoming squatters. In 1961 the police estimated the squatters at 20,000, a figure far in excess of that recorded in the previous year by the census.[7] Located in two main zones, on the fringe of the tenement area in West Kingston and on the outskirts of the built-up area of the city, these camps were usually located on land owned by the government or its agencies. The camps on the outskirts of the city had developed during the period of rapid population growth which took place after 1953. Moonlight City on the foreshore in West Kingston, for example, was set up during 1959, its adult population doubling from 54 to 106 between July 1960

[7] The figure of 20,000 squatters is probably closer to the truth. It is known that the Ras Tafari brethren, most of whom were squatters, were under-enumerated in the census.

and July 1961. The oldest squatter settlements were located at Trench Town and Back O'Wall on the fringe of the tenements; with interruptions, squatters had been living in the latter area since the 1930s. In both areas squatting had rapidly regenerated after the 1951 hurricane, and in Trench Town squatters had quickly captured government-owned land which had been cleared and prepared for rehousing. Population densities were much higher in the older than in the newer camps. Furthermore, large, almost impregnable, stockades had been raised around each parcel of captured land in Trench Town, whereas low fences sufficed as property boundaries in Moonlight City. The stockades in Trench Town were a reflection of competition for land which, in turn, was affected by the density of the population.

It was doubtful in Jamaican law whether the property at Back O'Wall belonged to its original owner. Private owners forfeited their land to squatters after six years of continuous residence, provided the land was fenced; otherwise the period was twelve years. Crown land, however, was relinquished only after 60 years of squatting, and this probably explains the greater tolerance shown by government. Disputes over privately-owned land were by no means rare. One of the best-known squatter camps in Trench Town was situated on land belonging to Boy's Town. The squatters claimed that the land was theirs, and most household heads were recorded in the census as owners.

Even in the older camps population densities rarely exceeded 150 persons per acre; these were lower than the figures recorded in the adjacent areas. However, the concentration of population within the squatter camps was out of all proportion to the facilities which were available. Dwellings consisted of one-room huts constructed from packing cases and fish barrels, cardboard and polythene. In an attempt to deter squatters the government had refused to supply public amenities, and pit latrines–though illegal–had to be dug and water collected from standpipes or stolen from fire hydrants. Although these conditions were later remedied, approximately 1,000 people shared one stand-pipe in the Boy's Town squatter camp at the beginning of 1961. In certain respects, however, the squatters enjoyed better conditions than the inhabitants of the tenements; they rarely slept more than three people to a room and paid no rent for their accommodation. But tenancy was by no means absent from some of these camps, for once squatters had captured a piece of land and built a high stockade around it, they frequently charged a ground rent to anyone who wanted to build on *their* land.

Squatting, together with secular unemployment, could be traced back to the 1930s. Furthermore, it created physical and social conditions reminiscent of those associated with the Negro huts which had surrounded Kingston during slavery. The runaway slaves who had inhabited them had been social outcasts; so, too, were the squatters. Both groups tended to occupy peripheral locations, and both lived outside the law. Squatting was illegal, and so were many of the activities of the squatters—their coal market at Three Miles, their pit latrines, and their source of water supply. This pattern of illegality was largely enforced by society.

Squatting was a way of life as well as an expression of extreme overcrowding. The social stigma attached to the inhabitants of the squatter camps and poorer tenements and yards made it extremely difficult for people from these areas to find employment; less than ten per cent of the factory workers on the Industrial Estate in West Kingston lived in that part of the city. Many squatters were lapsed literates or illiterate, malnourished and lacking in personal discipline; and most were regarded by businessmen as unemployable. The problem was compounded by the tendency of many people to describe themselves as skilled workers when they were semi-skilled or unskilled. Furthermore, some refused employment which, they felt, undervalued their ability. However, while the existence of full-time unemployment tended to encourage squatting, squatting gave rise to a form of unemployment which was not strictly speaking unemployment at all. The adult population of the squatter camps abandoned the search for paid employment, at least temporarily,[8] and relied upon 'scuffling,' or scraping a living from petty manufacturing, pimping and prostitution, begging, stealing, and selling scrap salvaged from the corporation dump or 'dungle' on the foreshore in West Kingston. People involved in these activities were, technically speaking, self-employed, but most regarded themselves as unemployed, and so did society at large. It is highly probable, therefore, that most who 'scuffled' for a living were classed by the census as unemployed. 'Scuffling' provided an important alternative to paid employment, especially in the areas in which the incidence of full-time or secular unemployment was high. The availability of this alternative, and partly illegal, system prevented wages from being depressed so that conditions of full and socially acceptable employment could develop. However, while the incidence of unemployment did not necessarily imply idleness, the very existence of 'scuffling' provided a socio-economic index of extreme population pressure and overcrowding.

The essence of this sub-culture of 'cotching' and 'scuffling' was summarised by the phrase 'living on the dungle.' During the 1930s people had literally done so. Even in 1960 one major squatter camp was situated on the seaward edge of the dump in West Kingston, while some of the poorest inhabitants 'cotched' in the wrecked car bodies which littered its surface. Furthermore, as most of the squatter settlements lay within easy reach of the dungle, it continued to act as a major source of saleable goods and building materials and of food discarded by groceries, supermarkets, restaurants and private households. Droves of squatters awaited the arrival of the garbage carts, and, as they disgorged their contents, competed for them with the John Crows. In this way the participants of the sub-culture maintained a parasitic relationship with the more prosperous inhabitants of the city. This relationship, however, was indirect, whereas that between domestic servants

[8] E. E. Hoyt, "Voluntary Unemployment and Unemployability in Jamaica," *British Journal of Sociology*, Vol. 11 (1961), pp. 129–36.

and their employers represented a more direct form of dependency.

The adaptations involving 'living on the dungle' were achieved at a level so low that it automatically involved the problem of disease. However, in one form or another social diseases affected most of the overcrowded sections of the city, and the squatter camps suffered no more conspicuously in this respect than the tenements and yards. As a result of improvements in public health since the 1930s, the major social diseases were confined to tuberculosis of the respiratory system, and typhoid, the former being associated with the overcrowding of rooms, and the latter with inadequate sewage disposal and the contamination of food and drinking water. The distribution of notified cases of tuberculosis occurring between 1 December 1959 and 30 November 1960, and of notified cases of typhoid recorded between 1950 and 1960 were both closely associated with the overcrowded sections of Kingston, and their incidence was particularly high in the west of the city. Moreover, there was a tendency for tuberculosis to be associated with the yards and tenements and for typhoid to be linked to the squatter settlements. The distribution of disease was an expression of the incidence of population pressure in Kingston, and an indication of the failure of individuals and the community alike to solve the city's fundamental and long-term socio-economic problems.

* * * *

Overcrowding was an integral part of the syndrome of poverty which circumscribed the lives of most persons of low socio-economic status, and especially those living in West Kingston. Within the working class population an important distinction existed between the unionized elite, and the unemployed and under-employed who were excluded from their ranks. The gap between the two widened considerably between 1940 and 1960, several informants attributed their difficulty in finding jobs to the restricting influence of the unions. A large body of unemployed persons certainly suffered from any rise in the cost of living. This led to an actual decrease in levels of living in West Kingston, at least relative to the other parts of the city, and undoubtedly encouraged squatting and the development of scuffling. By 1960 the high densities of population were an indication of desperate poverty as distinct from socio-economic efficiency.

The ecology of Kingston in 1960 remained basically similar to that of 1943. At both dates the tenements, parts of East Kingston, and almost all West Kingston were low ranking, while areas of higher status were located to the north and east, especially around Half Way Tree. This patterning of social statuses could be traced back to the 1870s, when King's House was established in St. Andrew, or, further, to the late eighteenth century, when city merchants began to purchase residential property on the Liguanea Plain. Furthermore, on the microscale, the incidence of overcrowding and disease in West Kingston were reminiscent of conditions in the same parts of the city in 1850, while the squatter camps resembled the Negro huts of the period of slavery. Despite the high degree of continuity in the spatial arrangement of social statuses since slavery, certain recent changes were noteworthy. Parts of Central and East Kingston declined in status between 1943 and 1960 as their inhabitants moved out to the suburbs. Population growth was heavily concentrated in West Kingston, but the high status areas in central and northern St. Andrew underwent considerable expansion. As a consequence, social polarisation was even more marked in 1960 than it had been in 1943. A major contributor to increasing polarisation in the city was the growth of the population and its concentration in West Kingston.

* * * *

It is possible to distinguish between several patterns of mobility in Kingston. Movement to the two largest middle-income housing schemes, and to most of the other new suburbs, too, was restricted to persons inhabiting at least median ranking areas. Many servants also penetrated these suburbs, but their status was essentially a dependent one. Mobility was highest in the tenements, but most of this was directed to similar areas and few of the inhabitants moved away to the suburbs. In 1961, for example, it was discovered that 43 per cent of the households in one tenement area in West Kingston had changed their address during the previous year without leaving the neighbourhood.[9] Finally, the squatter camps acted as the settling basins for the most impoverished element in the population, and together with the worst housing schemes, as at Majesty Pen, formed 'slums of despair' rather than 'slums of hope' from which new migrants might have ascended the social scale. These patterns indicate the rigid nature of the social stratification and its faithful reflection in spatial terms.

It is also possible to make a tentative distinction between cityward migration, internal migration within Kingston, and emigration, both with regard to the groups and areas which were involved. The migration of landless country people from the rural areas was directed to the tenements and yards of West Kingston which were characterised by high rates of residential mobility. Few migrants penetrated the source areas for the new housing schemes, and few settled immediately in the squatter camps. It is clear that the government's policy of not supplying basic amenities in the squatter settlements, thereby inducing population pressure, provided no deterrent to migrants. The slum dwellers were scarcely more able to afford to emigrate to Britain than to enter the suburbs. Emigration involved artisans, sugar-factory workers, tractor drivers, members of the land-owning peasantry and their dependants; many of the migrants from Kingston were drawn from the ranks of privileged, unionized labour and from some of the relatively higher ranking, low status areas. Emigration, like the move to the suburbs, involved the more prosperous inhabitants who had greater ability, if less necessity, to move. These migratory systems helped to expand and intensify the massive slums in the capital. The disillusion-

[9] H. Gordon, "Preliminary Report of a Socio-Economic Survey of Parts of West Kingston" (unpublished typescript; Kingston: Jamaica Social Welfare Commission, 1961).

ment and frustration experienced by young migrants who failed to find employment in Kingston constituted a major social problem; many lived under even worse conditions than those they had experienced in the rural areas.

9.

West Indians of all classes and levels of attainment have long been accustomed to emigrate in search of better opportunities than they can find at home. In earlier years they prospected for gold, helped dig the Panama Canal, taught school, worked on the railroads, and functioned as rulers or rebels in colonial Africa. Hundreds of thousands of West Indians are scattered throughout the Caribbean littoral and in various North American cities. More recently, large numbers of West Indians have emigrated to the United Kingdom, France, and other metropolitan centers. Some analysts, noting the loss of the skilled and better-educated part of the West Indian community, see this exodus as a detriment to local development. Others argue that emigration is a safety valve for overpopulation and aids rather than hinders economic growth. This selection, which assesses the local impact of heavy emigration from Jamaica to the United Kingdom during the 1950s, takes the latter position. The alleviation of population pressure and unemployment, the magnitude of remittances, and the rise of the Gross Domestic Product are pointed to as evidence of the positive effects of emigration.

GENE TIDRICK, an American trained in economics at Harvard University, is presently teaching at Williams College.

Some Aspects of Jamaican Emigration to the United Kingdom 1953–1962

Gene Tidrick[1]

Economists are generally agreed that the international movement of capital is a Good Thing. No such consensus exists concerning the desirability of the international flow of labour.

Some economists feel that factor flows of any kind may be treated with the same analytical tools. Hence, the movement of labour from an area where its marginal productivity is low to an area where it is high will increase the level of economic activity throughout the world, just as would a similar movement of capital. Dissenting voices take exception to this rosy view. The most pessimistic of these argue that migration from an area of low to higher marginal productivity of labour in the modern world means, in effect, migration from over-populated, less developed regions to more developed areas. In this view, migration merely postpones the day when birth rates must fall; unchecked migration would thus eventually drag the standard of living in the developed area down to the less developed level. A second group of dissenters take as their point of departure the viewpoint of the countries of emigration. Migration is seen to drain off the most enter-

From *Social and Economic Studies,* Vol. 15, No. 1, March 1966, pp. 22–39. Reprinted with permission of the author and the Institute of Social and Economic Research, University of the West Indies.

[1] I am indebted to Dr. B. I. Cohen and Mr. C. K. Harley, both of Harvard University, for suggestions on how to approach this analysis, and to Professor E. S. Mason of Harvard and Dr. G. E. Cumper of the University of the West Indies for helpful comments on an earlier draft of the paper.

prising members of the population, thereby prolonging the stagnation of the less developed economy.

The massive migration of Jamaicans to the United Kingdom, which began on a large scale in 1953 and was sharply curtailed in 1962 with the passage of the British Commonwealth Immigration Act, provides one of the few examples in recent history of an economically motivated population movement of significant size. The debate attending this movement has been inconclusive, not unlike the theoretical debate outlined above. The most serious misgiving on the part of academic observers has been that emigration would so deplete the skilled labour force that economic development would be impeded. The following statement, written in 1957, is typical:

> Thus against the picture of emigration as an agent for the reduction of population pressure, particularly as it tends to reduce the numbers in the ranks of those of working age, must be placed the picture of emigration as a source of depletion of the most valuable sections of the labour force. This seriously impinges on the prospects of economic and industrial development of the country.[2]

This paper will attempt to do two things: 1) to sharpen the focus of discussion concerning the effects of emigration upon Jamaican economic development by actually making some quantitative estimates of those effects, and 2) to assess the validity of the hypothesis that emigration seriously impinged upon "the prospects of economic and industrial development of the country." In some cases our quantitative estimates will only set minimum and maximum bounds upon the possible effects, but it is hoped that this will give us a basis for realistically assessing the impact of emigration. In all cases the costs and benefits of emigration will be analyzed from the Jamaican point of view. Part I of this paper will review the salient features of

[2] G. W. Roberts and D. O. Mills, *Study of External Migration Affecting Jamaica: 1953–1955* (Mona, Jamaica: Institute of Social and Economic Research, University College of the West Indies, 1958), p. 124.

Jamaican economic and demographic development during the decade under review. Part II contains the main body of our analysis and Part III will summarize the most significant conclusions.

I. JAMAICAN ECONOMIC AND DEMOGRAPHIC DEVELOPMENT 1953–62

In the early 50's Jamaica provided a classic example of a surplus-labour economy. It was, in fact, specifically cited as such by Professor Lewis in his path-breaking 1954 article.[3] Approximately half the labour force was engaged in agriculture with perhaps an additional 10 per cent employed as domestic servants.[4] Unemployment probably stood at about 15 per cent of the labour force and real *per capita* product had only recovered to its pre-war level in 1950.[5]

During the years following 1950, and especially during the early part of the period under consideration in this study, the Jamaican economy grew at a phenomenal rate. Table 1 details the growth of gross domestic product. From the beginning of 1953 until the end of 1961 real *per capita* GDP grew at an average annual rate of 6.8 per cent. (In 1965 a revised series of National Income and Product estimates for 1959–62 was published together with estimates for 1963. The constant value estimates, 1960 based, cover the period 1959–63 only and do not include the years 1953–56 which are the most important for this study.)

One development dominated this expansion–the exploi-

[3] W. Arthur Lewis, "Economic Development with Unlimited Supplies of Labour," *The Manchester School* (May, 1954), reprinted in A. N. Agarwala and S. P. Singh, *The Economics of Underdevelopment* (New York: Oxford University Press, 1958), p. 401.

[4] Jamaica, Department of Statistics, *Report on a Sample Survey of the Population of Jamaica, October–November 1953* (Kingston: 1957), Table 33, p. 67. Hereafter cited as *Sample Survey 1953*.

[5] A more detailed account of Jamaican development after World War II is given in Gene Tidrick, "The International Economics of Jamaican Growth," *Three Dimension* (Winter, 1965), pp. 79–98.

TABLE 1. GROSS DOMESTIC PRODUCT AT FACTOR COST: CURRENT AND CONSTANT VALUES.

	Current Values			*Constant (1956) Value*		
	GDP *£m*	*%* *inc.*	*per cap.* *£*	*GDP* *£m*	*%* *inc.*	*per cap.* *£*
1950	70.1	—	51	87.9	—	64
1953	106.7	12.3	74	117.2	14.3	81
1954	119.7	12.2	82	130.5	11.3	89
1955	136.4	14.0	91	143.6	10.0	96
1956	158.5	16.2	105	158.5	10.3	105
1957	191.1	21.1	125	181.5	14.5	118
1958	198.7	3.5	127	184.0	1.4	118
1959	212.1	6.7	133	195.0	6.0	123
1960	230.8	8.8	142	207.2	6.3	127
1961	244.3	5.8	149	212.3	2.5	130
1962	252.5	3.4	152			

Sources:
Jeanette Bethel, "Some National Income Aggregates for Jamaica, at Constant Prices, " *Social and Economic Studies,* Vol. 10, No. 2.
Jamaica, *Five Year Independence Plan* 1963–68.
Jamaica, *National Accounts, Income and Expenditure,* various years.
Population data for compilation of per capita figures is taken, for years preceding 1960, from the crude estimates of G. C. Abbott, "Estimates of the Growth of the Population of the West Indies to 1975," *Social and Economic Studies,* Vol. 12, No. 3; other years from Jamaica, *Economic Survey 1962.*

tation of bauxite beginning in 1952. Table 2 illustrates the impact which the inception of mining operations has had. In a decade the mining sector expanded from nil to the direct generation of nearly 9 per cent of GDP. By the late 50's Jamaica had become the world's leading producer of bauxite.

Other factors contributed to the prosperity of the period, however. The number of tourists increased from about 75,000 in 1950 to over 200,000 in 1962, thus making tourism the third largest "export" after bauxite and sugar, the traditionally dominant crop of all West Indian economies. Exports of sugar, too, expanded steadily and production was given an extra fillip by the American ban on Cuban sugar imports.

Manufacturing played a not inconsiderable role in Jamaican development. As may be seen in Table 2, the absolute expansion of the manufacturing sector paralleled that of the economy as a whole, its percentage share remaining roughly constant. Tax incentives and a major effort to attract foreign investment have stimulated the growth of the sector. In recent years, an increasing amount of industrial production has been geared to the export market. We shall have occasion to comment later on this significant development.

Table 3 underlines the important structural changes occurring between 1953 and 1960. In this short period the percentage of the population employed in agriculture declined sharply while secondary sector employment expanded from 15.6 per cent to 22.9 per cent of the whole. Precise figures for the mining sector are not available for the years indicated, but the direct employment provided was negligible—of the order of 1 per cent of the total labour force.

Rapid growth of GDP and significant structural shifts tell only half the story of Jamaican development, however. By the end of 1962 the island had a population density of 377 per square mile, higher than that of India. More significantly, Jamaica has a density of 1050 persons per square mile of agricultural land, and nearly twice that

TABLE 2. PERCENTAGE CONTRIBUTION MADE BY INDUSTRIAL GROUPS TO GROSS DOMESTIC PRODUCT.

	1950	*1953*	*1955*	*1957*	*1959*	*1960*	*1962*
Agriculture, forestry & fishing	30.8	21.2	19.2	13.8	13.3	12.4	12.5
Mining	nil	2.4	4.8	8.8	7.9	8.7	8.7
Manufacturing	11.3	13.8	13.5	12.7	13.2	13.4	13.3
Construction & installation	7.6	9.6	9.5	13.6	11.8	11.4	10.8
Transportation, utilities & communication	8.7	7.2*	7.8*	7.3*	7.6*	7.5*	8.0*
Distribution	15.2*	17.2	16.8	16.6	16.9	17.1	15.4
Ownership of dwellings	5.9	4.9	4.4	3.3	2.9	3.0	3.4
Government	6.1	6.5	6.6	6.5	7.3	7.5	8.4
Misc. services	15.0	17.1	17.5	17.3	19.1	19.1	19.4

* denotes storage included.

Source: Jamaica, *National Income, Accounts and Expenditure,* various years.

TABLE 3. PERCENTAGE EMPLOYED BY INDUSTRIAL GROUP.

	1953	*1957*	*1960*
Agriculture	48.9	44.2*	37.8
Manufacturing	12.3	12.8	14.7
Construction	3.3	5.9	8.2
Services	17.1	18.8	14.5**

* includes mining, forestry, and fishing which is unlikely to have exceeded 2 per cent of total employment.
** personal services only
Sources:
1953–Jamaica, *Sample Survey 1953,* table 33, p. 67.
1957–G. E. Cumper, "Employment and Unemployment in the West Indies," in G. E. Cumper (ed.), *The Economy of the West Indies,* ISER-UCWI (Mona, Jamaica, 1960), p. 169.
1960–Jamaica, *Census of Jamaica 1960,* table 8, p. 8-1866.

figure per square mile of agricultural land excluding permanent grassland.[6] Colin Clark, probably the most optimistic of those who have written on the economic implications of population, has asserted that, at Danish productivity and consumption standards, a country is overpopulated when its density per square mile of cultivable land exceeds 500.[7] Moreover, the crude birth rate of Jamaica was more than 40 in 1962, and the rate of natural increase exceeded 3 per cent.[8]

[6] Calculated from official population estimates, and from statistics of arable land area given in W. F. Maunder, *Employment in an Underdeveloped Area: A Sample of Kingston, Jamaica* (New Haven: Yale University Press, 1960), p. 24.

[7] Colin Clark, "Population Growth and Living Standards," *International Labour Review* (August, 1953), reprinted in Agarwala and Singh, *op. cit.,* pp. 40–41. It is not clear whether Clark's "cultivable land" includes permanent grassland. He does not consider India or China, among others usually so classified, to be overpopulated.

[8] Jamaica, Central Planning Unit, *Economic Survey 1963* (Kingston, 1964).

This undiminished population pressure helps explain what must on the surface appear to be contradictory developments–the coincidence of a period of rapid economic growth with massive emigration. A second factor accounting for this phenomenon is the nature of that economic growth. The leading growth sector, the mining of bauxite, did not provide direct employment opportunities at all commensurate with its impact on income. Hence, 13 per cent of the labour force was still unemployed in 1960.[9]

A detailed account of migration to the United Kingdom is given in Table 4.[10] Net emigration to the U.K. during the decade was 161,761, or 9.7 per cent of the population remaining on the island at the end of 1962.

We shall not enter into questions of the effect of economic conditions upon emigration, i.e., the age-old debate of whether the movement was a "push" or "pull" phenomenon.[11] Rather, we shall be concerned with the reverse relationship: how did emigration affect economic development? Did rapid economic growth occur in spite of, or because of, emigration?

II. THE REPERCUSSIONS OF EMIGRATION

Four "effects" of emigration, corresponding to those socio-economic variables of perhaps greatest concern to Jamaican policy-makers, have been isolated: the population, balance of payments, production, and employment effects. The list could be extended, e.g., by isolating a "savings effect," but these four should enable us to analyze

[9] See, for source, the next section under the employment effect.

[10] During the period under consideration there was additional net migration to other countries of some 20,000–30,000. We shall not be concerned with that flow in this analysis.

[11] It is sufficient to note here that, 1) economic conditions in Jamaica were far from ideal, 2) economic conditions in Jamaica were, however, improving though this is less certain in terms of employment opportunities, and 3) the rate of emigration tended to fluctuate directly with British economic conditions, e.g., emigration slowed down during the 1958 recession.

TABLE 4. MIGRATION TO THE UNITED KINGDOM.

	Emigrants				*Migrants returning from U.K.*			
	total	*males*	*females*	*children*	*total*	*males*	*females*	*children*
1953	2,210	1,284	875	51	*133	73	60	—
1954	8,149	5,178	2,861	110	*182	108	74	—
1955	17,257	10,911	6,145	201	*99	65	34	—
1956	17,302	9,144	7,577	581	757	n.a.	n.a.	n.a.
1957	13,087	6,257	6,097	733	1,376	700	439	237
1958	9,992	4,425	4,509	1,058	1,992	935	614	443
1959	12,796	6,410	4,955	1,431	2,318	833	816	619
1960	32,060	18,372	11,258	2,430	1,791	751	611	429
1961	39,203	19,181	16,276	3,746	1,558	705	493	360
1962	22,779	8,434	10,207	4,138	2,868	1,196	959	713

* from G. W. Roberts and D. O. Mills, op. cit., pp. 105–6.
Source of all other data: Jamaica, *Economic Survey 1958* and *Economic Survey 1963*.

the impact of emigration on some key factors in economic development.

The Population Effect

The absence of detailed statistics of the age structure and fertility of the migrant population renders a truly precise assessment of the impact of emigration upon population impossible. Nevertheless, though the crudity of our estimates might cause demographers to cringe, they will be sufficiently accurate to shed some light on economic problems.

It is presumed self-evident that a reduction in the rate of population growth in Jamaica would, *ceteris paribus*, favourably influence the growth of *per capita* income. While some economists might maintain that population growth is a stimulant to economic growth, surely none would argue that a 3 per cent increase per annum would have this effect in an already overpopulated country. It is instructive, therefore, to obtain some idea of the effect of emigration upon population growth. Net emigration to the U.K. during the period 1953–62 amounted to roughly 35 per cent of the natural increase of population. Assuming a smoothed curve in which emigration offset accessions through births at a constant rate, this would have had the effect of lowering population growth from a rate of 3 per cent to a rate of 2 per cent per year. Again, assuming the rate of economic growth to be independent of the rate of population growth, emigration would have raised the rate of growth of *per capita* product by the 1 per cent which the population growth declined.[12]

[12] This follows from the equation: % growth of *per capita* product = % growth of total product − % growth of population ($r = g - p$), which holds for small changes of the magnitude discussed here. See, for an example of a similar exercise, H. W. Singer, "The Mechanics of Economic Development," *Indian Economic Review* (August, 1952), reprinted in Agarwala and Singh, *op. cit.*, p. 396. I am not suggesting that growth of total product really is independent of the rate of population growth, particularly where emigration is involved. These considerations are taken up in discussion of the production effect.

Emigration reduced total population by more than the amount of net migration, of course. Most of the emigrants were adults, and a high proportion of these appear to have been in the fertile age ranges. By use of a rough and ready method, which yields estimates comparable to those of Roberts and Mills,[13] it is estimated that 38,700 births were lost to the island through emigration. While this estimate may be subject to an error of as much as 10,000 either way, it does suggest that, had there been no net migration to the U.K. during this period, total population would have been approximately 200,000 greater at the end of 1962.

It is clear that emigration affects the age structure of the population as well as total population. It should be equally clear that a reduction in the number of births equivalent to net migration would have profoundly different effects upon these two variables. The following exercise, the results of which are summarized in Table 5, illustrates the point with reference to the actual situation in Jamaica.

Row 2 shows the structure of the population at the end of 1960. This year was chosen, instead of 1962, because precise census data exist. "Productive population" is defined as the entire population between the ages of 15 and 60. This, rather than the actual labour force, is used as a measure of productive population to avoid the difficulties of dealing with unemployment, participation rates, etc. "Non-productive population" is consequently defined as the population less than 15 and greater than 60 years of age. We may reach an estimate of what would have been the situation had no net emigration to the U.K. occurred since 1953 by using the previous estimate of the number of births lost to the island. Combined with known totals of the net migration of adults and children (see Table 4), this figure yields the calculations of row 1. In the third case we have assumed that no net migration occurred but that births dropped by an amount (104,000) equal to the net migration which actually did occur 1953–60. The results are set out in row 3.

[13] Roberts and Mills, *op. cit.*, p. 63.

TABLE 5. EFFECT OF EMIGRATION ON THE STRUCTURE OF POPULATION 1960.

	total population	*productive population as % of total*	*non-productive population as % of total*
1. "Stable" population: no net migration to U.K. 1953–60	1,750,000	54%	46%
2. Actual situation as the result of net migration to U.K. 1953–60	1,625,000	52%	48%
3. Hypothetical case of a reduction in the number of births equal to net migration to U.K. 1953–60	1,645,000	57.5%	42.5%

It has already been pointed out that the happy result of emigration was to reduce total population by an amount greater than the migration itself by lowering the crude birth rate which would have obtained in its absence.[14] However, emigration also raised the proportion (though not the absolute number) of "non-productive" population from 46 per cent to 48 per cent of the total. By contrast, a reduction in the number of births would have *lowered* the non-productive population both relatively and absolutely.

A decrease in the ratio of non-productive to productive population (resulting from a falling birth rate) has, in part, the following beneficial effects: 1) by reducing the rate of

[14] Many demographers might argue that the trouble with migration is that it *does* affect fertility, i.e., provides an inducement for its maintenance at a high level. For simplicity, I have assumed here that migration affects birth rates only in the mechanical sense of transferring mothers from one country to another. But I would argue that in the short run this is a valid assumption.

population growth without affecting total output substantially, it raises *per capita* incomes; 2) it raises the potential rate of saving by reducing public expenditure necessary to maintain schools, etc., as well as by raising *per capita* incomes; 3) by reducing the size of the youngest age cohort it will, for a given rate of fertility among women of child-bearing age, reduce the rate of population growth in the next generation more than would a migratory movement of a comparable size; and 4) it will reduce the number of workers entering the labour force in the next generation, a benefit if a problem of long-term unemployment exists. It follows that the prime—perhaps the only —economic advantage to Jamaica of emigration over an equivalent reduction in the number of births is that the former may alleviate an acute unemployment problem *now.*

Emigration is, then, a "second-best" means of attacking the population problem. Some critics of emigration have argued, on this basis, that migration was detrimental to the Jamaican interest and should have been discouraged. It is true that the Jamaican Government has failed to come to grips with the need to induce the populace to exercise birth control, perhaps because a ready outlet for surplus population provided a convenient excuse for inaction. But it is certainly not true that such a precipitous fall in the birth rate as posited above was a feasible alternative to emigration.[15] The only relevant comparison, in the short run—and massive emigration had only a short run—is between the situation resulting from emigration and that which would have developed without it. The immediate population effect has been stated; total population was reduced, but the ratio of non-productive to productive population was increased. The economic implications of this will be examined shortly. It remains to comment on the long-run population effect.

Attempts to assess the long-run effect become highly speculative. We have already dismissed, rather summarily, the naïve view that emigration is a direct substitution for a

[15] This could be argued either by historical analogy or in terms of the mores of Jamaican society.

declining birth rate–a mere prolongation of the day of reckoning when birth rates must fall. A more sophisticated school argues that emigration may militate against a long-term solution of the population problem by a more devious route. Population is believed to grow as a logistic function of economic conditions. As prosperity increases, population growth begins to accelerate due to a falling death date and a stable or even rising birth rate. But at a certain threshold level of prosperity, the birth rate begins to decline. Thus, insofar as emigration lowers prosperity, the critical level or "prosperity threshold" may not be reached, *ergo* the birth rate will not fall.[16]

Per capita income did increase markedly during the decade of massive migration, though the possibility that it might have increased even more otherwise will be examined. More to the point, it may be questioned if population is a function of the level of prosperity.[17] Historically, birth rates have declined only after a long period of modern economic growth. This suggests that birth rates are functionally related to economic growth (and the associated urbanization, etc.) by the length of time the process has been going on, as much as by the level of prosperity achieved. Marked changes in attitudes are likely to occur only between generations. If it is accepted that the vast social changes necessary to induce birth rates to fall are a function of time, then it is uncertain whether a decade of emigration had any effect on the long-term birth rate. In this case, it merely provided a breathing space of reduced population pressure. But even if emigration did affect the birth rate, its influence must be presumed so slight that it was completely overwhelmed by the short-run population effect.

[16] See W. F. Maunder, "The New Jamaican Emigration," *Social and Economic Studies,* Vol. 4, No. 1 (March, 1955), pp. 58–59, who expresses fears in this vein.

[17] The argument here is based upon lectures given by Professor Simon Kuznets, Harvard University.

The Balance of Payments Effect

For many less developed countries a shortage of foreign exchange is one of the most serious bottlenecks impeding economic growth. Jamaica, however, has been quite favourably placed in this respect. Largely due to exports of bauxite, the income terms of trade (1954 = 100) expanded from 80.6 in 1953 to 152.1 in 1961.[18] Tourism and substantial foreign investment aided invisible items and the capital account, respectively. But the direct impact of emigration upon the balance of payments has been favourable as well. Moreover, foreign exchange benefits will continue to be derived in the future, for which the general prospects are less bright due to a slowing down in the rate of expansion of bauxite exports.

Calculation of the balance of payments effect is quite straightforward. The major cost of foreign exchange involved is the cost of passage and the prime benefit the remittances of emigrants.

In the first few years of the movement most migrants travelled by sea, but by 1961 about 75 per cent journeyed by air.[19] Fares apparently remained fairly constant from 1954 onwards at about £75 by sea and £85 by air.[20] R. B. Davison lists £80 as an appropriate estimate of the average cost of passage.[21] Roberts and Mills assume a loss to the island of only £70 per emigrant because they allow for the profits of local travel agents.[22] Since emigrants may have taken some savings with them (which would have been changed into sterling and spent in Britain), we will assume the real loss of foreign exchange to have been £80 per emigrant. One complication arises

[18] Jamaica, *Trade Indices 1948–61.*

[19] Information supplied by the Department of Statistics, Jamaica.

[20] See Maunder, "Jamaican Emigration," p. 55; Roberts and Mills, *op. cit.,* p. 125; and R. B. Davison, "West Indian Migration to Britain 1955–61," Part II, *West Indian Economist* (September, 1961), pp. 13–14.

[21] Davison, *loc. cit.*

[22] Roberts and Mills, *op. cit.,* p. 125.

due to the payment by relatives already in England of a portion of some fares. In so far as such gifts or loans were remitted to emigrants in Jamaica, it would be double counting not to include them as a cost to the island since they would show up as a benefit through remittances. Since the amount of fares paid in London, and thus never crossing the balance of payments, is not known,[23] and since we are particularly concerned not to understate the cost involved, it will be assumed that fares paid abroad represent an opportunity cost to Jamaica in the sense that an amount equal to the fare would have been remitted to the Jamaican resident had he chosen not to emigrate. Thus, complications notwithstanding, we assume a true loss of £80 in foreign exchange for each emigrant. Multiplying this by the total number of emigrants (not net migrants), the total estimated foreign exchange cost of emigration was £13,986,800 or about £14 million.

The amount of net remittances from the U.K. may be ascertained from records of postal and money orders. While this may understate the benefits thus derived, no attempt will be made to estimate the amount of remittances from other sources, such as the direct mailing of currency. The benefit has indeed been substantial. Remittances in 1962 totaled £6,264,000–an amount which covered 42.5 per cent of the visible trade deficit. Total net remittances from the U.K. 1953–62 were £28,566,000. The estimated amount for 1954 was £550,000 and for 1953, £250,000.[24] For simplification we will assume that all remittances in 1953 were from Jamaicans who had emigrated prior to the period under consideration, but that all remittances from 1954 onward were from those emigrating during the period. Total remittances from emigrants between 1953 and 1962, then, are assumed to equal total remittances 1954–62, or £29,116,000.

[23] Maunder does say that 25 per cent of those travelling to the U.K. by sea in his 1954 sample survey had their fares paid in London ("Jamaican Emigration," p. 55).

[24] Figures for 1955–62 from Jamaica, *Economic Survey 1961* and *Economic Survey 1963*. Other estimates are from *Economic Survey 1957*.

It is necessary to estimate the present value of future remittances from the cohort of emigrants 1953–62. To do this, we will call the entire period 1953–62 the present (year t), and assume that the flow of remittances after 1963 (remittances for that year = £5,798,000) will reduce by 10 per cent per year until 1977, after which they will continue in perpetuity at a constant rate. The present value will be calculated at alternative rates of discount for future earnings: 6% and 8%. Thus, in 1963 (year t + 1) the present (1962) value of actual remittances at a 6% discount rate was £5,460,000. By 1977 (year t + 15) remittances are assumed to have reduced to £1,326,000 per annum, at which rate they continue forever. The capitalized value of this flow is £22.1 million, the present value of which is £9.25 million (both at 6%). The results are summarized in Table 6. The sums have been disaggregated in case it is felt that a perpetual flow at the 1977 level is an unrealistic assumption. The minimum net foreign exchange gain (rate of discount = 8%, remittances stop completely in 1977) is £45,219,200. The maximum net gain (rate of discount 6%, remittances flow in perpetuity) is £57,439,200.

One other less important repercussion of emigration upon the balance of payments is worthy of passing mention. Since Jamaica imports certain basic items, e.g., codfish, a staple item in the Jamaican diet, it may be presumed that emigration reduced import requirements. Imports per capita of food, drink, and tobacco ranged from £5.8 in 1954 to £10.9 in 1962.[25] Arbitrarily assuming that each (net) emigrant reduced essential import requirements by £6 per annum, the total amount of foreign exchange saved in this way was about £4,115,000. The amount is so negligible that no attempt has been made to calculate the present value of future savings. Domestic demand for exportables is slight so that we may neglect this effect of emigration upon exports.

In addition to being slight, this consumption effect of emigration upon imports and exports is only meaningful

[25] Jamaica, Dept. of Statistics, *Annual Abstract of Statistics 1962* (Kingston, Jamaica).

TABLE 6. SUMMARY OF THE BALANCE OF PAYMENTS EFFECT (£ '000).

	Discount Rate 6%	*Discount Rate* 8%
Benefits:		
Total net remittances from U.K. through 1962	29,116	29,116
Present value of future remittances 1963–77	33,060	30,090
Present value of future remittances 1977	9,250	5,200
Total benefits	71,426	64,406
Costs:		
Passage to U.K. (174,835 emigrants at £80)	−13,987	−13,987
Net benefit:	57,439	50,419

if the marginal productivity of those emigrating was zero. For if marginal productivity was greater than zero, we should have to take into account the impact which changed production would have had on imports and exports. In the following section we shall attempt to assess the effect of emigration upon total production, but it would be impossible to make any meaningful estimates of how the level of exports, developmental imports, or foreign investment might be effected. Pertinent to this, it should be noted that the calculation of net benefit from remittances is additive to the production effect calculated in the next section. Regardless of how emigration affected total production, remittances would have been forthcoming as an added benefit.

The Production Effect

The conventional approach to the determination of the effects of emigration upon national income has been as follows.[26] The private and public cost of rearing a person until he has become a productive member of the labour force is viewed as an investment by the society in which he is reared. If this person should emigrate, the return on this investment is lost to the country of his birth and accrues as an external economy to the country to which he emigrates. Usually it is assumed that each emigrant would have earned the going wage for his productive services and hence the present value of his lifetime earnings are charged as a further loss to the country from which he emigrates. The most careful writers will calculate the true loss to be the present value of net earnings, i.e., the cost of living of the worker will be subtracted. Finally, the cost of passage is added to the debit column and the value of remittances is counted as the one real economic benefit derived from emigration. Almost invariably, a cost-benefit calculation of this kind shows emigration to have resulted in a substantial loss to the society of the migrant's birth.

We shall not use this approach, for several reasons. In the first place, it implicitly assumes full employment. Where unemployment or underemployment exists, the opportunity cost of emigration will not be equal to the wage of the emigrant. Secondly, the cost of rearing Jamaican youth to maturity should not be regarded as an investment, since the largest part of these expenditures would have been undertaken even if every child were known to be going to migrate at age 15. But if, despite these considerations, expenditure upon the rearing of children be looked upon as investment, then it should be regarded as a fixed cost. The cost of rearing a child should not be charged to emigration. Again, the relevant consideration is opportunity cost–given that Jamaica had a population of a certain size and age structure, was the country better off with or without emigration? Finally, the conventional approach is felt to be inadequate for our purposes because it is a partial equilibrium measure, valid only for the marginal analysis

[26] For examples of calculations similar to this applied to the West Indies, see Davison, *op. cit.*, pp. 22–25; and Roberts and Mills, *op. cit.*, pp. 83–86.

of very small outflows of emigrants. That is, the conventional approach uses *ceteris paribus* assumptions; we shall attempt to compare the actual GDP in 1962 with what it would have been, *mutatis mutandis,* had there been no net emigration to the U.K. 1953–62.

If labour were a strictly homogeneous factor, assessment of the production effect of emigration would be a simple task. So long as there was substantial unemployment—throughout the period in this case—the opportunity cost of emigration would have been zero.[27] To supply the actual figures, total GDP in 1962 would have been £252.5 million with or without emigration. *Per capita* GDP, assuming that total population without emigration would have been 200,000 greater, would have been £134 instead of the actual £152. On this basis of calculation, *per capita* product rose by £18 or 13.4 per cent as a result of emigration.[28]

It is unlikely that even the most ardent supporter of the reality of the surplus-labour model would suggest that total production was wholly unaffected by emigration. On the contrary, most scholarly studies of Jamaican migration have been replete with caveats about the ill effects of losing skilled labour to the U.K. Roberts and Mills, whose warning was quoted earlier, found that during the period 1953–55, 56.7 per cent of those emigrating to the U.K. were classed as skilled workers.[29] By their estimates during this short space of three years the number of masons, mechanics, electricians, and carpenters left on the island declined substantially.[30] Since a shortage of skilled labour is, al-

[27] Throughout this section we abstract from consideration the cost of passage and remittances.

[28] In a sense, we are avoiding welfare considerations by concentrating on the level of economic activity. However, they are brought back in again through the back door by concentrating on *per capita* as well as total product. It is best to make explicit my bias that only an increase in *per capita* product constitutes a favourable production effect.

[29] Calculated from tables 4M and 4Q, pp. 48 and 52, respectively, in Roberts and Mills, *op. cit.*

[30] *Ibid.,* p. 71. Masons by 16 per cent, mechanics and electricians by 13 per cent, and carpenters by 8 per cent.

most by definition, characteristic of an underdeveloped economy, regardless of its rate of general unemployment, loss of this scarce resource was bound to be viewed with alarm. One prophet of doom went so far as to suggest that the migration might be harmful to both Jamaica and Britain. Since even workers who were "skilled" by Jamaican standards were likely to be "unskilled" by British standards, emigration might lower the average level of skills in both countries.[31]

An attempt must therefore be made to evaluate the impact of this loss of skilled labour. Just as the estimated production effect under the assumption of homogeneity of labour attempted to set an upper bound on the benefit derived from emigration, the following estimate will attempt to set a lower bound.

In 1953, some 95,283 persons were classified as "crafts and production processes" workers, 81.8 per cent of whom were employed in the manufacturing and construction sectors.[32] As nearly as can be ascertained, this occupational category coincides with what might be called "skilled labour." In 1960, there were 126,568 persons classified as "craftsmen and technical workers," which appears to be a comparable category.[33] Of these, 70,964 were employed in manufacturing and 37,448 were employed in construction. Total employment in the two sectors had expanded to 89,523 and 49,828, respectively. Thus in the eight years between 1953 and 1960 the number of skilled workers in the two sectors increased by 30,478. During this same period total production in these two sectors rose in constant (1956) prices by £25.8 million.[34] Real output per skilled worker in the manufacturing and construction sectors rose from £334 in 1953 to £478 in 1960. In marginal terms, for each of the approximately 30,500

[31] Maunder, "Jamaican Emigration," p. 59.

[32] Jamaica, *Sample Survey 1953,* Table 48, p. 85.

[33] Jamaica, Department of Statistics, *Census of Jamaica 7th April, 1960,* Vol. I, Part D, Table 7, p. 7-1732. Sectoral breakdowns are from Vol. II, Part II, Bulletins 30 and 31. Hereafter cited as *Census 1960.*

[34] Jamaica, Department of Statistics, *National Accounts, Income and Expenditures,* various years.

new skilled labourers employed, production rose by £846. In current prices the increased value per marginal skilled labourer was about £1,060.

This marginal output/skilled-labour ratio will be used to estimate the total loss of production through emigration. While this tool is hardly expected to gain the position accorded the capital/output ratio in orthodox economic theory, it will serve our purposes here. The ratio was constructed for only the two sectors because 1) these two sectors employ 80–90 per cent of the skilled labour force, and scarcity of this factor can only be said to constitute a bottleneck in them,[35] 2) it would be unrealistic to attribute total increased output, so heavily influenced by bauxite investment, to skilled labour, and 3) potential for further growth, if it existed, must have lain in these two sectors. Thus, it is assumed that the marginal opportunity cost of a skilled migrant to the Jamaican economy in 1962 could not have exceeded £1,000 in current production potential and that the marginal opportunity cost of an unskilled emigrant was zero. It is further assumed that 50 per cent of all adult emigrants were skilled, as here defined. Between 1953 and 1962 Jamaica lost 75,194 skilled workers net, under these assumptions. Total GDP in the absence of emigration would have increased by £75,194,000 to £327.7 million. Per capita GDP, allowing for the 200,000 extra residents, would have increased to £173 or by 13.8 per cent. Table 7 summarizes the upper and lower estimates of the production effect.

It is important to recognize just how strong were the assumptions under which the lower bound was calculated. Use of an output/skilled-labour ratio assumes, *mutatis mutandis,* that all the necessary additional investment to employ the workers would have been forthcoming, that markets for the produce would have been found, that no balance of payments difficulties would have been encoun-

[35] See W. A. Lewis, *The Theory of Economic Growth* (London: Unwin University Books, 1955), pp. 208ff., for a discussion of the crucial role of skilled labour in construction and the crucial role of the expansion of the construction sector in development.

TABLE 7. SUMMARY OF THE ESTIMATED BOUNDS OF THE PRODUCTION EFFECT, 1962.

	total GDP (£ *m*)	*per cap. GDP* (£)	*net gain in per cap. GDP from emigration*
1. Actual situation as result of migration–1962	252.5	152	—
2. Lower bound. No emigration, half of adult migrants skilled	327.7	173	−21
3. Upper bound. No emigration, labour homogeneous	252.5	134	+18

tered, etc. In short, it assumes that skilled labour is *the* limiting factor in development, all the other ingredients of entrepreneurship, capital, markets, and foreign exchange being in excess supply. Moreover, it is unlikely that 50 per cent of the adult migrants were skilled. Nearly all of the female emigrants listed as skilled were dressmakers, and Roberts and Mills are dubious about classing these as skilled.[36] A 1961 survey conducted by the University College of the West Indies showed a far smaller proportion of the emigrants in that year to have been skilled.[37] Using the broadest possible definition of skilled, my calculations show only 31.9 per cent to have been in that category in 1961. We may certainly, then, take our lower bound estimate of the loss from emigration to be unrealistically large.

The question of the production effect of emigration

[36] Roberts and Mills, *op. cit.,* p. 51.

[37] R. B. Davison, "West Indian Migration to Britain 1955–61," Part 1, *West Indian Economist* (July–August, 1961), p. 28. The categories are not strictly comparable to those of Roberts and Mills.

must be pursued further, for the difference between the minimum and maximum estimates is substantial. A true determination of the production effect hinges upon the correct appraisal of the importance of loss of skilled labour. All attempts to establish a meaningful correlation between migration and production or investment, or all three together, either by using absolute figures or by relative and absolute first differences, proved fruitless. Hence, we may only offer the following evidence in support of the view that the loss of skilled labour was relatively unimportant.

Firstly, the phenomenal growth of the economy during the period militates against attributing a great deal of weight to the loss of skilled labour. Rapid expansion of total product may reasonably be said to have occurred, in spite of unfavourable countertrends, due to the peculiar role of bauxite. But surely exports of manufactures (see Table 8), which must compete in world markets, could not have expanded at an exponential rate had a shortage of skilled labour force been a serious factor.

TABLE 8. DOMESTIC EXPORTS OF INDUSTRIAL PRODUCTS. (Sections 6, 7, & 8 of the S.I.T.C.)

	£'000
1954	337.8
1956	518.4
1957	650.2
1958	1,002.5
1959	1,102.5
1960	2,034.5
1961	2,843.2
1962	4,023.0

Source: Jamaica, *External Trade of Jamaica 1962.*

Secondly, the fact that the skilled labour force increased by over 30,000 in eight years while the total experienced labour force declined is surely significant. This does not prove that skilled labour did not emigrate, nor does it say anything about possible deterioration in quality. It does, however, point up quite strikingly an essential characteristic of skilled labour frequently overlooked by those bemoaning its loss–it may be trained. Labour is not homogeneous, but neither is there the marked dichotomy in its essential nature assumed in calculating the lower bound estimate of the production effect.

Finally, it is subject to question whether even skilled workers were fully employed during the period. Maunder's 1954 survey of migrants going to the U.K. to seek work showed that 18 per cent of them were unemployed and an additional 38 per cent had been neither working nor seeking work in Jamaica.[38] By this measure, some skilled workers among the emigrants were necessarily at least voluntarily unemployed, for a greater percentage were skilled than were employed. In the week preceding the census of 1960, only 72.3 per cent of those employed at all during the week in manufacturing worked a full (5–7 day) week. The corresponding figure for construction was 65.6 per cent.[39] While some of this underemployment may have been voluntary, and though skilled workers in these sectors may have been more heavily employed than unskilled, it still seems likely that some degree of underemployment among skilled workers existed. Involuntarily unemployment was 4.5 per cent in manufacturing and 12.3 per cent in construction during the week preceding the census.[40] These statistics, too, indicate that there may have been slack in the demand for skilled labour.

These considerations, along with the recognition of the extreme assumptions used in calculating a lower bound, create a presumption that the production effect of emigration was nearer the upper bound than the lower. It seems likely that total GDP was somewhat lower than it would have been without emigration, but that *per capita* GDP was

[38] Maunder, "Jamaican Emigration," p. 54.

[39] O. C. Francis, *The People of Modern Jamaica* (Kingston, Jamaica: Department of Statistics, 1963), Table 7.12, p. 7-25.

[40] The corresponding figure for the whole economy was 6.1 per cent. *Ibid.*, Table 7.9, p. 7-20.

higher.[41] In addition, it should be remembered that the net benefits accruing from remittances were not included in the above estimates. If account is taken of production by Jamaican migrants resident in England, then it seems safe to conclude that the total product as well as the *per capita* product of Jamaicans (as opposed to the product of Jamaica) rose as a result of emigration. There is little value in dogmatism on these points, however, and in the absence of more refined statistics, it is possible that other observers will reach different conclusions.

The Employment Effect

Estimates of the employment effect will be the least certain of any undertaken. But something must be said of the effect of emigration upon this most crucial parameter in the belief that, "In a poor country, it may be better to fail in answering important questions than to succeed in answering unimportant ones."[42]

It is maddeningly difficult to compare the actual employment situation in 1953 with that in 1960, the two years during the period for which reliable data exist.[43] The data of the 1960 census are relatively free of ambiguity. Total unemployment was 84,902 of a labour force of 651,354, a rate of 13 per cent. A large number of these were seeking a first job, however, and the comparable figures for "experienced" workers was 37,143 unemployed

[41] At the risk of appearing to give a wholly spurious precision to the production effect, one more estimate, which I believe to be realistic, will be made. Assume that in reality 25 per cent of the emigrants were skilled and that their opportunity cost equalled the average product per skilled worker in manufacturing and construction in current prices in 1960 (£527). Then, total GDP would have been £272.1 million and *per capita* GDP £145 without emigration.

[42] J. K. Galbraith in foreword to Werner Baer, *The Puerto Rican Economy and United States Economic Fluctuations* (Barcelona: Social Science Center, University of Puerto Rico, 1962), p. xv.

[43] See G. E. Cumper, "A Comparison of Statistical Data on the Jamaican Labor Force, 1953–1961," *Social and Economic Studies,* Vol. 13, No. 4 (December, 1964), pp. 430–39.

of a total 603,595 or a rate of 6.1 per cent.[44] The 1953 *Sample Survey* indicates that 90,400 experienced workers were unemployed, though other figures are also given,[45] whereas an additional 20,000 were seeking a first job.[46] Dr. Cumper claims the figures which are really comparable with those of 1960 are 65,800 experienced unemployed of a total labour force of 609,900,[47] or a rate of unemployment of 10.7 per cent. On this basis, the comparable figure for the total unemployment rate would be 13.6 per cent. From this morass of confusion it is perhaps safe to conclude: the total experienced labour force declined 1953–60 and with it the rate of unemployment, whereas the total labour force increased. Total unemployment either declined or remained about the same; total employment increased.

Methods similar to those used to analyze the production effect may be utilized to gauge the employment effect of emigration. Under the assumption of homogeneity of labour, emigration merely served to reduce total unemployment by an amount equal to the number of net adult migrants leaving to seek work in the U.K. Even if the migrants were themselves employed before leaving the island, under this assumption their departure would have meant that their job would be taken by previously unemployed workers. Taken literally, this would have meant that unemployment in 1960 would have been about 185,000 and the rate of unemployment 24.6 per cent in the absence of emigration. In practice, many of these potentially unemployed would have found non-productive employment in agriculture, petty trading, etc., and structural shifts in employment would have been less marked.

If we assume that half the emigrants were skilled and that these would have found productive employment, the effect would have been reversed. Professor Lewis estimates that every job created in manufacturing in the West Indies

[44] Jamaica, *Census 1960,* Table 6, p. 6-1634.
[45] Jamaica, *Sample Survey 1953*, p. 87.
[46] *Ibid.,* p. 66.
[47] Cumper, *op. cit.,* Table 1, p. 431.

creates another job elsewhere in the economy.[48] For each additional employed skilled worker, therefore, it seems reasonable to assume an employment multiplier of two. Under these conditions, employment would have risen by an amount equal to net adult emigration, or 99,643 in 1963. Total unemployment would have remained unchanged, and the rate of unemployment would have dropped to 11.3 per cent in the absence of emigration. Table 9 summarizes the two estimates. It may be seen that the (favourable) effect of emigration under the first assumption is much greater than the (unfavourable) effect under the second. Without emigration, the rate of unemployment would have risen to 24.6 per cent in the first case, but have fallen to only 11.3 per cent in the second.

TABLE 9. SUMMARY OF THE ESTIMATED BOUNDS OF THE EMPLOYMENT EFFECT, 1960.

	total employed	*total unemployed*	*rate of unemployment*
1. Actual situation as result of emigration 1960	566,452	84,902	13%
2. Lower bound. No emigration, half of adult emigrants skilled	666,092	84,902	11.3%
3. Upper bound. No emigration, labour homogeneous	566,452	184,454	24.6%

Again, we must confine ourselves to a probabilistic estimate of which tail of the distribution of possible outcomes

[48] W. A. Lewis, "The Industrialisation of the British West Indies," *Caribbean Economic Review* (May, 1950), reprinted in W. Arthur Lewis, *Industrial Development in the Caribbean* (Port-of-Spain, Trinidad, 1951), p. 32.

was actually approached. Many of the same arguments for regarding the lower bound of the production effect unrealistic are applicable in this case: the estimate of the number of skilled emigrants is too high, some of the skilled emigrants were unemployed, and "skill" is not a God-given attribute, as evidenced by the expansion of the skilled labour force in spite of emigration. However, emigration might have affected the level of employment by a more circuitous route not accounted for by the above calculations. Cumper has asserted that a shortage of skilled labour has raised the general wage level in Jamaica.[49] This could, of course, aggravate unemployment, and insofar as emigration was responsible for such a shortage, it could thereby have indirectly increased unemployment. A rising wage level may very well have been a major factor in curbing the expansion of employment opportunities, but it by no means follows that emigration affected the wage level. The influence of high wages in the bauxite industry, coupled with the existence of strong labour unions, appear to have been the decisive factors affecting the general wage level. However, it would be very difficult to assess quantitatively the effect of the wage level upon employment in Jamaica, much less to determine the impact of emigration upon the wage level. It seems likely that any adverse indirect effects of this nature would be slight in comparison to the direct effects of emigration upon employment.

Two things may be said of the employment effect with some assurance. Firstly, emigration did not solve the unemployment problem. Secondly, if the above estimates of the possible effects of emigration are at all realistic, the unemployment problem would not have been solved under the best of conditions. Even if the employment effect was nearer the lower than the upper bound, emigration probably reduced unemployment both relatively and absolutely.

[49] G. E. Cumper, "Labour and Development in the West Indies," *Social and Economic Studies,* Vol. 11, No. 1 (March, 1962), p. 10.

III. SUMMARY

The following points are pertinent by way of summary and conclusion:

1. Jamaica had one of the highest rates of economic growth in the world 1953–62. Associated with this rapid economic expansion, however, were continued population pressure, heavy unemployment, and a massive emigration of working-class Jamaicans to the United Kingdom to seek employment.

2. The migratory movement reduced population pressure to some extent. Total population was probably 200,000 less in 1962 than it would have been without emigration. A reduction in births would have been a more desirable means of reducing population pressure, but it is naïve to think that such a massive reduction in births was ever a realistic alternative to emigration.

3. Migration brought, and continues to bring, substantial earnings of foreign exchange to Jamaica.

4. The migration of skilled workers may have reduced total production somewhat, but *per capita* production was probably greater in 1962 as a result. The growth of real *per capita* GDP by 6.8 per cent per year 1953–61 probably occurred more because of than in spite of emigration.

5. Emigration did not solve Jamaica's unemployment problem, but it may have alleviated it.

6. On balance, emigration appears to have aided rather than impeded economic development. Nothing has been said of the social consequences of emigration in this paper.

7. Nor has this paper dealt with the possibility of a return flow of migrants to Jamaica after 1962. In 1963, net emigration to the U.K. still exceeded 3,000, and a similar trend could be seen in the first half of 1964. A massive reversal of the movement does not, therefore, appear imminent. Against the adverse population and, possibly, employment effects a return flow would have must be set the probability that returning migrants would bring savings and increased skills with them.

8. If there is little net migration, particularly of skilled workers, in the next decade, it should be possible to draw firmer conclusions about the economic effects of emigration in the decade 1953–62.

10.

Features that set Caribbean economies apart from those of other underdeveloped lands are discussed in this selection by an eminent West Indian planner and economist. Focusing on Jamaica, Trinidad and Tobago, Guyana, and Barbados, the author assesses the constraints imposed on economic development by West Indian traditions of political democracy and free trade unions—institutions more generally characteristic of developed than underdeveloped nations. He stresses the negative implications of an agricultural system sharply dichotomized between plantation and peasant cultivation, consumer aspirations aroused by close proximity to, and long contact with, Western ways of life, and continuing dependence on foreign capital for bauxite and petroleum development. The restriction of emigration, the growth of population, and a lag in industrialization combine to make structural transformation of Caribbean economies a necessity.

WILLIAM G. DEMAS, a Trinidadian, has been in the forefront of Caribbean economic planning and development efforts. Trained in economics, he has been Research Fellow and Visiting Professor of the Centre for Developing Area Studies at McGill University and Head of the Economic Planning Division of the Government of Trinidad and Tobago. He is presently Secretary General of the Caribbean Free Trade Association (CARIFTA).

Characteristics of the Caribbean Economies

William G. Demas

In this chapter I shall outline very briefly what I conceive to be the principal characteristics and problems of the Caribbean economies and indicate also very briefly my reasons for believing that development is urgently required today in the area. The discussion of characteristics and problems does not seek to be exhaustive nor is there any attempt to present a thorough survey of the structure and recent history of these economies.[1] This is a task which in itself would require volumes. All I shall seek to do is to present the characteristics which are relevant to the general framework previously outlined and to the problems of planning discussed in the next chapter. In other words, the data I shall present here are meant to be purely illustrative and are by no means exhaustive.

The first problem is to define the term 'Caribbean'. Here I take the Caribbean to include the ten former members of the West Indies Federation: Jamaica, Trinidad and Tobago, Barbados, the four Windward Islands and the three Leeward Islands, and British Guiana. In other words, I am referring to what used to be called the British Carib-

From *The Economics of Development in Small Countries with Special Reference to the Caribbean*, Montreal, McGill University Press, 1965, pp. 95–118. Reprinted by kind permission of McGill University Press.

[1] A very competent macro-economic study of the economic development of Trinidad and Tobago in the 1950's is to be found in Frank Rampersad's 'Growth and Structural Change in the Trinidad and Tobago Economy 1951–1961', Central Statistical Office, *Research Papers No. 1* (Port-of-Spain, Trinidad, December, 1963).

bean and which, now that Jamaica and Trinidad and Tobago have become independent, is now called the Caribbean Commonwealth countries. It should be noted, however, that in terms of regional integration the Caribbean might have to assume a wider meaning and include the Dutch and French mainland and island territories, Puerto Rico, and the independent republics. The broader definition would give the region a total population of 21.8 million as against a population of 3.8 million in the narrower definition.

As Table I indicates, individual units of the Caribbean Commonwealth countries are very tiny economies and the area as a whole, even if economically integrated, would still be a very small economy. Even so, I think a useful distinction can be made between the 'larger' territories of Jamaica, Trinidad and Tobago, British Guiana, and perhaps Barbados, on the one hand and the 'smaller' territories of the Leeward and Windward Islands on the other hand. It should not be forgotten that the Leewards and Windwards are separate islands, most of them having between 70,000 and 90,000 inhabitants: Montserrat, the smallest, having 13,000. Moreover, British Guiana is in many respects a small island since, in spite of its total area of 83,000 square miles, only a narrow coastal strip is inhabited. Finally, the high population densities and high rates of natural increase should be observed.

While I shall include the Leeward and Windward Islands in the description which follows, what I have to say about planning in the next chapter will relate principally to the 'bigger' countries of Jamaica, Trinidad and Tobago, British Guiana, and Barbados.

The Leeward and Windward Islands are so small as to fall into a separate category and, while this factor in itself does not preclude the development of manufacturing industry, it appears to me that their future is much more closely bound up with exports of traditional primary products, the growth in productivity of the domestic food-producing sector and the development of the tourist industry. Moreover, the economies of the 'larger' territories are

TABLE I

CARIBBEAN POPULATION DATA

	Population 1961	*Area Square Miles*	*Density per Square Mile*	*Natural Rate* of Increase during 1960 %*
Jamaica	1,630,000	4,411	370	3.3
Trinidad and Tobago	859,000	1,980	418	3.1
British Guiana	580,000	83,000	7	3.3
Barbados	235,000	166	1,395	2.5
Leewards and Windwards	437,600 (1960)	1,182	370	3.2

* Excludes emigration and immigration.

SOURCE: 'Estimates of Inter-Censal Population by Age and Sex and Revised Vital Rates for British Caribbean Countries 1946–1960', Census Research Programme Publication (Port-of-Spain), 1964, and official government publications.

capable of sustaining more sophisticated financial institutions.

The Caribbean, by reason of its long historical association with the Western world and its close proximity to the North American continent, has been overcome—perhaps more than most other areas—by the revolution of rising expectations. In consequence of this and as a result of the impact of advertising through the news media, consumption functions have been pushed upwards. There is a widespread desire for many of the more expensive durable consumer goods associated with North American civilization, and consumer credit (or hire-purchase) facilities are increasingly providing the means to satisfy this desire. In addition, increasing demands are being made for the provision of expanded and improved governmental welfare services.

In considering the development of the Caribbean economies we have to bear in mind two fundamental institutional constraints: the existence of political democracy on classic Westminster lines and the existence of a strong independent and forceful trade-union movement sharing the philosophy of North American, and to a lesser degree, British trade unionism. These constraints are not of course unique to the Caribbean—although I suspect that in few other underdeveloped countries is the trade-union movement so imbued with ideas and attitudes more appropriate to the advanced countries. This stems not only from the commendable, though often misplaced, idealism of certain international organizations but from the close proximity to North America and the general 'openness' of the society which makes for very close contacts with the trade-union movements in Britain and North America.

The consequences of these social and institutional parameters for the development process are not difficult to discern. First, the existence of political democracy and the possibility of alternative governments can bring to the forefront the quite justifiable demands of the population for immediate and badly needed improvements, especially in social services; and since resources are always limited, this can conflict with long-run objectives of promoting structural changes in the economy. Second, the trade unions can and often do pursue policies which secure short-term gains in real wages and working conditions for their membership at the expense of the expansion of employment opportunities, capital formation, and the government budget.

Even a nodding acquaintance with the historical development process of the advanced countries–the U.K., Japan, and the U.S.S.R., to take only three extreme types–suggests that full-blown political democracy and a free unfettered trade-union movement can impose severe constraints on the growth process. For historically these institutions are to be viewed as the *products* rather than the *concomitants* of the developed process. To recognize this is not of course to deny the intrinsic value of these two institutions. Even though the economist may accept such intrinsic values, he is professionally bound to draw attention to the wide area of incompatibility between them and the desire for rapid economic development. The point that is being made here is that the preservation of parliamentary democracy and an independent trade-union movement is conditional upon an even greater development effort than would otherwise be necessary.

I have emphasized some of the negative features of the institutions of parliamentary democracy and free trade unionism. Yet it would be wrong to ignore the positive aspects.

In an underdeveloped country trade unions can play a positive role in giving dignity to the wage relationship; in promoting increased productivity; in inculcating discipline, in providing welfare facilities, and in encouraging and mobilizing savings from their membership. Most important in the Caribbean, the trade unions in the modern sector of the economy can do much for employment by pursuing wage policies which are appropriate to Caribbean conditions rather than those copied from the wholly different situation of advanced countries.

Generally speaking, it is remarkable how little thought has been given either in the advanced or the underdeveloped countries to the role of the trade-union movement in a nationalist ex-colonial society aiming at rapid economic development. In a totalitarian one-party state the problem does not arise, since the interests of associations such as trade unions are made to coincide with those of the state and of the society. In fact, in such a country all associations are appendages of the state. But in a pluralistic society the dilemma has to be squarely faced and possible solutions devised.

From a nationalist standpoint, trade unions have undoubtedly been a progressive force in Caribbean society. The movement has been from its inception intimately associated with, and often in the vanguard of, the struggle for political independence. It has also been responsible for removing the grosser forms of exploitation by foreign capital which existed even up to the 1950's. But it is clear that, now that the case of political nationalism has been won in Jamaica, and Trinidad and Tobago and is on the verge of being won in the other territories and now that important economic concessions have been won from foreign capital, the unions have a somewhat different role to play in future.

It is too easy to say that the unions are to blame for not having perceived their new role. The problem goes very deep and involves the whole community. For a new role can be devised for the unions only as part of the wider task facing Caribbean society of evolving economic and social arrangements which provide for the needs of the rural population, the unorganized urban workers and the unemployed as well as those of organized labour, while at the same time ensuring that the income produced by foreign capital is equitably divided between the companies on the one hand and the people and government of the community on the other hand. One of the effects of the dual economic structure of the Caribbean has been to create an aristocracy of organized labour in the modern sector. The gap between organized labour on the one hand and the rest of the labour force has two consequences. The first is that it tends to increase the amount of migration to the urban areas, the consequences of which are obvious. The second aspect of the gap is more social than economic. It unfairly stratifies the population of working age into the privileged and the underprivileged under circumstances unrelated to any rational criteria.

I have also said that full-blown parliamentary democracy has a negative influence on development in so far as demands for immediate improvements do not sufficiently take into account the economic resources of the country. This negative influence is enhanced in countries experiencing a rapid growth of population. There is therefore the important task for political leaders and social scientists in the Caribbean of determining how far plans should go in meeting popular demands without compromising the basic objectives of long-run improvement.

The positive side of democracy in economic planning is that it can provide the opportunities for the participation of the people in the development process. But the exploitation of such opportunities is not automatic. It depends on political leadership and on the development of appropriate mechanisms to make such participation a reality.

It is a fact that *per capita* incomes, especially in Trinidad and Tobago and Jamaica, are higher than in many underdeveloped countries; further, both these countries experienced high annual growth rates in the Gross Domestic Product of the order of 8 per cent per annum throughout the nineteen-fifties.

Neither of these facts necessarily reflects the achievement of an advanced stage of structural transformation. The large divergence between the Gross Domestic Product on the one hand and the Gross National Product and the National Income on the other hand, as revealed in Table II, is a reminder of continued heavy foreign investment in the enclave export industries without which the high growth rates could never have been recorded.

The relatively high *per capita* income of the smaller territories as compared with many of the economies of Africa and South-East Asia is probably due to a greater degree of specialization, reflecting the greater pervasiveness of the money as opposed to the subsistence economy and also perhaps a longer period of participation in international trade. The fast rates of growth of *per capita* real product, real income, and real consumption in Trinidad and Tobago and

TABLE II

G.D.P., G.N.P., AND NATIONAL INCOME (WEST INDIAN DOLLARS)

		G.D.P. at Factor Cost per capita	*G.N.P. at Factor Cost per capita*	*National Income per capita*
Jamaica[1]	(1962)	734	706	658
Trinidad and Tobago[2]	(1962)	1180	1058	920
British Guiana[3]	(1960)	469	450	414
Barbados[4]	(1961)	502	n.a.	n.a.
Leewards and Windwards[4]	(1961)	337	n.a.	n.a.

SOURCES

[1] *Jamaica, Five-Year Independence Plan 1963–1968* and *Economic Survey 1963.*

[2] *Trinidad and Tobago, Draft Second Five-Year Plan 1964–1968.*

[3] A. Kundu, 'Inter-Industry Table for British Guiana 1959 and National Accounts 1957–1960', *Social and Economic Studies,* Supplement to Vol. XII, No. 1.

[4] C. O'Loughlin, *Survey of Economic Potential and Capital Needs of Barbados and the Windward and Leeward Islands* (London: H.M.S.O., 1963).

Jamaica are in part deceptive in that they were the reflection of fortuitous circumstances which are hardly likely to recur —such as the rapid expansion of the mineral-exporting sectors—oil in Trinidad and Tobago and bauxite in Jamaica. In Jamaica, there was in addition the emigration outlet for surplus labour in the U.K. In fact favourable fortuitous circumstances operated in all the territories. Apart from the existence of emigration outlets, there was the guaranteeing of sugar markets in the U.K. under the Commonwealth Sugar Agreement, the development of the tourist industry, and the development of the banana industry in the Windward Islands. Many of these favourable factors are unlikely to operate with the same force in the 1960's, in particular the availability of emigration outlets and the rapid growth of production of bauxite in Jamaica and of oil in Trinidad and Tobago. Even the Commonwealth Preference system is in question.

Within their limited resources, the governments of the territories have done as much as they could for education, health, and the other public services. Compared with many other poor countries, social services have attained a fairly high standard in the Caribbean, although availability still lags woefully behind the levels demanded by the population and their quality is often deficient.

This is not the place to attempt an inventory of the physical and natural resources. Suffice it to say that in each territory the range of resources is highly skewed. For the area as a whole the only major natural resources, apart from agricultural land and tourist attractions, are petroleum and natural gas in Trinidad and bauxite in Jamaica and British Guiana. Coal and iron ore are generally speaking nonexistent. The resource potential of British Guiana—apart from bauxite—is still largely an unknown quantity.

Thus we have a correspondingly skewed type of export trade, heavily dependent on two basic resources: bauxite and alumina plus sugar and sugar products account for 76 per cent of Jamaican domestic exports, while petroleum, sugar and sugar products account for 90 per cent of Trinidad and Tobago domestic exports.

Further, earnings from exports constitute a very high

proportion of national income. All of this is to be seen in Table III, which shows characteristics of the area's foreign trade.

If tourist income were added, the dependence on external sources of income would be even greater, especially in Jamaica, Barbados, and the Leewards and Windwards.

We may also note the low share of manufactures in total exports. If we exclude the processing of primary export staples (e.g. alumina, sugar, rum and molasses, and petroleum products) we find that exports of manufactures are practically non-existent, except in Jamaica where they amounted to 6.9 per cent of total exports in 1962.

Another aspect of the dependence on petroleum, bauxite, and sugar is the high rate of domestic capital formation, heavily financed by foreign resources. (If we were to include depreciation allocations, the share of foreign resources would be even greater.) We may note the complementary, low share of the public sector in total capital formation (Table IV).

The importance of mining and processing of minerals in Jamaica, British Guiana, and Trinidad and Tobago again emerges from an examination of the industrial origin of G.D.P. as shown in Table V. In the case of Trinidad and Tobago the mineral sector dominates the economy, accounting for 30 per cent of G.D.P. Manufacturing, including the processing of agricultural crops, but excluding the processing of minerals, has attained fairly respectable levels in Trinidad and Tobago (12.6 per cent of G.D.P.) and in Jamaica (13 per cent of G.D.P.), but contributes little or nothing in the smaller islands and in British Guiana. This sector includes a limited amount of intermediate and capital goods such as building materials and paints, but the bulk of the output consists of consumer goods in both Jamaica and Trinidad and Tobago. The importance of agriculture in the smaller islands is apparent.

It is important to note that the low share of agriculture in Trinidad and Tobago and in Jamaica does not represent an advanced degree of transformation. Rather, in both islands it is simply a reflection of the profound *malaise* of food production for the home market. In Trinidad and To-

Table III

CHARACTERISTICS OF FOREIGN TRADE

A. Exports

	Year	*Ratio of Exports to G.D.P.* %	*Ratio of Imports to G.D.P.* %
Jamaica[1]	1961	24.8	30.9
Trinidad and Tobago[2]	1961	59.3 (1962)	64.5 (1961)
British Guiana[3]	1960	50.0	55.5
Barbados[4]	1961	32.0	68.8
Leewards and Windwards[4]	1961	27.0	59.3

B. Imports

SELECTED COMMODITY GROUPS AS A PERCENTAGE OF TOTAL IMPORTS

	Jamaica[1] %	*Trinidad and Tobago*[5] %	*British Guiana*[6] %
Food, Drink, and Tobacco	21.2	13.8	18.7
Raw Materials	21.5	51.8	18.6
Manufactured Goods	34.7	20.6	32.7

[1] *Jamaica Independence Plan 1963–1968.*
[2] *Trinidad and Tobago Five-Year Plan 1964–1968.*
[3] Kundu, 'Inter-Industry Table for British Guiana'.
[4] O'Loughlin, *A Survey of Economic Potential and Capital Needs.*
[5] Rampersad, 'Growth and Structural Change in Trinidad and Tobago'.
[6] Calculated from official government reports.

TABLE IV

CAPITAL FORMATION IN THE CARIBBEAN

		Gross Domestic Capital Formation $ millions (W.I.)	*Share of Domestic Capital Formation in G.D.P.*	*Share of Foreign Capital Inflow* in Total Capital Formation*	*Share of Public Sector in Total Capital Formation*
		%	%	%	%
Jamaica	(1960)[1]	248.6	23.3	30.9	10.0
Trinidad and Tobago	(1962)[2]	298.3	29.8	33.6	21.6
British Guiana	(1960)[3]	85.4	28.6	34.6	n.a.
Barbados	(1961)[4]	32.1	13.8	49.0	n.a.

* Balance of payments deficit on current account, which includes *all* net accruals of foreign profits even where they may be reinvested in the country.

SOURCES

[1] *Jamaica Independence Plan 1963–1968.*
[2] *Trinidad and Tobago Five-Year Plan 1964–1968.*
[3] Kundu, 'Inter-Industry Table for British Guiana'.
[4] O'Loughlin, *A Survey of Economic Potential and Capital Needs.*

TABLE V

INDUSTRIAL ORIGIN OF GROSS DOMESTIC PRODUCT (PERCENTAGES)

	1961 *Jamaica*[1]	*1961* *Trinidad and Tobago*[2]	*1960* *British Guiana*[3]	*1956* *Barbados*[4]	*1961* *Leewards and Windwards*[5]
Agriculture, Forestries, and Fisheries	12.7	11.8	27.2	33.7	38.6
Mining and Processing	8.6	30.8	8.6	0.6	1.9 (Mining and Processing, and Manufacturing combined)
Manufacturing	13.3	12.6	10.2	17.4	
Construction	11.2	5.0	11.2	7.6	9.6
Government	7.9	9.8	9.8	10.0	17.7
Public Utilities	1.1	3.5	0.9		included in manufacturing
Transport and Communications	6.9	3.8	7.0	6.3	2.2
Distribution	15.8	12.8	14.6	10.8	14.7
All Other Sources	22.5	9.9	10.4	13.6	15.3

SOURCES

[1] *Economic Survey*, Jamaica, 1962.
[2] Rampersad, 'Growth and Structural Change in Trinidad and Tobago'.
[3] Kundu, 'Inter-Industry Table for British Guiana'.
[4] J. Bethel, 'A National Accounts Study of the Economy of Barbados', *Social and Economic Studies*, IX, No. 2 (June, 1960).
[5] O'Loughlin, *A Survey of Economic Potential and Capital Needs.*

bago between 1951 and 1961 the rate of growth of this sector (excluding poultry and livestock) was slower than the rate of population increase, while in Jamaica it probably stagnated.

In fact, there is sharp dualism within the agricultural sector of most Caribbean countries. On the one hand, there is the estate or plantation producing crops usually geared to the export market and using relatively large amounts of capital per man and relatively advanced techniques. On the other hand, there is the peasant who produces either export staples or food for the home market or, as is common, both at the same time. Here capital per head is smaller and the techniques employed less advanced than in plantation agriculture and this fact reflects itself in lower yields per man and lower yields per acre in peasant agriculture.

The export sector, although more efficient, is also vulnerable. In the case of several crops—bananas in the Windwards, sugar in Jamaica, Trinidad and Tobago, Barbados, British Guiana, and the Leewards, citrus in Jamaica, and Trinidad and Tobago—remunerative production is vitally dependent on special preferences or special commodity agreements granted principally by the U.K. and to a smaller extent by Canada. These preferences are important because the Caribbean countries are high-cost producers of these commodities.

Dualism within the agricultural sector is only a manifestation of the more general phenomenon of dualism in the Caribbean economy. Thus a comparison of employment by industrial sector with output by industrial sector reveals striking contrasts in output per man: in Trinidad and Tobago, for instance, average output per man was $22,393 in petroleum mining and processing, some eight-and-a-half times as high as average output in manufacturing—$2,585—or in agriculture—$2,040. Employment by sectors is shown in Table VI.

Incidentally, we must note that the relatively low percentage of employment in agriculture in Trinidad and Tobago (21 per cent) should not be taken as an index of transformation. Like the small share of output, it is a sign of *malaise,* and it represents both the dominance of oil and

TABLE VI

EMPLOYMENT BY SECTORS 1960 (PERCENTAGES)

	Jamaica	*Trinidad and Tobago*	*British Guiana*	*Barbados*	*Leewards and Windwards*
Agriculture	39.0	21.1	37.0	26.4	46.0
Mining and Quarrying	0.7	4.9	3.8	0.6	0.2
Manufacturing*	14.8	15.5	16.3	15.2	11.2
Construction	8.2	11.4	8.0	10.5	10.8
Transport and Communications	3.2	6.2	4.8–	5.2	3.7
Distribution	9.9	13.3	11.3	17.3	9.7
Other Services	24.2	27.5	18.8	24.7	18.3
Total	100.0	100.0	100.0	100.0	100.0

* Includes processing of mineral and agricultural products, except in British Guiana, where alumina processing is included under 'Mining'.

SOURCES: 1960 Census Data; and J. Harewood, 'Employment in Trinidad and Tobago', Central Statistical Office, Research Papers, No. 1 (Port-of-Spain, December, 1963).

the neglect of agricultural production for domestic consumption.

Third, the important share of the tertiary or service sectors does not only reflect transformation but also the large volume of underemployment and lack of opportunities for more productive employment.

The unemployment picture is somewhat confused because of the conceptual and definitional problems of measuring unemployment and underemployment. In particular, two sets of estimates are available, based on different definitions. The definition which we use here is 'those persons of working age, able to work, wanting and having actively sought work within one month prior to the survey'. On this basis unemployment in 1960 amounted to 12.7 per cent, 10.6 per cent, and 11.3 per cent of the respective labour forces in Jamaica, Trinidad and Tobago, and British Guiana. Underemployment is also very severe; in the absence of generally agreed definitions and procedures for measurement we do not give any data. Suffice it to say that underemployment is severe whether measured in terms of numbers of the labour force engaged in low-productivity and low-income occupations or in terms of man-months worked.[2]

One of the most remarkable phenomena of contemporary social science is that total output can grow quite rapidly without a corresponding, or indeed significant, increase in employment. Many of the Caribbean economies have exhibited this phenomenon in greater or lesser degree. For example, in Puerto Rico, while very rapid rates of growth of output have been experienced since the institution of the 'Fomento' programme in the forties, unemployment has remained at a very high level of some 13 to 14 per cent of the labour force. Other countries, too, outside the Caribbean have undergone similar experiences: in India the absolute amount of unemployment actually increased over the period of the second Five-Year Plan in spite of the notable

[2] A good analysis of the employment situation in Trinidad and Tobago for the period 1946 to 1960 is given in Jack Harewood, 'Employment in Trinidad and Tobago', *C.S.O. Research Papers No. 1* (Port-of-Spain, 1963).

progress achieved in total output as well as in infrastructure and other fields.

The genesis of the employment problem in the Caribbean is the high rate of growth of the labour force (currently 2.4 per cent per annum in Trinidad and Tobago) combined with the capital-intensive nature of modern technology. This is the simple but fundamental explanation and is of course not peculiar to the Caribbean. Not only have capital-intensive processes characterized many of the new industries, but labour-saving devices have been introduced into major existing industries–especially petroleum and sugar, where employment has actually declined in recent years.

However, as we have seen, the employment problem in the Caribbean has been further aggravated by recent wage tendencies which have had three effects.

The first is one we have already referred to: the understandable urge by trade unions to extend to other less productive sectors the wage levels obtaining in the highly productive sectors, which then have neither the incentive nor the means to create jobs. The relatively high wage rates obtainable in the modern sector also convert underemployment or low-productivity employment into open unemployment by raising the 'supply price' of labour. This occurs because the expectations of what constitutes a 'reasonable' income are raised and, short of receiving this 'reasonable' income, individuals prefer to remain unemployed rather than engage in low-productivity occupations such as peasant agriculture, services, or handicrafts.

This effect is quite distinct from the influence that a rapid rate of increase in wage rates in a particular industry may have on the substitution of machines (always imported in the Caribbean) for local labour. This argument, although often put forward dogmatically, should not always be uncritically accepted. Its validity depends on the ratio of wage costs to other costs in the particular industry concerned and on the extent to which the product it makes has to face competition abroad. The truth of the matter may well be that in many modern industries more mechanized techniques are simply more efficient than less mechanized ones, even where wage rates are relatively low. To recognize this, however, is not to deny that big increases in wage rates or the desire to minimize the numbers employed in conditions of unsettled labour relations may *accelerate* the introduction of more mechanized techniques.

The third effect has also been analysed already. It is based on the Seers model of the functioning of an open petroleum economy in the short period when an increase in wage rates which is faster than the rate of increase in exports may, through the operation of a sort of 'wages-fund' mechanism, check the expansion of employment.

Many–in fact nearly all–underdeveloped countries have 'surplus labour'. But what makes the situation in the Caribbean so explosive potentially is the large amount of open unemployment in the towns, especially among young people. On the other hand, in less urbanized countries, surplus labour which takes the form of disguised unemployment in the rural areas may perhaps be tolerated by its victims for a longer period.

It has often been pointed out–quite correctly–that there has been real progress in the employment situation in the Caribbean in that the jobs created in modern industry have been well-paid high-productivity jobs, even though these have been inadequate in number and often at the expense of existing lower-productivity jobs (as in Puerto Rico). It is clear, however, that from a social point of view, such a state of affairs cannot entirely be regarded with equanimity by policy-makers.

The public finance system in the Caribbean has three features worth mentioning.

The first is the pressure on governmental capital and recurrent expenditures exerted by the rapid rate of growth of population. This pressure is felt particularly in the field of education. The consequence of the decline in death rates in recent years is the large number of children of school age; and this group is growing even faster than the general population. In Trinidad and Tobago the percentage of the population aged fifteen years and under is as high as 42 per cent.

Second, there is no capital market in any of the countries and this restricts the ability of governments to borrow large amounts locally for the financing of capital expenditures.

Third, incentives in the form of income-tax holidays and other fiscal concessions are granted to the growing sectors of the economy, in particular manufacturing, tourism, and petroleum. This means that the increase in revenue tends to lag behind the growth of the Gross Domestic Product; and this of course adversely affects the recurrent balance of the government's budget. It also means that personal incomes and personal expenditures bear a disproportionate share of the burden of fiscal imposts as compared with company income.

The result of these three features is heavy reliance on foreign aid in spite of very commendable fiscal efforts by the governments.

Except in Jamaica, which has a central bank, the monetary system of the Caribbean is the characteristic colonial Currency Board system. In its pure form, this system, which in essence is a very rigid form of the Gold Standard, requires 100 per cent backing in the form of sterling assets for local currency. Recently the system has been modified to allow for a small fiduciary issue. The Currency Board system implies that sterling and local currency are automatically convertible into one another at fixed rates of exchange in unlimited amounts. This in turn implies that Caribbean governments cannot impose exchange controls against the pound sterling. Further, the commercial banks are all branches of banks with head offices overseas. In theory this monetary system could work to ensure that the rate of growth of the money supply—and so of domestic expenditure—is rigidly tied to the state of the balance of payments (on both current and capital account); but the connection may not be so rigid because of 'autonomous' action by the commercial banks in extending credit locally independently of the state of the balance of payments.[3]

[3] See Analyst, 'Currency and Banking in Jamaica', *Social and Economic Studies,* Vol. 1, No. 4 (August, 1953); and C. Y. Thomas, 'The Balance of Payments and Money Supplies in a Colonial Economy', *Social and Economic Studies,* Vol. 12, No. 1 (March, 1963). The first is the pioneering and the second the definitive study of colonial monetary arrangements in the Caribbean.

But even if the commercial banks bring in funds from outside to create local credit, independently of movements in the balance of payments, the local managers of the economy have no control over the monetary situation.

It should also be noted that the establishment of the Central Bank in Jamaica has not created an independent currency nor does the Bank possess any real possibility of monetary management of the economy.[4]

It should be emphasized that in this dependent monetary system deficit financing is ruled out and consequently there is not much possibility of domestic inflation, the domestic price level being largely determined by movements in export and import prices. Thus Caribbean economic development has not been plagued with the monetary vicissitudes which have affected so many other developing countries.

Commercial and exchange control policies have been characterized by a high degree of openness. We have seen that there can be no exchange controls against sterling because the monetary system requires automatic convertibility between the local currency and sterling. When Britain moved to sterling convertibility in 1958, all the Caribbean Commonwealth countries followed automatically. Import licensing on the whole is not widely used to protect local industry, except in Jamaica which has recently acceded to the G.A.T.T. and which may therefore be expected not to intensify such controls. The tariff is in fact the main instrument of protection in the Caribbean. In 1962 Trinidad and Tobago modernized her tariff structure by increasing duties on durable consumer goods and on commodities being produced or capable of being produced locally and lowering duties on, or freeing, machinery and raw materials in order to protect local industry and assist the balance of payments. This was an important and historic step away from the colonial economic system; but by and large the Caribbean economies, including Trinidad and Tobago, still remain highly open in terms of commercial and foreign exchange policies.

[4] See Lloyd Best and Alister McIntyre, 'A First Appraisal of Monetary Management in Jamaica', *Social and Economic Studies,* Vol. 10, No. 3 (September, 1961).

It is interesting to observe one of the absurd aspects of the open economy in the Caribbean. This is the availability of consumer credit (or hire-purchase) facilities for the purchase of imported durable consumer goods. Hire-purchase booms have in more than one case been financed by an inflow of foreign capital! Not only does the system permit of external borrowing to finance consumption; such borrowing is used to finance imports of luxuries or semi-luxuries when there is a large amount of domestic unemployment and when the glaring necessity exists to mobilize domestic resources for development. Needless to say, advertising conspires with the existence of consumer credit facilities to lure people to the delights provided by the gadgets of modern civilization.

The extent of Caribbean economic co-operation is at present limited. Intraregional trade in 1962 amounted to only 6 per cent of total trade. Petroleum from Trinidad and rice from British Guiana are the main items. The economies have all been geared to metropolitan markets and sources of supply. During the days of Federation a customs union plan was drawn up but the breakup of the Federation prevented its implementation.

After this very brief survey of the characteristics and problems of the Caribbean economies, I think it legitimate to draw three conclusions.

First, structural transformation, even in Trinidad and Tobago and Jamaica, has still a long way to go—in spite of the relatively high *per capita* income.

Second, the economies are very dependent, not only structurally in the sense that there is a high ratio of foreign trade to Gross Domestic Product, but also in that there is great reliance on foreign private capital inflows and foreign aid, there is little financial and monetary autonomy, and there are still important gaps in the domestic financial structure. Foreign decision-making is all-pervasive and touches many parts of economic and financial life.

Third, because people have begun to taste the fruits of development as a result of the fortuitous combination of circumstances of the 1950's, any slowing down in the pace of development is fraught with dangers of social and political unrest. The development effort in the years ahead has to be intensified in order to accommodate the rising population with their heightened expectations of material improvement; in order to compensate for the expected decline in the rate of growth of the leading mineral export sectors of bauxite and petroleum; in order to compensate for the removal of opportunities for emigration; and in order to preserve the intrinsically valuable institutions of political democracy and a free trade-union movement.

In order to summarize the foregoing and to promote clarity of thought, let us now recall the principal structural and institutional characteristics and the major problems of the Caribbean economies relevant to economic planning. Let us further very schematically divide these into three types: those typical of many underdeveloped countries, those typical of small open economies, and those peculiar to the Caribbean. As in all classifications, the distinction between the three types of characteristics is somewhat rough. For example, a developed country may have one or more of the characteristics listed under all three heads, while a large underdeveloped country may exhibit some of the characteristics of small open economies, and so on. The purpose of the classification is purely that of convenience.

1. Typical of many underdeveloped countries:
   (*a*) an unfavourable ratio between population on the one hand and the stock of capital and of natural resources on the other hand (the Malthusian constraint);
   (*b*) the dualism of the economic structure as reflected in the varying levels of productivity in different sectors and in the large volume of unemployed, whose productivity is of course zero;
   (*c*) a domestic agricultural sector, the growth of whose production is lagging behind the increase in demand for food;
   (*d*) the absence of a developed capital market.
2. Typical of small open economies:
   (*a*) a high ratio of foreign trade to Gross Domestic Product;
   (*b*) the domination of the export trade and in some

cases the whole economy by one particular export —petroleum in Trinidad and Tobago, bauxite in Jamaica, sugar in Barbados and the Leewards, bananas in the Windwards;

(*c*) the absence of a diversified resource base and the narrowness of domestic markets;

(*d*) the almost complete lack of domestic interindustry transactions, most transactions being with the outside world;

(*e*) the possibility of the export of savings as a result of the branch nature of banking and financial institutions, the automatic functioning of the currency system, and the absence of rigid exchange controls;

(*f*) as a corollary of (*e*), the absence of serious domestically generated inflationary pressures.

3. Peculiar to the West Indies:

(*a*) the dichotomy between plantation and peasant agriculture, a peculiarly West Indian manifestation of dualism;

(*b*) a high-cost export agriculture, sheltered by special and other preferential arrangements in the U.K. and Canadian markets;

(*c*) the firm commitment by present leaders to full-blown political democracy and a free trade-union movement;

(*d*) the pressure to generalize wage rates obtaining in the modern sector, but which are beyond the capacity of the less advanced sectors to pay;

(*e*) the sharply rising expectations of the population as a result of long contact with and proximity to the Western way of life;

(*f*) the dependence on foreign capital for the development of the mineral-producing, manufacturing and, to some extent, the sugar industries and the consequent large gap between the domestic product and the national income;

(*g*) the nature of the public finance system as a consequence of large educational and other recurrent expenditures, revenue foregone through tax incentives and the diseconomies of scale in providing administrative services for small populations.

Having set out the characteristics of the economies very baldly, we may now summarize the problems of the Caribbean in equally bald fashion:

1. The Caribbean economies, in spite of their relatively high *per capita* income, still need to undergo further transformation, especially in view of the slowing down in the rate of growth of the leading mineral-exporting sectors and the disappearance of opportunities for emigration.

2. However broadly or narrowly defined, the Caribbean illustrates many of the characteristics of small open economies as well as some of those of the large underdeveloped countries, and has many peculiar features of its own as well.

3. These peculiarities include the obsessive urge for North American standards of consumption; the dichotomy between plantation and peasant agriculture; the dependence of export agriculture on Commonwealth Preference and special marketing arrangements; the influence exercised by the wage levels in the dominant enclave sectors on the rest of the economy; the peculiar nature of the public finance system; and the great dependence on foreign capital.

II INTERPRETATIONS OF DOMESTIC ORGANIZATION

11.

For an understanding of the familial and household patterns of West Indians of African ancestry, it is historically and theoretically appropriate to open with an essay by Melville J. Herskovits, who pioneered anthropological studies of the New World Negro, or, as he termed them, Afroamericans. In this article, he proposes a general program of Afroamerican research, indicating its scope, complexity, and potential scientific contributions and linking with it such concepts as retentions, syncretisms, and reinterpretations, which have since made their way into the anthropological lexicon. Herskovits' framework for the study of African culture survivals in the New World provides a point of departure for black studies in general as well as for explanations, exemplified in this section, of sociocultural patterns among West Indians of African descent.

MELVILLE J. HERSKOVITS (1895–1963) was born in the United States and received his anthropological training and doctorate from Columbia University. For many years he was Professor of Anthropology at Northwestern University and Director of its program of African Studies. His major research in the West Indies was carried out in Surinam, Trinidad, and Haiti and in western Nigeria, Dahomey, and among the Ashanti in Africa. Among his major publications, *The Myth of the Negro Past, Life in a Haitian Valley,* and, with his wife Frances, *Trinidad Village* and *Rebel Destiny* are of special interest to West Indianists.

Problem, Method and Theory in Afroamerican Studies

Melville J. Herskovits

I

This paper will discuss three elements in the scientific study of the New World Negro and his African background that, hitherto in large measure implicit in my writings on the subject, suggest their timeliness for explicit formulation. These comprise a definition and delimitation of the field, which is essential for clarity of purpose in research and for directing future effort; some of the methodological concepts and techniques that have been successfully employed; and some of the hypotheses which have guided investigation and developed out of experience in the field.

It is not always realized how recent is systematic study of the Afroamerican field. Little of the present substantial store of facts concerning New World cultures, or the civilizations from which they derive, or the historical circumstances of their formation were available two decades ago, so that it is apparent why the need to amass data took first place in the attention of students. This continuing emphasis was particularly relevant in view of the vastness of the area in which New World Negroes live and the variety of their cultures, the complexity of the African civilizations from which they derive, the technical difficulties in the way of studying provenience and the intricacy of the acculturative processes to which they have been exposed.

Today, the scientific importance of Afroamerican studies as a field for research is firmly established. A climate of

From *Afroamerica,* International Institute of Afroamerican Studies, Mexico, Vol. I, 1945, pp. 5–24.

opinion, both lay and scholarly, which encourages further research, has been created, while the body of factual materials and comparative analyses that has been amassed by those working in the field allows hypotheses and procedures to be assessed in terms of collected data and achieved results rather than of probable validity and possible return. It thus appears a logical moment for stock-taking, for the explicit statement of theoretical assumptions, and for a refinement of techniques.

II

An outstanding characteristic of the field of Afroamerican studies is its interdisciplinary nature, which must be taken into account whenever problems of definition or method are under discussion. But more than that, Afroamerican studies not only cross disciplines, but are also intercontinental, treating of peoples living in North, South and Central America, the Caribbean, and Africa. The implications of this interdisciplinary and intercontinental scope, when thought of in terms of the conventional organization of scholarly study, are many. For the field cuts across so many boundaries that it cannot be defined in terms of any commonly accepted categories—a fact that accounts for its late recognition as a definable area of scholarship and for certain practical difficulties that at one time or another have faced those who have worked on its many problems.

That the ramifications of such studies extend into the social sciences, the humanities and the biological sciences, follows from the nature of the data. In this our field is no different from any research that is concerned with obtaining a rounded view of the life of man, or of any group of men. It is nonetheless worthwhile to recall how in Afroamerican studies investigation has had to have recourse to the resources of anthropology, history and psychology to reach an understanding of the social structures, the accepted patterns of behavior, and the past development of the societies studied; how linguistics, musicology and comparative literature have had to be called upon to contribute their techniques for insight into some of the most revealing data in the field; and how such problems as the incidence and effects of race-crossing, of the dynamics of Negro population formation and the like have had to be studied in terms of the techniques and orientations of human biology and demography. Not every student can study every problem, but most students of the Negro have come to realize that their competence in the discipline of their primary affiliation gives them but a starting-point for further effort; and that their field of interest has characteristically broadened as the data have been followed where they led, even when these called for disregard of current delimitation of scholarly concern.

In similar fashion, accepted regional approaches to the ordering of research have had to be transcended. Researches restricted to Latin American problems, or to the United States, or to Africa or to an island of the Caribbean alone, of course, make their contributions to Afroamerican studies. For where data are as sparse as in this field, all contributions are welcome. But those whose perspectives have not been so circumscribed know well how much researches in these areas are enriched by a broader point of view. One of the most telling instances of this is the aid which the study of New World Negro peoples can bring toward a fuller comprehension of the cultures of Africa itself. This is striking because it reverses the customary order of thought, which focuses on African survivals in the New World. That the study of African ways of life is essential to an understanding of survivals of these customs is a truism; but what, it may be asked, can the analysis of survivals contribute to comprehension of their own sources?

Though the matter cannot be documented here, it need merely be recalled that survival is an index of tenacity, which in turn reveals general orientations in parent cultures that may at times not be given proper stress without such background. This is the case as concerns the place of religion in African cultures, whose theoretical importance will be considered in a later page. Furthermore, specific complexes of significance that have been quite overlooked in Africanist studies are to be revealed by investigation on this side of the Atlantic. A recent example of this is had in the instance of the place of drummers, not only in cult-rituals, but in the life of the community as a whole. First noted in a New World Negro culture, it required only brief questioning of Africans to reveal itself as an important facet of social organization in Africa itself, that had hitherto not been explored at all.

Though overlapping many disciplines and a number of geographical regions, the field of Afroamerican studies is distinct from all those on which it impinges, from which it follows that it is therefore often a matter of emphasis and intent just where a given piece of research is to be classified. This is the source of many practical difficulties. Papers on African cultures, deriving from studies stimulated by an interest in the New World descendants of Africa, may appear in Africanist journals where much of their usefulness to those who concentrate on New World Negro societies is lost, while reports on historical aspects of the field, often published in historical journals, are not seen by those studying Afroamerican problems whose primary affiliation is with other disciplines. Conversely Africanists who confine their work to the peoples of that continent, or historians of the Negro whose range of interest is defined by their discipline, fail to benefit from New World studies, or from work on other than historical phases of Negro life that might open new vistas to them.

This may meet with the reasonable suggestion that there is enough justification for the existence of the conventional disciplines in their achieved results to give us pause before we cross their boundaries, tested by time and experience. In the final analysis, however, the ordering of the most fruitful results can be had only when the facts are studied as they lie, without those preconceptions which, in a case such as that under discussion, lead to distortion if not considered in terms of all interrelated aspects.

This leads us to the nature of the contributions Afroamerican studies can be expected to make, for the point is basic in discussing the importance of the field for scientific research. More than anything else, it comprises data that, because of the available historic controls and the range of related materials, go far toward approximating those laboratory situations which, in the study of man, are more difficult to achieve than any other single methodological factor in the repertory of science. Thus the very fact that to conduct Afroamerican studies calls on the techniques of many disciplines, and is carried on in many different areas, gives it a special significance for the scientific study of man. For here can be prosecuted those comparative researches of mixtures of physical types, of languages and of modes of behavior in terms of known rather than of assumed past contacts. And while in this, Afroamerican research does not differ in kind from studies among other groups of differing backgrounds between whom contact has taken place or is in process, it is to be distinguished from them in degree, as expressed in the very broad variety of situations that, in this field, are to be investigated.

It is not difficult to phrase the manner in which the Afroamerican field differs from the several disciplines on which it draws. To the extent that its problems are to be comprehended within their areas of interest, such problems have an affiliation immediately recognizable. Thus a study of land-tenure in a Caribbean island might find ready reception in a journal devoted to economics, the analysis of a Negro musical style in a musicological publication, the description of the physical characteristics of a North American Negro community in an organ devoted to the problems of physical anthropology. Even where cross-disciplinary considerations have entered, publication can be achieved in journals devoted to the discipline of principal emphasis or, more often, in the subject with which the student is technically affiliated. This is one of the reasons why bibliographic problems are so difficult in Afroamerican research.

To draw the line between area fields and Afroamerican research requires somewhat more careful distinctions, for here the problem of efficient historic relationships enters. It is simple to state that study of the Negro in Latin America contributes to the Latin American field; even though, in this sense, we once again encounter overlapping. Yet it is open to question how much a detailed investigation of certain Negro social conventions or music or religious beliefs that have not significantly diffused to other population elements in a given Latin American country is to be regarded as a contribution to the Latin American field, except in a secondary sense.

In the Africanist field, the matter is somewhat different. In earlier years, before the provenience of New World Negroes was known as well as it is at present, it was held that a knowledge of African culture in general was essential to effective comparative study of the New World Negro. Today, however, one may ask why, except for general background, this is needed. Field research on the cultures of East Africa, the study of the slave trade in Zanzibar, the analysis of Bushman art, or investigation of Zulu physical types deal with peoples who are outside the range of effective historic impact on New World Negro patterns, since so few individuals from the parts of Africa where they live were brought to the New World that their influence in the formation of New World Negro types and cultures could only have been negligible.

A further point to be made in clarifying the limits of the Afroamerican field has to do with the study of those situations of everyday life in many countries which, as they affect the Negro, present practical problems of great moment that press for immediate solutions. Because the student is also the citizen, with heightened awareness of the needs engendered by these situations, the temptation is great to give over the long-term view in favor of *ad hoc* solutions of such issues. This has been especially true in the United States, where for many years an almost exclusive preoccupation with action programs discouraged the type of broad research which characterizes the Afroamerican field. This is not the place to consider the problem of applied science as against research on a long-term basis, yet it is important that the distinction be made and maintained. For even in the short view, the broader base of comprehension that the results of Afroamerican studies can give those whose task is to frame policies for practical procedures would, of itself, justify the position that such studies must be held distinct from remedial programs in the troubled field of race relations.

Finally, it must be stressed that Afroamerican studies are not to be limited to the study of Negro populations and their cultures alone, but must follow through to assess the contributions Africa has made to the peoples among whom the Negroes live. Thus when race-crossing carries Negroid elements into the genetic composition of the non-Negroid groups, this is quite as significant a subject for research as it is to determine the physical traits of the Negroid group. Parallel cultural phenomena have not been systematically studied at all, except, perhaps, in Brazil. Yet just as race-crossing invariably follows on contact between peoples of different physical types, so cultural borrowing,—two-way borrowing—also ensues. The theoretical importance of this fact is clear. Here the problem is stated to emphasize the necessity of including, in the repertory of Afroamerican research, investigation not only into the maintenance of African tradition in the New World, but also into how, and to what extent African custom was diffused to the aboriginal Indian peoples and to those of European derivation who experienced prolonged contact with Africans and their descendants.

III

To the extent that the problems of Afroamerican research fall within the compass of established disciplines, or require interdisciplinary consideration of a type already employed outside the Afroamerican field, the question of method presents no difficulty. A comparative study of Negro music utilizes the techniques of the musicologist, one of language employs the methods of the linguists, research into the present-day Negro family or of living standards of Negro populations uses the approaches of the sociologist or the economist. Overall descriptions of any of these cultures, whether in Africa or the New World, require ethnological field techniques, while analyses of psychological problems arising out of the way of life of Negro peoples utilizes the methods of social psychology. Studies of the slave trade, or of the economics of the plantation, though cross-disciplinary, find research techniques at hand in the modes of investigation employed by economic historians.

Strangely enough, the resources of ethnology and history have only recently been welded into a usable tool. Despite the fact that there are historical schools of ethnology and social historians, there has been but little contact across these disciplines. The "history" of these ethnological schools has been based on the reconstruction of events rather than on documentation; while the social historian, despite the illumination his writings have thrown on the development of the institutions with which he has dealt, has worked primarily as an historian and only rarely and recently has had recourse to the methods of the social sciences. There are, of course, some exceptions to this statement. Studies of certain Indian groups in the United States afford instances of how the use of historic sources has been able to illuminate ethnographic problems, while historians of the American frontier are more and more finding it essential to take into account the relevant ethnographic facts.

Experience is teaching us that the methods of these two disciplines, more than any other two, must be jointly called on if the varying situations that are to be studied comparatively in the Afroamerican field are to be analyzed with comprehension. It must be stressed that this field, constituting as it does, a special instance of culture contact, derives its greatest significance from the fact that it so superbly documents the problems of cultural dynamics. Now in studies of culture contact it is essential to establish the cultural base-lines from which the processes of change began, to know facts concerning the culture or cultures that have emerged, or are emerging from the contact, and to comprehend how, and under what circumstances, the phenomena as observed in the culture that has resulted from the contact actually developed. The first of these requires ethnographic study, and in some measure the second. But the second also requires historical treatment, while the third demands an attack that is essentially historical.

The *ethnohistorical method,* as this combined ethnological and historical approach is to be termed, has been basic in systematic Afroamerican research, for until the use of this method was fully established, it was found difficult to achieve perspective, and comparative studies were but elusive. It is through the use of this method, and only by its use, that it has been possible to recover the predominant regional and tribal origins of the New World Negroes and, with this information in hand, to turn to ethnographic research in Africa with a certainty that the materials gathered there would be relevant to the problems of cultural retention and cultural change met with in the New World. Similarly this method has made it possible to test the validity of the rich store of existing documentary information concerning slaves and slaving, plantation life and the responses of the Negro to it, and the like, and to realize much of the potential contribution of these materials. Most important, also, has been the continuous comparison of ethnographic facts as found on the two sides of the Atlantic; for ethnohistory, as employed in the study of Afroamerican problems, consists essentially of the application of a comparative ethnographic technique in unravelling, on the basis of written sources, the historic progression of events that led up to the establishment and functioning of New World Negro cultures as they exist at the present time.

Not only has the ethnohistorical approach been able to fix the African origins of New World Negro cultures, but it has been of great value in accounting for differences that are found between the cultures of Negroes living in different parts of the New World. Thus comparative ethnographic studies have revealed that the cultures of the Dutch Guiana Bush Negroes and of the Maroons of Jamaica manifest their Africanisms predominantly in terms of Gold Coast retentions, while those of Haiti are of Dahomean and Yoruba derivation. The documents tell us that Dutch and English planters preferred Gold Coast slaves, not only because they were more likely to find these for sale by their own nationals, but because of rationalizations that came to be set up concerning the worth of Negroes from tribes of this area compared to other kinds of Negroes. On the other hand, they make it equally clear that Latin slave owners preferred Dahomean and Yoruba slaves, for the same reasons, and thus resolve what would otherwise be a difficult problem.

Another methodological device that has proved of outstanding value in analyzing the problems of Afroamerican research is that of a scale of intensity of Africanisms over the New World. This implies a logically conceived continuum which ranges from retentions that are completely African, or almost so, to those least African and most European–the Indian elements having been so little studied that they cannot be classified. Such a continuum permits an arrangement of the data that gives insight into the processes of cultural change by allowing comparisons to be drawn between cultures whose various aspects lie at different points on it. This, in turn, facilitates analysis of the processes that have operated to bring about the cultural changes observed in the course of field research.

It must be emphasized that, as in all scientific study, a classificatory device such as the scale of intensity of Africanisms is but a means to an end rather than an end in itself. In this case, the end that is envisaged is that comprehension of process which alone can lead to valid prediction. To be revealing in terms of this end the classification must be derived through induction, and flow from the data, rather than be imposed upon it after the fashion of *a priori* categories that tend to force materials into groupings that do violence to the scientific reality. Scientific analysis is impossible without classification of data, and herein lies the importance of this series of categories; but it cannot be too strongly emphasized that classification, of itself, can tell us nothing about causes, or relationships, or the processes of change.

A *scale of intensity of Africanisms* was first established somewhat more than a decade ago. At that time, however, the data were meager compared with present resources, so that of necessity the listing was tentative, and had to be in terms of whole cultures or areas or countries. That is, places were assigned to such Negro groups as those of the Guianas or the Virgin Islands, or Haiti, on a scale ranging from most to least African. A revision of this original statement was made several years later, but still in overall terms, though additional data from various regions were utilized to amplify and rectify the listing. While preferable to the earlier statement, this revision proved to be simpler than the nature of the materials has come to demand. For overall categories of this character do not adequately illuminate the complexities of the data, and often indeed, hide relationships rather than reveal them, which is their intent.

The scale given in this paper represents an application to Afroamerican studies of certain techniques of analyzing cultures that have been increasingly employed as greater acquaintance with human ways of living have been gained. That is, we now know that the broad divisions of culture, even particular institutions, behave differently in different situations. This does not mean that a given body of tradition is to be thought of as other than a unified whole, whose elements are all closely interrelated. But it has come to be recognized that the historic forces that are operative in any given situation–forces which, by their very nature, are unique in each circumstance–will eventuate differently in different instances as far as differing aspects of culture are concerned, or where different institutions within a given cultural category are involved.

The principle of cultural focus, discussed in later pages, is helpful in this connection, since its implications for the dynamics of culture in this situation, as in all others, is that it offers an important leverage to bring about changes in certain aspects of a people's way of life as against others or, under contact, to make for differential resistance to change. Thus pressures from outside the Negro groups to give over economic patterns were far greater in the New World than those militating against the retention of folktales or secular musical forms, so that the latter two manifest far more of an African character than the former. On the other hand, inner compulsions derived from the focal concerns of Africans with the supernatural tended to resist varying pressures, in varying countries, employing the different kinds of adjustments that have been described, with the result that Africanisms figure prominently in New World Negro religious behavior everywhere.

A refinement of the earlier scale of intensity of Africanisms, not in terms of total cultures, but of aspects within each culture, such as our data now make possible, is given here. In addition, a further refinement has been achieved by subdividing the areas which earlier appeared as units, where the materials indicate that within a given region districts can be distinguished wherein the pattern and degree of African retentions differ. But since it is apparent that in every part of the New World where Negroes live, excepting only the Guiana Bush, class differences operate so as to make for variation in the number and intensity of Africanisms within each Negro group, our table will record only that degree of retention for each group which is closest to African custom.

Because this point is crucial for a proper reading of the table, and an adequate understanding of its significance, it may be amplified here. Bahia, for example, is rated as most African in language because only there have certain African tongues been retained, as against retention, at most, of no more than African words or phrases or grammatical structures elsewhere. In their daily usage, as a matter of fact, the Bahian Negroes show perhaps less African elements than elsewhere, since they speak the same Portuguese as is spoken by other Brazilians, with fewer elements of African vocabulary, pronunciation or grammar than is found in the speech of almost any other New World Negro group.

It cannot be too strongly stressed that in every area of the New World, except in the Guiana Bush, variation in African forms of behavior stretches from the point of greatest intensity indicated in our table to almost conformity with European ways of life. The problem thus becomes one of accounting for differing degrees of variability in the different populations studied. But since the variation does in almost every case extend to the limit set by the conventions of European custom, it can be seen how significant is the analysis of retentions of African convention if we are to discover how far the distribution extends toward the patterns that made up the cultural endowment of the ancestors of present day Negro populations that are the central concern of Afroamerican research.

Table I presents, then, these degrees of intensities of Africanisms, listed by aspect of culture and by region in terms of the most African-like manifestation of a given cultural aspect or institution. The assignment of values in each instance has either been on the basis of my own field research in the regions listed, or on the reports of trained and competent observers in areas where I have not had first-hand contact. The weightings given the entries are broadly conceived, as is indicated by the terms used to denote the categories of intensity—"very African," "quite African," and the like. To be more specific would be merely to enlarge the area of possible disagreement between students, and to no purpose, since all classifications of such data must be subjective, at least at this point in our knowledge and with the technical resources for cultural analysis at hand. The sources are indicated in the note appended to the text of this paper.

Greater refinement in the treatment of these data might also be more revealing, but the technique of trait-analysis seems to be too mechanical, and to work too great violence to the unity of the cultural elements involved, to be profitably employed in this case. In like manner, the designations are to be regarded as having been set down for convenience only, and to consider them as anything more than useful symbols would be to introduce a note of spurious accuracy against which too great warning cannot be given.

It is apparent, from scanning the table, that the overall listings in the earlier ratings are in the main borne out by the tabulations of this more refined treatment, the principal clarification being in the direction of indicating variability of retention within a given country. Especially interesting is the indication that extension of the continuum toward the pole of African traditions can be greater in certain traits manifested in centers of population than in Brazil. Taken as a whole, however, the progression of

TABLE I*

SCALE OF INTENSITY OF NEW WORLD AFRICANISMS

(Only the greatest degree of retention is indicated for each group)

	Technology	*Economic*	*Social Organization*	*Non-kinship Institutions*
Guiana (bush)	b	b	a	a
Guiana (Paramaribo)	c	c	b	c
Haiti (peasant)	c	b	b	c
Haiti (urban)	e	d	c	c
Brazil (Bahia-Recife)	d	d	b	d
Brazil (Porto Alegre)	e	e	c	d
Brazil (Maranhão-rural)	c	c	b	e
Brazil (Maranhão-urban)	e	d	c	e
Cuba	e	d	c	b
Jamaica (Maroons)	c	c	b	b
Jamaica (Morant Bay)	e	c	b	b
Jamaica (general)	e	c	d	d
Honduras (Black Caribs)**	c	c	b	b
Trinidad (Port of Spain)	e	d	c	b
Trinidad (Toco)	e	d	c	c
Mexico (Guerrero)	d	e	b	b
Colombia (Choco)	d	d	c	c
Virgin Islands	e	d	c	d
U.S. (Gullah Islands)	c	c	c	d
U.S. (rural South)	d	e	c	d
U.S. (urban North)	e	e	c	d

a: very African b: quite African c: somewhat African d: a little African

*Derivations of the listings in Table I are given in a note at the end of the chapter.

Guiana, Haiti, Brazil, Jamaica, Trinidad, Cuba, Virgin Islands, the Gullah Islands, and southern and northern United States comprise a series wherein a decreasing intensity of Africanisms is manifest. The series will be filled in after field-work has been carried on in areas as yet unstudied, but there seems little prospect of finding New World Negro cultures more African than those of the interior of Dutch Guiana, nor, in recognizable form, less so than among certain Negro groups in the northern part of the United States.

Religion	*Magic*	*Art*	*Folklore*	*Music*	*Language*
a	a	b	a	a	b
a	a	e	a	a	c
a	a	d	a	a	c
b	b	e	a	a	c
a	a	b	a	a	a
a	a	e	a	a	c
c	b	e	b	b	d
a	b	e	d	a	b
a	a	b	b	a	a
b	a	e	a	a	c
a	a	e	a	a	a
b	b	e	a	b	c
b	a	e	b	c	e
a	a	e	b	a	e
c	b	e	b	b	d
c	b	e	b	?	e
c	b	e	b	e	e
e	b	e	b	b	d
c	b	e	a	b	b
c	b	e	b	b	e
c	b	e	d	b	e

e: trace of African customs, or absent ?: no report

**Carib Indian influences are strong in this culture.

Turning now to consider the different degree to which differing elements in each of these cultures have responded to contact with non-African ways of life, we see that the carry-over of Africanisms is anything but uniform over the individual cultures, being far greater in some aspects than in others. Certain generalizations can, however, be drawn. Music, folklore, magic and religion, on the whole, have retained more of their African character than economic life, or technology, or art, while language and social structures based on kinship or free association, tend to vary through all the degrees of intensity that are noted.

These differences are probably due to the circumstances of slave life, and confirm common sense observations made during the period of slavery. Slave owners were primarily concerned with the technological and economic aspects of the lives of their slaves, while the conditions of life as a slave also of necessity warped whatever patterns of African social structures the Negroes felt impelled to preserve. On the other hand, what tales were told or the songs that were sung made little difference to the masters, and few external blocks were placed in the way of their retention. In the case of religion, outer controls were of varying kinds and were responded to in varying degree, as is reflected in the intermediate position of this cultural element. Magic, which tends to go underground under pressure and can most easily be practised without direction—the force of the specific psychological compulsions here being of special importance—persisted in recognizable form everywhere, particularly since the similarity between African and European magic is so great that the one cultural stream must have operated to reinforce the other. The failure of African art to survive except in Guiana and to a lesser degree in Brazil is understandable when the life of the slave, which permitted little leisure and offered slight stimulus for the production of art in the aboriginal African style or, indeed, in any other style, is recalled.

One further fact which emerges from our table is the differing variability, over the New World as a whole, of the several aspects of the cultures as these have been listed. Only religion and language comprehend in maximum extension toward African patterns, all degrees of intensity. Minimum variation in this respect is shown by music, which everywhere has been retained in at least "quite African" form. The degree of variation within each of the groups is likewise interesting, since it is seen how the Bush-Negro culture, the most African, is also most homogeneous as far as the African nature of its several elements is concerned, while the cultures of the Negroes of the United States, though manifesting a comparable degree of homogeneity, expresses its homogeneous quality at the opposite end of the scale.

The facts thus shown hold both particular and general significance. To students of Afroamerican problems, differentials offer leads for further historical and ethnological analysis, since it is to be assumed that the explanation for such differentials is to be discovered in the modes of conducting slaving operations and in the circumstances of slave life, as these reacted upon the aboriginal patterns of individuals derived from the various relevant cultures of Africa. From the broader point of view of understanding culture as a whole, however, such treatment documents the concept of culture as a series of interrelated, but quasi-independent variables that undergo processes of change in accordance with the particular historical situation under which impact of new ideas and new customs has taken place, and the focal concerns of the peoples who, like the Negroes of the New World, made the cultural and psychological adjustments that were called forth by their historical experience.

IV

The hypotheses that underlie the study of African cultural survivals in the New World derive from a conception of human civilization that holds social behavior to be something learned rather than inborn and instinctive. This means that though there are as many cultures—that is, accepted modes of conduct, configurations of institutions, and systems of values and goals—as there are societies, every culture, or any of its elements, can be mastered by any individual without regard to race, or by any group that has the will and the opportunity to master it.

It follows from our concept of culture as something learned that the borrowing of traditions by one people from another is a simple matter, and research has actually established that cultural borrowing is a universal in human social experience. It is today clear that no two peoples have ever been in contact but that they have taken new ideas and new customs from each other, and this quite independently of whether that contact was friendly or hostile, whether it was between groups of the same size or of unequal size, whether differences of prestige existed between them or they met on a plane of equality.

The conception of culture on which our hypotheses are based thus envisages the operation of the principle of constant change—through borrowing and internal innovation—but at the same time assumes a high degree of stability in every culture, which is assured by the transmission of habits, customs, beliefs and institutions from one generation to the next. That is, the individual member of a society learns how to behave in a given situation, how to operate the techniques which assure his society its living, how to adapt to a given system of drives, rewards and values because he is taught or observes all these things. The resultant cultural conservatism gives to every way of life a tenaciousness, a toughness—in many writings not sufficiently recognized—which comes to be of special importance in the study of Africanisms among the Negroes of the New World.

If we assume, then, that culture is in constant change because it is learned, and not inborn, but is learned by the individuals that constitute any given society so well that the tendency of human beings to conserve tradition gives to every culture great stability, the problem next presented is to resolve this seeming paradox by studying those circumstances in which changes are instituted, or in which retention of conventions makes for successful resistance to change. It is essentially the problem of balancing the drives that induce acceptance of new customs as against the mechanisms that preserve earlier sanctioned modes of behavior. It is here that the field of Afroamerican studies can make its greatest contribution.

We may say that the basic hypothesis of culture as something learned is sharpened when it is perceived that under contact elements of a culture are the more effectively retained in the degree that they bear resemblance to newly experienced patterns of behavior or institutions. This, in turn, is further refined by references to the process of *syncretism,* the tendency to identify those elements in the new culture with similar elements in the old one, enabling the persons experiencing the contact to move from one to the other, and back again, with psychological ease. The outstanding instance of syncretism is the identification, in Catholic countries of the New World, of African deities with the saints of the Church—a phenomenon so well documented that it need but be mentioned here to make the point.

The discovery that the same principle is operative in West Africa, at the southern border of Mohammedan influence, where among the Hausa the pagan *iska* are identified with the *jinn* of the Koran extends its validity. But if we turn our analysis to Protestant countries, where syncretism of this sort is not possible, we find that though the names of African deities have been but rarely retained, syncretisms take other, more generalized forms. An example of this is the retention of the African requirement of initiation into religious groups through its syncretization with the Christian concept of sanctification achieved through preparation for baptism, or as expressed in the institution of the "mourning ground."

At this point another principle must be stated—that of *reinterpretation.* For where it is not possible to set up syncretisms, the force of cultural conservatism seeks expression in substance, rather than form, in psychological value rather than in name, if the original culture is to survive at all. Here the hypothesis of the importance of resemblance of the old element to the new is again involved. Though to a lesser degree than in the instance of syncretism, reinterpretation also requires that some characteristic of the new cultural element be correlated with a corresponding part of the original one by those to whom it is presented, before the mechanism can operate effectively.

In this fashion, the pattern of polygynous family structure has come to be reinterpreted in terms of successive, rather than of simultaneous plural matings, something which has set in motion an entire train of adjustments. Not the least of these has been the rejection, within the Negro group, of the European interpretation of illegitimacy as applied to offspring of unions not sanctioned by law, and to legal divorce, since these laws are meaningless in terms of aboriginal conventions. The extent to which new orientations of this kind find distribution among Negroes everywhere in the New World demonstrates the effectiveness of the mechanism, not only to achieve cultural but also psychological adaptation to the new setting. This could also be documented from other aspects of culture—economic life, or religion, or music—if considerations of space permitted. Here, however, the example given suffices to illustrate the principle that has been derived.

Retention of original custom under contact, whether through syncretism or reinterpretation is, however, merely one side of the problem, the other being the acceptance of what is newly presented. Here many imponderables enter, the most important being the degree to which outer acceptance involves transfer of values and interpretations in the psychological as well as in the institutional sense. This, of course, raises one of the most difficult problems in the entire field of cultural dynamics—whether any element of culture is ever taken over without some degree of reinterpretation, however free the borrowing.

If this particular question be for the moment disregarded, however, it is to be seen that just as syncretism and reinterpretation are means by which retention of the old is achieved, they are by the same token effective in encouraging the adoption of the new. A succession of matings entered into by a man or woman implies an acceptance of the monogamic principle, at the same time that it points to the method by which, through reinterpretation, the old polygynous tradition has been retained. Where African gods are syncretized with Catholic saints, the significance of the fact that the Negroes, as professing Catholics, have accepted the new religion must not be lost sight of by focusing attention too closely on the retention of aboriginal deities.

When we press the matter, however, we find that the problem is further complicated by the selective nature of borrowing on another level. On the basis of a comparative analysis of African and New World Negro cultures, it is apparent that even under the compulsions of the dominant culture of whites, Negroes have retained African religious beliefs and practices far more than they have retained economic patterns. But when we examine the patterns of African cultures, we find that there is no activity of everyday living but that it is validated by supernatural sanctions. And consequently, these figure far more in the total life of the people than does any other single facet of the culture such as those matters having to do with making a living, or family structure, or political institutions. This weighting of the concerns of a people constitutes the focus of their culture. *Cultural focus* is thus seen to be that phenomenon which gives a culture its particular emphasis; which permits the outsider to sense its special distinguishing flavor and to characterize its essential orientation in a few phrases.

The role of cultural focus is of such great importance in situations of cultural contact that a further hypothesis may be advanced to the effect that more elements which lie in the area of focus of a receiving culture will be retained than those appertaining to other aspects of the culture, acceptance being greater in those phases of culture further removed from the focal area. Where a culture is under pressure by a dominant group who seek to induce acceptance of its traditions, elements lying in the focal area will be retained longer than those outside it, though in this case retention will of necessity be manifested in syncretisms and reinterpretations.

For example, in the interior of Dutch Guiana, almost the only Europeanisms to be found are those which lie in the realm of material culture. In Brazil, where the Negroes accept most of the dominant European economic order, they adjust to the exigencies of the Church by syncretizing their African deities and continuing to worship them as they are worshipped in Africa. In the United States, where pressures have been most severe, almost no African economic patterns have persisted, but adaptation to Protestantism has been marked by the retention of many Africanisms through reinterpretation.

Still another point that must receive attention has to do with the degree to which elements of a culture that may be peripheral to the focal area, but that ride high in the consciousness of the people—that require thought, or call for decision—are retained under contact when compared to those which, so to speak, are carried below the level of consciousness. These may be termed *cultural imponderables*. Prominent among these are linguistic patterns and musical style, and such sanctions as are comprehended in those determinants of behavior that include types of motor habits, systems of values, or codes of etiquette. Research has demonstrated that manifestations of African culture, wherein there is little conscious awareness, have persisted in the New World to a far greater degree than those cultural elements that lie outside the area of cultural focus. This is not surprising when the factors involved are considered, since the cultural imponderables, being those elements in culture that intrude but slightly upon consciousness are taken for granted, and are thus far more difficult to dislodge from the thought and behavior patterns of individuals subjected to a new culture than those which must be given continuous attention.

Language and musical style may be cited here to illustrate the point. In the case of the former, the analysis of New World Negro dialects in English, French and Spanish, and their African counterparts in English and French, has shown that the underlying structure of the aboriginal tongues persists longest, and is most resistant to change, while vocabulary and pronunciation exhibit the most non-African elements. But it is just the grammatical configurations of any language that lodge deepest in linguistic habit-patterns, and that present the greatest difficulties where a new language is to be learned—far more so than either phonetics or vocabulary, though this last is easier learned than pronunciation. One does not think about the structure of his speech when he uses his own language; he need only "choose his words," as the saying goes.

Such patterns are laid down very early in life; so that, under contact, they are highly persistent. In like manner it is musical style, the "grammar" of music, that most resists change under contact, so that while music proves to be among the most African elements of Negro culture everywhere, yet in such regions as the United States, or in such a country as Peru, where the retention of Africanisms has been least extensive, the elusive elements of style remain in songs where an aspect such as melodic line has given way to a more European type of musical expression.

On the basis of the findings, then, the hypothesis can be advanced that in situations involving change, cultural imponderables are more resistant than are those elements of which persons are more conscious. It is important to stress in this connection, however, the distinction between this assumption and the hypothesis which holds that material culture is more acceptable under contact than non-material culture. All those phenomena which have been mentioned do fall within the latter category, it is true, but this is incidental to the hypothesis that has been advanced, since the principle is one that concerns process and does not concern form.

An exhaustive treatment of the theoretical basis of Afroamerican research would require the statement of still further hypotheses, dealing with such matters as the effect of population mass, of isolation, and of opportunity for acquiring a new culture, or discussion of the operation of such intangibles as pride in an original culture that is under assault, and a resulting determination to retain it against odds. It would require the evaluation, on the basis of available materials of hypotheses that have been advanced as a result of research in other cultures, or of the more *a priori,* philosophical speculations, such as the principle which correlates a supernaturalistic approach to life with a primitive or rural setting, or that which assumes a special type of mentality for non-European peoples.

Enough hypotheses which have guided Afroamerican research or have developed out of it have been indicated, however, to demonstrate how significant its contribution can be, and indeed, already has been, in furthering the wider ends of the scientific study of man. We have here been concerned with principles that can be applied to culture; we have mentioned one instance where language is to be drawn on; we could, in the same manner, document the point further with reference to the problems of human biology. But whatever the problems to be studied, the advantages presented by the field of Afroamerican studies in the way of breadth of scope and historic control of data, permit assumptions within the field to be tested adequately, before advancing them as applicable to other areas, under differing situations of historical development.

NOTE

The derivations of the listings given in Table I are as follows:

Guiana, Brazil (Bahia and southern Brazil), *Trinidad,* and *Haiti,* field research, and various published works bearing on the Negro peoples of these countries.

Brazil (north-urban and rural), unpublished reports of field-work by Octavio Eduardo in Maranhão.

Jamaica, first-hand contact with the Maroons and other Jamaican Negroes, though without opportunity for detailed field research; and for the general population, the volume *Black Roadways in Jamaica,* by Martha Beckwith.

Cuba, various works by F. Ortiz, particularly his *Los Negros Brujos,* and on R. Lachetãneré's *Manuel de Santeria.*

Virgin Islands, the monograph by A. A. Campbell entitled *St. Thomas Negroes–a Study of Personality and Culture,* Psychological Monographs, Vol. 55, No. 5 (1943), and unpublished field materials of J. C. Trevor.

Gullah Islands, field-work by W. R. Bascom, some results of which have been reported in a paper entitled, "Acculturation among the Gullah Negroes," *American Anthropologist,* Vol. 43 (1941), pp. 43–50.

United States, many works, from which materials of African derivation have been abstracted and summarized in my own work, *The Myth of the Negro Past.*

12.

The strengths and weaknesses of the Afro-American research approach are rigorously examined here by a West Indian-born, English-trained social anthropologist, whose field experience in the West Indies and in West Africa is as wide-ranging as that of Herskovits. This selection is part of *A Framework for Caribbean Studies,* in which M. G. Smith sets forth a general theoretical and practical perspective for social science in the West Indies.

M. G. SMITH is identified on page 66.

Afro-American Research: A Critique*
M. G. Smith

Afro-American research merits consideration first, not merely because it was the first major development with a direct Caribbean reference but also because it has been largely developed on the basis of materials from Caribbean societies, and therefore has a direct and obvious relevance for us. Afro-American studies owe a very great deal to Professor Herskovits, who has not been content to study African survivals in the New World, but has also sought to fill gaps in the ethnographic knowledge of parent societies on the West Coast of Africa by his own field work. Sociological literature on the Caribbean has also been enriched greatly by the accounts of Melville Herskovits and his wife of their field work in Surinam, Trinidad, and Haiti; and by other researches of like orientation, falling within this area or its broader context.[1]

* [Editors' title]

From *Framework for Caribbean Studies,* Caribbean Affairs Series, pp. 11–18. With permission from the author and the Editors, Department of Extra-Mural Studies, University of the West Indies, Mona, P.O. Box 42, Kingston 7, Jamaica.

[1] W. R. Bascom, "Acculturation among the Gullah Negroes," *American Anthropologist,* Vol. 43 (1941), pp. 43–50, "The Esusu: A Credit Institution among the Yoruba," *Journal of the Royal Anthropological Institute,* LXXII (London: 1952), 53–70, and "Two Forms of Afro-Cuban Divination," in Sol Tax, ed., *Acculturation in the Americas* (Chicago: University of Chicago Press, 1952), pp. 169–79; Andrew T. Carr, "A Rada Community in Trinidad," *Caribbean Quarterly,* Vol. 3, No. 1 (Trinidad: 1953), pp. 35–54; O. D. Eduardo, "The Negro in Northern Brazil: A Study in Acculturation," *Memoirs of the American Ethnological Society,* XV (New York: 1948); An-

Briefly, Afro-American researches consist in the study of changes or persistence of African traditions and cultural forms that have marked the historical association between whites and persons of African origin or descent in the Americas. Culture here connotes the total body of learned and transmitted behavior that characterizes a population and distinguishes it from others. Thus Afro-American research is focused on the problem of "acculturation"; or cultural change in a situation of contacts between carriers of different cultures. In particular, such research studies the processes by which the African immigrants and their descendants have retained, lost, or adapted elements of their initial African cultures within the contact situation provided by association with whites in the New World. The method employed in pursuit of this inquiry is a combination of history and ethnology; and the general object is to contribute to the study of cultural persistence and change by unraveling some of the factors

---

drew Pearse, "Aspects of Change in Caribbean Folk Music," *UNESCO International Folk Music Journal,* VII (1955), 29–36; George E. Simpson, "The Vodun Service in Northern Haiti," *American Anthropologist,* Vol. 42 (1940), pp. 236–54, "Haitian Magic," *Social Forces,* Vol. 19 (1940), pp. 95–100, "Sexual and Familial Institutions in Northern Haiti," *American Anthropologist,* Vol. 44 (1942), pp. 655–74, "Four Vodun Ceremonies," *Journal of American Folklore,* Vol. 59 (1946), pp. 154–67, "Acculturation in Northern Haiti," *Journal of American Folklore,* Vol. 64 (1951), pp. 397–403, and "Discussion of Dr. Price-Mars' Paper," in Sol Tax, ed., *op. cit.;* D. M. Taylor, "The Black Caribs of British Honduras," *Viking Fund Publications in Anthropology,* No. 17 (New York, 1951); Emilio Willems, "Race Attitudes in Brazil," *American Journal of Sociology,* LIV (Chicago, 1949), 402–8, "Caboclo Cultures of Southern Brazil," in Sol Tax, ed., *op. cit.,* pp. 231–43; see also M. J. Herskovits, *Acculturation, A Study of Culture Contact* (New York: J. J. Augustin, 1938), *Dahomey,* 2 vols. (New York: J. J. Augustin, 1938), *Man and His Works* (New York: Knopf, 1948), "The Contribution of Afro-American Studies to Africanist Research," *American Anthropologist,* Vol. 50 (1948), pp. 1–10, "Introduction," in Sol Tax, ed., *op. cit.,* "Some Psychological Implications of Afro-American Studies," in Sol Tax, ed., *op. cit.,* and M. J. and F. S. Herskovits, *Trinidad Village* (New York: Knopf, 1947).

and processes of acculturation, through detailed studies of Negro-white contacts in the New World.

Now clearly the determination of results of this culture-contact must precede the investigation of the processes by which these effects developed. Hence, Afro-American research is initially concerned with an examination of contemporary Afro-American cultures to discover survivals, retentions, syncretisms, or reinterpretations of African cultural elements obtaining within them. As the results of such examination accumulate, they also raise problems about the processes of acculturation, especially with regard to the differential survival of African cultural elements of various kinds, and in differing environments. A useful tool developed to facilitate such comparative analysis is the concept of *a scale of intensity of Africanisms,* which permits a classificatory comparison of New World cultures from Brazil to the United States, distinguishing between Africanisms in economic, social, religious, and aesthetic life.[2] Such a scale shows a greater concentration of Africanisms in such fields as folklore, music, and religion, than in technology and economic life; but there is a notable absence of political and governmental institutions from this catalogue of Africanisms. The differential intensity of Africanisms in these various fields invites some explanation. This analysis is undertaken with the aid of various hypotheses and concepts, the most important of which distinguishes the focal aspects of cultures as those most tenacious in situations of contact, and of greatest interest to the populations concerned, and conceives of cultural persistence in terms of survivals or retentions on the one hand, syncretism and reinterpretation on the other. *Survivals* have greatest direct resemblance to original forms. *Syncretisms* involve a combination of parallel forms from the cultures in contact; while *reinterpretations* adhere to the substance or content of the original culture, although departing from its initial forms.

[2] M. J. Herskovits, *The Myth of the Negro Past* (New York: Harper, 1941), and "Problem, Method and Theory in Afro-American Studies," *Phylon,* Vol. 7 (1946), pp. 337–54.

Finally the concept of *cultural imponderables* connotes that category of Africanisms which are clearly not included in the *cultural focus,* but nonetheless have a high level of intensity in New World populations. It appears that values and automatic motor patterns constitute the bulk of these surviving cultural imponderables. Within this frame of research the ethnohistorical method has hitherto been employed principally to determine the cultural provenience from which Africans were recruited for the various New World slave-states, and the types of condition to which they were subjected under the slave regime. In the attack on problems of differential intensities of Africanisms, that is, the variable effects and processes of acculturation, the ethnohistorical method has played a less prominent part than the development of the hypotheses and concepts just mentioned.

This seems to constitute one of the major weaknesses of current Afro-American studies. Instead of undertaking the examination of those *processes* of acculturation which form the stated object of such research by the more vigorous employment of the ethnohistorical method which documentary materials, autobiographical, and other studies permit, with a view to the unraveling of detailed processes in limited fields, the tendency has been rather to develop and systematize a set of concepts which, taken together, obscure the problems of process rather than otherwise. We can illustrate some aspects of this weakness by a brief examination of these concepts and their interrelations, ignoring for the moment questions of variable distributions of African elements within the populations concerned, or the nature of Africanisms as such.

The scale of intensity of Africanisms shows a variable tenacity of African cultural elements distinguished in terms of technology, economy, social organization, nonkinship institutions, religion, magic, art, folklore, music, and language. The problem of variation in these different fields leads, after a discussion of syncretism, retention, and reinterpretation, to the following formulation by Herskovits:

> Even under the compulsions of the dominant culture of the Whites, Negroes have retained African religious beliefs and practices far more than they have retained economic patterns. But when we examine the patterns of African cultures, we find that there is no activity of everyday living but that it is validated by supernatural sanctions. And consequently, these figure far more in the total life of the people than does any other single fact of the culture such as those matters having to do with making a living, or family structure, or political institutions. This weighting of the concerns of a people constitutes the focus of their culture. . . . The role of cultural focus is of such great importance in situations of cultural contact that a further hypothesis may be advanced to the effect that more elements which lie in the area of focus of a receiving culture will be retained than those appertaining to other aspects of the culture, acceptance being greater in those phases of culture further removed from the focal area. Where a culture is under pressure by a dominant group who seek to induce acceptance of its traditions, elements lying in the focal area will be retained longer than those outside it, though in this case retention will of necessity be manifested in syncretisms and reinterpretations.[3]

We can summarize the relations between the conceptual system and the scale of intensity in the following terms: greatest intensity of cultural survivals occurs in the area of cultural focus, if cultural imponderables are excluded. The cultural focus is the area of greatest tenacity in cultural retentions; consequently, assuming equal pressures on all fields of cultural activity from outside, it will show the highest degrees of purity in these retentions, and will also contain the last elements to disappear. Purity of retention diminishes as it passes from direct survival to syncretism, and so to reinterpretation. The relative proportions of these particular modes of persistence in different cultural spheres is reflected in the scale of intensity; and this illustrates or defines the focus. So the circle is completed; and the variable persistence of cultural elements of dif-

[3] *Ibid.*, p. 352.

ferent kinds is simply restated in the form of a system of hypotheses and concepts, ostensibly developed to further the analysis of this variability, only to be canvassed thereafter as its explanation.

Even so, the distinction between cultural focus and periphery in terms of tenacity and persistence is not borne out by the scale of intensity on which it is based. Thus, Herskovits' comparison of folklore with magic or religion in terms of levels of intensity of African elements of these kinds for the fifteen areas concerning which materials were then available shows that folklore elements persist on an average to a higher degree than do either magic or religion. Similarly, Africanisms in music have a higher level of intensity than those in any other field, in terms of this scale.[4] Now it is possible to exclude music from the comparison effectively by treating it as a pattern of motor behavior of the type which is liable to persist in a very marked degree, even though marginal to the culture focus. But this treatment cannot be extended to cover folklore. Nor is it useful to define folklore, religion, and magic coterminously, although this would remove the problem of peripheral elements showing a higher degree of tenacity and persistence than focal ones. On the other hand, if folklore is included among the cultural imponderables on grounds of the value-systems which it often expresses, the question arises whether all other departments of culture are not equally open to similar treatment, notably of course, religion, and kinship. In such a case, the notion of cultural focus as distinct from periphery would cease to be of much use.

There is always grave danger in exaggerating the relative importance of one aspect of culture at the expense of others; and this difficulty is involved in the concept of cultural focus. The type of conclusion which emerges from Fortes' thorough study of an African society is relevant here.

> To study Tale kinship institutions apart from the religious and moral ideas and values of the natives would

[4] *Ibid.*, p. 352.

> be as one-sided as to leave out the facts of sex and procreation. On the other hand, our analysis has shown that it is equally impossible to understand Tale religious beliefs and moral norms apart from the context of kinship. A very close functional interdependence exists between these two categories of social facts.[5]

Similarly Forde, reviewing African cosmologies, finds that "belief and ritual tend, in other words, to mirror the scale and degree of social integration."[6] Fortes and Evans-Pritchard reach a parallel conclusion from their review of African political systems. "Myths, dogmas, ritual beliefs and activities make his social system intellectually tangible and coherent to an African and enable him to think and feel about it. Furthermore, these sacred symbols, which reflect the social system, endow it with mystical values which evoke acceptance of the social order."[7] These observations indicate the very great need for caution in the classification of cultural elements as focal or otherwise and direct attention to their close interdependence. Clearly, insofar as religion and kinship are essential to the understanding or practice of one another, their separation and ranking in terms of cultural priorities is liable to do violence to this relation.

We can perhaps more usefully and easily distinguish foci in the culture-contact situation itself than in the cultures themselves. Herskovits makes frequent reference to this variability in the pressures of the contact situation, but does not systematize concepts to treat it. In the historical situation of Afro-American culture-contact these foci of contact reflected the interests of the dominant group in its control of the subordinate as slaves. Consequently the social organization, technological, and economic practices of the subordinate Negroes were subject

[5] Meyer Fortes, *The Web of Kinship Among the Tallensi* (London: Oxford University Press, 1949), p. 346.

[6] Daryll Forde, "Introduction" in Daryll Forde, ed., *African Worlds* (London: Oxford University Press, 1954), p. xvii.

[7] Meyer Fortes and E. E. Evans-Pritchard, "Introduction" in Fortes and Evans-Pritchard, eds., *African Political Systems* (London: Oxford University Press, 1940), p. 17.

to pressure of a kind without parallel for intensity and continuity in such other fields as religion, music, or folklore. Language, the essential mode of communication between the dominant and subordinate groups, occupied an intermediate position in this variable pressure of cultural elements between the two groups. The advantages of conceiving the contact situation as a field of variable pressure over time as well as at any moment are many and varied. It directs attention consistently to the study of social relations between and within the two culturally differentiated groups as the matrix of these acculturation processes, and thereby invokes employment of historical and sociological research together to relate these processes to the structures and situations through which they matured. It allows relatively simple and precise determination of the focal and peripheral fields of culture-contact on the basis of documentary analysis. It thereby permits the study of persistence of different categories of elements in their differing degrees of intensity or purity to proceed without supplementary postulates which are hardly verifiable about focal and peripheral sectors within the cultures themselves. It directs attention to the fact that purity of form in survival might simply indicate marginality within the acculturative situation, rather than any central significance of the elements retained in the original culture; whereas relative impurity of form in persistence might simply indicate the relative intensity of pressure on the elements concerned, rather than their marginality to the original culture. A good many possible fallacies are ruled out at once by such conceptualization of the contact continuum, and effort is thereby redirected from the development of broad classificatory conceptions such as retention, reinterpretation, and syncretism, and imprecise and unverifiable hypotheses such as that of cultural focus, toward the formulation of more limited propositions capable of being tested against historical materials on the contact situation within the particular fields for which they are separately developed.

Hitherto we have been discussing certain aspects of Afro-American research which focus on the processes by which acculturation proceeded among New World Negroes. We must now turn to consider its conceptual system especially with reference to the classification and study of the forms produced by such processes. Here we are mainly concerned with the precision or generality of the principal concepts, although we must commence with the problem of attribution. Clearly, Afro-American research can only yield tentative ascriptions of provenience for contemporary custom, to the degree that the African centers from which New World Negroes and their ancestors were recruited are unknown, or to the degree that parallel European practices, or the measure of influence exercised by these forms on the development of contemporary Africanisms are not fully determined. Systematic study has shown that the areas from which most of the New World Negro slaves were recruited lie along the densely populated West African Coast. This reduces the problem of the provenience of Africanisms, leaving only the question of their accretions of European or Amerindian elements. Amerindians, being largely peripheral to the areas of Negro-white contact, may be ignored in this general discussion.

Herskovits is careful to weigh the influence of European cultural practice on African tradition, particularly where elements of folklore are involved; but the issue is greatly obscured by his postulate of common denominators for European and African cultures in the concept of the Old World as a single cultural province.[8] A concept of this level of generality is of dubious value. It implies a division of the world into two cultural provinces, the New and the Old. Yet this could easily be criticized, partly on the evidence that points to the movement of Old World populations into the Americas to become their "aboriginals"; but more importantly on the ground that the absence of such elements as the wheel or writing from fifteenth-century America, or of tobacco from the Old World at that date, forms an inadequate basis for such a distinction, since cultural differences of a similar order have

[8] M. J. Herskovits, *The Myth of the Negro Past.*

been overlooked within the cultures of the Old World province itself. Yet if this criticism was granted, it would place some strain on the conceptual framework of Afro-American studies.

It is difficult to reconcile specific studies of Afro-American acculturation with statements such as the following:

> It is here we must turn for an explanation of the seemingly baffling fact, so often encountered, that given traits of New World Negro, and especially of American Negro behaviour, are ascribable equally to European and African origin. This may well be viewed as but a reflection of the fact that deep beneath the differences between these varied civilisations of the Old World lie common aspects which, in generalized form, might be expected to emerge in situations of close contact between peoples, such as Europeans and Africans, whose specialized cultural endowments are comprehended within the larger unity.[9]

Similarly, in comparing the wider persistence of Africanisms in magic than in religion, Herskovits notes the advantages of magic in being private and difficult of detection where pressures are brought to prohibit both practices; and concludes that Africanisms in magic "persisted in recognizable form everywhere, particularly since the similarity between African and European magic is so great that the one cultural stream must have operated to reinforce the other."[10] It is doubtful in what sense the predicated similarity of European and African magic can be taken to contribute to the survival of Africanisms in this field, as is clear from a glance at such patterns in West Indian Obeah. As is well known, a good deal of the magical rites of the Obeahman are taken in whole or in part from imported literature such as *The Sixth and Seventh Books of Moses, The Black Arts,* and the like. These books describe techniques which are significantly different from

[9] *Ibid.,* p. 18.
[10] M. J. Herskovits, "Problem, Method and Theory in Afro-American Studies," p. 348.

African practices, especially in the use of cabalistic signs, writing, and foreign languages. They present a type of magic which is distinguished locally in terms of its literary and learned pretensions as "book magic." In contrast, pure Africanisms in Obeah rely mainly on the employment of herbal or animal substances, and the casting of spells in dialects or African tongues. These two categories of Obeah, the literary and the "African," are at least as much in competition as they are active in reinforcing each other. Thus acceptance of the one form may mean displacement of the other. Something similar has been recently reported from Africa also by Nadel, who found the native pagan magic of Nupe being displaced by imported forms enjoying the higher prestige of Islamic civilization.[11] Now, unless a careful analysis of the magical systems of New World Negroes is made to determine exactly what proportion and type of practice has European or African provenience, the attribution of these forms to African culture whether as syncretisms, reinterpretations or retentions, begs the question of their "origin." The concept of a "generalized form" which permits this type of attribution is thus confusing rather than helpful to the analysis.

These observations direct attention to the levels of generality on which the search for Africanisms and their attribution proceeds; and these levels vary widely indeed, from meticulous correspondences between Haitian and Dahomean *vodun,* or Afro-Cuban and Yoruba divinatory practices on the one hand, to such conceptualizations as those which reduce "matriarchal" family patterns and loose mating associations among New World Negroes to the level of "reinterpretations" of African polygynous patterns by the device of successive, rather than simultaneous, plural matings.[12] Important questions concerning the

[11] S. F. Nadel, *Nupe Religion* (London: Oxford University Press, 1954).

[12] M. J. Herskovits, *Life in a Haitian Valley, Dahomey, The Myth of the Negro Past,* pp. 169 ff.; Bascom, "The Esusu: A Credit Institution Among the Yoruba," "Two Forms of Afro-Cuban Divination."

levels of generality in such conceptualization of family-types, mating patterns, and reinterpretations remain to be answered before the attributions involved can be discussed profitably. An alternative approach to such problems as changing family structures present for acculturation studies may be made by comparing parallel situations and developments in other parts of the world.

Let us examine this matter of family forms for a moment since its handling by Afro-Americanists has promoted some controversy, their opponents attributing the contemporary "disorganization" of New World Negro family forms to "the historic condition of slavery," under which, as is well known, stable matings among the Negro populations were inhibited by a variety of factors.[13] Afro-Americanists, as we have seen, derive these "deviant, disorganized" family patterns of New World Negroes from African practice by reinterpretation. Much ink has already been spilled on these conflicting ascriptions, and their antithesis has directly affected the study of family patterns in the British Caribbean.

[13] Frazier, *The Negro Family in the United States,* "Theoretical Structure of Sociology and Sociological Research," *British Journal of Sociology,* Vol. 4 (1953), pp. 293–313; Fernando Henriques, "West Indian Family Organization," *Caribbean Quarterly,* Vol. 2, No. 1 (1952), p. 24, Letter to the Editor, *Caribbean Quarterly,* Vol. 2, No. 3 (1953), p. 56, review of *Personality and Conflict in Jamaica* by Kerr in *Caribbean Quarterly*, Vol. 3, No. 1 (1953), pp. 61–62; Simey, *op. cit.;* Matthews, *op. cit.;* cf. also M. J. Herskovits, "Some Psychological Implications of Afro-American Studies," in Sol Tax, ed., *op. cit.,* and Letter to the Editor, *Caribbean Quarterly,* Vol. 2, No. 2 (1952), pp. 44–45.

13.

In this extract from their book *Trinidad Village*, the Herskovitses argue that rural Negro marriage and family patterns in Trinidad reflect West African cultural elements, such as polygyny and household organization, which have been retained and reinterpreted ever since the Middle Passage.

MELVILLE J. HERSKOVITS is identified on page 246. FRANCES S. HERSKOVITS actively collaborated with her husband in anthropological research and writing. In addition to *Trinidad Village* and *Rebel Destiny*, they together wrote *Surinam Folk-Lore* and *Dahomean Narrative*. Mrs. Herskovits has since edited *The New World Negro: Selected Papers in Afroamerican Studies*, a collection of her late husband's articles.

Retentions and Reinterpretations in Rural Trinidad*

Melville J. Herskovits and Frances S. Herskovits

It has been shown that both legal marriage and the informal union termed "keepers" share in the formation of the Toco family; that both these enjoy social sanction, though they are endowed with differing degrees of prestige; and that in terms of the patterns of Toco conventions there thus is in this dual system nothing reprehensible. We are, indeed, here faced with one of the most interesting series of reinterpretations to be found in the entire range of Toco or, for that matter, of New World Negro custom. For here is a translation, in terms of the monogamic pattern of European mating, of basic West African forms that operate within a polygynous frame.

In West Africa and the Congo, where the children born of a mating belong to the man's family, and are under his control, certain ritually decreed fees must be paid to a prospective bride's family, and certain tasks must be performed for her father and mother. Should the girl merely join the man and form a union, living together without his paying these fees and discharging these obligations, children born to the couple remain under the control of the woman, or her family, no matter how enduring the match.

In Trinidad, practices governing the payment of fees, or the control of children have disappeared. What is left is the classification of unions into marriage and keeper types, the

* [Editors' title]

From *Trinidad Village,* by Melville J. and Frances S. Herskovits.

looseness of the bonds that bind a man and woman in a union—here applying to both classes of matings—and the attitudes derived from the existence, in Africa and later under slavery, of the nucleus of mother and children as the basis of the family structure.

The substance, if not the form of the obligations of a suitor toward the parents of the girl he wishes to marry are to be discerned in legal marriage. The formal letter, which under the law carries contractual force, is the reinterpretation of what, in Africa, are addresses to the parents of the girl made through an elder member of the family acting as an intermediary, and the contractual nature of betrothal; in Haiti, it is known as the *lettre de demande*. The investigation of the family of the young man by that of the girl, and of her family background by his, is similarly fundamental in African practice. The informal convention that a young man work for a few days during the planting season in the garden of his girl's father is a truncated expression of the African requirement that he prepare a field for his prospective father-in-law; though there, unlike Toco, he continues to do this or a comparable task periodically after his marriage. The contributions of food given if a close relative of a fiancé or spouse dies, not mandatory in Toco, is one of the most rigorously observed requirements of a man or woman in West Africa. The need to obtain the consent of the ancestors to the match, by holding a reel dance and giving the *sakara* sacrifice, is entirely African, deriving from the sanctions of the ancestral cult which, in uninstitutionalized form, are represented in Toco by the beliefs in the power of the dead members of the family that, as has been seen, function widely there.

It would be expected that with the disappearance of the sib, and the tradition of counting descent on only one side of the family, African patterns of exogamy would also disappear. In Toco, all that remains of this is a feeling on the part of the old people that one should not marry a second cousin, though even this rule is being dismissed with the dictum, "Second cousin no family." Only fragmentary, also, are the retentions of West African traditions of the sororate and levirate. There, when a man dies, his brothers and sons customarily marry his wives, and among some West African peoples, when a wife dies, the widower takes one of her sisters. In Toco, however, such marriages are sanctioned only if the original mating produced no offspring.

In all matings, the importance of "having the family behind you" is to be looked on as the retention of a complex of attitudes and relationships so deeply rooted in African culture that not even the experience of slavery could change it. Europeans also have family ties that strike deep, yet the quality of this feeling is one which, in kind and degree, is quite different from that of Europe. One recalls the shocked reactions in the courtroom when a mother and son bitterly contested the ownership of a plot of ground. A woman does everything she can to obtain the consent of her parents before entering into a marriage or a "keepers" relationship of which they are inclined to disapprove; a wayward daughter is brought under control by a rite denouncing her conduct to the ancestors. All this is a part of the pattern which, with the sanctions imposed and guardianship granted by the spirits of the family dead, gives stability to family life in full African fashion, even where unions often do not endure.

This also explains the importance of the household in the rearing and training of children. In essence, this is based on the retention in Toco of the nucleus of African kinship structures which, as explained, consists of a mother and her children living in a hut within her husband's compound, also inhabited by her co-wives and their children. That this nuclear unit has evolved into such a household as the one headed by the elderly woman, previously described in detail, where her grown daughters are still more or less under her direction and some of their children entirely given over to her care, merely represents in one respect the logical development of this African institution under the influence of slavery and of the particular socio-economic position of the Negroes after slavery was abolished.

Further examination of this household reveals attitudes

that are to be ascribed to other reinterpretations of African custom. We have seen that in this grouping, since the father assumed financial responsibility for a daughter and subsequently for her first child, these two members remained under his guardianship. Unlike the case in West Africa, in Toco the concept of the children "belonging" to a man has neither ritual nor economic import. Nevertheless, whenever the man provides the support of children born to him, his authority over them is recognized. Of equal significance is the attitude of the woman who heads this household toward the grandchild she has supported from infancy. She had been given no contributions toward the child's rearing, and therefore the child's mother could make no claim to it.

Thus in considering the forms taken by the family and the behavior associated with it, we are faced with a retention of African custom that has been reinterpreted so drastically as to make the resulting institutions not only susceptible of description as pathological manifestations of the European family but ones which, in fact, have been frequently so described. Nevertheless, as we have seen, these forms of the family are not pathological at all, but rather demonstrate how tenaciously a tradition can be held to, and how the process of reinterpretation can give to custom resilience and malleability in the face of new circumstances.

In examining the customs surrounding birth and training of children during the first years of their lives we shall find it useful again to recall our hypothesis that in the New World the process of stripping from the Africans the larger institutions in their culture left them only the more intimate aspects of earlier ways of life, for here retentions of this order abound. That abortion is held socially repugnant and must be practiced, if at all, in secrecy, is not particularly restricted to Africa; but that the enforcing sanction is in the fear that the ancestors, in their resentment, will cause barrenness is African. Another Africanism is found in the fact that a diviner is consulted when a woman has a first pregnancy, or has experienced miscarriages, or her previous children have died.

Notifying the family dead that a first child has been conceived, and asking their aid and that of the saints—transmuted from the African deities, although here European belief enters as well—for a good parturition or, should there have been a series of still-births, for the survival of the infant, is similarly in accordance with African custom. The measures taken by the lookman to counteract the evil magic that, in Toco, is believed to have "tied the baby" in the womb of the mother, or where a woman is held to have a "jumby belly," represent retentions of African belief and behavior in forms but little changed.

Toco has carried over from Africa many of the practices surrounding childbirth, and many of the beliefs concerning the significance of various characteristics of the newly born child. Depositing the umbilical cord in a hole over which a fruit-bearing tree is planted is found in many parts of Africa, though there the tree usually becomes the property of the child. In Africa, as in Toco, it is held that a baby with extra fingers or toes will be lucky, and that an infant born feet foremost is a dangerous being. The custom of giving a child born after a series of miscarriages a "funny" name, acting toward it as though it were disliked, dressing it poorly, taking precautions to nullify the magic that had caused the previous still-births, and vowing the child to a saint—reinterpreted from African deities—all constitute a complex widely spread among those who live in the areas from which the African ancestors of the Toco Negroes were obtained.

The African derivation of the cult of twins can be localized, for its form indicates the influence of the "Yarriba" component in the Trinidad Negro population. The fact that twins are held to bring good luck, the elaborateness of the rite of emergence from the house held for them, as compared to that for ordinary infants, their being taken to nearby houses to receive gifts that must be given in two equal parts, and the customs that follow the death of one of the pair are all variants of the Yoruban-Dahomean tradition, even to some of their details. These customs are also found in Brazil, Guiana, Haiti, Cuba, and elsewhere in the New World in similar specific form, where twins are given either their Yoruban or Dahomean designations *ibeji* or *hohovi*. In the Gold Coast, the Ashanti regarded twins as so important that, if they were girls, they became wives of the king, if boys, his servitors; and they were brought to him in a golden bowl. But eastward of the Yoruba, twins are destroyed at birth, for the respect in which the more westerly peoples hold them, because of the supernatural power they are believed to wield, turns to fear.

Other Africanisms found in the care of infants and rearing of children, in addition to the rite of emergence of mother and child from the house nine days after birth, . . . can be reviewed briefly. Baptism is a Christian rite, but the interpretation of its need to keep the child from joining the spirits of the forest is African; while the one baptismal name that in Toco is held secret is the counterpart of the "real" name given an infant in Africa, a name whose use exposes him to the force of any magic set against him. That an infant must never be left alone or, if this is unavoidable, must have magical or supernatural protection is a tenet of belief found everywhere in West Africa, its reinterpretation in Toco being manifested in placing an open Bible or prayer book at the side of the child whose mother is urgently called away from it, and has no one with whom to leave it.

The convention of giving an infant a gift when the first tooth appears, and the little ceremony performed when the first deciduous tooth falls out, come directly from Africa. In Dahomey as in Toco, this first tooth is thrown on the roof of the house–though by the child rather than the mother–and a little dance is held by its playmates, who sing,

> "I don't want the teeth of a pig,
> They're big!
> I want the teeth of a goat,
> They're small!"

The experiences–almost inevitably, it would seem, traumatic in effect–of those who soil the sleeping-mat are paralleled in West Africa, even to attaching a live frog to the offender, and sending the child out in the street to be shamed by the taunting songs of its playmates.

Other aspects of growing up which are African either in form or sanction include the manner in which a child is trained in household duties or in working the field, the importance for black magic of a girl's first menstrual cloth, the punishment of wayward children by the ancestors. But most important, to return to the household as a unit, are the attitudes toward father or mother. Here we must once again refer to the hypothesis advanced in the first chapter of this work, since the instances of the relationships within the household that were given show how, in the lower socioeconomic strata of Toco society at least, the father, as in Africa, remains on the periphery of the nucleus constituting the household, whose center is the mother, a grandmother, an aunt.

14.

In this selection a Trinidadian Catholic clergyman trained in the social sciences opposes Herskovits' view. Not Africa, but the institutions of slavery and the plantation, are seen as responsible for West Indian family structure. Comparisons between West Indian concubinage and Yoruban polygyny are shown to lack validity; in Dom Basil's view, the exigencies of the slave system led to the characteristic mating and family forms of West Indian Negroes. And here he reviews the historic pressures of plantation life in Trinidad.

DOM BASIL MATTHEWS, a Trinidadian in the Benedictine Order, trained at Louvain University in Belgium and at Fordham University in the United States, where he received his doctorate. For a number of years he served as Principal of St. Benedict's College, Trinidad, and presently is in the Department of Sociology and Anthropology at Howard University.

The Plantation and the African Heritage*

Dom Basil Matthews

THE PLANTATION

In the year of Our Lord 1842 there appeared a book which, because of its singular value as source material for Trinidad social and economic history, may very well be styled the book of the century. The title of the book is "Observations On The Present Condition of The Island of Trinidad and The Actual State of The Experiment of Negro Emancipation". The book was written by William Hardin Burnley, Chairman of the Agricultural and Immigration Society in Trinidad and acknowledged Dean of Trinidad Planters. The book was written in support of a plea to the Imperial Government to make available for plantations in Trinidad a cheap supply of free immigrant labour from the coasts of Africa. In this book is contained the findings of the Agricultural Society's sub-committee appointed "to inquire and report respecting the state of the agricultural interests of the colony since the abolition of apprenticeship in August, 1838, their present condition and future prospects, and to recommend such measures as they may think conducive to the general prosperity". The essential features of the economy of the plantation appear in bold relief in Mr. Burnley's book.

* [Editors' title]

From *Crisis of the West Indian Family*, Caribbean Affairs Series, Port of Spain, Trinidad, University College of the West Indies, 1953, pp. 27–43. Reprinted with permission of the author and from the Editors Department of Extra-Mural Studies, University of the West Indies, Mona, P.O. Box 42, Kingston, Jamaica.

Here is a summary of the observations of the Chairman and his Society "On the Present Condition of the Island of Trinidad".

> In the period following emancipation the general conditions of the Island–much uncultivated land available for purchase (p. 60, 107) or squatting (p. 66, 100, 111, 112), the relatively scanty, population (p. 4) and the fact that only necessity could compel free labour to work on plantations–caused a rise in wages (p. 64, 66) and a decrease in the number of working hours.
>
> At this time it was customary to pay part of the wages in allowances of food, rum and rent (p. 51, 80, 131). The custom of rum allowances was mainly responsible for the general increase in drunkenness which was the major cause of cases of disorderly conduct (p. 59, 85). However, despite this, the general moral and religious conduct of labourers in the post-emancipation period was greatly improved (p. 94, 95); one of the evidences of this is the increase in marriages (p. 56, 58, 95), another is the increased support of churches, schools, and benefit societies (p. 95, 98), particularly those of the Catholic Church which was most deeply rooted in the native Trinidadian population (p. 76); and there was relatively little crime (p. 164) despite the inadequacy and inefficiency of the police (p. 53, 84).
>
> During this period many ex-slaves purchased property (p. 54) and there was a large increase in the number of cottage settlers (p. 119), but not enough to make any appreciable difference in the economy (p. 105). Most gardening was done for home consumption (p. 54), undoubtedly in many instances because of the inaccessibility of markets (p. 63).
>
> Vagrancy increased during this period, especially among the immigrants (p. 18, 66, 96) many of whom deserted "their former employment to engage in trade or other more pleasing occupations" (p. 116, 161).
>
> Squatters had been encouraged to settle on Crown lands before emancipation (p. 111); however, immediately afterwards, the planters with government approval and assistance tried to eject squatters (p. 111, 168). "The object is . . . . . to condense and keep together

the population in such a manner that it may always contain a due proportion of labourers" (p. 139, 140).

Another means by which the government co-operated with the planters to maintain "a due proportion of labourers" was "by diminishing the facilities of obtaining land . . . . . by fixing the price of fresh land so high as to place it above the reach of the poorest class of settlers" (p. 138).

There was a large increase in the influx of immigrant labourers (p. 123) who were encouraged by the planters (p. 68, 124) because additional workers meant competition for jobs and this in turn would lead to lower wages.

Despite occasional differences between the proprietors and the colonial government as to means and methods (p. 158) we find that in the basic matter of economic relationships the government acts to the benefit of the proprietor, frequently at the expense of labour (p. 130, 131, 132, 138, 139, 140, 111, 168). Fear of the growth of economic independence among the people and of political democracy–loss of profit, loss of autocratic powers–underlies this mutuality of interest between the proprietors and the state in this period (p. 10, 12).

The annual export of labourers from Africa was advocated "for the purpose of raising sugar in our colonies" (p. 33). Twice the amount of sugar produced with African slave labour could be produced by the same amount of free African labour (p. 33) and at a greatly reduced expense. "We could therefore furnish a more abundant supply to the sugar market at a cheaper rate" (p. 33). It is "easily reducible to calculation that one-sixth part only of the cultivable surface of Trinidad would more than supply the actual demand of Great Britain for sugar" (p. 40). Trinidad possesses "peculiar fitness for a great sugar producing colony" (p. 41).[1]

Thompson has described the plantation as characterized by forced labour, open resources and concentration on a staple crop. By forced labour must be understood not slavery exclusively, but also the application of economic, moral

[1] W. H. Burnley, *Observations on the Present Condition of the Island of Trinidad* (London: Longman, Brown, Green & Longmans, 1842).

or social pressure. Associated with forced labour is cheap wages. Open resources means an abundance of available agricultural lands; and concentration on a staple crop is a die-hard insistence upon the maintenance of a one-crop economy as the main resource of a country. Burnley's "Present Conditions of the Island of Trinidad", fits into this pattern exactly. And, as we shall see presently, the features of the Trinidad plantation as described by Burnley for the period 1833–45 continued essentially the same after that date.

The predominant features of the plantation economy in Trinidad were the same not only after Burnley's time, but also before. Consider the case of the aboriginal Indians on the encomiendas, the cocoa plantations of the Spaniards in Trinidad during the seventeenth and eighteenth centuries. The encomienda was a system by which Queen Isabella allotted Indians to work for Spanish planters overseas in return for fair pay, adequate food, and instruction in the Christian religion. The labour contract was to be free, was to have a definite term, and was not to apply to hazardous or over-strenuous work. The Indians had a right to time to work for themselves, and to rest if they were tired or ill, and to be instructed in Christianity. They were to reside in missions under the immediate supervision of the missionaries. At least so Queen Isabella had planned it. The system was introduced to Trinidad in 1687.

But, alas, the Spanish planters welcomed the encomienda not in the spirit of Isabella but in that of the exploiting Commander de Lares, the West Indian Governor who, in order to commandeer the Indian labour force, advised the Queen to entrust the native Indians to the immediate care of the planters. For, he argued, let alone, the Indians ran away both from work and from religious instruction. The Spaniards in Trinidad had long resented the missionary control of the labour force. Now they urged that the colony's agriculture was threatened for lack of labour. And besides, they added, life in the shelter of the missions made the Indians indolent and gave them time to foment revolts. They supported their argument by pointing to the Indian revolt at San Francisco de los Arenales in 1699 in which a Governor and three missionaries were massacred. The planters obtained control over the labour of the Indians. Already under the former system the Indians returned from the cocoa fields exhausted, sick with hunger, untaught and unpaid. The Church intervened directly to protect the workers from the rigours of the regime and to soften and to mitigate the regime itself. It was by way of concession to ecclesiastical action that the Government appointed a corregidor or civil magistrate to take care of the social welfare of the Indians. But conditions grew steadily worse. In the hands of the planters the encomienda became an instrument not of uplift but of oppression. The Indians retaliated by promptly deserting and taking to the mountains. The story of the plantation then, as later, is a story of forced labour, open resources, and concentration on a staple crop.

From the facts so far presented it is apparent that the plantation as known to tradition is an economic system which, somewhat like the system of slavery, achieves its own effects and does so by methods proper to itself regardless of who operates the system. The race or nationality or personal character of the planter has made no difference to the essential nature and operation of the system. It is therefore idle to discuss the plantation in terms of planters as individuals. And this is a point which I should like to underscore heavily at this stage both for its own sake and for the sake of those of my friends and readers associated with the planter class. This chapter is not a discussion of personalities or of social classes, but of the nature and operation of an impersonal system of economics. If we cannot help speaking of planters, then we speak of them considered not as individuals or as families but merely as the agents and operators of a system the creation of which they had little to do with. In any event, the planters, even considered as a social class, have little to fear from the verdict of history. For when all is said and done it remains true that the West Indies, as Professor C. Y. Shepherd observes, have not known better friends. Nevertheless there is a logic in the plantation, and it works itself out independently of interference, and the planters themselves became, in their own way, victims of its inexorable logic.

The plantation in freedom is the heir and repository of a vast New World tradition, a living tradition of customs and attitudes, adopted or adapted, established and developed within the institution of slavery and as part of the institution. The general attitude of the descendants of the master class towards the descendants of the servile class and of these towards their masters and towards themselves is part of this tradition. By way of illustration let us consider an instance noted in a 1939 British administrative report on labour conditions in the West Indies. The slave labour tradition on the free plantation shows itself in the wage earner's persistent belief that he belongs to the estate owner almost as much as the estate itself, and therefore ought to be taken care of as much by his employer as by himself. Even the plantation owners, continues the report, have grown into that tradition. They feel pressed by the prescriptions of custom, even though the law of the land abolished certain patriarchal duties formerly binding upon the ex-slave owner towards the ex-slave. For example, estate owners felt bound to provide residence on the estate for the body of workpeople although the tradition no longer enjoyed legal support. The free worker today, states the report, tends to expect not only housing, but medical attention and other privileges beyond his wages. He still tends to regard the squalid, dilapidated barracks as his home and to protest vigorously if required to leave.

Along with slavery traditions the slave mentality was also carried over into the era of the free plantation the whole structure and operation of which were calculated to foster and promote the continuance of the servile mentality. Unfortunately, the propagation of the slave mentality by the plantation system also meant the reinforcement and, in effect, the sanctioning of the ideals and practices developed by the servile class in respect of marriage under the system of slavery. Things that were heretofore done under a system repudiated by the decree of

Emancipation now became on the free plantation the new order of an emancipated society. In particular, the sexual nomadism of slavery settled down on the free plantation to become the non-legal union. In slavery a secure union between the sexes was practically impossible. Slaves were subject to sale or transfer at any time; to the slave owner the slave family was incidental; among Trinidad slaves marriage was the exception, concubinage the rule, writes De Verteuil. And concubinage was of the random and irresponsible type. Marital unions among slaves in Trinidad, we are told by Mrs. Carmichael, the Tacarigua slave owner, were eclectic, and "for trial", and accordingly subject to frequent change. Children owed obedience first and foremost not to their parents but to the plantation owner and to his deputy, the Nannie in charge of the child-rearing farm. All these conditions operated against the establishment of stable unions and of family life on the slave plantation. But on the free plantation people were free to settle down with whom they wished for as long as they wished; partners could not be sold away any more; women were no longer economically dependent on the plantation owner but upon the mate who now provided both support and protection. Children belonged to their parents. A measure of security in family life now became possible and the non-legal union swung into being as a way of family organization–a thing previously impossible for all but a negligible few of the servile class. Thus the free plantation became, in its own right, the matrix of a complex of ideas and practices concerning marriage the roots of which went back into the system of slavery. The free plantation is indeed the inaugurator of the non-legal union as a social institution. For although all the elements of this union had already been forged on the anvil of slavery the slave, we stress once more, did not have a chance of forming a union either durable in time or familistic in its organization or stable in its anchorage.

Besides being of its very nature a favourable breeding ground for the non-legal union, the free plantation carried over from slavery a tradition of indifference to marriage in so far as the servile class was concerned. And so, the plantation–symbol of the social order of its day–can be seen quite clearly to preside at the formation of public opinion in the matter of non-legal unions for the populace.

Along with its indifference to marriage as regards the labouring class, the plantocracy was traditionally and notoriously hostile to the education of this class. This means that the helpless inhabitants of the plantation village, already isolated from the centres of civilization, were further not effectively exposed to the civilizing influence of Christianity and education. In 1838 Lord Grey, then Secretary of State for the Colonies, instructed Lord Harris, Governor of Trinidad, that the emancipated should be made "to look to labour on neighbouring estates as their main dependence". The peasants should be put "in circumstances in which a greater amount of labour than at present shall be required to supply their wants".[2] To meet the educational needs of the Negro Lord Grey proposed a new type of school. Its object, Lord Grey pointed out, was to correct the deficiency of labour. The school programme should be largely industrial. Every school would have a garden attached to it. And, if possible, a cane field! This education would create new wants and tastes and would stimulate "a love of employment". The end in view, comments the fair-minded historian Mathieson seemed "not so much mental as sugar cultivation".[3] One of the weighty objections to the implementation of this scheme, reports Mathieson, was the attitude with which Catholics would view the fate of religious teaching in such a school. The scheme failed but its hostile spirit towards the education of the people is unmistakable. And it was the spirit of the traditional plantation. If anything is clear in the social history of Trinidad it is this, namely, that the more Christian and the more civilized the people become the more they abandon the non-legal union as a way of life. The greater the isolation,

[2] W. L. Mathieson, *The Sugar Colonies and Governor Eyre, 1849–1866* (London: Longmans, Green and Company, 1936), pp. 15, 87ff.

[3] *Ibid.*, pp. 52, 53.

ignorance and illiteracy of the rural population the greater, generally speaking, is the prevalence and the entrenchment of the non-legal union.

One result of his ignorance was that the freed man of the plantation was ill prepared for the responsibilities of economic freedom. In 1824 a law was passed enabling slaves to purchase their freedom. Many preferred to purchase land rather than freedom. When freedom bells rang out in August, 1838 there was a mad rush on the part of the freed men to acquire lands. They bought up lots of fifty by a hundred feet fronting the public road at $116 a lot, and lots of seventy by a hundred feet immediately behind at $110 a lot. So widespread was the acquisition of land and so rapidly did the emancipated settle down into villages that planters were haunted by the fear that few freed men would remain working as labourers above a year.[4] The years 1780 to 1920 constituted the golden age of peasant proprietorship in Trinidad. Not a great deal of good husbandry was called for. There was a great deal of wild and irresponsible spending, careless borrowing, injudicious mortgaging of properties, and blind improvidence for the future. This was true of all people but more especially true of the recently emancipated. Despite this tempting of fate Prosperity flowed with the tide and wealth was there for the taking. As late as 1939 seventy per cent. of cocoa planters were persons who cultivated less than ten acres of land, and roughly half of all land under cocoa was owned by planters having less than fifty acres each. But already by 1920 a tide of adverse circumstances had set in. Few were prepared to breast it. The race of small owners is today practically extinct. The multitude of small homesteads have been absorbed into the big business enterprises. Why have so many people lost title to ownership of their native land? There were economic factors beyond the control of the local proprietors. But greater than all these is the one which seems to

[4] Burnley, *op. cit.*, pp. 155, 54, 102, 108; Mrs. Carmichael, *Domestic Manners and Social Conditions of the White, Coloured and Negro Population of the West Indies* (2 vols., London: Whittaker, 1834), Vol. II, p. 220.

be fundamental. And to describe it the words of Charles S. Johnson in his study of "The Shadow of the Plantation" can be made our own: "Such families as escape from the prevailing economy of dependence into the new responsibilities which go with independence find economic complications and shades of social conflict which manifest themselves in various ways, sometimes prompting them to migration, but as often leading to resignation and relapse from the ownership status to tenantry."

If the freedman was unprepared for the responsibilities of economic life, he was still more unprepared for the moral responsibilities of civilized life in the West. Cut adrift from the controls of the tribal organization, ineffectively exposed to the influence of Christian religion and education, the freedman was abandoned to his own designs, that is to say, to the promptings of impulse, the call of passion and the sway of concupiscence. The attitude of all but two of the slaves on Mrs. Carmichael's estate at Laurel Hill is revealing and suggestive of a great truth about life within the orbit of the plantation. These slaves preferred to hang themselves in the estate forest rather than contemplate monogamous marriage or, indeed, any binding form of marriage with their own kind. This attitude on the part of the men was shared by the women slaves. Why? Because, as the women put it, on the plantation "Negers run 'bout here, dere and everywhere"—a statement which is borne out by a review of the illegitimate birth rate down through the years. The free people spoke more truly than they perhaps realized when they explained freedom to mean that "there is to be no massas at all".[5]

Unrestraint is not the whole story of the free plantation, that repository of so many of the traditions of slavery. The shiftlessness and social stagnation that stem from the one-crop economy helped to cripple in a newly free people that initiative which was already so badly broken in the machinery of slavery. Worse still, the one-crop economy set in motion forces which made for the

[5] Carmichael, *op. cit.,* Vol. I, p. 246; Vol. II, pp. 177, 178.

servile dependence of the worker upon the landlord, and of both upon the fluctuation of seasons and markets and the imperatives of Empire trade. This economy had the effect of binding the worker hand and foot to the estate owners who themselves were largely robots in the overall system of the plantation. We took notice of Lord Grey's directive to make estate labour the main dependence of the emancipated. His Lordship further directed that the price of Crown lands be raised "very considerably", that "village lots be sold at a high price". The Negroes replied to these conditions by resorting to wholesale squatting. The planters pressed the Colonial Office hard to obtain the ejection of squatters and the prevention of squatting. A step in this direction was a change in the Prisons' regulations which ordered the heads of debtors shaved. A squatters' riot ensued. A tumultuous deputation was ejected from the Council Chamber. It retaliated by breaking the windows. The summoned troops were violently stoned. In reply they fired upon the crowd killing two persons and wounding one mortally. The Governor's carriage was pelted, his coachmen severely wounded. Several estates were fired.

Other methods employed to restrict free labour to the estates were less forcible in character. The following familiar plantation device needs no commentary. In the second quarter of the nineteenth century "John Lamont was taking practical measures to ameliorate his labour difficulties in Naparima. (He) sold off 44 small parcels of land at Canaan to emancipated slaves in order to settle them on the estate. On these lots they built their own houses, and worked on the estates, instead of drifting to the towns. Thus was formed what is known as Bamboo Village at the junction of the Dumfries Road and the Southern Main Road."[6]

In the 1860's a nice legal arrangement was made by which the negroid squatters of 1849 were allowed to retain their holdings. The move "assured the continued sup-

[6] Trinidad Historical Society Publications, "The Life of John Lamont," Public Lecture Series 1935–36 (Port of Spain, Trinidad: Government Printing Office, 1936), p. 23.

ply of produce", and there arose "a prosperous peasantry whose production swelled the exports of the Colony". Sugar exports stepped up from 20,000 tons in 1850 to 67,000 tons in 1879; cacao from less than four million pounds in 1850 to nearly twelve million pounds in 1879. In similar strain we read that "Owing to the difficulty of securing adequate capital for carrying on estate cultivation, and with the additional object of persuading East Indians, whose period of indenture had expired, to remain in the island, the sugar estates began, in the nineties, to encourage the production of cane by peasants for sale to the factory."[7] Employers offered the Indians small tracts of land either rent-free or at a nominal rent. But there was a condition. The land was to be cultivated in cane and in food crops, but primarily in cane. "Two-thirds of the said land fully in sugar-cane" runs the formula of the contract. The terms of this contract may be read on page 69 of Council Paper No. 70 of the year 1926.

Servile economic dependence upon the plantation and the economic insecurity that was necessarily associated with that dependence did not help to stabilize or to regularize the shattered family life of the ex-slave. Moreover, low wages and poor working conditions seem to be inherent in the plantation economy as known to tradition. This fact is amply and specifically borne out by an official document as recent as Command Paper 6179 on Labour Conditions in the West Indies. The writer may therefore be dispensed from any further display of the unpalatable details of the historical evidence. The low wages and working conditions, in conjunction with the moral and social handicaps of the plantation previously discussed, have operated to consolidate those low standards and that low grade mentality which the scourge of slavery during four hundred years burnt into the souls of the subject folk. What is the bearing of this on the non-legal union? It is common knowledge that this low grade mentality con-

[7] C. Y. Shepherd, *Agricultural Labour in Trinidad* (Port of Spain, Trinidad: Government Printing Office, 1936), p. 5.

stitutes the moral climate in which the non-legal union flourishes. There can be no gainsaying that fact.

The arrangements of the plantation, whether in slavery or in freedom, wrought its evils on all alike, regardless of race. Thus we see lower class free white men on the West Indian slave plantation cultivating the organized non-legal union which their free Negro counterparts could only pursue effectively on the free plantation after Emancipation. On this point there is a striking passage in Mrs. Carmichael's diary:

> "Before concluding this imperfect sketch of the white population, I would offer a few observations upon the condition of the secondary class of whites, with reference chiefly to the demoralizing influence of slavery upon their characters and habits,–facts applicable to all West Indian colonies. Slavery operates prejudiciously on the higher classes; but its demoralizing effect operates in a different manner, and still more prejudicially, upon the lower orders of white people, who, having seldom or ever any females in their own situation in life to associate with, and to whom they might be respectably married, they get a negro (probably belonging to the estate they are employed upon) to live with them, until they gradually forget their country, and their early instructions, and become as the expression is, almost a white negro. These, I think, are the effects of slavery among those whose business it is to manage slaves."[8]

The passage is valuable not only for what it openly states. It is a solid warning that the existence of the authentic non-legal union can be explained without recourse to either an African heritage or to personal or group enslavement on the plantation.

THE AFRICAN HERITAGE

Fragments of the African heritage entered into the moulding of West Indian attitudes towards marriage in

[8] Carmichael, *op. cit.,* Vol. I, p. 59.

general. Other fragments lent support to the sexual nomadism of slavery, and yet other fragments helped to fashion patterns of behaviour within the non-legal union itself. However, the initiation of the characteristic relationships between the sexes on the slave plantation was not an ordinance of the African tradition, but rather, and quite obviously the creation of the machinery of slavery itself. Indeed the relationships between the sexes on the slave holding represented an almost complete travesty of the arrangements in West African society. The abnormal in Yoruba society became the normal on the Trinidad slave plantation; what was perverse there became standard here. This was the case, for instance, with sexual relations between persons who had no intention of getting married. This was the case, too, with concubinage.

The non-legal union of the West Indies or the organized family-like concubinage of the free plantation received aid and comfort not from the standard West African code but from marginal practices within the twilight zone of that code. And just as the African heritage did not ordain the nomadic sex arrangements of slavery, so also this heritage did not initiate or sponsor the non-legal union. At most it underscored something which, as history is there to show, issued directly from the play of factors quite distinct from the heritage of Africa. If we wish to saddle Africa with the authorship of the non-legal union of the West Indies then that responsibility is more nearly correctly placed not on the African heritage but on the heritage of African abuses—a very different thing. But even this kind of negative African authorship of the non-legal union in the West Indies cannot be established from the relevant facts of the situation.

For firstly, the arrangements of the plantation economy suffice, as we have already shown, to explain the emergence of the authentic non-legal union among lower class plantation folk of both races, or indeed of any race. In the case of the Negro, if we take into account the sexual anarchy of his slavery background, the impact upon him of the supervening agency of the plantation in freedom offers an even fuller explanation of the origins of the non-legal union.

Secondly, those who propound the African heritage theory in respect of the non-legal union rest their case on two traditions or institutions in the culture of West African society, namely, polygyny or the plurality of wives, and concubinage. Now polygyny and concubinage as practised in West Africa, and particularly so in Yoruba land, constitute a singularly insecure foundation upon which to base the theory in question.

What is the frequency and distribution of polygyny among the Yoruba? Polygyny is of two kinds. It is, reports Father Ward, simple or multiple. It is simple when one man has from two to four wives. It is multiple where a husband has five or more wives, acquired in the usual marriage fashion. Although multiple polygynous unions are to be found in every district however remote, it can be stated as a general rule that where polygyny exists it is of the simple type. Father Ward says that both from systematic observation and from the analysis of population statistics, the practice of polygyny cannot be very widespread, and it is certainly not as widespread as is commonly believed.

> "In the Official Government Statistics of 1912 the Yoruba people were numbered as follows: Males, 996,320; females, 1,117,091; total, 2,113,411. Percentage of totals: Males 47%; females, 53%. According to these figures there were, when taken analytically, in every one hundred persons in the Yoruba population, six more females than males . . . . . If we are to place any reliance on the carefully prepared government statistics which tell us of the relative equality of the sexes, and on the fact that the majority of males find a mate sometime in life, we are forced to the conclusion that the number of (polygynous) unions cannot be so very high."[9]

And in the accumulation of wives, even among the big men, sex interest plays only a minor part; in some cases

[9] Edward Ward, *Marriage Among the Yoruba* (Washington, D.C.: Catholic University, 1937), pp. 24–27, 33.

only a relatively slight part. The achievement of status is the major interest.

The majority of the marriages, as far as he sees, are, Father Ward insists, monogamous, that is, one man is married to one woman. "This form is rarely found among the marriage unions of kings, chiefs, or people with money. I have never known a pagan chief to be monogamous. And in the whole of the land, only a few of those chiefs who profess to be Christian are content with one wife. Among the rank and file, however, monogamy is the common form."[10] As the overwhelming majority of West Indian slaves were rank and file it is evident that they boasted no heritage of the practice of polygyny. It is therefore difficult to see how this heritage enters as a factor in the production of the non-legal union so universally and so suddenly all at once. This solution is unnecessarily far-fetched.

The case for West African concubinage as a start for the non-legal union in the New World rests on no better foundations than the case for polygyny. Concubinage as a cultural unit in the West Indies can be shown to be essentially different from the cultural unit which constitutes concubinage in West African society. Once more we must revert to Yoruba land because of its intimate and necessary connection with Afro-West Indian society in Trinidad. There are two component parts of concubinage as a social institution. There is the external fact of the marital union of two people outside of wedlock, and then there is the other and more important element of the social significance of the external fact within a particular society. The social significance is revealed by the attitude of society towards the external fact. The same fact may be viewed and valued differently in different societies, and this will alter its true character and meaning from society to society. Unless we take the whole institution, body and soul, matter and meaning, it is impossible to tell whether an institution is really common to two or more given societies. One man's meat may be another man's poison. The glory of one is the shame of another. When concubinage in Trinidad is com-

[10] *Ibid.*, p. 41.

pared in this way with concubinage among the Yoruba the result is not a comparison but a contrast.

The external fact is the same in Trinidad as in Africa or in any other part of the globe. But the social attitudes towards the fact in Trinidad and in Yoruba land are poles apart. Among the Yoruba there exists a truly formidable public censure against concubinage, not indeed on moral but on social grounds. Let me quote from Ward.[11]

> "In the Yoruba country, public opinion is not against a man living with a concubine. People do not see anything morally wrong in the sexual angle of that . . . . . It seems to be chiefly the question of status which is involved. The chief means of acquiring status in the Yoruba country is by paying the dowry for a number of wives and by taking them with ceremonies in the accustomed way. A man pushes up his social position a peg with every wife he acquires. Concubines do not count much. They are not included among the legitimately acquired wives. Social status means too much to the ordinary native for him to neglect this" (p. 16).

People speak derisively "of a woman acquired without the customary marriage ceremonies as a 'lover', a concubine in other words" (p. 15). Again, "A girl attached to the harem of a polygynist without having had the marriage ceremony performed, occupies, in the opinion of society, a lower place in the harem than do the other wives. Dowry may have been handed over for her and in reality her husband may class her among his wives, but the people do not see this. There has been no marriage ceremony performed. Consequently, the girl's people are not slow to cry out against a husband who might want to follow this course. The girl herself is very apt to resent such treatment for the same reason and may give him plenty of trouble in his marital experience if he persists. On the other hand, when the full marriage has taken place, both she and her group are always proud to advertise the fact in order to show the world that she has the full status of a wife" (pp.

[11] Edward Ward, *The Yoruba Husband-Wife Code* (Washington, D.C.: Catholic University, 1938).

16, 17). Among the Yoruba, concubinage is resorted to by daredevils and by those who hope to escape detection by absorption into the harem of a rich man's married wives, or who hope to deflect social criticism by attachment to a single man of overwhelming social prestige.

The Yoruba attitude towards unwed mothers is also noteworthy. The unwed mother is usually debarred from getting married in the ordinary ceremonial way. She has lost status and her parents will not receive the full dowry or bride-price for her. Here again it is the loss of social status and not the stigma of giving birth to a child outside of wedlock that matters. No such stigma seems to be present as a general rule. Such a depreciated girl is nearly always certain to find a man with whom to live, who will protect and care for her and the child in return for services. Concubinage in this case is a *refugium peccatorum,* and, as before, the status of the girl will be beneath that of legitimately married women.[12]

How does the Trinidad situation compare with the West African? It is true that in Trinidad the concubine, both in her own eyes and in those of her social set as well as of society at large, is held to be socially quite beneath the "respectable married woman"; it is true that when she succeeds in pulling off a marriage the Trinidad concubine, like her African counterpart, is proud and eager to advertise the fact in order to show the world that she has the full status of a wife. It is also true that among the lower classes in Trinidad parents themselves sometimes give their daughter in concubinage to a "bigger" man if formal marriage is not forthcoming. But here the similarities end. And, be it noted, these points of similarity are not characteristic of Africa and the West Indies; they are commonly associated with concubinage in most parts of the Western world. And as to parental connivance in a concubinal arrangement for their daughters, that is easily and naturally explained by the circumstances surrounding a girl of humble and insecure station, or of uncertain prospects, particularly if she has happened to conceive in fault for a

[12] *Ibid.*, p. 34.

"bigger" man or even for one who is not so "big" but who is able to fend for his own and for her support. Such negotiations with lower class white and other men by free coloured mothers in the interest of their own daughters were notorious in nineteenth century Trinidad society, and are recorded by Mrs. Carmichael: "The majority of (coloured) parents have little anxiety upon the subject; and to make a good bargain—that is, a good legal settlement for their daughter—is all they aim at; and if this be properly and legally managed, they consider marriage of little import." And when the connexion is with a white man "the coloured women always glory in the tie".[13]

The tempting similarities suggesting lineage between African and West Indian concubinage lose their plausibility when confronted with the significant differences between the two. And not only this; the West Indian features of resemblance then appear to be quite fortuitous and to form no part of the genuine African article. Is the West Indian concubine the object of derision or of carping criticism in her social set or in society at large? Not at all. On the contrary, while her state is not admired, she is the object of a sort of benign sympathy, the sort of sympathy with which one looks upon the victim of a necessary evil. I am not saying that concubinage is a necessary evil; I am saying that whereas in Africa the evil is a deliberate choice contrary to accepted standards and duly castigated, in the West Indies the lower class patrons of concubinage generally seem to feel that they have little or no choice in the matter. Hence the attitude towards them of that certain kind of sympathy so difficult to describe because so complex. Complex because it proceeds from a dual outlook by which one part of the mind, so to speak, sympathizes, and the other part disapproves on both social and religious grounds. Disapproval, overt or covert, on religious and moral grounds is another difference that puts West Indian concubinage in an entirely different category from the African institution.

Again: Do lower class West Indian parents cry out and

[13] Carmichael, *op. cit.*, Vol. I, p. 73.

take vigorous action against a suitor who plans to enter into concubinage with their daughter? No indeed; they almost encourage him. There are, of course, exceptions. Does the West Indian girl candidate for concubinage resent that course, or does she plot reprisals on the man if she is forced into that state? She is the most obliging and obsequious partner in the world, incomparably more obsequious and obliging than lawfully married women are, and more obliging than she herself will be when she succeeds in pulling off that marriage. Her attitude is explained by her need of security on the one hand, and on the other by the absence of public censure. Is West Indian concubinage a *refugium peccatorum* in the sense of a hiding place or an escape for fallen girls? It is this in some instances. But in general it is neither hiding place nor escape; nor is it reserved for women fallen by strange men but is an ordinary career for a man and his chosen spouse.

Considered as a whole or complete social phenomenon, that is, considered as an organic social institution, concubinage in the West Indies does not appear to derive from its African counterpart. It is more simply and more naturally and historically explained independently of specific West African influence. And, finally, concubinage in the West Indies turns out, upon close examination, to be essentially different from that item in West Africa. The connection between the two things in the concrete is external and accidental, and the integral West Indian article is naturally well explained without recourse to African concubinage.

In summary, then, it is my finding that West African polygamy and West African concubinage have no significant bearing upon the structure and the patterns of behaviour within the non-legal union in the West Indies. I am satisfied, however, that there are portions of the West African heritage which have exerted a direct and substantial influence on certain West Indian attitudes towards marriage in general, and upon certain patterns of behaviour within the non-legal union in particular. Not even slavery and the plantation could fashion the West Indian Negro out of nothing. Only God can do that. The slave could not help bringing to the plantation that which he was. It was upon what the Negro was that slavery wrought and the plantation in freedom re-wrought. It is therefore important to know what the rank and file Negro was and thought and did for ages and ages in West Africa before he came as a slave to the West Indies. And here we are concerned with the field of marriage organization only.

Among the Yoruba a man usually has sex relations before formal marriage with the first girl whom he is engaged to wed. As the rank and file marry but one wife it can be said generally that among the Yoruba the engaged usually get to know each other sexually before marriage. The purpose of this relationship is to find out whether the girl can conceive.[14] Because this practice is so universal among the Yoruba it is easy to see the connection between it and similar beliefs among the descendants of the Yoruba in the West Indies. There is a lingering belief in Trinidad that sexual intercourse as between persons engaged to be married does not fall under the proscriptions of the sixth and ninth commandments of the Decalogue. It is also common to find concubines postponing marriage on the ground that the woman must first "prove herself", that is, bear a child. For, says the man, I do not want to marry a mule.

Another important item with the Yoruba is solemnization of the marriage ceremony and the great emphasis on the elaborateness of the festival to follow. These rituals are intended both to mark and to augment social prestige. Forms of marriage ceremonial differ from region to region, tribe to tribe, and even within the same tribes. Of the forms best known all include a bridal procession involving a great deal of conference with the prospective bridegroom. In remote regions the procession also involves considerable ceremonial ill-treatment of the bridegroom by the parents, relatives and friends of the bride. In all cases the formal marriage ceremony ends with the introduction or admission of the bride to his home by the bridegroom. This is the moment and the ceremony of climax. On the night of the wedding all are entertained lavishly by the host, the bridegroom, and the night is spent in a riot of song,

[14] Ward, *The Yoruba Husband-Wife Code*, pp. 11, 29.

drunkenness and dance. The elaborate entertainment provides "plenty of the best pounded yams of the place, good, well-cooked bush meat and palm wine in abundance." The feast is dear to the heart of every Yoruba. All look forward to it. It costs them nothing and the host spends himself and is spent even "though he may have to go begging for the future."[15] In Trinidad we know with what eagerness neighbours and friends look forward to the "freeness" of a wedding feast. And the West Indian attaches such importance to the elaborateness of his wedding festival that, unlike other Western peoples who also love wedding pomp and splendour, he would rather not go through with the wedding ceremony if he cannot provide the elaborate festivity. Once more the connection between this distinctive trait and its West African archetype is easily and naturally established.

The sexual liberty allowed married men among the Yoruba is also pertinent to behaviour within the non-legal union. It is by no means the whole explanation of extramarital relationships, but since all husbands practised it in the old country it cannot but be an influence on the conduct of the male partner in the new country. The liberties allowed in the West African code grew in part out of the lengthy periods of abstention from his wife during pregnancy and lactation imposed by the tribal code. Partly also out of consideration for the man who was financially unable to afford the price of a new wife.[16] This man may, without incurring the censure of his people, have recourse to outside women. A certain type of woman with whom married men thus associate is designated a "friend". The West Indian expression "to be friendin" with somebody is used in exactly the same way as among the Yoruba.

[15] *Ibid.*, pp. 12–17.
[16] *Ibid.*, pp. 150, 151.

15.

The significance of slavery for the characteristic West Indian mating and family patterns was recognized long before Dom Basil Matthews' writings. In this article, a Jamaican sociologist contends that West Indian family forms "are in fact a product of the peculiar conditions of slavery." Neither Africa nor Europe need be looked to for sociocultural continuities or survivals: the unique pre-emancipation West Indian reality explains present-day West Indian domestic groupings. Following the lead of T. S. Simey's *Welfare and Planning in the West Indies,* Henriques sets forth a typology of domestic groups based on forms of cohabitation—the Christian family, faithful concubinage, the maternal or grandmother family, and the keeper family. Fuller details and examples of these types are supplied in Henriques' more recent monograph, *Family and Colour in Jamaica.*

FERNANDO HENRIQUES was born in Jamaica, trained in social anthropology, and received his doctorate from Oxford University. Previously attached to the University of Leeds, he is currently Professor at the University of Sussex and Director of the Centre for Multi-Racial Studies in Barbados.

West Indian Family Organisation

Fernando Henriques

West Indian Negro society is bounded by poverty and color frustration. The island of Jamaica is taken as typical of society in the Caribbean. The family or domestic group in this society can be regarded as a phenomenon *sui generis.* Four types can be distinguished: Christian family, faithful concubinage, maternal or grandmother family, and keeper family. These familial forms exhibit a marked degree of stability. But they can be regarded as indicative of the disequilibrium inherent in the society. The contemporary family structure of the Negro in the New World is the result of plantation slavery rather than of a West African tradition.

When discovered by Columbus in 1492, the West Indies were inhabited by Tanala, Arawak, and Carib Indian tribes. In a comparatively short time through the rigors of enslavement these tribes became, in most areas, almost entirely extinct. As the European powers turned from the vain search for gold to tobacco—and sugar-planting, the demand for a labor force began to grow. At first the experiment with European indentured labor was tried under conditions very like actual slavery. The experiment was a failure, and the Europeans were soon replaced by African slave labor.

The Negro slaves in the New World were drawn from a great area of Africa stretching from northern Nigeria to south of the Congo. It was not only the coastal regions which were involved for there are references in the liter-

From *American Journal of Sociology*, Vol. 55, No. 1, July 1949, pp. 30–37. Reprinted with permission of the author and University of Chicago Press.

ature to Negroes from eastern and central Africa brought across the continent by coffle to slave ports on the western coast. There are even some references to slaves from Madagascar. Some of the designations utilized in old Caribbean slave lists, too, may give an indication of the variety of tribal groupings concerned: Fan, Whydah, Mocoe, Fanti, Nago, Yoruba, Coromantyn (Ashanti), Egba, Ibo, Ewe, and Madagass.

Crossing the Atlantic meant for the Negro a complete break with his traditional type of society. Customs, social sentiments, and patterns of behaviour could survive only as ideas and oral traditions, for there were no special mechanisms in the new society by which they could be perpetuated.

The society into which the Negro was inducted was radically different from any type of African society. Plantation slavery in the West Indies involved a constant supply of Negroes, who constituted the actual labor force both in the fields and in the homes, the supply being maintained both by frequent importations and by local breeding, chiefly the former. Slaves were forced to live in barracks or in huts. As the slave might be sold at any time to another local owner or into the American colonies, there was no real security. Obviously this affected his domestic behaviour, since any union he might contract with a woman was liable to be broken up. Again the owner would often encourage his female slaves to breed from a number of men, even offering prizes for this purpose, in the mistaken belief that intercourse with a number of men increased fecundity. In other words, slaves were not permitted to form permanent unions on either an African or a European model. Family life under these conditions was impermanent. Thus the emphasis in the contemporary slave family was upon the mother-child relationship.

It was the common practice among the owners and European plantation employees to take concubines from among the better-looking of the female slaves. Two patterns can be discerned here. One was the setting up of an independent household for the concubine and her children, both being well cared for by her master-protector.

The other was for the concubine to be temporarily lodged in the plantation house. But, after she had out-grown her use, she was returned with her children to the barrack or hut. The female children of such unions quite often became in their turn the mistresses of Europeans. To the female slave concubinage offered an avenue of escape, even though temporary, from oppressive field labor.

These practices were to have a profound effect not only on the forms of the family but on the whole class-color hierarchy of the society. It can be said that concubinage was the foundation of the present color-class grading system in the West Indies. Christianity with its advocacy of monogamous marriage was unable to make much headway in these conditions. The planters as a group were opposed to the conversion of their slaves lest it increased slave rebellions.

The radical changes introduced by emancipation in 1834 profoundly modified this system. The chief reaction of many of the freed slaves was to get away as far as possible from the plantation and its associations. To begin with, there was great enthusiasm in favour of the orthodox Christian churches, many of which had been in the forefront in the fight for abolition. But this enthusiasm quickly waned, and local 'native' churches began to develop.

Although the freed Negro could remove himself from the plantation in a physical sense, he was unable to destroy the patterns of behaviour evolved under the system of plantation slavery. This is strikingly seen in the contemporary family structure.

Professor Herskovits' view is that the original West African forms of the family survived in the Caribbean and in the New World generally. My own contention is that the forms of the family in the West Indies are *sui generis*. They are in fact a product of the peculiar conditions of slavery. To some extent these forms may have been influenced by the fact that slaves were largely drawn from polygamous groups, but the dominant influence has undoubtedly been that of slavery.

To substantiate the contrary view–that West African forms have survived into the contemporary scene–it would be necessary to show that patrilineal influence, for example, in Haiti, had produced a different type of family from that existing in Jamaica, where the predominant influence appears to have been matrilineal. Professor Herskovits' own field material on Haiti shows that this is not the case.

Again Leyburn has pointed out that Haitian slaves were drawn from at least thirty-eight African groups, and Freyre has produced similar evidence for Brazil. Since the slaves in the New World were drawn from a great area of Africa, it would have been impossible for any one culture to survive as a whole. In other words, the throwing-together of matrilineal and patrilineal groups in a particular area would have prevented the development of a society of one specific type or the other.

What in fact occurred was that these diverse groups were subjected to the uniformity of slavery. The manifestations of slavery in the New World were very similar. Localized differences illustrated by religious cult groups have persisted through verbal traditions. There are obvious differences between the Yoruba cults in Trinidad and Brazil and similar cults in Jamaica. But in the sphere which was controlled by the master, family life, the slave was forced into a new mould. That mould was the same in its major aspects all over the New World. The pattern of European-African concubinage and the impermanence of slave sexual relationships is repeated from Brazil to the United States.

Patterns of family life could not survive as a verbal tradition. Whereas the slave could, and did, practice his magic and divination in secret, he could not perpetuate his ancestral family forms in secret. The pattern of his family life was governed by the will of his master. With the exception of the 'bush Negro' of Dutch Guiana who has, through isolation, evolved a matrilineal family pattern which owes little to slavery, the contemporary family structure among the New World Negroes can be distinguished as a phenomenon due mainly to the influence of slavery.

Illegitimacy figures for the territories in the Caribbean area fall between 50 and 70 per cent. of the total of live births. Thus, the so-called 'deviation' from the norm of Christian monogamous marriage is fairly uniform over the whole area, and a similar type of family organisation exists through-out the region. A discussion of family life in Jamaica supports my contention that the Negro family in the New World is *sui generis.*

The class structure in Jamaica can be seen as a division into three classes: lower (85 per cent. of the population), middle, and upper. These classes are determined by a variety of factors, including color, income and prestige.

The primary group is the elementary biological family, consisting of a man, a woman, and their children, real and socially ascribed. There has been a tendency to equate family and marriage, but, as Linton points out, 'the personnel and function of this (conjugal) group may coincide with those of the authentic family in certain societies but they do not do so for human societies as a whole. Marriage and the family are really separate institutions and must be considered separately'. The tendency to equate marriage and the family is due to the fact that in western Europe this coincidence often takes place, and it is difficult for Europeans to dissociate them dealing with other societies.

Domestic groupings can be divided into those with a conjugal and those with a consanguineous basis; that is, into groupings which stress the husband-wife relationship and those which stress the blood relationships of either the father or the mother. Western Europe exemplifies the former while parts of Africa exemplify the latter.

Jamaican family structure does not fall clearly into either category but appears to combine qualities of both. There is however, a tendency in certain types of family grouping to stress the husband-wife relationship. But there is not the same recognition of the monogamous conjugal union as the licit and morally approved means of satisfying sexual needs as there is in western Europe. If this deviation is recognized, the best method of classifying family groupings appears to be the adoption of the term 'domestic group' as the unit of family structure in the island.

In Jamaica the domestic group is the residential unit

which constitutes a household. This group may, but this is not always the case, consist of the elementary biological family, that is, of a man, a woman and their real and socially ascribed children. It exists to satisfy the needs of sexual gratification and parent-child relationships (i.e., procreation and child-rearing), common housekeeping and other domestic needs associated with social standing in the community. A domestic group may serve all these needs or only some of them, according to its actual constitution.

Four types of such groups can be distinguished: (*a*) Christian family, (*b*) faithful concubinage, (*c*) maternal or grandmother family, and (*d*) keeper family.

The classification is not rigid, since a domestic group can in its history experience all these forms. Also there are groups which exhibit features of more than one group. But for the purposes of analysis it is necessary to make a broad classification.

Marriage is the cohabitation of a man and woman with the legal and social sanction of a particular society. Type A is the only form of family group which is based on marriage; the others have apparent community tolerance but no legal sanction. Jamaica is thus a society in which there is a contradiction, as regards conjugal unions between what is legally accepted as the norm for the whole society and what is actually socially accepted. This contradiction or opposition between legal and social acceptance applies to other situations, beside the family.

Cohabitation is the mark of the domestic group of Types A, B, and D, but it is not apparent in the case of Type C. A domestic group does not depend on cohabitation, for cohabitation helps to determine the type of family but not the existence of the family.

It must be emphasized that the classification of family groups is not of such fundamental importance as an understanding of the functions of such groups in the society.

Stability and continuity in the family are more assured where there is a greater emphasis on the consanguineous as opposed to the husband-wife relationship. That stability is exhibited to a marked degree by the society considered.

The total number of mothers in Jamaica in 1942 was

258,842. Approximately 34 per cent. were listed as married, 54 per cent. as unmarried, and 12 per cent. as widowed or divorced.

The attitude toward legal marriage is ambivalent. Unmarried mothers questioned will express a desire to be married, but frequently the same persons will say that they are not sure of the man and wish to wait until they are or until the 'right' man comes along. Although no social stigma attaches to the unmarried state, and 'living in sin' is not a term of reproach, marriage is regarded often as an ideal not within the woman's reach. Marriage, to the lower-class woman, means a better home and, above all, a servant. Many Christian households were found in which a servant was kept. In other words, the economic condition is of some importance in determining legal marriage. The majority of cases of monogamy was found among the better-off members of the lower class. A typical case is that of a man who combined peasant proprietorship with work as a carpenter or factory hand. Since the Jamaican insists on a 'show' for his wedding, another obstacle is the actual cost of the ceremony. People must be entertained with music, rum, and food; if this can not be done, it would not be a 'proper' wedding.

Another fear expressed by unmarried mothers is that marriage will lead to undue domination of her by the man. This may be a very real fear, as there is no doubt that the monogamous union is a family strictly ruled by the husband-father, whereas in Types B, C, and D the woman is quite often the dominant member of the family. In practice the unmarried union leads to equality between the sexes.

Color does not enter much into the situation. The majority of the lower class is black, as is the majority of the better-off section of this class. Color only operates in the usual way in governing the choice of a mate; an attempt is always made to secure a woman lighter in complexion and with 'better' features and hair.

The typical monogamous family lives in a three-room wooden house with a corrugated iron roof. One room will be a living room, the others bedrooms. There may be more than one bed for the children, and this is of great importance, since it affects their early sexual habits. The fact that children do not sleep in the same room with their parents is of equal importance. The family gathers in the evenings on the veranda, and friends are entertained there. If in a town, the house has electric light. In physical layout the home will correspond with a simplified version of the middle-class home.

The father will have a regular job and a small cultivation either adjacent to the house or up in the 'bush'. He will be the sole wage-earner unless sons are of sufficient age to be working (about fourteen). He will give his wife money for household expenses, but there is no question of his turning over his weekly earnings to her. He is the final authority in all disputes in the home. The children attend school regularly and have more or less adequate clothing to do so. The whole family will be assiduous in its church-going. Diet will be sufficient if not sufficiently nutritious. Such a household may consist of the man and his wife, from two to eight children of the couple, the man's mother, rarely with wife's mother, the father's sister and her children, and the servants.

In all small matters the mother is the authority, that is to say, in the daily running of the house. She gives the servant orders, goes to market, &c., but anything requiring a more-than-routine decision is referred to the father. In disputes between the husband and wife, the grandmother often sides with the wife although normally she does not interfere. The wife does not attend to the cultivation unless she wishes to, and she is not forced to do so by the husband. He works the cultivation much as the English allotment holder, that is, in his spare time and at week ends. The wife may sell the produce in the market or get a friend to do so, but she has to account to the husband for the money.

Disputes are frequent in the family during the adolescence of the children. They may come about through the choice of work for the sons or at the girls' running wild with boys. In some cases the children will leave home either to get a job in the capital or to live with some other family. From an early age children are subjected to physical punishment, the father often enforcing his authority with a belt or strap. Meals are taken in common, and this acts as a binding force for the whole family.

The picture which emerges is reminiscent of the respectable Victorian working-class family in which the husband was a sober and steady person in regular employment. The atmosphere is markedly religious, and the patriarchal position of the father is reinforced by frequent reading of the Bible.

The maintenance of this type of family is governed by the regularity in the man's employment, which gives to it economic stability. His sexual needs are satisfied within marriage. If he does feel the temptation to go outside, religion and respectability are liable to prevent him: to do so would be to betray the group and place him with the undesirable elements of his class. This feeling is very strong.

Increased income is a contributory factor of monogamy. There are many instances of better-off couples in the lower class classified under Type A who have preserved some of the tradition of peasant people who after emancipation were extremely religious, as many authorities testify. Such families will be proud of their church connection which dates back two generations or more. It is, however, impossible to say precisely what the motives are which cause one section of the lower class to adopt the manners and morals of the middle class as opposed to the majority of their own class.

The line of demarcation between Type B, the faithful concubinage; Type C, the grandmother or maternal family; and Type D, the keeper family is not so clearly defined as between these forms and Type A, the monogamous union. There is a tendency for Types B, C, and D, to coalesce; that is, a given family unit in its lifetime may experience all three forms.

Type B can be described as the kind of family in which the man lives with the woman as if he were married to her and performs all the functions of a legal husband. There is, of course, the most profound psychological difference between such a household and that described above. A much greater sense of equality exists between the couple. Many women will say that they dislike the idea of marriage since it means being under rule of the man. Such expressions are more common among the couples who have been together only a few years, and they tend to disappear as the household persists.

The grandmother family (Type C) is so called because the grandmother or some female relative, perhaps a sister, usurps the function of the father and, at times, the function of the mother. Such a family may originate through a girl's becoming pregnant while still living at home. The girl's father may not be living at home. The household will possibly consist of her mother, her mother's sister, and the girl's siblings. The girl may continue at home and look after her child, but in case she leaves, the child is reared by its grandmother, being treated in the same way as the other children in the household. If the girl's father lives in the house, he will act toward his grandchild as if it were his child. There are thus two types to be distinguished in Type C: one in which there is no male head of the family and the grandmother or other female relative fulfils the function of both father and mother; another in which the grandmother may stand in the place of the mother, but a man is normally the head of the household.

Pressure may be brought to bear by the girl's family on the father of the child to make him contribute to her and the child's support. She may even have him brought before the court and seek a bastardy order. But neither remedy is effective if the man's whereabouts are unknown. Additional income may be brought into the family. In many instances the girl may move away and send money to her mother and, in other cases, when she has settled down with a man, send for her child.

In the case of Type D, the keeper family, the man and woman live together in a temporary union. He will contribute to the woman's support, but she may continue to work, depending upon how much money he brings home. If the union persists over a period of years, it will come under the heading of a settled concubinage. The arrival of children does not affect the continuance of the union; in fact, the presence of several children tends to drive the man away, as it makes greater demands on his income.

It can be seen from the description of Types B, C, and D that the psychological and domestic atmosphere of these households differs radically from that of the monogamous union. In Type C the child grows up with no knowledge of its father. The same can be said of Type D, since, by the time the child is of an age to notice its parents, the father may have left the home. It is only in the case of faithful concubinage that conditions do approximate to that of the monogamous union. The female partner in the keeper family is constantly aware of the insecurity of her position, which is the price she pays for her freedom from any restrictions. Although the latter union is on a basis of equality, either partner is likely, if the union is broken up against one or the other's will, to resort to obeah or violence. This may occur in all four types of family, with the lowest incidence for Type A.

It is difficult to make any accurate estimate of the incidence of the different types of families, since the Jamaica census has no classification. A rough estimate from observations in the field would be that, of all households, 25 per cent. would come under the heading 'monogamous unions' and 25 per cent. under 'faithful concubinage' with the remaining 50 per cent. being divided in unknown proportions between Types C and D. Types C and D tend to occur more in the younger age groups in the period of sexual experimentation, although they are by no means confined to such groups. The incidence for town and country does not seem to vary in any marked way. The latter statement is of great importance, since it illustrates the fact that the Jamaican family structure is not due to the degeneration of a rural culture by corrupting urban or industrial influences, as was the case of the southern Negro migrating to the northern cities in the United States, but that it is a natural development of Jamaican society. Actual living conditions, therefore, are of vital importance not in determining the type of family but in affecting the norms of behaviour inside a particular type.

It is not suggested that the four types of family are fixed categories but that there is an essential unity of them all, in part provided by color, and in part by poverty. Again, the rigidity of these divisions is softened by the numerous examples of domestic groups which pass through these forms. That is not to say that there is little form or order in these groups; the contrary is the case. A typical example from any one of the categories will exhibit a definite type of behaviour which justifies its inclusion in its particular category.

Color provides a general uniformity, as the majority of the lower class is black. Again, poverty is the essential background of all lower-class families. If a scale of poverty be made on the level of income, the majority of families will decrease from Type A to Type D. That is to say, those families coming in the category of the Christian family would form the better-off group in the lower class. Those in the keeper family would be nearest to the extreme poverty line. There are, of course, exceptions—examples of Christian families, and the reverse, households in the latter category which enjoy the same level of income as many Christian families. But poverty exists in all groups; it is merely a question of degree.

Low income as opposed to high income will produce poor living conditions, and the actual housing of the lower class is sufficient proof of that. Outbreaks of violence and brutality are due to the cheek-by-jowl existence in overcrowded houses. Bad housing may affect children's attendance at school. With poor sanitary conditions the disease rate is greater; it undoubtedly creates anxiety about the future and may prevent the development of an active desire for change. In fact, poverty pervades the entire structure of the Jamaican lower-class family. But what it does *not* do is to create the forms of that structure. In that context economic insecurity merely becomes one of several conditions.

The problem confronting the Jamaican peasantry and proletariat is that which is presented to all societies: how to satisfy the needs of sex, procreation, domesticity, prestige, &c. The solution of the problem is determined by the society's past and by its contemporary environment. In the case of Jamaica the freed slave inherited a tradition of slavery. Emancipation meant, for the vast bulk of the slaves, translation to a new world. It meant that after generations of dependence they could now choose the way they would live. That transition from dependence to freedom was, and still is, of supreme psychological importance to the Jamaican.

It cannot be stressed too often that the slave could not marry. The example of his masters was indeed one of marriage, but it was of marriage in conjunction with concubinage. The West African heritage of the ideal polygamy and the dissolubility of marriage may have persisted in a verbal tradition and may have been reinforced by the semblance of polygamy in the slave forms of mating.

The psychological atmosphere of freedom found expression in the almost complete revulsion of the Negro from the estate labor. Similarly there existed the active desire to carry freedom into all forms of life. If this be granted against the background of the factors mentioned, the development of the present family structure can be seen.

The Jamaican lower-class woman both in social and in family affairs has a prominence which is absent in the equivalent European society. Often in a mixed social group, whether a party or a trade union, it is a woman who is the leader, openly or covertly. In the maternal family no male is in authority over the grandmother. In the keeper family there is generally an equality of status and authority between the man and the woman. In any group where the woman is the chief wage-earner she tends to be the final authority and the administrator of the family.

One of the distinctive features of Jamaican lower-class family life is the strong sense of kin beyond that of the immediate family. In any domestic group taken at random there are likely to be adopted children, an aunt, some distant male relative, or perhaps someone who cannot claim any blood relationship whatsoever. All children in the household are treated by the biological siblings as their brothers and sisters. The mother and father make no distinction between the adopted and real children. Those members of the group who do not possess a clearly defined position, as for example, that of an uncle, are addressed as 'Coz' or 'Cousin'. To the child deference is due to all those older than himself, as to his parents. Such persons will, if able, contribute to the upkeep of the household. They are treated as full members in every sense of the word.

Collateral relatives in a domestic group are more often those of the mother than the father. Thus in the maternal family, with the grandmother as its head, there will be a number of her relatives of both sexes. In this type of family the sense of kin is stronger than in the other types. In all matters connected with the family in Jamaica, except in the upper class, there appears to be both an unconscious bias toward the maternal.

In Jamaica lower-class society, because of the general social and economic insecurity, which is reflected in the lower forms of the family, there is a tendency to stress relationships between individuals. As the insecurity diminishes the tendency diminishes. In the upper class there is less of kin feeling, though it is much greater than in the equivalent class in England. This economic interpretation of kinship does not ignore the historical factor, but what may have had historical causation is now supported and controlled by the economic fabric of the society.

The lower-class domestic family satisfies the needs of sex, domesticity, prestige, &c., but it also subserves another important function. Jamaican society is in an acute state of disequilibrium. A vast lower-class population lives barely above the subsistence level. This class is opposed to a small upper class, which, comparatively speaking is extremely wealthy. The contrast between the two modes of living presented to the submerged group results in feelings of envy and frustration. There are no means whereby equality of status can be achieved, for on either hand are the barriers of color and of lack of economic opportunity. This has led to an intensification of family relationships as a substitute for the individual's social and economic advancement. In English society where such barriers do not exist except in fragmentary form there has been a steady decline in the emphasis on family as opportunities for advancement and social security increase.

Although the society is in a state of disequilibrium, this does not mean that the family groupings described are themselves disorganized, as some writers have suggested. In fact, they have exhibited a high degree of stability over a long period. This criticism is due to the error of regarding the family structure of the Jamaican lower-class as a deviant from the West European ideal, evidence of which are the strictures on the so-called illegitimacy rate of 71 per cent. This attitude negates any attempt at a proper analysis of the family structure.

A comparable society in a state of disequilibrium would be that of an occupied European country during the war. The members of the Jewish community, for example, in Holland, although oppressed and persecuted, established a definite behaviour pattern which exhibited stability, yet its existence was a symptom of the disequilibrium inherent in Dutch society at that time.

This article has attempted to show that the Jamaican family structure illustrates the thesis that the forms of the family among the New World Negroes is *sui generis* a phenomenon which owes its character to the historic condition of slavery.

16.

In this selection from her book *My Mother Who Fathered Me,* Edith Clarke carries forward the debate on West Indian family forms by classifying rural Jamaican varieties of cohabitation and household patterns. Class and economic differences, in her view, play a major role in determining forms of household structure, marital union, and parental roles. Comparisons of three communities–a sugar town, an impoverished agricultural village, and a relatively prosperous peasant village–show how present-day conditions directly affect the types of cohabitation and household organization predominant in each social setting. Specific socioeconomic and ecological variables are seen to result in distinctive combinations of family types on the community level.

EDITH CLARKE, a member of a distinguished Jamaican family, joined that island's civil service in 1936, serving as Secretary to the Board of Supervision for the administration of poor relief and as the first woman member of the Legislative Council. She earned her diploma in Anthropology from the University of London and is a recipient of the Order of the British Empire.

Variations in Jamaican Domestic Patterns*

Edith Clarke

I

The year 1938 may well come to be recognized by historians as marking the beginning of a new phase in the social and political development of Jamaica, if not of the West Indies as a whole. Inevitably the emergence in Jamaica, in that year, of a labour movement, aggressively expressing the needs of the working class, and the beginnings of Trade Union organization, meant the direction as never before of public interest to problems of work and wages, unemployment and poverty.

Alongside the political activity there were new and important developments in the voluntary social services. In particular, the formation in 1936 of Jamaica Welfare Limited under the dynamic leadership of Mr Manley marked the beginning of a new approach to welfare work with the emphasis on an improvement in the standard of living of the working classes through self-help.[1]

Inevitably the inquiries which were set on foot attracted attention to wider aspects of the organization of society and particularly to the structure of the family. In this respect

* [Editors' title]

From *My Mother Who Fathered Me: A Study of the Family in Three Selected Communities in Jamaica,* London, George Allen & Unwin, 1957, 2nd edition, 1966. Reprinted with permission of the author and publisher.

[1] For a history of Jamaica Welfare Limited (now the Jamaica Social Welfare Commission), see Roger Marier, *Social Welfare Work in Jamaica* (Paris: UNESCO, 1953).

it was clear that both ideals of behaviour and actual practice varied widely between different social classes: the principles which operated in the upper and middle classes were not even accepted as ideals in peasant and working class society.

Popular interest concentrated mainly on two closely related aspects of family organization: the fact that among the poorer Jamaicans concubinage was a substitute for marriage, and the high rate of illegitimacy. It was also very widely believed that a rate of population increase which was regarded with alarm was directly related to sexual promiscuity, parental irresponsibility and the looseness of conjugal ties.

There followed a dangerous, because sterile, approach of seeking to explain dissident elements in contemporary social institutions in one of two ways: either by reference to the historical facts of slavery or in terms of both the cultures which have contributed to Jamaica's history–the European and the African. Thus the 'maternal' family was said to be characteristic of Jamaican peasants either because West African societies were supposed to have been matriarchal, or because during the period of slavery Negro children were wholly dependent on their mothers; the existence of concubinage as a socially recognized relationship was accounted for sometimes as a local version or adaptation of African polygamy and sometimes as a consequence of prohibition or discouragement of marriage between slaves. To many of those who were giving sincere and anxious thought to the problems of the family in Jamaica, it appeared simply as the European family 'gone wrong' owing to a series of historical events, the chief of which was slavery.

It is true that the principal features of slavery had the effect, intentionally or unintentionally, of obliterating African institutions and that at a later period there developed a coloured middle class which not only adopted European values but was highly sensitive to any reminder of African antecedents. It was largely from this class there came criticism of comparative studies which aimed at isolating the different cultural strains either in institutions, myth or folklore. To many, the different class patterns appeared as the result of a choice between two cultural traditions: the European, defined in terms of Christian monogamy and stress on the father role, and the 'African', defined in terms of the maternal family, concubinage, illegitimacy, etc.

Even if we reject those theories which explain contemporary institutions in terms of elements derived from parent cultures, we must take into account those historical events which have clearly influenced family life in Jamaica.

There was, under slavery, no room for the family as a parent-child group in a home; still less for the development of those stable relationships among a wider circle of kin such as can be maintained only if kinsmen live in permanent contact or are able to travel freely and visit one another. The residential unit in the plantation system was formed by the mother and her children with the responsibility for their maintenance resting with the slaveowner. The father's place in the family was never secure. He had no externally sanctioned authority over it and could at any time be physically removed from it. His role might, indeed, end with procreation. Occasionally a father was able to undertake responsibility for his family to the extent of supplying them with food from land which he cultivated but he was only able to acquire such land through the benevolence of his owner. In general, he was not the source of protection and provision for mother and children. This might come directly from some other man or from the system itself which, while a woman was of child-bearing age, secured to her and her children at least their minimum material necessities. It is against this background of the weakness of the father role in the system of family relationships that those of mother and grandmother assume particular importance.[2]

It would be a mistake, however, to stop here in our analysis. The fact of Emancipation did not in itself create a set of conditions, social or economic, in which the freed

[2] See E. Franklin Frazier, *The Negro Family in the United States* (Chicago: University of Chicago Press, 1939), and T. S. Simey, *Welfare and Planning in the West Indies* (Oxford: The Clarendon Press, 1946), pp. 79–80.

Negro could at once assume the role of father and husband in the new society. While, at Emancipation, the slave-owners were compensated for loss of property by the British Government, so far as the slaves were concerned the assumption apparently was that they should remain as wage-labourers on the estates to which they had been attached. The British Government in the nineteenth century was not concerned to interfere in the social and economic adjustments created by the new situation. The local administration, representing the planters as it did, was still less prepared to introduce measures which, by giving the newly created peasantry an alternative to wage labour, would have threatened to deplete their labour supply.

Nevertheless conditions in Jamaica differed in an important aspect from those in the Southern States after Emancipation, where the ex-slaves were still tied inevitably to the old plantations and to wage labour at rates fixed and conditions prescribed by their previous owners.[3] In Jamaica they had not only the right to move but there was somewhere to which they could move and start a new life. Many trekked to the 'back lands' of the plantations, unsuitable for cultivation and unused by the planters, others established themselves as squatters on the Crown lands and in the forest reserves. Others gradually bought small holdings helped by the early Land Settlement Schemes of the Christian missions. Others, still, received grants of land from their ex-owners to own in perpetuity. . . . But from the period following Emancipation, because it was felt to give the greatest freedom from white domination, a special value came to be attached to 'owned' as distinct from rented land. It became one, if not the most important, indication of improved, higher status.

There thus developed an association of certain ways of life and of earning a livelihood with status and class structure: as also with the patterns of behaviour accepted within the higher class. For example 'ownership' of land and marriage came to be associated with the highest class

[3] Frazier, *op. cit.*

status, and manual labour or working for wages as 'a common labourer' with the lowest.

As far as the family was concerned, Emancipation, by making it possible for a man to own land and sell his produce, or offer his labour where he pleased, created conditions in which he could assume the role of father and husband without the threat of external interference in these relationships. Family patterns were, however, already prescribed by status and class structure. The slave-owners, in opposing the teaching of the Christian Missionaries on marriage, as inappropriate for the slaves, were in fact primarily concerned with the possible effect of this on their right of free disposition of their chattels. But they also appeared to be arguing that Christian monogamy was the prerogative of the white man, and associated with the caste structure. But, in fact, the white man's monogamy almost invariably had concubinage as its concomitant. White planters often accepted responsibility for their children by negro mistresses. Not only were the status and material conditions of the mother better in these cases, but the children often had the advantage of a better education than would otherwise have been available locally for them. They moved up in the social structure, becoming small landowners or entering one or other of the professions.

Thus was created a coloured middle class which Lord Olivier, writing in 1907, saw as the liaison between the two races through which cultural homogeneity would eventually be achieved.[4] The emerging coloured middle class, from the outset, aligned itself with the white upper class, adopted its systems of values, both in regard to occupation and marriage as opposed to concubinage, and stood aloof from the peasantry and the landless field-labourers, who, in their turn, developed both suspicion and distrust of the 'brown man', with his superior advantages. It was not until the turn of the century that the mutual resistances broke down sufficiently for this middle-class to emerge and be

[4] Sydney Olivier, *White Capital and Coloured Labour* (London: Independent Labour Party, 1910).

accepted by the workers as leaders, both in the political and Trade Union fields.

So far as the family is concerned there are still profound class differences in form, in household structure, in the basis of the union in marriage or concubinage and in the parental roles. And it is our thesis that these differences are not explicable either by reference to the different inherited cultural patterns or solely by the historical facts of slavery.

The important point for an understanding of the contemporary situation is that conditions which make it impossible for men to perform the roles of father and husband as these roles are defined in the society to which they belong, *persist in present-day Jamaica* and it is in conditions as we find them today that we shall most profitably look for the explanation of the 'unstable' features of family life to which such prominence is being given.

For this reason we set ourselves the task of investigating the different types of family structure in Jamaica. Finally, we made it our task to describe the actual relationships covered by the terms 'marriage' and 'concubinage', both between the couple and with reference to the children born to them.

We assumed the existence of the family as a social group: in other words we assumed that children were born and nurtured in some form of social institution. We did not, that is, expect to find that mating was truly casual and unorganized or that there was no parental responsibility—as Margaret Mead has put it, that there was 'no set of permanent arrangements by which males assist females in caring for children while they are young'; though if this should prove to be the case, we should consider that such a unique situation would all the more merit study.[5]

II

The three communities which form the basis of my research, Sugartown, Mocca and Orange Grove, show impor-

[5] Margaret Mead, *Male and Female* (New York: William Morrow, 1946), p. 188.

tant differences. The first is in regard to size. Our records show the number of households in Mocca and Orange Grove to have been approximately the same—119 and 117 respectively—whereas we have 433 family records for Sugartown without taking into account the interviews recorded with 170 men and women who arrived during the early part of our stay seeking work, the majority of whom had no fixed place of abode, and 315 who came in daily from the neighbourhood villages to their jobs. The total population for the three Centres is shown in Appendix 2 to be: Sugartown 1,191, Orange Grove 677, and Mocca 412.

Sugartown, unlike the other two, was a township imposed upon a post-Emancipation settlement where the families lived upon family land and practised subsistence farming. The urbanization began in the beginning of the century with the turn over from banana and coconut production back again, as in the old days, to sugar. Present-day Sugartown centres about the factory, surrounded by thousands of acres of cane. Along the main road are the shops. The few two-story wooden houses are the Chinese grocery and rum shops, where the family live on the upper floor. Small one-, or at most two-, roomed shops are owned or rented by the local butcher, cake-maker, shoemaker, bicycle repairer and the like. On the pavement outside the grocery shops, the women higglers spread their trays of fruit and vegetables for sale. On two or three of these small shops is the red and white striped barber's 'pole', although one of the barbers plied his trade in the open under a large tree. Behind this main road run narrow footpaths leading into the family holdings which are now congeries of one- or two-roomed thatched huts with here and there an old wooden house, in the last state of disrepair, inherited from the 'old people'.

There is a middle-class section where housing conditions are better, situated on a steep lane on one side of the village and within the estate compound the company houses for junior and senior staff. On the side of the main street facing the factory are the estate barracks; long wooden ranges divided into single rooms with outside kitchens, intended by the Company only for seasonal male workers, but in our time, owing to the housing shortage, occupied in fact by couples, sometimes by whole families, sometimes by two men and one woman. The management, it is only fair to say, were anything but complacent about these conditions. Some years previously they had offered ninety acres of land to the Government for a housing scheme and the use of their bulldozers to clear the sites, but up to the time we were there their gift had not yet been accepted. When it eventually was, the offer of the bulldozers was refused because, it was said, of the necessity to provide relief work, with the result that the cost of development put the houses beyond the means of many of the people who had applied for them. None of this, however, happened while we were there and over-crowding in the one- and two-roomed wattle-and-thatched shacks made any sort of decent home life within them impossible for the majority of the population. The family in Sugartown lived in the family 'yards', ate in the tiny smoke-blackened wattle kitchens, and drew water for all domestic purposes from the Company stand-pipe outside the barracks in the main street. Babies and small children were washed in pans in the yard; adults and the older children bathed in the river, where, also, the women did their laundry.

The special pattern of society in Sugartown derives from conditions of work in the sugar industry. It requires a large labour force for some seven months and only limited numbers for the rest of the year. There is no difficulty in getting the additional labour required owing to the extent of unemployment and much larger numbers than can be absorbed begin to pour into Sugartown from the beginning of 'crop' as the busy season is called, both from the neighbouring villages and from other parts of the Island. The incoming population creates, as it were, a recurrent social revolution transforming the ordinary routine and rhythm of life. The housing shortage is aggravated and the newcomers create changes in the constitution of households and both set up new, and alter existing, conjugal relations. Earnings fluctuate from a relatively high level in the crop season to bare subsistence level, or below it, in the *tempo moto* (slow time) as the slack period is graphically described.

The population of Sugartown is too large, too mixed and too mobile for the development of any strong community sense. What associations there are tend to be sectional and do not provide a relational system which involves continuous mutual cooperation and interdependence. The largest and most influential organization is the Trade Union, but it is an organization of sugar-labourers, and mainly confined to men. Other sectional associations are the Cane Farmers' Association and the Rice Growers' Association. The dances held occasionally on the Masquerade Ground bring another section of the community together–mainly the younger folk. The largest non-sectional gathering while we were there was on the occasion of the death of a prominent citizen. During the Nine Nights ceremonies which followed the funeral, a large and diverse section of the community participated at one time or another in the feasting and singing. But there is nothing in Sugartown to compare with the kinship solidarity of Mocca, or the opportunities which occur regularly in Orange Grove for the entire group, men, women and even children to meet together and act as a corporate whole.

In Mocca, where there is neither a source of employment nor land for mixed farming, there is no mobility of population. No one comes into the village; only a few of the younger folk move out. The community is historically as old as the original village of Sugartown on which the estate pattern has been imposed. Houses, in Mocca, are built on family land and family and kindred cling together, united in the struggle to find a means of livelihood in a hostile environment where the process of mechanization and changing industrial conditions have passed them by.

Although the village is only ten miles by road from Sugartown its men do not seek employment in the factory or canefields during crop, and in fact we found few contacts between the two Centres.

The Mocca folk are agriculturalists at heart. They produce what foodstuffs they can on the family land on which their houses are built. Here, also, they keep their small stock–pigs, goats and chickens. A few own cattle which they graze on the roadsides or run surreptitiously on the back-lands of adjoining properties. As many as can rent 'grounds' on which they grow foodstuffs for the local markets and for home consumption. These 'grounds' may be, and in fact generally are, situated many miles away from Mocca and much time is wasted in travelling to and from them. They are usually visited at regular intervals, for planting, bushing and weeding, and then at the reaping period. Inevitably, the cultivator suffers from praedial thieves and invariably the crops suffer from lack of regular care. Tenancy is on a short-term basis. They have no training in any trade; the only work on the sugar estate for which they would be qualified would be as cane-cutters and this does not attract them. Their poverty is extreme and varies little with the seasons. By far the majority of the homes are one- or two-roomed wattle-and-thatched houses, which do not keep out the rain and are expensive to maintain. The diet consists almost entirely of home-grown starchy foods seasoned with salt-fish bought at the shop. The principal families are all connected by marriage or concubinage and the village is tiny enough for the members to be acutely aware of each other's affairs. Most of the inhabitants trace their ancestry back to the founders of the village. One or two people who have come in since then are still called 'strangers' (the local term is 'bluefoot') although they have lived there most of their lives.

One's first glimpse of Orange Grove is a red dirt roadway running through a fertile valley of farms with neat citrus groves and solid, well-built houses, often with an upper story, set among flower and vegetable gardens. Some of the farmers own horses, practically everyone has at least one cow, donkey, goat or other small stock. Eggs are sold through a co-operative marketing organization, and milk supplied to the Condensary. They are subject to the vicissitudes of farmers everywhere; but their mixed farming is competent, their orange groves well-cared, the soil is fertile, the climate healthy and temperate, and they have a market at satisfactory prices for whatever they produce. Levels of income are relatively high and there are no violent fluctuations as in Sugartown. This Centre is larger than Mocca, but the community sense is highly developed and there are recurrent occasions, such as meetings of the Crop Associations, when the community can exchange views on matters which concern them all. It was interesting to note that at the monthly meetings of the various organizations, in the Community Hall, the programme always included songs and recitations by the young people so that even the children in the village participated.

Land has a particular meaning for the people of Orange Grove since it is the sole means of livelihood for everyone and the whole life of the farmers, their wives and children are bound up with it.

To summarize, in Sugartown there are fluctuations between relatively high earnings and bare subsistence living, in Orange Grove there is a more even and relatively high level of economy, and in Mocca there is consistent and extreme poverty. These are the general economic backgrounds of the three Centres.

It is important to have these differences between the Centres in mind because they are obviously influential when we come to consider the forms of conjugal union and kinship roles. For example we shall later be showing that there are certain pre-requisites which have to be fulfilled before marriage can be considered. A man should, in the ideal at any rate, be able to offer a wife, as distinct from a concubine, an assured social position. He should, if a wage earner, be in a position to buy his own house and land on which they can make a permanent home or have inherited land or house, and be regularly employed, even if this does not in fact imply relatively higher actual earnings.

In Orange Grove the possibility of fulfilling these requirements exists. It is probable that only the better off farmers in Orange Grove derive as high an income from their farming as do the best paid sugar-workers. But their income is more evenly distributed over the year; and is demonstrably the result of the amount of foresight, energy and intelligence they themselves put into their work. They are sure of a market for whatever they produce and they have the land they need. Their ambition is to improve their farms and add to their stock; emulate their neighbours in the better furnishing of their homes and provide for the future of their children.

These are all incentives to saving. In Sugartown the labourer feels that he is at the mercy of forces over which he has no control; the demand for his labour is always less than the manpower available. The principal incentive to thrift—the possibility of buying house or land—is lacking. There is no land to buy. The period of crop and high wages is like a boom following an acute depression, and it has all the instability of a boom. Part of the new wages go to pay off debts accumulated during the *tempo moto,* part in replenishment of a depleted wardrobe, and much of the rest is dissipated in gambling or drinking.

For this reason alone, it is not surprising that Orange Grove has the most stable form of family life and highest marriage rate in any of the Centres. But there is also the fact that, if we may so phrase it, marriage induces marriage. In Orange Grove it is part of the class structure and is reinforced with strong social sanctions which do not exist in either of the other two communities. Concubinage in Orange Grove is practised by the poorer families, or those of the younger folk who have broken away from strict parental control, but it is regarded with disfavour by the respectable farmers and their wives. Where an irregular relationship results in pregnancy marriage generally takes place.

Where there are not the clear-cut class distinctions, such as we find in Orange Grove, to reinforce the legal or religious basis and outlaw the irregular union, and where the method of earning a living and the conditions of employment do not in general allow of the realization of the ideal which is associated in people's minds with the institution of marriage, the ratio is much lower. Whereas in Orange Grove these unions represent a falling away from the accepted social standards, and can be co-related with other social and economic factors, there is no such observable distinction in the other two Centres. In Sugartown and Mocca there is, in fact, no apparent real association of marriage or concubinage with economic status or class structure.

III

The anthropologist in search of the family *sees* first the house, surrounded by other houses in yards on family land: separated by barbed wire fences, along village streets or country roads; appearing as a thatched roof in the distance, emerging between trees of breadfruit, ackee or mango on the edge of a yam field; or as a white painted wooden cottage behind regular lines of orange trees with their green and yellow fruit. Within that house, be it hut or cottage, is contained, for some time of the day or night, part of the group which he is about to study.

But what part of it? Will he find the majority of these households to contain parents and their children; or mothers only with their daughters and their daughters' children; or a man and woman with some only of their offspring? Or, instead, will he find a heterogeneous collection of kin, brought together by some new pattern of association, based on a system of relationships fundamentally different from that found in other societies elsewhere?

Before we can answer these questions it is necessary to be quite clear as to the meaning of the terms we shall be using to describe different types of relationship, since it is largely the loose use of language which is responsible for the existing confusion and false assumptions on the subject of family relations in Jamaica.

The terms to be defined fall into three categories: those which describe types of union, those which describe types of grouping based on kinship, and those which describe types of grouping based on residence.

It is particularly in regard to the first that language is popularly used in a misleading way. The meaning of *marriage* is clear: it is a conjugal and domestic union formally entered into in the manner prescribed by the law and approved by the religious authorities, and involving the implicit or explicit recognition by the parties of duties towards each other and towards their children. Where only one form of conjugal union has the sanction of law and religion, all others are correctly described as *irregular*. But these are of many different kinds and it is of the greatest importance to be able to discriminate between them.

In popular discussion, and in some published work, terms like concubinage, common-law marriage, prostitution, promiscuity and polygamy are applied, without distinction, to any type of irregular union. For our purpose these terms need to be either clearly defined and differentiated or else abandoned.

We may deal first with the two terms which are sometimes used to describe irregular unions in Jamaica but which do not correctly describe any of the unions which we have observed. The first is *common-law marriage*. This term is used without definition in the 1943 Census of Jamaica and also by Henriques, who defines it as 'the union of a man with a woman which lasts indefinitely without the full sanction of law', and adds that the distinction between Christian marriage and common-law marriage is sociologically useless.[6] Common-law marriage is a legal term describing a type of union which at one time was recognized by the law as marriage although it had been entered upon without all the formalities which the law prescribes. It is therefore not appropriate to apply it to unions which are clearly distinguishable from marriage, both by the partners and by the society at large, and, in my experience, it is never used of any type of union by the Jamaicans who are themselves participants in these forms of union.

Polygamy, the second term, is the legal marriage of a man to more than one wife at the same time. Henriques' definition of polygamy as 'a man or woman co-habitating with more than one of the opposite sex' would not be accepted by anthropologists in general.[7] If standard usage is followed, polygamy can only exist where the law recognizes it.

Of the terms which can appropriately be applied in Jamaican conditions, we define *concubinage* as the conjugal union in co-habitation of a man and woman without legal and religious sanction. *Casual mating* is a sexual congress

[6] Fernando M. Henriques, *Family and Colour in Jamaica* (London: Eyre & Spottiswoode, 1953), pp. 84, 106.
[7] *Ibid.*, p. 84.

without co-habitation or any intention to form a permanent relationship. *Promiscuity* is indiscriminate casual mating. *Prostitution* is the practice of promiscuity for payment.

Groupings based on kinship can be divided into the *simple family,* consisting of parents and children, and the *extended family,* which includes, in addition, kin of a higher or lower generation.

In regard to legitimacy: the law recognizes as *legitimate* only children born in wedlock; but in the case of couples living in concubinage it is necessary to distinguish between children of the union and other children of either partner. We have used the terms *socially legitimate* of the former and *outside* of the latter.

In differentiating between residential groupings, or household types, we may distinguish, first, *simple family households* and *extended family households. Consanguineous* households include (a) *denuded family* households in which there is only one parent and which may be of either the simple or extended type, and (b) *sibling households* in which adult brothers and sisters live under one roof. Finally there is the *single person* household and households of unrelated men living together or women sharing a room, which are common only in Sugartown.[8]

This was, of course, a broad classification. For it to be useful in the later stages of our inquiry, into the behaviour patterns between members of the household and the kin outside the household, we had to make a number of distinctions within the groups. For example, in *simple family households* we distinguished between couples with children of their own and those which included *outside* children of either the man or the woman, or both. By this means we were able to show, for example, that outside children in the home were more likely to be those of the woman than of the man; that they were most likely to be included where the current union was childless and where that union was based on concubinage rather than marriage.

[8] For a distribution of these types in the Centres and a detailed analysis of their structure, see Edith Clarke, *My Mother Who Fathered Me* (London: Allen and Unwin, 1957), Chapter 5 and Appendices.

17.

The preceding selection dealt with variations in cohabitation and household structure from place to place. The present article examines variation and change in household structure through time. From field data collected in three Guyanese Negro communities, R. T. Smith delineates a developmental cycle through which most lower-class Negro households pass. In the first phase of this cycle, young adults form relationships and become parents without leaving their parental households; in the second, a young couple live together with their children in their own house; in the third, the household becomes matrifocal, that is, authority and control shifts to the mother. This cycle originates and is perpetuated not on the community level but in the total Guyanese social system, which ascribes low status to Negro villagers. The analysis is more fully developed in the author's book *The Negro Family in British Guiana.*

RAYMOND T. SMITH was born in England and received his doctorate in social anthropology from Cambridge University. He was for many years on the staff of the Institute of Social and Economic Research and the Department of Sociology at the University of the West Indies in Jamaica, and is presently Professor of Anthropology at the University of Chicago.

The Family in the Caribbean

Raymond T. Smith

This paper does not attempt to cover every aspect of family organization nor to review the literature on the family in the Caribbean. Instead it will discuss the problem of relating variations in the form of family structure to other factors in the social system, using the author's own field material for purposes of illustration.

It is convenient to begin by examining the structure and activities of household groups. These are easily isolated for study and most writers are agreed that the main functioning family unit in the Caribbean is a household group. It will be defined as a group of people occupying a single dwelling and sharing a common food supply. The term "family" can be used to denote many different types of group, depending upon its definition and qualifications, and it is also used to refer to an institution, i.e., a standardized mode of co-activity.[1] In discussing the household group as a family unit, this distinction between the mode of co-activity and the group which activates it will be made. Although kinship ties extend beyond the household group, no organized enduring group structures based upon kinship and comparable to a corporate lineage are reported for the larger territories,

From *Caribbean Studies: A Symposium,* edited by Vera Rubin, Institute of Social and Economic Research, University College of the West Indies, Jamaica, and Program for the Study of Man in the Tropics, Columbia University, New York, 1957, pp. 67–75. Reprinted by permission of the Institute of Social and Economic Research, the Research Institute for the Study of Man, and the author.

[1] S. F. Nadel, *The Foundations of Social Anthropology* (London: Cohen and West, 1951), p. 108.

though M. G. Smith speaks of patrilineages in Carriacou,[2] and of course the Bush Negroes of Surinam are another special case.[3]

As a preliminary step in analysis it is useful to distinguish the following elements of household group activity. The comments refer to the situation in Negro villages in British Guiana but the elements themselves can be generally applied.

1) *Child Care:* This is an almost universal activity of household groups and is normally under the control of a woman in the status of "mother," who is not necessarily the biological mother of all the children in the group. Males do not participate directly in this activity, but the existence of the role of "father" is important to the socialization process and male contributions to the household economy are essential in the majority of cases.

2) *Sexual services:* Within the household these are provided only between spouses in non-incestuous unions,[4] but they may be provided across the boundaries of household groups between persons who will be referred to as "lovers."

3) *Domestic services:* These are provided by adult females for all members of the household group, and consist mainly of cooking and washing clothes. They are rarely provided across the boundaries of household groups.

4) *Economic support:* Economic support is provided by adult males and channelled to the woman in the status of wife-mother or mother. It consists mainly of cash with which to buy essentials such as certain kinds of food, clothing, and other consumer goods but it also includes farm produce. It may also be provided by males outside the household group in return for sexual services or as a paternity obligation. In a few cases economic support may

[2] M. G. Smith, "Transformation of Land Rights by Transmission in Carriacou," *Social and Economic Studies,* Vol. 5, No. 2 (1956), pp. 103–38.

[3] M. J. and F. S. Herskovits, *Rebel Destiny* (New York: McGraw-Hill, 1934).

[4] Because of the existence of different kinds of marital status, the terms "spouse" and "conjugal union" are used without differentiation between legal and non-legal unions. The terms do imply co-residence.

be wholly provided by female members of the household through their trading, farming, or wage-earning activities. But this is rare.

These are the four main elements relevant to a discussion of the village data but two more may be added since we shall need them later on for comparative purposes.

5) *Managerial functions:* This only applies in cases where a farm or business provides the basis of the household economy and where co-ordination of activities in the ownership and operation of the enterprise invests one person with some measure of control over the other members of the group.

6) *Status-defining functions:* This occurs where the definition of the status of the household group in the society at large depends upon the activities of one or more of its members and not primarily upon the ascribed characteristics of the whole group. Status-defining functions will normally refer to the activities of males in the external occupational system, but this element will not be considered present if that activity does not confer a higher or lower status than if it were absent.

In these Guianese Negro villages, household groups, with few exceptions, come into being when a man and a woman enter a conjugal union and set up house together. The relationships between the members of a newly constituted household group may have been in existence for some time and the couple may have several children as a result of their previous ties as lovers. The woman may have been providing the man with sexual services in return for a measure of economic support, but until they live together there is no explicit recognition of the man's exclusive rights to her sexual services. Also she is unlikely to have provided him with domestic services while they were living in separate households.

Young women tend to remain in their parents' households during the period of maximum instability in their sexual relationships, and they may have several children by different men before they acquire a more permanent lover. Once they go off to live with a man in a separate house, the relationship is usually much more stable regardless of whether they are legally married or not. The majority of unions endure at least until the woman finishes her period of child-bearing.

The position may be rather different in an urban or semi-urban area where women live with a series of common-law husbands, perhaps sending any offspring to be cared for by their mothers. In such areas there are usually more employment opportunities for women, particularly as domestic servants. A companionate type of union may develop with an absence of child-rearing functions or a very inadequate type of child care leading to delinquency and so on. But even in urban areas this is not likely to be the predominant type of household.[5]

Once the household group is established, its size gradually increases by the birth of children, and their care takes up a good deal of the time and energy of the mother.

All household groups in these Guianese communities are kinship groups, and a detailed examination of the categories of kin which are included shows that there are definite regularities in their composition. In households with male heads, the largest single category of kin is children of the head and his spouse, followed by daughter's children. A small proportion of other kin is found, but these are mainly children of a deceased sister of the head or his spouse. Households with female heads contain a large proportion of the head's daughter's children and a larger proportion of her siblings' children than is found in households with male heads. These differences in the composition of household groups are related to the fact that households with female heads grow out of the male-head type, and the increase in the number of persons related to the "mother" (whether she is in the status of spouse or of head) reflects her increasing authority within the group as she grows older. The proportion of kin more distantly related to the head than sibling's grandchild never exceeded 1.5 per cent in any of the communities studied.[6]

[5] L. Braithwaite, "Social Stratification in Trinidad," *Social and Economic Studies,* Vol. 2, Nos. 2 and 3 (Oct. 1953).

[6] R. T. Smith, *The Negro Family in British Guiana* (London: Routledge and Kegan Paul, 1956), Chap. IV.

During this early stage in the life of the household group the woman is quite dependent upon her spouse for economic support, for he is the sole provider for herself and her small children. She becomes less completely dependent upon him as her eldest children begin to leave school and to enter the labour market, thereby acquiring the means to make some contribution to the economic support of the group. Sons rarely work with or for their fathers, but they always give support to their mothers, who perform domestic services for them. Although young men rarely set up a household of their own before they reach the age of twenty-five, they do begin to have affairs with young women and to divert part of their earnings to the support of children they may have fathered. They do not normally bring a spouse to live in their parents' household, nor can they expect at an early age much assistance in setting up a household of their own. Gradually they accumulate enough capital to provide for a house of their own and they may then enter into a conjugal union.

Girls of the household group help their mother with domestic tasks and child-rearing. They too may go out to work if there are employment opportunities locally. Almost certainly they will begin to have affairs with young men, and it is likely that they will have their first child while living with their parents. The girl who has children while living in her mother's home will relinquish many of the functions of child care to her. However, some girls contract a legal marriage before having a child and others marry when they are pregnant.

From now on men in the status of husband-father begin to drop out of the group, usually because they die, but also because they may just leave the group to go and live alone, or to enter another union. Whether they leave or not, the focus of authority and control gradually shifts to the wife-mother, so that, irrespective of whether there is a husband-father present, the household group at this stage can be referred to as "matrifocal." The fact that women generally live longer than men means that there is a large number of widows, and these women just automatically become household heads. Sons and daughters begin to leave as they develop sufficiently stable relationships with a lover to set up a household of their own, but daughters will usually leave some of their children to be cared for by their mother. Some women spend the whole of their child-bearing period in their mother's home, having no more than casual affairs with a series of men from whom they receive some economic support.

There are really three phases in the development cycle of the household. In the first phase, young men and women are forming relationships with a series of lovers and becoming parents without living with a spouse. This is really a latent phase for it is only when they enter phase two and begin to live together that the life of a new household group can be seen to begin. The second phase involves the isolation of a nuclear family unit in its own house. In the third phase the household has become matrifocal, and it usually includes the members of a three generation matri-line: mother, daughters and maybe sons, and daughters' children. At this stage it may also incorporate other categories of kin, more particularly the mother's sisters or sisters' children. Clearly, phase one and phase three of this cycle overlap in time. In some cases the second phase may be bypassed completely, and in others it may be extended either way so that phases one and three disappear completely. In the villages under discussion all three phases normally exist as a part of the system.

A striking characteristic of the system is the close relationships between mother, daughters, and daughters' children, relationships which are rooted in the activity of child care. However, there is no discrete type of household group which contains only the members of this primary coalition. If families are viewed as units with a time dimension, then it can be seen that the vast majority of women spend at least a period of their lives in some sort of conjugal union. Matrifocality, a feature remarked upon by every writer on the New World Negro family and by many writers on Latin American societies, is a matter of degree rather than some absolute quality of the system. So far as this writer is aware, one never finds a whole community made up of households in which there is no husband-father.

In the absence of any enduring group structure to organize the economic support of women and children, males provide this support in their roles as husbands, sons, and lovers. There is a limit to the extent to which men, in their role as sons, can provide support for the household. Once the mother dies, the system breaks down and men do not give economic support directly to their sisters. Outside the mother-son relationship economic support is closely bound up with the provision of sexual services, and the brother-sister relationship is subject to a strict incest taboo. The system permits a woman with children to select a male in the status of husband, common-law husband, or lover from a wide range of possible individuals. The strength of the ties between mothers and child-bearing daughters is directly related to the way in which men perform their roles in the family system. An analysis of the time sequence of household group development shows up the changing position of mothers and children in relation to the sources of economic support and the varying structural arrangements which go with it.

Professor and Mrs. Herskovits have pointed out that on the New World slave plantations it was impossible to maintain those fields of male activity, such as the clan and the extended family, which had been important in Africa. While the mother-child cell remained relatively intact, the male's functions as production manager, ritual leader, and jural head of the lineage disappeared.[7] There is much more in this than a statement of historical fact, and it is profitable to follow up this lead and to examine the contemporary social system in order to see how the functions of males in the society at large react back upon their status in the family structure.

It was mentioned earlier that managerial functions and status-defining activities are absent from the type case we have been examining. Farming is certainly a part of the economic life of the village, but it does not mobilize household or kinship groups for work under the direction of one person. A minimum of labour and enterprise is ex-

[7] M. J. and F. S. Herskovits, *Trinidad Village* (New York: Alfred A. Knopf, 1947).

pended on the small scattered holdings which comprise these farms, and the focus of attention is wage labour in large-scale organizations such as plantations, government works, bauxite mines, etc. In other parts of the Caribbean an entirely different situation exists. In Jamaica, for example, there are areas such as Miss Edith Clarke's Orange Grove[8] where the management and operation of medium-sized farms introduces a new element of co-activity into the household group and results in a greater emphasis upon the position of husband-father. Jamaica is typical of situations where complexities arise from the range of variations according to ecological area, and these variations provide one useful basis for comparison.

In spite of variations, the general type of family structure I have outlined for the Guianese villages seems to be fairly widespread in the Caribbean, and something very like it is found in other parts of the world. It is never the norm for a total society and one may venture the suggestion that it is always found under certain conditions. It is characteristically confined to low-status sections of a more inclusive society, such sections being differentiated primarily on the basis of ascriptive criteria.[9] They may be differentiated on the basis of ethnic, occupational, or cultural factors. Membership in such sections is almost invariably defined by birth, though it is not patrifiliation which in itself determines membership in the group. Apart from the broad differentiation between children and adults and the hierarchical differentiations within household groups, there is no significant degree of hierarchical differentiation within such sections. But they are integrated into the larger society of which they are a part in such a way that their members all fill subordinate roles in wider systems of organization. There is, at best, very limited possibility of upward social

[8] Edith Clarke, "Land Tenure and the Family in Four Jamaican Communities," *Social and Economic Studies,* Vol. 1, No. 4 (1953), pp. 81–118.

[9] It may be that in some cases the status sections so differentiated are very small and marginal to systems of differentiation according to achievement criteria. An example would be small pockets of slum dwellers in an otherwise open-class type of society.

mobility. The importance of cash income from wage labour in the Guianese case has already been stressed, and this, or the corollary that ownership of income-producing property is a marginal consideration, seems to be another associated feature. It is unlikely that this system will develop in a situation where the ownership, control, and use of real property is the sole basis of family economy, as it is in a true peasant society.

However, it is never the absence of productive property which alone determines the form of family structure. This is easily borne out by an examination of the West Indian middle class. (This term is used loosely because we are not concerned with an exact description of the status system here.) Within such middle-class sections there is a fairly wide range of internal status differentiation and the definition of status is a task of the household group. There are several factors which militate against the development of an isolated nuclear family whose status is defined by the occupation of the husband-father, as in the urban middle class in the United States.[10] There is generally less mobility, both spatial and hierarchical, and ethnic factors, which are the basis of ascribed status, are constantly reasserting themselves. Braithwaite comments upon the lack of authority of the Trinidadian middle-class husband-father, but he gives little indication of the variations in this condition either over time or within the middle class as a whole. He does state unequivocally that ". . . the status of the kinship group derives from the occupational and social status of the father."[11] Marriage and co-residence are necessary preliminaries to child bearing and one does not find unmarried daughters with their children living in the parental home. The lack of authority of the husband-father may be marked, particularly in a situation where it is common for men to validate their occupational status by marrying lighter coloured women, and where they may have to keep incrementing their occupational status in order to prevent the centre of status interest from swinging back

[10] Talcott Parsons, *Essays in Sociological Theory* (Glencoe, Ill.: The Free Press, 1954).

[11] Braithwaite, *op. cit.,* p. 103.

onto the wife-mother. So long as the man's income provides the basis for the style of life that is important in maintaining the status of the whole group, then there is a point beyond which his position in the family is unlikely to deteriorate.

In the lower class where neither status definition nor managerial functions are important male activities, the husband-father role is extremely circumscribed. It does not disappear; there is never complete promiscuity; and the incest taboo operates with full force. In rigidly stratified societies such as that of British Guiana, where social roles are largely allocated according to the ascriptive criteria of ethnic characteristics, the lower-class male has nothing to buttress his authority as husband-father except the dependence upon his economic support. The uncertainty of his being able to carry out even this function adequately because of general economic insecurity undermines his position even further.

One of the problems in discussing family structure is to pin down the large number of factors influencing it and to separate out those which appear to vary significantly from one society to another or from one group to another. In the first half of this paper an attempt was made to show that one set of apparent variations can be reduced to greater order by taking into account the changes which occur over time and by discussing family structure as a cyclical process. Variations over time are thus a part of the system, and what appear to be different types of family viewed simultaneously are perhaps different growth stages of the same system.

Another point made was that there is a significant relationship between the form of family structure and economic and status factors. Variations within and between status sections and between different ecological areas are best seen against the background of the structural differentiation of the total society. At its simplest such a view can concentrate attention upon the role of husband-father or upon the dual role of males in the family and in the total social system.

Although this paper has dealt with Negro groups, there

is no reason why the method of analysis cannot be applied generally, regardless of ethnic factors. Cross-cultural typologies may be constructed when it is decided what the theoretical basis of their establishment shall be. It is suggested that in the case of the family the typology must rest upon some prior consideration of structure and function rather than upon a simple list of elements which may or may not be present (e.g., presence or absence of legal marriage, particular forms of child-training techniques, or specific bases of family economy).

The type of family system with which this paper has been primarily concerned bears some resemblance to those reported from other societies culturally and ethnically dissimilar. A short report on certain aspects of the family in a section of East London deals with the existence of what Young refers to as the "matrilateral" family.[12] Dealing with a random sample of ninety-six working-class families, he concludes that the close relationships between "Mum" and her daughters and daughters' children is related to the insecurity which working-class women have to face in a situation in which males may easily become unemployed, die, or just desert their wives. Superficially at least, there are marked resemblances between these families in London's East End and those in a Scottish mining community reported on by Miss Wilson.[13] In the latter community there appears to be a basic correlation between the nature of lower-status family relations and the relative absence of vertical social mobility. In both the East London and Scottish studies, the evidence suggests that the existence of a three generation matriline with an emphasis upon the matrifocal household group is associated with a social structure in which males neither control income-producing property nor wholly determine, by virtue of their occupa-

[12] M. Young, "Kinship and Family in East London," *Man*, Vol. LIV, Art. 210 (1954).

[13] C. S. Wilson, "The Family and Neighborhood in a British Community" (M.Sc. dissertation, Cambridge University Library, 1953). For a fuller discussion of this work, see R. T. Smith, *op. cit.*, pp. 247–51.

tional or political role, the status position of their families of procreation.

Similar types of family structure are also found in some Latin American countries where the culture is predominantly Iberian, often mixed with aboriginal Indian elements. The Peruvian village of Moche is an outstanding case which has been discussed elsewhere.[14] The Paraguayan town of Tobati described by E. R. and H. S. Service provides an interesting comparative case, especially as the authors submit some quantitative data on household composition which show quite clearly the tendency toward matrifocal families in the lowest status group of the *gente*.[15]

In all these cases there is a definite similarity to the Caribbean lower-class matrifocal family pattern, and although much research needs to be done to determine the degree of structural similarity, at least they shift our attention from a purely historical treatment of Caribbean Negro family patterns. There is no doubt that the present position of the Negro group and the Negro family system had their origin in the extreme type of society created by plantation slavery. Even so, it may be less profitable to regard slavery as the cause of present-day family structure than to examine the correspondence between the various parts of the contemporary system. In this way it is possible to widen the comparative framework to include societies with a different historical background but similar structural features, as well as to recognize the fact that Negroes participate at higher status levels in the present society and live in varying types of family system.

A correct use of the comparative method requires more than a search for identity between particular structural features in widely differing societies. We must also explain such negative cases as there may be, or comparison leads

[14] J. Gillin, *Moche: A Peruvian Coastal Community*, Institute of Social Anthropology Publication 6 (Washington, D.C.: Smithsonian Institution, 1945). Discussed in R. T. Smith, *op. cit.*, pp. 240–45.

[15] E. R. and H. S. Service, *Tobatí: Paraguayan Town* (Chicago: University of Chicago Press, 1954).

nowhere. In this respect the East Indian community in the Caribbean forms an extremely valuable test case. In British Guiana the economic position of Indians is in many ways similar to that of Negroes, but their family system is quite different. This is not merely a matter of cultural persistence. A number of group structures have been developed in which males play important roles, and there is an Indian status system which is distinct from that of the total society. This is not to say that Indians do not participate in the ranking system of the total society, for they certainly do, but they have not been ranked at the bottom of a scale of colour values as Negroes have, with all that that implies so far as social mobility is concerned.

It is apparent therefore that in speaking of the family in the Caribbean we are dealing with a number of varying types, which we may either distinguish and classify in terms of a series of specific characteristics, or which we may attempt to distinguish in terms of their structural characteristics and functional relation to other elements of the social structure.

18.

This essay critically and sometimes acidulously examines the major viewpoints of the West Indian family structure including all of those presented in this section. The author's own research in this field is set forth in his *West Indian Family Structure,* which compares family and household data from Grenada, Carriacou, and Jamaica.

M. G. SMITH is identified on page 66.

A Survey of West Indian Family Studies

M. G. Smith

1

The family life of West Indian 'lower class' Negroes or folk presents a number of equally important academic and practical problems. In this region family life is highly unstable, marriage rates are low, especially during the earlier phases of adult life, and illegitimacy rates have always been high. Many households contain single individuals, while others with female heads consist of women, their children, and/or their grandchildren. The picture is further complicated by variations in the type and local distribution of alternative conjugal forms; and, characteristically, differing communities, social classes and ethnic groups institutionalize differing combinations of them. Excluding legal marriage, mating is brittle, diverse in form and consensual in base among these Creole or Negroid populations. The implications of this mating structure for the composition and stability of familial groups is perhaps most easily appreciated by comparing these Creole patterns with others current among East Indians of comparable socio-economic position in British Guiana and Trinidad.

Among these local East Indians, men settled in differing villages arrange the first unions of their children during early adolescence and celebrate these marriages by tradi-

Originally published as the Introduction to *My Mother Who Fathered Me* by Edith Clarke, 2nd edition, London, George Allen & Unwin, Ltd., 1966. Reprinted with permission of the publisher and the author.

tional Hindu or Muslim rites. The girl then leaves her natal village to join her husband in his father's community. Between one-fifth and one-quarter of these arranged marriages recurrently dissolve, usually not long after their celebration and before children are born to the couple. Following this the girl almost always resumes cohabitation with another partner, often after returning briefly to her parental home. If the earlier marriage had not been registered as legal, this second union may be legalized by such registration. Otherwise, although non-legal, it is usually lifelong.[1]

Creole 'lower class' mating patterns differ from those of the local East Indians in two important ways. Firstly, all Creole systems for which we have adequate data institutionalize extra-residential, non-domiciliary, or visiting relations as one of several alternative conjugal patterns. In this conjugal form the partners live apart with their separate kin while the man visits his mate and contributes to the support of herself and their children. According to Stycos and Back, this extra-residential pattern is the most common form of mating among 'lower class' Jamaicans, especially during the earlier adult years.[2] It is also the most diverse in its content and social contexts, the most brittle and formally unstable type of union; and, given the partners' domestic dispersion, the most vulnerable to disruptive in-

[1] Morton Klass, *East Indians in Trinidad: A Study of Cultural Persistence* (New York: Columbia University Press, 1961), pp. 93–136; R. T. Smith and C. Jayawardena, "Hindu Marriage Customs in British Guiana," *Social and Economic Studies,* Vol. 7, No. 2 (1958), pp. 178–94; R. T. Smith and C. Jayawardena, "Marriage and the Family Amongst East Indians in British Guiana," *Social and Economic Studies,* Vol. 8, No. 4 (1959), pp. 321–76; R. T. Smith, "Family Structure and Plantation Systems in the New World," in *Plantation Systems of the New World,* Social Science Monographs VII (Washington, D.C.: Pan American Union, 1959), pp. 154–55; G. W. Roberts and L. Braithwaite, "Mating Among East Indian and Non-Indian Women in Trinidad," *Social and Economic Studies,* Vol. II, No. 3 (1962), pp. 203–40.

[2] J. Mayone Stycos and Kurt W. Back, *The Control of Human Fertility in Jamaica* (Ithaca, N.Y.: Cornell University Press, 1964).

fluences of various sorts. For this reason among others, durable visiting relations are generally converted into co-habitation, whether legal or consensual by their principals. When these unions break down, the children usually re-main with the unmarried mother or her kin.

Among East Indians in Trinidad and British Guiana this pattern of extra-residential mating is either absent or ex-tremely rare;[3] and in consequence the great majority of East Indian children usually grow up in their father's home and under his care. Among West Indian Creoles, given their predilection for unstable extra-residential unions, the reverse is more nearly the case. For example, of children living in the Creole households studied in Carriacou, Latante and Grenville in Grenada, and in Kingston and rural Jamaica, only 37.6 per cent, 52.6 per cent, 35.7 per cent, 34.7 per cent, and 49.3 per cent were found in homes containing their fathers;[4] and as Edith Clarke shows [in *My Mother Who Fathered Me:* see selection 16, above], the pattern of domestic dispersal by which children are separated from their fathers is heavily influenced by the character of their parents' conjugal union and by the chil-dren's birth status.[5] Clearly these differences in the mating organizations of the 'lower class' Creoles and East Indians correspond with parallel differences in their modes of in-stitutionalizing paternal roles and in their emphases on nu-clear families as the basis of domestic organization. De-spite comparable 'denudation' of domestic nuclear families through widowhood, migrancy and other conditions, these ethnic differences in family patterns are striking.[6]

The second major difference between these Creole and East Indian family systems consists in the age and condi-

[3] R. T. Smith, "Culture and Social Structure in the Carib-bean: Some Recent Work on Family and Kinship Studies," *Comparative Studies in Society and History,* Vol. 6, No. 1 (1964), p. 42; Roberts and Braithwaite, *op. cit.,* pp. 207–12.

[4] M. G. Smith, *West Indian Family Structure* (Seattle: Uni-versity of Washington Press, 1962), Table 17, p. 239.

[5] Edith Clarke, *My Mother Who Fathered Me* (London: Allen and Unwin, 1957), pp. 127–33, Appendices 5–8, 16 & 17.

[6] Klass, *op. cit.;* R. T. Smith and Jayawardena, "Marriage and the Family Amongst East Indians in British Guiana."

tions under which cohabitation and marriage are institutionalized. In the Caribbean, as elsewhere, East Indians prescribe cohabitation by customary rites of marriage at an early age for both sexes. Among lower-class Creoles the ideal and modal ages of marriage are both much higher; and typically consensual cohabitation with the same or other partners precedes marriage by several years. Thus, whereas East Indians marry before having children, lower-class Creoles normally marry in middle or later age after the women have ceased to bear children or are already grandparents.[7]

These differences in the age and conditions of marriage among the East Indians and Creoles have obvious and important effects on the organization and stability of family life and on the average number of mating unions that characterize the two ethnic groups. Few East Indians engage in more than two conjugal unions and despite differences of ecological and social context, apparently at least three-quarters have only one.[8] *Per contra,* among 'lower class' Creoles few individuals have only one conjugal union, however this may be defined; and a substantial proportion engage in three or more. Thus whereas East Indian mating practice institutionalizes lifelong unions following early 'marriage', that of the Creole lower class encourages serial matings of varying form and conditional character, with legal marriage as the terminal type of union. In consequence, whereas East Indian families are nucleated in separate domestic groups, among the Creoles nuclear or elementary families are systematically fragmented and dis-

[7] Stycos and Back, *op. cit.,* pp. 318–24; Roberts and Braithwaite, *op. cit.,* p. 205; Jamaica, Department of Statistics, *Population Census* (1960); *Some Notes on the Union Status, Marital Status and Number of Children of the Female Population of Jamaica* (n.d. ? 1962), pp. 15–16, 21; O. C. Francis, *The People of Modern Jamaica* (Jamaica: Department of Statistics, 1964), Ch. 5.

[8] C. Jayawardena, "Marital Stability in Two Guianese Sugar Estate Communities," *Social and Economic Studies,* Vol. 9, No. 1 (1960), pp. 78–81; R. T. Smith and Jayawardena, "Marriage and the Family Amongst East Indians in British Guiana," p. 368; Roberts and Braithwaite, *op. cit.,* pp. 204–17.

persed throughout two or more households as a direct effect of their mating organization; and whereas among East Indians paternity is relatively fixed and constant in its form, content and context, among the Creoles its modes and effectiveness vary as a function of differing conjugal forms and their combination.[9]

2

The numerous practical or social problems presented by the characteristic patterns of West Indian (Creole) mating and lower class family life have attracted continuous attention ever since 1938 when a Royal Commission appointed by the British Parliament to survey the social and economic conditions of this region and to recommend appropriate programmes for action, dwelt on the evident 'disorganization' of family life and on the apparent increase of 'promiscuity' as against faithful concubinage, the 'common law' or consensual cohabitation which had hitherto been accepted as the Negro peasant's equivalent of marriage, and the basis of his family life. To halt this presumed spread of 'promiscuity', in 1944–45 Lady Huggins, wife of the then Governor of Jamaica, launched an island-wide campaign to marry off consensually cohabiting couples and any others whose mating status and relations seemed to warrant this. This Mass Marriage Movement was initiated in response to the Royal Commission's demand for 'an organized campaign against the social, moral and economic evils of promiscuity'.[10] However, being based on ignorance of Jamaican folk society and family life, the movement was equally misconceived in its methods and goals, and proved unsuccessful. At its greatest impact the movement lifted the Jamaican marriage rate from 4.44 per thousand in 1943 to 5.82 in 1946. By 1951 the marriage rate and the correlated illegitimacy ratio among annual

[9] Clarke, *op. cit.*, pp. 97–111, 159–64.

[10] *West India Royal Commission Report* (Moyne Report), Cmd. 6607, London, H.M.S.O., 1945, pp. 220–22.

births had reverted to their earlier level.[11] By 1955 the Mass Marriage Movement had petered out.

Several conditions ensured the failure of this Mass Marriage Movement, despite the energy and skill with which its director, Lady Huggins, marshalled the churches, schools, press, radio, welfare agencies and 'national' associations behind it. Above all, the campaign was based on the erroneous notion that because the élite and lower class employed a single word, marriage, to denote a particular conjugal institution, this had identical or very similar meanings, value and significance among these social strata. We now know that this view is only superficially correct, for reasons indicated below. Being thus conceived in error, the Mass Marriage Movement could hardly succeed; and its early signs of failure indicated the need for systematic sociological studies of those unfamiliar familial institutions with which the problems of 'promiscuity', marital instability, defective paternity and child socialization, high illegitimacy birth rates and low rates of marriage were all evidently linked, though in obscure and problematic ways. It was in this context that T. S. Simey visited the West Indies to survey its social conditions and to advise the recently constituted agency responsible for Colonial Development and Welfare. It was in these circumstances also that the Colonial Social Science Research Council in Britain asked Edith Clarke to undertake and direct a formal study of Jamaican family life. During the course of field-work she was joined by Madeline Kerr, a social psychologist from Bedford College, London. 'The object of the Survey was to obtain factual information on family and social life in a selected number of villages.'[12] While Edith Clarke studied the sociological contexts and features of the family organization, Dr Kerr concentrated on the social psychology of Jamaican class and community life, and on the distinctive features of socialization among its rural people. Together these two reports still represent the most com-

[11] Jamaica, *Digest of Statistics, No. 13,* Central Bureau of Statistics (1953), p. 5.

[12] Madeline Kerr, *Personality and Conflict in Jamaica* (Liverpool: Liverpool University Press, 1951), p. xi.

prehensive and detailed account of any West Indian family system yet published; and despite their different orientations, data and emphases, the two studies are remarkably congruent in their major conclusions and in the picture that they separately present.

Several of the most intractable social problems that confront West Indians centre on these conditions and patterns of mating and family life. The complexity of these problems is easily illustrated. For example, in its report the Royal Commission stressed that 'the policy of land settlement to which some West Indian governments are heavily committed depends for its success on the existence of a cohesive family unit';[13] but, as Edith Clarke demonstrates, land ownership often promotes 'cohesive family units', sometimes to an excessive degree. Similar uncertainties apply to public programmes in the fields of health, housing and especially education. Grossly inadequate as are the local school systems in their physical and educational provisions, these deficiencies are magnified by the desultory attendance, and high drop-out rates associated with extensive child dispersal, weak family organization, defective paternity, and other social and economic conditions.[14] As regards the effects of such disturbing familial and educational contexts on the development of stable and well-adjusted adult personalities, Madeline Kerr concludes that the modal personality type of the Jamaican 'lower class' or folk is characterized by deep-set defensive mechanisms and tendencies to shift blame or responsibility for any lapse or misfortune to other persons or to external circumstances —an orientation which clearly minimizes adult learning capacities and reflects childhood experience.[15] In Kerr's view, two of the 'five major social situations giving rise to tension in Jamaica are: (1) dichotomy of concepts over parental roles: (2) lack of patterned learning in child-

[13] *West India Royal Commission Report,* 1945, p. 424.

[14] C. A. Moser, *The Measurement of Levels of Living with Special Reference to Jamaica* (London: H.M.S.O., 1956); Kerr, *op. cit.,* pp. 74–84.

[15] Kerr, *op. cit.,* pp. 115 ff., 165–74.

hood.'[16] Both are directly connected with the modes of family organization and child rearing.

The material difficulties of West Indian economic and social development are thus compounded by instabilities and fluidities in the family organization on which the society depends both for the effective socialization of its young and for the adequate motivation of its adult members to participate vigorously in the social and economic life. These familial conditions affect labour productivity, absenteeism, occupational aspirations, training and performance, attitudes to saving, birth control, and farm development, and to programmes of individual and community self-help, housing, child care, education, and the like.[17] West Indian social and economic development accordingly presupposes adequate scientific study of these basic institutions, in order that programmes of public action to improve living standards, national integration, productivity and the quality of citizenship may be appropriately designed and effective. If the Mass Marriage Movement did little else, it should surely have served to demonstrate this vital need for adequate knowledge of West Indian social conditions in advance of the 'organized campaigns' mounted to remedy or reduce them. Intensive sociological research designed to elucidate the forms, 'causes' and implications of West Indian family organization should thus rank very high on the list of essential steps towards the reconstruction and development of local society; and the very limited and costly advances achieved by various schemes of social development launched during the past twenty years merely demonstrate the fundamental character of this need

[16] Madeline Kerr, "The Study of Personality Deprivation through Projection Tests," *Social and Economic Studies*, Vol. 4, No. 1 (1955), p. 83.

[17] G. E. Cumper, "Two Studies in Jamaican Productivity," *Social and Economic Studies*, Vol. 1, No. 2 (1953); M. G. Smith, "Education and Occupational Choice in Rural Jamaica," *Social and Economic Studies*, Vol. 9, No. 3 (1960); M. G. Smith and C. J. Kruijer, *A Sociological Manual for Extension Workers in the Caribbean* (Jamaica: Extra-Mural Department, University College of the West Indies, 1957).

for scientific knowledge of these social conditions before proceeding with further schemes of this sort.[18]

3

Jamaican family life cannot be adequately understood in isolation. The Jamaican family is merely one of several similar systems which share many common properties of form and history, while differing in consequence of their particular social contexts and internal constitution. Most of these related systems are to be found in the Caribbean, especially among its Creole populations; but systems of similar character and historical derivation are current also among the Negroes of the United States, where they were first subject to careful study and controversial interpretation during the late 1930's and early 1940's. In that initial phase the late Franklin Frazier, who pioneered this enquiry, debated with Melville Herskovits the relative influences of African cultural persistence of New World slavery and *post bellum* socio-economic contexts on the determination and distribution of family forms, especially among the Negroes of the United States.[19]

This debate was essentially directed at problems of social causation and historical derivation. Both Herskovits and Frazier agreed that the Negro family in the U.S.A. and Caribbean was especially distinctive in its high rates of illegitimacy, marital instability and 'maternal' households consisting of a woman and her children, with or without her grandchildren. Herskovits argued that these organizational patterns were of African derivation; and that they

18 See George Cumper, ed., *Social Needs in a Changing Society: Report of the Conference on Social Development in Jamaica,* Council of Voluntary Social Services (Kingston: 1962); *Children of the Caribbean–Their Mental Health Needs: Proceedings of the Second Caribbean Conference for Mental Health* (San Juan, P.R., 1961).

19 E. Franklin Frazier, *The Negro Family in the United States* (Chicago: University of Chicago Press, 1937); Melville J. Herskovits, *The Myth of the Negro Past* (New York: Harpers, 1941), pp. 145–88.

were effects or correlates of practices through which Old World polygyny had been modified and reinterpreted by institutionalized serial matings. Frazier countered this argument by assembling voluminous data on the social history and situation of Negroes in the United States to demonstrate the influence of differing social and economic contexts on their mating and family patterns. For example, among Negro professionals and propertied families in Northern cities of the United States, marriage is the normal basis of family life and illegitimacy is very rare. Conversely, among southern rural immigrants in these cities, 'maternal families' and illegitimacy were common, while marriage rates were relatively low.

Although, like many other scientific controversies, this debate between Frazier and Herskovits was inconclusive, most subsequent students of Negro families in the New World have adopted Frazier's orientations and hypotheses rather than those of Herskovits. Thus, in discussing West Indian family organization, Simey and Fernando Henriques both accept Frazier's thesis that the social and economic conditions of slavery precluded development of stable nuclear families among New World Negroes; and both writers stress that the continuing 'disorganization' of West Indian family life expressed by the high incidence of conjugal turnover, illegitimacy and 'maternal' households, reflect the continuing situation of the West Indian Negroes as an economically and socially depressed class.[20] Both Simey and Henriques however emphasize that in Jamaica and other West Indian societies, 'illegitimacy', maternal families and concubinage or common-law marriage are socially accepted and statistically modal conditions of lower class life.[21] Henriques further distinguishes West Indian family structure from that of the Negroes in the U.S.A. as a natural development of local society and a system with its own

[20] T. S. Simey, *Welfare and Planning in the West Indies* (London: Oxford University Press, 1946), pp. 50–51, 79; Fernando Henriques, *Family and Colour in Jamaica* (London: Eyre and Spottiswoode, 1953), p. 103.

[21] Simey, *op. cit.*, pp. 53, 85–87; Henriques, *op. cit.*, pp. 84–119.

distinctive properties.[22] Both Henriques and Simey emphasize the relations between differences of mating and family organization and differences of socio-economic class; and both writers provide similar typologies of West Indian domestic families in this connection.

For Simey, the four principal 'family' types to be found in West Indian society were as follows: (1) 'Christian' families, defined as 'patriarchal' units based on legal marriage; (2) 'Faithful concubinage', also 'patriarchal' but without legal sanction; (3) 'Companionate' unions or consensual cohabitations of less than three years' duration; and (4) 'Disintegrate' families, consisting of women with their children or grandchildren. Henriques merely renamed the 'disintegrate' family as the 'maternal' or grandmother family and the 'companionate' as the 'keeper' family or union.[23]

Though suggestive, neither of these classifications was grounded on detailed study of the household or conjugal units to which they referred; and although both these familial typologies rested on distinctions of conjugal form and status, neither Henriques nor Simey gave explicit attention to extra-residential mating as a widespread institutional pattern. In brief, these early studies, however illuminating, lack the data essential for an adequate analysis of West Indian mating and family organization.

4

Only in 1956–57 were the first systematic studies of West Indian[24] family systems published, by R. T. Smith on Guianese Negroes and by Edith Clarke on Jamaica respectively. These two studies share numerous common features. Each reports and compares family organization in three selected communities by analyses of detailed censuses of household composition in these areas. Both studies emphasize the influence of current social and economic con-

22 Henriques, *op. cit.*, pp. 103, 111.

23 Simey, *op. cit.*, pp. 82–83; Henriques, *op. cit.*, pp. 105–7.

24 R. T. Smith, *The Negro Family in British Guiana* (London: Routledge & Kegan Paul, 1956).

ditions on the organization and development of household groups; and both seek to 'explain' the observable variety of domestic groups by reference to current social and economic conditions and practices rather than by reference to the past. The two studies also differ in certain fundamental ways, notably in their analytic models and implied or expressed 'explanations', and since these differences have influenced subsequent work, they merit special attention.

R. T. Smith offers an analysis of family life among the Guianese and West Indian 'lower class' Negroes which rests on a series of interconnected propositions. These may be summarized briefly as follows: (1) the household is the natural unit of family organization and its sociological analysis.[25] (2) 'Common-law' unions and legal marriage are sociologically identical, at least in these lowly strata of West Indian society. It is neither necessary nor appropriate to distinguish between them.[26] (3) Children derive nothing of any importance from their fathers, who are marginal and ineffective members of their families of procreation, even when resident. It is indeed indifferent whether these husband-fathers live with their families or not, or even whether their children know them personally.[27] (4) Most or all Negro 'lower-class' households are 'matrifocal' and dominated by women in their combined roles of mother and wife; and this female dominance increases as children grow up and daughters bear other children whose fathers live elsewhere.[28] (5) Most or possibly all households begin as domestic nuclear families and all share a common cyclical pattern of growth, expansion and decay which

[25] *Ibid.*, pp. 51–52, 94–95, 108–13, 146, 257; R. T. Smith, "The Family in the Caribbean," in Vera Rubin, ed., *Caribbean Studies: A Symposium,* Jamaica, Institute of Social and Economic Research, University of the West Indies, 1957, pp. 67–68; R. T. Smith, "Culture and Social Structure in the Caribbean: Some Recent Work on Family and Kinship Studies," pp. 30–34.

[26] R. T. Smith, *The Negro Family in British Guiana,* pp. 97, 167–68, 178–79.

[27] *Ibid.*, pp. 147, 153, but also see p. 258; R. T. Smith, "The Family in the Caribbean," pp. 71–73.

[28] R. T. Smith, *The Negro Family in British Guiana,* pp. 102, 142, 150, 223–24; "The Family in the Caribbean," p. 70.

varies in its phases within fixed limits, but which generally involves a period when its matrifocal character and organization is most pronounced and short matrilines of mother, daughter and daughter's children (Frazier's 'maternal' family) are usually present, with or without resident husbands and sons.[29] (6) Such matrifocality of household organization and the correlative marginality of men as husbands and fathers, is characteristic of low ranking sections in ascriptively stratified societies; these patterns are directly associated with ascriptive stratification, low rates of social mobility, restricted public roles for adult men, and an absence of 'managerial' functions, political responsibilities and status differentiation among them.[30] Thus wherever such rigid, typically racial, status ascription obtains, we should find similar conditions of male marginality in familial contexts and matrifocality in domestic organization, coupled with a single standardized developmental cycle for household groups based on the nuclear family in its initial phase. (7) Only those patterns of sexual association which involve co-residence of the partners merit classification as 'conjugal' unions or direct analysis in the study of family life. This is so because the family involves close and continuous association of its members; it is therefore inherently a domestic unit, and households and families are identical. Hence, men are truly marginal members of families begotten in extra-residential mating.[31]

Thus having eliminated several critical elements of the local family structure by denying their relevance, and having identified the nuclear family as the necessary basis for domestic organization, R. T. Smith has to seek the factors which determine the development and matrifocal qualities of these units in extrinsic conditions of social stratification. In his view the common distinctions between legal and consensual cohabitation, and between legitimate and illegiti-

[29] R. T. Smith, *The Negro Family in British Guiana,* pp. 108–22, 228, 257; "The Family in the Caribbean," pp. 69–71.
[30] R. T. Smith, *The Negro Family in British Guiana,* pp. 142–43, 221, 226–29; "The Family in the Caribbean," pp. 67–75.
[31] R. T. Smith, *The Negro Family in British Guiana,* pp. 51, 108–10, 184–85, 223–24.

mate children are sociologically irrelevant. He likewise excludes extra-residential mating from the category of conjugal union relevant to analysis of these family systems; and finally he dismisses the internal differentiations among these villagers as irrelevant to his analysis, asserting that such differentiations are minimized because they are 'inconsistent with the criteria on which the colonial system of social stratification is based, and to which the inferior stratum *must* normatively subscribe'.[32] Why either of these two latter conclusions should hold is never revealed; and during Smith's field work in British Guiana, both the Negro and East Indian low status sections of the colonial society supported a political movement which he describes as 'truly revolutionary' since it sought to disrupt and discard 'the existing authority system' and explicitly rejected the European domination on which the ascriptive colonial stratification was based.[33]

Later, among the Guianese East Indians who rank beside or below the Negroes on ethnic and occupational grounds, R. T. Smith and his colleague Jayawardena found a distinctive 'Indian' system of status differentiation linked with prevailingly 'patrifocal' family organization, despite status deprivations imposed by the wider society quite as severe as any to which the Negroes were subject.[34] Smith accounts for the patriarchal character of family organization among these low-ranking East Indians by appealing to conditions of ethnicity, cultural autonomy and social separation;[35] but the Negro villages he first studied enjoy very similar conditions of isolation and ethnic homo-

[32] *Ibid.*, pp. 181, 195–96, 210–12, 223; see also pp. 39–47, 191–220.

[33] *Ibid.*, pp. 199–200.

[34] R. T. Smith, "Family Structure and Plantation Systems in the New World," pp. 153–59; "Culture and Social Structure in the Caribbean: Some Recent Work on Family and Kinship Studies," pp. 41–43; R. T. Smith and Jayawardena, "Marriage and the Family Amongst East Indians in British Guiana."

[35] R. T. Smith, "Family Structure and Plantation Systems in the New World," pp. 158–59; "Culture and Social Structure in the Caribbean: Some Recent Work on Family and Kinship Studies," pp. 42–43.

geneity. It is also clear that these villagers are part of a culturally distinct section of Guianese society; and as such they possess some autonomy which, however limited, is imposed on them by their social situation. Under these conditions it would be remarkable if the villagers lacked their own internal system status differentiation.[36] Evidently Smith made little attempt to study this system in detail, or to appreciate its criteria and functions in sustaining the cohesion and solidarity of these 'black people's villages'.[37] Instead he dismisses the villagers' internal differentiations of age and sex as trivial, although his careful tabulations indicate that legal marriage is closely associated with increasing age in both sexes;[38] and it is also evident, despite his attempt to equate them, that marriage is regarded by these Negro villagers as having greater prestige than other forms of mating, and as the appropriate status for men and women of middle or senior age. If so, then marriages late in life can rarely fail to enhance the status and authority of men as 'husband-fathers' within and outside their homes, by simultaneously legitimating their unions and children and by conferring higher status on their wives while achieving corresponding increments themselves through their personal fulfilment of community norms.

Despite such data, R. T. Smith prefers to treat the people's community values and status structure as irrelevant or trivial and to analyse their familial institutions within a 'frame of reference' of the 'total social system' in which, by virtue of their low ascribed status, internal differentiations among these Negro villagers are indeed irrelevant, together with their institutional practice. Thus although 84 per cent of all domestic unions in the three villages studied were based on legal marriage, Guianese élite regard common-law unions as 'exclusively lower-class custom' and as 'part of the lower-class cultural tradition'.[39] From this vantage point, Smith ignored the distinction between

[36] R. T. Smith, *The Negro Family in British Guiana*, pp. 45–46, 89–90, 208, 223; see also pp. 203–20.
[37] *Ibid.*, pp. 183 f., 203–6.
[38] *Ibid.*, pp. 116–19, 178–81.
[39] *Ibid.*, p. 182; see also p. 259.

common-law and legal marriage which his villagers' conduct show that they emphasize.

Such procedures represent a remarkable departure from the standard practice of social anthropologists, whose work repeatedly demonstrated that social analyses which are not based on a thorough and infinite appreciation of folk values, distinctions, conceptions and modes of thought can rarely if ever avoid serious error and misrepresentations of the people's way of life and social organization. Some illustrations of this truism in R. T. Smith's work have already been cited; for example, the arbitrary exclusion of extra-residential mating from the category of conjugal relations on which his analysis of nuclear family organization rests; the unsubstantiated assertion that resident husband-fathers are simultaneously marginal members of their own homes, and undifferentiated members of their local communities; the misleading equations of legal and common-law marriage, household and nuclear family; and the surprising assertions that differences in the closeness, continuity and quality of father-child relations are socially irrelevant, or that these Negro villagers fully accept the low social status ascribed to them and the criteria on which this ascription is based, although they supported a political movement expressly committed to overthrow the colonial social order.

In Grenada, Jamaica, Haiti, Trinidad and in other West Indian societies where ascriptive systems of stratification also employ racial criteria, distinctive status structures have been reported even among the lowliest people in all rural communities where they have been sought.[40] These com-

[40] M. G. Smith, *Stratification in Grenada* (Berkeley and Los Angeles: University of California Press, 1965), pp. 49, 158, 237; *Kinship and Community in Carriacou* (New Haven: Yale University Press, 1962), pp. 59–84; "Community Organization in Rural Jamaica," *Social and Economic Studies,* Vol. 5, No. 3 (1956), pp. 306–9; E. P. G. Seaga, "Parent-Teacher Relations in a Jamaican Village," *Social and Economic Studies,* Vol. 4, No. 3 (1955); M. G. Smith and G. J. Kruijer, *A Sociological Manual for Extension Workers in the Caribbean,* pp. 34–45; Melville J. Herskovits, *Life in a Haitian Valley* (New York: Knopf, 1937), pp. 86–87, 123–35; S. Comhaire-Sylvain, "Courtship, Marriage and *Plasaj* at Kenscoff, Haiti," *Social and Economic Studies,* Vol. 7, No. 4 (1958), pp. 227–32; Remy

munity status systems do not always, or perhaps even usually, involve stratification by 'class', occupation, colour and other variables which are institutionalized in the societal stratification. For this reason, they are all the more distinctive, and repay careful study. Conversely, nowhere in this Caribbean region has any other student found men to be always 'marginal' as husbands and fathers. Nor has anyone observed the close association of nuclear families and household groupings on which the assumption of a uniform developmental cycle for domestic units is based. Instead several scholars have criticized these generalizations on theoretical and empirical grounds alike.[41] For decisive evidence on these topics, one needs look no further than the present text, which systematically demonstrates how differences in the forms of mating relation are associated with differences in men's roles as husbands and fathers, and with differences in their performance. Further, the present book shows how widely communities may differ in the combinations of mating patterns that they institutionalize; and how such differences in community mating systems determine parallel differences in their domestic organizations, as shown by local differences in the incidence of household groups of differing type, in their average size, stability, generation depth and conjugal base.

Bastien, "Haitian Rural Family Organization," *Social and Economic Studies,* Vol. 10, No. 4 (1961), pp. 496, 502; George E. Simpson, "Sexual and Familial Institutions in Northern Haiti," *American Anthropologist,* Vol. 44, No. 4 (1942), pp. 661–63; Melville J. Herskovits and Frances S. Herskovits, *Trinidad Village* (New York: Knopf, 1947), pp. 30–37.

[41] Clarke, *op. cit.,* pp. 28–31, 113; Nancie L. Solien, "Household and Family in the Caribbean," *Social and Economic Studies,* Vol. 9, No. 1 (1960); M. G. Smith, *West Indian Family Structure* (Seattle: University of Washington Press, 1962), pp. 6–11, 20–23, 221–25; Sidney M. Greenfield, "Socio-Economic Factors and Family Form," *Social and Economic Studies,* Vol. 10, No. 1 (1961); W. Davenport, "The Family System in Jamaica," *Social and Economic Studies,* Vol. 10, No. 4 (1961), pp. 452–54; G. E. Cumper, "Household and Occupation in Barbados," *Social and Economic Studies,* Vol. 10, No. 4 (1961), pp. 410–17; K. F. Otterbein, "The Household Composition of the Andros Islanders," *Social and Economic Studies,* Vol. 12, No. 1 (1963), pp. 78–83.

By combining specialized definitions, value judgments, exclusions of relevant data, and by assimilating dissimilar units and relations, R. T. Smith seeks to generalize Frazier's theory of the influence of the depressing social and economic conditions on the family organization of American Negroes to all low-ranking sections of ascriptively stratified societies. As hypothesis or generalization, this formula is only meaningful on the following assumptions: (1) that the members of these disprivileged strata accept the system of values with which the structure of social inequality and their own deprivation is identified as normatively valid; (2) that they lack distinctive status structures for their own internal differentiation which are relevant to the familial roles of men as husbands and fathers; (3) that alternative patterns of mating, parenthood and nuclear family organization current among such people are irrelevant to the constitution and development of their family and household units alike. Unless these three conditions are simultaneously present, the generalization cited above cannot apply.

5

Like other social institutions, family systems have internal and external aspects which are clearly related, though variably so in differing cultures and societies. These family systems may thus be analysed with primary reference to their internal constitution and consistency, or with primary reference to their congruence and articulation with the wider social system in which their adult members participate. However, analyses of this second sort presuppose prior detailed knowledge of the internal organization of the family systems and societies concerned.

As social systems with clearly defined boundaries, family systems consist internally in a variable organization of several distinct modes of social relation, such as mating and affinity, filiation and parenthood, or descent and extended kinship, through which such units as nuclear or extended families, households and conjugal unions are established. Thus to analyse such systems we must examine closely their intrinsic components, that is, the elements and relations that give them their particular qualities and form; and in this task it is necessary to observe carefully all local distinctions between different types of relation whose mutual connections and relative weight constitute the system. In such analyses, mating forms and conditions clearly deserve most meticulous attention, since these relations are prerequisites of parenthood, and affinity and nuclear or extended families alike.

In this regard R. T. Smith's method of family analysis is most instructive. He begins by excluding extra-residential mating, with which the conditions of 'matrifocality' and 'male marginality' are closely linked, and by assimilating legal and 'common-law' unions, although these are clearly distinguished by the community and society alike. In this way, Smith defines conjugal relations exclusively by the criterion of co-residence, though the villagers clearly do not; and on this ground he identifies the formation of household groups with the establishment of nuclear families consisting of couples and their children, whereas many nuclear families are never co-resident, and many households neither begin nor develop on this basis.[42] By the same token, since he denies the conjugal status of the widespread extra-residential form of mating, Smith denies the sociological relevance of paternity in such unions and accordingly interprets the presence of young women and children in their mothers' homes as evidence of familial matrifocality rather than as necessary and inevitable consequences of the mating pattern. Likewise, having identified the formation of household groups with the establishment of nuclear families by his exclusive definitions of conjugal and paternal relations, Smith concludes that a single model of their domestic form and development applies to virtually all these Negro families with limited variation. Indeed, having ignored locally significant differences between the roles of men as fathers and husbands in extra-residential, 'common-law' and legal unions, all must be equally 'marginal' or central to family life; and since most children generally remain with their mothers during and

[42] R. T. Smith, "The Family in the Caribbean," pp. 67–71.

after extra-residential or other types of union, male marginality is rather more evident than the alternative. Thus by eliminating these internal differences of mating form and parenthood, and by ignoring their implications for domestic grouping, Smith is free to seek the 'causes' or correlates of this male marginality in other spheres of the social system which, being non-familial, can only be either communal or societal. Here again, for reasons which are not quite clear, he elects to ignore the external social system of greatest immediacy and significance to the people concerned–their local community–and derives instead the predicated marginality of these Negro men from their uniformly low status in the colonial society. In short R. T. Smith combines a cavalier treatment of the features intrinsic to the family system with major emphases on the decisive influence of extrinsic societal conditions.

In his pioneer studies of American Negro family life, Frazier had tried to combine both planes of analysis, although he also over-emphasized the influence of external conditions and devoted little attention to its intrinsic elements. Since he was mainly concerned to contrast the family organization of plantation slaves and share-croppers in the Deep South with those of rural immigrants and 'black bourgeoisie' in the Northern cities, Frazier's failure to analyse the internal components of these differing structures, and particularly the relations between their patterns of mating and family form and development, escaped general notice; but it was precisely on these grounds that Herskovits challenged the general thesis of socio-economic determination of family form on which Frazier's analysis rested.

Following Frazier, and being unaware of the statistical and structural significance of the extra-residential mating pattern, Simey first sought to interpret West Indian family patterns in terms of economic conditions, 'companionate' and 'faithful' concubinage being associated with low levels of income while 'Christian' marriage was linked with higher income levels, and the 'disintegrate' family was inferentially derived from the two preceding 'lower class' types.[43] In

[43] Simey, *op. cit.*, pp. 80–88.

his turn Henriques, following Simey, noted differing social histories of West Indian and American Negroes and emphasized that West Indian family forms are *sui generis,* natural developments of local society, and not by-products of migration and urbanization such as Frazier had observed in Chicago and New York. However, like Simey, Henriques also failed to isolate the extra-residential mating pattern which Stycos and Back have recently shown to be the most common form of mating and the almost universal practice in early unions among 'lower class' Jamaicans. Accordingly, like Frazier and Simey, Henriques had to seek explanations for the prevalence of 'grandmother' or 'disintegrate' families in extra-familial social conditions. Like Simey too, he distinguished between stable and unstable consensual cohabitations on the one hand, and Christian marriage on the other, primarily by reference to differences of economic situation.[44] The 'grandmother' family was again derived from unstable 'keeper' unions, at least by inference. However, once we recognize the prevalence of extra-residential mating, especially during the early years of adult life, its pivotal significance for the organization and development of elementary and domestic families alike is immediately evident; and these earlier attempts to 'explain' West Indian family forms and their variations by reference to extrinsic economic and societal conditions lose their relevance and validity until the effects of these inner components have been clearly identified.

As an elementary rule of sociological method, it is always first essential to examine the interrelations, requisites and implications of elements intrinsic to any social system, family or other, in order to determine its structure and conditions of change or self-perpetuation, before seeking extrinsic determinants. By ignoring these intrinsic components and their integration within the family system, and seeking instead their determinants, requisites, or correlates in external social spheres, R. T. Smith combined an over-simple model of Guianese Negro family organization with a premature and misleading explanation which substitutes the societal stratification for earlier emphases on eco-

[44] Henriques, *op. cit.,* pp. 85–87, 103–19.

nomic and social contexts of 'disorganization'. But this 'stratification' theory of the 'matrifocal' West Indian family organization which treats men as marginal husband-fathers, assumes that local differences of conjugal union and paternity are irrelevant, and also ignores local status structures which differentiate people by reference to sex, age, land ownership, conduct, marital and familial status and by locally relevant occupational and economic differences. Such an interpretation depends for its value on the demonstrable validity of the various assumptions, value-judgments and exclusions of data on which it rests. Instead of seeking 'explanations' of institutional systems in the remoter conditions of their social context, we must first attend meticulously to the specific distinctions, relations, and forms institutionalized within them, to determine the limits, degrees and conditions of their closure as self-perpetuating bodies of custom, and so to identify their extrinsic requisites and susceptibilities.

Indeed, by its careful analyses of household composition in relation to the mating status of household principals and the fragmentation of nuclear families within and beyond them [*My Mother Who Fathered Me*], conclusively indicates the deficiency of those attempts to 'explain' West Indian family patterns which assert the influence of extrinsic conditions on grossly oversimplified models of them. Whereas R. T. Smith chose to interpret West Indian family organization, kinship and mating from the perspective of the household group, and to interpret the community differentiation from the perspective of the colonial society, Edith Clarke shows how alternative types of mating relation influence the constitution and stability of household groups, and how differences in the organization and character of local communities are associated with significant differences in their patterns of family organization.

6

One of the major contributions of *My Mother Who Fathered Me* is to demonstrate the influence that community organization and ethos have on local patterns of family life.

Such community variations show how misleading it is to assume an undifferentiated and uniform pattern of family organization among the Creole 'lower class' which may be analysed without further qualification, as R. T. Smith, following Simey and Henriques, seeks to do. Careful comparisons of varying community patterns of family organization also show that simple economic differences are not themselves evident 'determinants'. Thus, despite its higher level of average income, Sugartown, for obvious reasons, has a lower ratio of domestic nuclear families and higher rates of individual isolation and marital instability than Mocca; and despite their differences of wealth and status, 'Mocca and Orange Grove, in their different ways, are integrated societies in which kinship plays an important role, whereas Sugartown is . . . a conglomerate of disparate sections, held together only by common involvement in a sugar estate'.[45] In Mocca, despite its 'extreme poverty'[46] 'where the conjugal pattern is concubinage for life, the family is all-important',[47] and 'the pattern of descent is predominantly patriarchal'.[48] In Orange Grove, marriage is 'part of the class structure and is reinforced with strong social sanctions'.[49] By contrast, 'there was no adult pattern of male conjugal or paternal responsibility' in Sugartown. 'It is to Orange Grove and Mocca that we have to turn to find examples of fathers lavishing care and affection on their children and carrying out conjugal and paternal duties.'[50]

The typical basis and form of cohabitation, the modal size, composition and stability of household groups, the differing modes of paternity and their statistical distribution, and the quality, range and density of family relations, all vary directly with differences in the composition, character and cohesion of the communities concerned. Clearly the 'integrated societies' of Mocca and Orange Grove possess dis-

[45] Clarke, *op. cit.*, p. 182.
[46] *Ibid.*, p. 26.
[47] *Ibid.*, p. 92.
[48] *Ibid.*, p. 62.
[49] *Ibid.*, p. 27.
[50] *Ibid.*, p. 98; see also p. 82.

tinctive status structures which are normatively effective in regulating individual conduct at the familial and community levels. At Orange Grove this status system takes the familiar form of internal class divisions which, however insignificant at the national level, are locally influential and reinforce male responsibility and authority in conjugal and paternal roles. At Mocca, our data indicate that status allocations rest primarily on criteria of sex, age and familial position; thus while one-third of the Mocca girls aged between 15 and 19 marry—presumably for religious reasons and to men some years older than themselves—'concubinage increases rapidly in the next ten years until it reaches . . . 61 per cent for the 25–29 age-group, marriages decrease in the same period, but climb again between 30 and 40, until at 35 the entire population is living in a conjugal union, fairly evenly balanced between marriage and concubinage'.[51] Such data indicate that while cohabitation in legal or common-law unions is prescribed for adults in their mid-thirties at Mocca, among younger people, mating is modally extra-residential. As age increases, so do the ratios of married and consensually cohabiting couples whose nubile daughters are beginning to bear children in their parents' homes through early extra-residential liaisons. Among Grenadian and Jamaican peasants this customary prescription of alternative conjugal forms as appropriate or inappropriate at successive phases of the adult life cycle has a similar character and supports very similar family structures at both the domestic and extra-domestic levels. By contrast, in the Grenadian and Jamaican towns of Kingston and Grenville, conditions very similar to those at Sugartown prevail, consequent on the disruption of this peasant mating sequence by proletarianization, migration and exposure to élite pressures and stimuli.[52] For Jamaica the independent enquiries of Stycos and Back have recently confirmed these general findings.[53] A careful reading will reveal that these recent advances in our knowledge have their foundation in the present book.

[51] *Ibid.*, p. 115.
[52] M. G. Smith, *West Indian Family Structure*, pp. 198–242.
[53] Stycos and Back, *op. cit.*, pp. 318–41.

Briefly and schematically, among the West Indian Creole folk or 'lower class', young people typically begin their mating career with extra-residential relations of varying duration and publicity. According to folk tradition these unions should receive the consent of the girl's parents;[54] but often they are clandestine. Particular unions may or may not lead to childbirth or to consensual or legal cohabitation; but when sanctioned by parental approval and public recognition, these extra-residential relations provide an adequate institutional context for the young couple's mating. They also ensure in advance acknowledgment of paternity for any children begotten in these relations. During such mating the young girl normally remains in her parental home until such time as she has achieved her 'womanship' by bearing one or two children. Normally she will then be willing to set up a joint household with her current mate; and if their union later breaks down, she returns to her former home until she finds another. Most successive matings begin as extra-residential liaisons, but in each later union the interval between the initiation of mating and of cohabitation typically decreases; and by their thirtieth year most women are living in conditional but often stable consensual cohabitation (concubinage) with a man and their common children. At this stage, unless their union is childless, the couple's children by previous matings are usually dispersed in other homes, typically with the children's maternal kin, lineal or collateral.

Such consensual cohabitations face three possible courses of development: disruption by desertion, conjugal disagreements or widowhood; conversion into legal mar-

[54] Clarke, *op. cit.*, pp. 104–5; M. G. Smith, *Kinship and Community in Carriacou*, pp. 105–16, 221–26; *Dark Puritan: The Life and Work of Norman Paul* (Jamaica: University College of the West Indies, Extra-Mural Department, 1963), pp. 34–35; *West Indian Family Structure*, p. 251; K. F. Otterbein, "The Courtship and Mating System of the Andros Islanders," *Social and Economic Studies*, Vol. 13, No. 2 (1964); Greenfield, *op. cit.;* Davenport, *op. cit.;* Comhaire-Sylvain, *op. cit.;* Bastien, *op. cit.;* M. Herskovits and F. Herskovits, *op. cit.*, pp. 81–86.

riage; or persistence without formal change until widowhood occurs. At Mocca, and in those communities which Stycos and Back designate as the 'Jamaican foothills', for example, in the parishes of St Catherine and coastal St Thomas, consensual cohabitations are prevalent and often lifelong, while marriage is statistically marginal.[55] However, in most peasant communities of Jamaica, marriage is prescribed as the appropriate form of cohabitation for women in their forties, and few women remain in consensual cohabitation as 'common-law' wives past their 54th year.[56]

The serial distribution of these alternative mating forms as normatively appropriate or inappropriate at successive phases of the adult life cycle is inevitably identical for both sexes, except that men typically begin their mating careers rather later than girls, are typically some 5 years older than their current partners, and generally die first, leaving their legal or consensual widows with or without children and kin at home.

Ideally in those peasant systems that institutionalize all three conjugal alternatives, a young couple may convert their relation from visiting to consensual cohabitation and so to marriage at their own discretion. Alternatively a young girl may marry one of her earliest suitors, who is then generally several years her senior. Both possibilities are rarely realized, and as a rule adults of either sex move through these successive phases of their mating careers by unions of varying form, length and fertility. Some women never cohabit, but maintain visiting relations with a succession of men whose children they bear, as for example in the case of Nesta described below.[57] For various reasons, this type of adaptation is also relatively rare. So are reversions from marriage to 'common-law' cohabitations, which are strongly disapproved in settled peasant communities whose age-graded status structure ensures elders

[55] Clarke, *op. cit.*, pp. 82, 121–23; Francis, *op. cit.*, Ch. 5, pp. 7–11; Stycos and Back, *op. cit.*, pp. 327–30.

[56] M. G. Smith, *West Indian Family Structure*, Table 7, p. 147.

[57] Clarke, *op. cit.*, pp. 58–59, 103, diagram p. 72.

the immunities required to act as spokesmen for the local mores. Thus, as individuals increase in age, social maturity, parental responsibilities and local prominence, they are normally constrained by individual and social conditions to convert their non-domiciliary liaisons into stable consensual cohabitation, and in most peasant communities of Jamaica and Grenada, to convert these 'common-law' unions into marriage during middle or late middle age, marriage being institutionalized as the appropriate mating status for senior members of the community.

In rural and urban proletariats this serial order by which these alternative mating forms are integrated with advancing social maturity in the individual life cycle has limited validity, though many rural immigrants use it to orient their conduct. In these proletarian contexts, of which Sugartown is an excellent instance, all forms of mating are always simultaneously available to anyone, without normative restriction; and, if my data from Grenville are valid and generally representative, under these conditions marriage lacks finality, and after their desertion, separation or widowhood, men often revert to consensual cohabitation.[58] In such conditions many cohabitations are 'non-purposive', 'companionate' or 'keeper' households in contradistinction to the 'faithful concubinage' characteristic of peasants during and after their thirties. Likewise, in these proletarian contexts, non-domiciliary relations are often casual and promiscuous rather than sexually exclusive and durable. By comparison with settled peasant communities, among these proletariats the proportionate incidence of single-person households is generally higher, together with the ratio of 'denuded' households, especially those consisting of women, their children and/or grandchildren; but, while the ratio of households containing three generations declines, the ratio of households based on cohabitation remains constant at about 40 per cent, although the proportional incidence of marriage falls sharply.[59] In short, increased instability of mating organization in pro-

[58] M. G. Smith, *West Indian Family Structure,* Table 7, p. 114.

[59] *Ibid.,* p. 242.

letarian contexts is associated with increasing fragmentation of nuclear families and with the dispersal of their elements in smaller households of shallower generation depth. It is also associated with a general increase in the diversity and instability of household groupings.

This analysis demonstrates the orderly arrangement of alternative conjugal forms in a series integrated with advancing social maturity and status at successive phases of the individual life cycle in these peasant communities. It serves to show how differences in local systems of mating underlie differences in the domestic and familial organization of these communities; and it also shows how these family structures vary in consequence of differences in the complement, organization and incidence of these conjugal alternatives.[60] For illustrations immediately to hand we need only compare the proportionate distributions of households classified in Appendix 9 by family type and by the conjugal status of their principals at Sugartown, Orange Grove and Mocca. The relevance for studies of marital stability and fertility of these differing community mating structures, which are clearly integrated with the local systems of status allocation, has lately been shown by Stycos and Back.[61]

7

Recently also K. F. Otterbein has attempted to show how imbalances in the adult sex ratios of local populations, produced by movements of men to seek wage employment, 'determine' the 'family systems' of Caribbean communities.[62] To demonstrate this determinism, Otterbein calcu-

[60] M. G. Smith, *Kinship and Community in Carriacou,* pp. 116–22, 189–94, 216–21, 311; *West Indian Family Structure,* pp. 198–265; K. F. Otterbein, "The Courtship and Mating System of the Andros Islanders"; R. T. Smith, "Culture and Social Structure in the Caribbean: Some Recent Work on Family and Kinship Studies," pp. 41–43.

[61] Stycos and Back, *op. cit.*

[62] K. F. Otterbein, "Caribbean Family Organization: A Comparative Analysis," *American Anthropologist,* Vol. 67, No. 1 (1965), pp. 68, 77.

lates correlation coefficients between adult sex ratios on the one hand, and percentages of consensual unions in local cohabitations and of homes with female heads, on the other. Both calculations yield high positive correlations, indicating close associations between the variables concerned; and both are vitiated by unnecessary errors or inappropriateness in the data on which they are based. For example, to derive ratios of homes with female heads in Sugartown, Mocca and Orange Grove, Otterbein selects from Appendix 9 below the percentage ratios of denuded and single-person households classified as 'female', and simply sums them. Thus, although Edith Clarke expressly refrains from classifying domestic groups based on conjugal couples by the sex of their head, Otterbein treats all such households as units having male heads. Likewise he assembles the wrong data on the percentage of consensual unions among cohabiting couples from my survey analyses.[63] However, these errors of data compilation are more easily corrected than the conceptual blunders on which his analysis rests.

Briefly, Otterbein assumes the detailed and uniform constitution of the family system whose 'major determinant' he identifies as imbalances in the adult sex ratio. It is easy to show that this procedure and analysis is empirically and theoretically invalid. For example, in my rural Jamaica sample where the adult sex ratio was virtual parity (1 male: 1.04 females), 30.1 per cent of the households had female heads and 41.2 per cent of all cohabitations were consensual. In Latante and Grenville, Grenada, and in Carriacou, where sex ratios were considerably less equal (1: 1.24, 1: 1.29, and 1: 1.92, respectively) consensual cohabitation accounted for 26.4 per cent, 42 per cent and 8 per cent of all domestic conjugal units.[64]

Otterbein's argument assumes stable ratios of 'single' males and females engaged in extra-residential mating *inter se;* and it also assumes that all other extra-residential

[63] *Ibid.*, p. 72, Table 1; Clarke, *op. cit.*, pp. 205–6, Appendix 9; M. G. Smith, *West Indian Family Structure*, Table 22, p. 242.

[64] *Ibid.*, pp. 226–27, 243.

relations hold between married men and 'single' women, most of whom presumably live in homes with female heads. But clearly the relative incidence of extra-residential matings and cohabitations, whether legal or consensual, is a function of the mating organization rather than of simple shifts in the adult sex ratios. The addition of another 50 men in a population of x adults with a previous surplus of 100 females will leave the percentage ratios of homes with female heads and consensual cohabitation completely unchanged if this male increment is accommodated in extant units, and if they remain celibate, mate extra-residentially, or contract consensual and legal cohabitations in already current proportions. Alternatively, this increment may decrease the ratio of households with female heads if its members establish so many single-person units, as for example at Sugartown where 34 per cent of the households surveyed contained single individuals, 110 men and 41 women.[65] In such a case, this change in the ratio of households with female heads proceeds without any corresponding change in the ratio of consensual unions. The point surely is that increases or decreases in the adult sex ratios depend for their familial effects on the local patterns of mating, kinship and domestic organization which accommodate them and regulate their effects. That a large surplus population of adult women need not entail the presence of any households with female heads whatsoever would be apparent to anyone who has studied an African polygynous society.[66] To say that such African comparisons are irrelevant merely indicates that the 'determination' of West Indian family systems by differential sex ratios presumes the specific patterns it seeks to account for. If West Indian societies institutionalize consensual cohabitation and other modes of mating together with female household headship, these are surely features

[65] Clarke, *op. cit.*, p. 205.

[66] M. G. Smith, *The Economy of Hausa Communities of Zaria* (London: H.M.S.O., 1955), pp. 17–26; Vernon R. Dorjohn, "The Factor of Polygyny in African Demography," in W. R. Bascom and Melville J. Herskovits, eds., *Continuity and Change in African Cultures* (Chicago: University of Chicago Press, 1959), pp. 87–112.

of the social organization rather than simple functions of demographic and economic structures. Consequently shifts in the relative incidence of female household headship or of common law unions represent changes or adjustments of the domestic organization, and may proceed without any changes in the local adult sex ratios.

These demographic factors cannot possibly 'determine' the 'family system'–by which Otterbein evidently means the statistical distribution of certain arbitrarily selected features of the domestic organization–for the obvious reason that family systems and demographic ratios are drawn from quite different levels of social organization. For example, in Carriacou, St Helena, and the Long Bay Cays, Bahamas, the marginal incidence of consensual unions is clearly a function of distinctive kinship and mating structures rather than the 'demographic-economic' variable to which Otterbein appeals.[67] Indeed, his entire argument rests on the cultural prescription that men should own their homes in order to undertake marriage. This institutional prerequisite is said to motivate male migration in search of the necessary money. If so, the resulting disbalances of adult sex ratios are themselves 'determined by' the mating and familial organization whose conditions and variability they are then employed to explain. Otterbein's argument is another illustration of the deficiencies of 'causal' analyses of unfamiliar systems in terms of inappropriate extrinsic variables.

8

Another favourite method for such extrinsic causal analyses involves the interpretation of West Indian family organization by reference to economic conditions. This tra-

[67] Otterbein, "Caribbean Family Organization: A Comparative Analysis," p. 72, Table 1, and p. 78, footnote 2; "The Courtship and Mating System of the Andros Islanders," pp. 282, 299; M. G. Smith, *West Indian Family Structure,* pp. 245–46; R. T. Smith, "Culture and Social Structure in the Caribbean: Some Recent Work on Family and Kinship Studies," p. 42; Roberts and Braithwaite, *op. cit.,* pp. 207 ff.

dition has persisted from Macmillan onwards.[68] In general, these 'economic interpretations' concentrate on 'explaining' the variable incidence of marriage and common-law unions by reference to differences of income and economic situation; and sometimes the present text is cited as evidence of this relation. Certainly Edith Clarke dwells on the economic preconditions and correlates of marriage in contrast to those of concubinage. Thus she says, 'in general marriage is associated with a higher economic status . . . [and] by and large concubinage is an institution of the poor'.[69] But besides stressing the similarities between 'purposive concubinage' and marriage, Edith Clarke insists that the incidence and stability of unions of either type is a function of the community organization; and she observes that 'in Sugartown and Mocca, there is, in fact, no apparent real association of marriage or concubinage with the economic status or class structure'.[70] At Orange Grove 'marriage . . . is part of the class structure'.[71] Elsewhere it 'occurs . . . as a later stage in an association begun in concubinage . . . the seal of a proven conjugal union'.[72]

Other students who have closely investigated the relation between differential mating forms and economic levels have come to similar conclusions.[73] These are most succinctly expressed by Cumper, who concludes a detailed analysis of these relations in Barbados with reservations about the influence of economic conditions on family organization, due to the presence of intervening 'cultural prescriptions'.[74] For Jamaica, Stycos and Back have also

[68] W. M. Macmillan, *Warning from the West Indies* (London: Penguin, 1938), pp. 49–53.

[69] Clarke, *op. cit.,* p. 109.

[70] *Ibid.,* pp. 28, 105.

[71] *Ibid.,* p. 27.

[72] *Ibid.,* p. 84.

[73] R. T. Smith, "Family Structure and Plantation Systems in the New World," pp. 148–60; G. E. Cumper, "The Jamaican Family: Village and Estate," *Social and Economic Studies,* Vol. 7, No. 1 (1958), pp. 76–108; "Household and Occupation in Barbados," *Social and Economic Studies,* Vol. 10, No. 4 (1961), pp. 386–419; Greenfield, *op. cit.;* Davenport, *op. cit.*

[74] Cumper, "Household and Occupation in Barbados," p. 414;

tried to measure the associations of alternative conjugal forms with such variables as age, community type and employment statuses of husband and wife. They find salient differences in the distributions of these conjugal alternatives between women of identical age groups settled in different types of communities; and also between women of differing age groups in the same type of community; but they fail to find any direct evidence of correlations between marriage rates and the 'occupations'–by which they refer mainly to differences between wage and own-account employment–of these women's partners. Such differing incidences of marriage as these writers find in the unions maintained by men of differing 'occupations' are complicated by differences in the average age of these groupings. 'Age is still a most important correlate, marriage increasing and visiting decreasing with age in every instance. The woman's employment status is also important. . . . The occupation of husband is still related, but its relation is neither as pronounced nor as clear-cut as the other two variables.'[75]

These scholars then investigate relations between the marital and employment status of women of different age groups whose 'spouses' are classified as wage or own-account employed. They conclude that, irrespective of the woman's age and of her 'husband's' employment status, marriage is associated with higher rates of female unemployment than other forms of mating; but this conclusion is only borne out by their data for women in their thirties. Among women aged between 15 and 24 years, few legal wives are found among the unemployed; and in the succeeding age-group, 25–29, 'common-law' and legal wives are represented equally among unemployed women. Thus even as regards the women's employment status there is no evident difference between legal and 'common-law' marriage before the 30th year, by which time most women are busy with children and home.

---

see R. T. Smith, "Culture and Social Structure in the Caribbean: Some Recent Work on Family and Kinship Studies," pp. 37–41.

[75] Stycos and Back, *op. cit.*, p. 330, and Table 133 on p. 331.

Stycos and Back also investigate the system of economic support for non-domiciliary mates and for the children of broken unions. They report that over 85 per cent of the 1,359 women in their sample who were engaged in extra-residential mating received economic support from their mates. Excluding their current partners, many women also received external support for their children, generally from their own kin or from the children's fathers; but as the woman's marital status changes from 'single' to consensual and to legal cohabitation, the contributions received from these absent fathers decline, and it seems quite clear that many men contribute little towards their children's care after their conjugal unions have ended. Even so, more than one-third of the current mates of these women, and close to two-thirds of their extra-residential mates over 40 years of age, contributed to the support of 'outside' children. Approximately one-half of all the men aged over 40 with whom these women were mating contributed towards the support of at least some of their children by former unions. Stycos and Back conclude that 'a remarkably consistent picture of adjustments of the family system to the exigencies of the fluid pattern of mating and childbearing emerges, a system in which resources are pooled in order to provide economic and child rearing support for children occurring out of wedlock'.[76]

9

Its normative character and status present yet another important focus of current interest in the study of West Indian marriage and family systems. T. S. Simey and Madeline Kerr both explored this problem in different ways, but perhaps Henriques first expressed the central issues most cogently. He described Jamaica as 'a society in which there is a contradiction as regards conjugal unions between what is legally accepted as the norm for the whole society and what is socially accepted. This contradiction or opposition between legal and social acceptance applies to

[76] *Ibid.*, p. 338; see pp. 332–39.

other institutions as well as the family.'[77] On other grounds also Henriques dismissed the social distinctions between legal (Christian) and 'common-law' marriage as 'official and legal but quite useless sociologically';[78] but although treating stable common-law unions and legal marriages as functional equivalents, he distinguished between the familial and household groupings they identified.

Following Henriques several writers, including Edith Clarke, have documented this thesis of normative dualism and institutional alternatives in mating and family organization of West Indian societies.[79] In general these analyses have confirmed Henriques' observation that among the West Indian 'lower classes' 'the attitude towards legal marriage is ambivalent. . . . Although no social stigma attaches to the unmarried state and "living in sin" is not a term of reproach, marriage is often regarded as an ideal which is not within the woman's reach.'[80]

On these questions among others our most systematic data lie in this text, in chapters 3 and 4. This shows clearly how folk attitudes to marriage and its alternatives vary in the different communities that Edith Clarke studied; and it also shows that while legal marriage ranks above other forms of mating in folk opinion, in some communities, e.g. Sugartown, there is 'no social disapprobation of concubinage nor bias towards marriage'.[81] Although at Orange Grove, 'concubinage is disesteemed', at Mocca 'the conjugal pattern is concubinage for life'.[82]

[77] Henriques, *op. cit.,* p. 106.

[78] *Ibid.,* p. 106; see also pp. 86–89.

[79] Clarke, *op. cit.,* pp. 77–84, 104–5, 108–10, 157–58; M. G. Smith and Kruijer, *op. cit.,* pp. 52–60, 242–50; L. Braithwaite, "Sociology and Demographic Research in the British Caribbean," *Social and Economic Studies,* Vol. 6, No. 4 (1957), pp. 542–45; W. Davenport, "Introduction," in Sidney W. Mintz and W. Davenport, eds., "Caribbean Social Organization," *Social and Economic Studies,* Vol. 10, No. 4 (1961), pp. 383–85; "The Family System of Jamaica," *Social and Economic Studies,* Vol. 10, No. 4 (1961), pp. 425–35; Stycos and Back, *op. cit.,* pp. 99, 122–23.

[80] Henriques, *op. cit.,* p. 107; see also p. 86.

[81] Clarke, *op. cit.,* p. 82.

[82] *Ibid.,* p. 92.

Nonetheless, though these communities differ in the norms that they institutionalize and in the weight and sanctions that they attach to their observance, in all areas 'sexual exclusiveness is the ideal mode of behaviour, whether in marriage or concubinage'.[83] In extra-residential relations women are also required to remain faithful to their partners; and it is by reference to these norms of sexual exclusiveness that adultery and unfaithfulness are distinguished from casual or promiscuous intercourse to which no such conditions attach.[84]

That the normative dualism identified by Henriques is not restricted in Jamaica to modes of mating is further evident from Edith Clarke's discussion of family land in Chapter 2, and from the distinction she draws between social and legal legitimacy[85] and between adoption and the rearing of 'schoolchildren'.[86] But many instances of this pervasive normative dualism could be cited from other fields of social life, particularly religion, politics and social stratification.

However, Judith Blake has recently asserted that marriage is the only form of mating which Jamaican women of the 'lower class' approve and desire;[87] and by so doing, she has concentrated current interests in the normative structure and integration of West Indian society directly on the analysis of mating and family norms among West Indian folk. In discussing R. T. Smith's work above we have touched on another aspect of this basic problem.

Blake rests her analysis on replies to questionnaires on attitudes to mating and fertility which were administered to 99 women and 53 men in Jamaica in 1953–54 by a

[83] *Ibid.*, p. 77.

[84] See W. Davenport, "The Family System of Jamaica," pp. 425–35, for a particularly sensitive presentation of these issues and the relevant data.

[85] Clarke, *op. cit.*, p. 30.

[86] *Ibid.*, pp. 174–77.

[87] Judith Blake, "Family Instability and Reproductive Behavior in Jamaica," *Current Research in Human Fertility* (New York: Milbank Memorial Fund, 1955); *Family Structure in Jamaica: The Social Context of Reproduction* (Glencoe, Illinois: The Free Press, 1961).

staff of 'trained' interviewers drawn from the local 'middle class'. The appropriateness of her sample and field procedures has already been criticized;[88] but her conclusions are also suspect on other grounds. Briefly, Blake's thesis is that Jamaican 'lower class' women regard legal marriage as a norm and disapprove morally of illegitimacy and extra-legal mating in all its forms. As evidence, she cites her questionnaire responses which indicate the women's expressed preferences and attitudes; and she refers to the familiar increases in the ratios of married persons as age advances.[89]

To account for the grave divergences between actual behaviour and expressed preference or 'norm'—an inference or equation for which Braithwaite properly criticized her[90]—Blake relies on two major arguments, both supported by her questionnaire replies. First she tries to show that young Jamaican girls become pregnant in their early liaisons through innocence and ignorance about sex, in consequence of their inadequate and misguided socialization and their exploitation by philandering males.[91] Secondly she argues that in consequence of these early errors, 'the bargaining position' of these unmarried mothers deteriorates 'in the courtship market',[92] since no men want to marry such women and to bring up other men's children. The woman is thus driven by economic need and by her expressed desires for marriage into a further series of extra-marital unions of visiting or co-residential types, in each of which she willingly risks further pregnancies in

[88] Braithwaite, *op. cit.*, pp. 541–51; R. T. Smith, Review of J. Blake, "Family Structure in Jamaica," *American Anthropologist,* Vol. 65, No. 1 (1963), pp. 158–61; Hyman Rodman, "On Understanding Lower Class Behavior," *Social and Economic Studies,* Vol. 8, No. 4 (1959), pp. 441–50; see also Judith Blake, "A Reply to Mr. Braithwaite," *Social and Economic Studies,* Vol. 7, No. 4 (1958), pp. 234–37.

[89] Blake, *Family Structure in Jamaica,* pp. 110–11, 133, 170–71, 180.

[90] Braithwaite, *op. cit.*, pp. 541–45; see also Rodman, *op. cit.*, pp. 444–49.

[91] Blake, *Family Structure in Jamaica,* pp. 51–52, 56–57, 76–109, 135, 146.

[92] *Ibid.*, pp. 134–35, 142–43, 146–48, 160, 168.

the hope of 'cementing' the current union and 'earning' its conversion into marriage.[93] These are the two basic arguments by which Blake seeks to account for the observable gap between women's expressed 'ideals' or norms and their actual conduct.

Though these Jamaican lower-class women are said to express active discontent and hostility to extra-legal associations and to the bearing of illegitimate children, we are informed–somewhat inconsistently–that whereas these women put the 'median ideal age' of marriage at 20 years, they put the 'median ideal age' of their first union–defined by Blake as any association involving sexual contact from rape to lifelong marriage–at 18.4 years; and that in fact half of them began mating during or before their sixteenth year, the median age of first union for Blake's sample being 17.0 and of (actual) marriage 25.6.[94] Thus to adopt Blake's method of reasoning, these women clearly distinguish sexual intercourse (unions) and marriage at both the ideal and behavioural levels. Instead of identifying, they segregate them, and apparently they regard premarital intercourse as a normatively indispensable prerequisite for marriage. Under such conditions, granted the virtual absence of any attempts to prevent conception, their premarital pregnancies seem inevitable, and it is thus pointless to attempt to transfer the responsibility for these developments to licentious males or to inept and restrictive parents, as Blake tries to do. In short, Blake's questionnaire responses themselves reveal the normative dualism she seeks to disprove.

Moreover, both the arguments by which Blake seeks to accommodate the evident discrepancies between these women's expressed 'norms' and actual behaviour are controverted by the data furnished by Stycos and Back. These writers show that only one-half of the women in their much larger sample became pregnant during their first unions, which they carefully define as 'sexual association

[93] *Ibid.*, pp. 134–35, 146–69.

[94] *Ibid.*, on unions, see pp. 14 footnote, 50–51, 135; on median and actual ideal ages of marriage and first intercourse, see pp. 45–47, 50–51, 135.

lasting for more than 3 months', thereby excluding casual liaisons.[95] Even so, very few of these women entered their second union in marriage. Accordingly it appears that these young girls are not entirely the victims of innocence and ignorance, male exploitation and parental folly, as Blake would have us believe; and this, coupled with their expressed desires for premarital intercourse, disposes of her argument from 'ruined innocence'.

Furthermore Stycos and Back conclusively show that in Jamaica the chances of lower-class women securing marriage on entering each successive union are unaffected by the presence or absence of children by previous unions.[96] This finding disposes of Blake's second assumption, and her supplementary argument of the 'deteriorating bargaining position' of unwed mothers by showing that in the local 'courtship market' this condition is irrelevant for marriage. Indeed, if Jamaican men prefer to seduce and abandon virgins, and refuse to marry unmarried mothers, it is difficult to see how anyone ever got married in the island at all.

There remains the statistical pattern of increases in marriage ratios with increasing age, which Blake cites in support of her thesis that women are normatively committed to marriage as the *only* morally appropriate basis for reproduction and family life. In doing so she commits precisely the same methodological sins of which she accuses Simey, Henriques and others,[97] but more grossly. W. J. Goode, who employs the same argument, at least commits no overt inconsistency in the process.[98]

Clearly Blake's elaborate argumentation rests on serious misconceptions of the meanings of 'family' and 'marriage' among her respondents—with whom indeed she had very little, if any, personal contact. As marriage is evidently

[95] Stycos and Back, *op. cit.*, pp. 110, 134–37, 145–46.
[96] *Ibid.*, pp. 345–49.
[97] Blake, *Family Structure in Jamaica,* pp. 19, 110–17, 133, 170–72.
[98] William J. Goode, "Illegitimacy in Caribbean Social Structure," *American Sociological Review,* Vol. 25, No. 1 (1960), pp. 21–30.

neither normatively prerequisite for mating, nor parenthood, and as most couples marry late in life, often after the woman's reproductive career has ended, many married couples lack common children although either partner may have several by previous matings. These simple facts —that 'lower-class' Jamaicans begin mating extramaritally at an early age and typically marry rather late in life after having had several children—should indicate to anyone that the folk conception of marriage differs sharply from that of the local upper classes, for whom it is the essential precondition of procreation and family life—at least in class-endogamous matings. Blake however has chosen to give these folk concepts of 'marriage' and 'legitimacy' their standardized middle-class meanings in American and West Indian middle-class society, thereby creating the false problem of apparent differences between conduct and norms at which she addresses her dialectic in a futile effort to 'prove' that marriage is the only 'norm' recognized by Jamaican women, who are the unwilling victims of social circumstance, forced against their will to mate and bear children outside of wedlock, and thus neither responsible for their actions, nor deviant from their own moral convictions.

This is precisely the pattern of self-vindication which Madeline Kerr identified as distinctively Jamaican and perhaps West Indian; and the administration of Blake's questionnaire which left respondents free to attribute responsibility as they willed, without any objective checks, and to misrepresent or rationalize their attitudes, motivations, goals, experiences and circumstances, provided a perfect opportunity for these women to demonstrate by their vicarious self-exculpations the validity of Madeline Kerr's psychological analysis. It is therefore interesting that throughout her discussion Blake should ignore the much-publicized Mass Marriage Movement which was still under way in Jamaica in 1953 during her visit, and with which her respondents may quite well have confused her questionnaire enquiries, especially because the topics and personnel engaged in both campaigns were strikingly similar. Surely if Jamaican lower-class women were as fervently committed to marriage and as hostile to other forms of union as Blake asserts, this Mass Marriage Movement under militant if misguided leadership, backed by a well-organized Federation of Women with access to ample funds, should not have proved such a dismal failure. But then neither should the 'median ideal ages' of marriage and first sexual intercourse be so sharply separated by these female respondents.

Rodman has stressed the dangers of applying 'middle-class' meanings and assumptions to such common terms as marriage, family, legitimacy and land ownership in sociological studies of West Indian folk.[99] Blake's analysis merely demonstrates the relevance of Rodman's caution. All our data presently go to show that whereas marriage, household and family are often congruent, their association is neither ideally prescribed nor empirically modal among West Indian Creoles of the folk or 'lower class'. Many, perhaps most, individuals and couples throughout Jamaica and other West Indian territories bear and rear children outside of wedlock; and in such Jamaican parishes as St Thomas and St Catherine, rates of consensual cohabitation have remained equally high and stable from 1943 to 1960.[100] On such evidence it is not merely meaningless but misleading to predicate a uniform 'lower-class' regard for marriage as the normative basis for family life. Mocca, described in this book, is a quite representative instance of those communities in which marriage is not prescriptively institutionalized. In urban proletariats and plantation areas such as Sugartown, marriage, despite its high public esteem, can neither be regarded as a local ideal, nor as the binding and morally obligatory rule of conduct which corresponds to the accepted sociological meaning of 'norm'. Among the West Indian upper and middle classes there is no doubt that marriage is normatively requisite in their matings with one another, though

[99] Rodman, *op. cit.*

[100] Jamaica, Department of Statistics, *Population Census, 1960. Some Notes on the Union Status, Marital Status and Number of Children of the Female Population of Jamaica* (Jamaica, 1960), pp. 7–11.

taboo in their matings with the folk; and, with due exceptions, among West Indian peasants in general, marriage is institutionalized as the appropriate personal status and basis for cohabitation during middle or later age. It is thus rather as an essential condition of maturity and social status in these rural communities than as the basis or 'context of social reproduction' that marriage has its decisive and distinctive significance for the West Indian rural folk; but of course, once this is realized the apparent divergence between expressed norms and actual conduct on which Blake and Goode both dwell, simply disappear. There is in fact no contradiction between statements that marriage is preferred or required and participation in premarital unions during early and middle life–provided only that marriage is usually reserved for later years. Likewise there is no contradiction between normative emphases on legitimacy and high illegitimacy ratios in the annual birthrates, provided only that we distinguish as Edith Clarke does, between folk concepts of social legitimacy which require free acknowledgment of paternity, and legitimacy as defined by law and the upper classes.[101] In most West Indian rural communities, marriage is indeed valued as the appropriate status for mature and independent couples of middle or senior years. The unmarried age-mates of these elders lose social status by their failure to fulfil these norms where the community institutionalizes marriage in this way. Thus in these West Indian communities marriage has dual meanings, as a condition of personal status, and as the most esteemed form of mating, though neither the sole nor the obligatory one. Its association with parenthood and the family accordingly varies individually and for couples as an effect of differences in their community situation and in their individual mating careers. In consequence its general equation with 'common-law unions' among these people is a major sociological error, as Edith

[101] Clarke, *op. cit.*, p. 30; Braithwaite, *op. cit.*, p. 542; M. G. Smith and Kruijer, *op. cit.*, p. 54; M. G. Smith, *Kinship and Community in Carriacou,* p. 93; see also Bronislaw Malinowski, *Sex, Culture and Myth* (New York: Harcourt, Brace & World, 1962), p. 63.

Clarke carefully indicates.[102] This is so because the people concerned distinguish these conditions sharply, and invariably ascribe marriage higher status. Moreover, as we have seen, differing communities may institutionalize the alternative patterns of mating in differing ways.

10

In summarizing these recent developments in the study of family organization among the West Indian folk or Creole 'lower class' I have touched on no subject that is not treated concretely and with insight in this book, but perforce I have omitted several topics, such as the dispersion of children, diversity of parental roles and surrogates, differential fertility rates associated with different types of mating, land tenure, and recent changes in family organization associated with urbanization, and increases of social mobility. Several of these topics have been studied by others; but undoubtedly much work remains to be done, especially in the critical areas of social economics, psychology, education, legal reform, fertility control, and in the study of the processes and conditions of socialization begun by Madeline Kerr nearly twenty years ago. In attempting to review these recent developments and advances in this branch of Caribbean sociology, I have dwelt rather on the strictly sociological issues of method and theory, in an attempt to summarize the present state of our knowledge and to indicate recent advances in West Indian family studies by elliptic discussions of certain central themes and controversies. Perhaps there are few other tropical areas in which family organization presents as many academic and practical problems and opportunities as the West Indian area; and perhaps in no other comparable region has the family been studied so extensively over the past decade. Inevitably these later studies have raised new issues and interpretations, some of which have been mentioned here; but they also rest on earlier work; and in

[102] Clarke, *op. cit.*, pp. 29–30, 73–77, 108–9.

this context the present book, which provides the most careful and systematic account of this family system and its principal variations available to us, holds a central position.

SELECTED READINGS

ANDIC, FUAT M., and Mathews, T. G., editors, *The Caribbean in Transition: Papers on Social, Political, and Economic Development,* Proceedings of the Second Caribbean Scholars' Conference, 1964, Río Piedras, Institute of Caribbean Studies, University of Puerto Rico, 1965.

BECKFORD, GEORGE, *The West Indian Banana Industry,* in *Studies in Regional Economic Integration,* Vol. 2, No. 3, Jamaica, Institute of Social and Economic Research, University of the West Indies, 1967.

BENOIST, JEAN, editor, *Les Sociétés Antillaises: études anthropologiques,* Montreal, Department of Anthropology, University of Montreal, 1966.

BLAKE, JUDITH, with Stycos, J. Mayone, and Davis, Kingsley, *Family Structure in Jamaica: The Social Context of Reproduction,* New York, Free Press, 1961.

CLARKE, EDITH, *My Mother Who Fathered Me: A Study of the Family in Three Selected Communities in Jamaica,* 2nd ed., London, George Allen and Unwin, 2nd ed., New York, Humanities Press, 1966.

COMITAS, LAMBROS, *Caribbeana 1900–1965: A Topical Bibliography,* Seattle, University of Washington Press for the Research Institute for the Study of Man, 1968.

CUMPER, GEORGE E., editor, *The Economy of the West Indies,* Jamaica, Institute of Social and Economic Research, University of the West Indies, 1960.

DAVISON, R. B., *Black British: Immigrants to England,* London, Oxford University Press for the Institute of Race Relations, 1966.

DEMAS, WILLIAM G., *The Economics of Development in Small Countries with Special Reference to the Caribbean* (Keith Callard Lectures, Ser. 1), Montreal, Mc-

Gill University Press for the Centre for Developing-Area Studies, 1965.

EDWARDS, DAVID T., *Report on an Economic Study of Small Farming in Jamaica,* Jamaica, Institute of Social and Economic Research, University of the West Indies, 1961.

EISNER, GISELA, *Jamaica, 1830–1930: A Study in Economic Growth,* Manchester, England, Manchester University Press, 1961.

GERBER, STANFORD N., editor, *The Family in the Caribbean,* Proceedings of the First Conference . . . , Río Piedras, Institute of Caribbean Studies, University of Puerto Rico, 1968.

GIRVAN, NORMAN, *The Caribbean Bauxite Industry,* Jamaica, Institute of Social and Economic Research, *Studies in Regional Economic Integration,* Vol. 2, No. 4, University of the West Indies, 1967.

GONZÁLEZ, NANCIE L. SOLIEN, *Black Carib Household Structure: A Study of Migration and Modernization,* Seattle, University of Washington Press, 1969.

GREENFIELD, SIDNEY M., *English Rustics in Black Skin: A Study of Modern Family Forms in a Pre-Industrialized Society,* New Haven, College and University Publishers, 1966.

HAREWOOD, JACK, editor, *Human Resources in the Commonwealth Caribbean* (Report of the Human Resources Seminar, University of the West Indies, Jamaica, August 1970), Trinidad, Institute of Social and Economic Research, University of the West Indies, 1971.

HENRIQUES, FERNANDO, *Family and Colour in Jamaica,* 2nd ed., London, MacGibbon and Kee, 1968; New York, Humanities Press, 1969.

HERSKOVITS, MELVILLE J., *The New World Negro: Selected Papers in Afroamerican Studies,* edited by Frances S. Herskovits, Bloomington, Indiana University Press, 1966.

HERSKOVITS, MELVILLE J., and Herskovits, Frances S., *Rebel Destiny: Among the Bush Negroes of Dutch Guiana,* New York, McGraw-Hill, 1934.

——, *Trinidad Village,* New York, Alfred A. Knopf, 1947.

HOROWITZ, MICHAEL M., *Morne-Paysan: Peasant Village in Martinique,* New York, Holt, Rinehart and Winston, 1967.

LOWENTHAL, DAVID, *West Indian Societies,* London and

New York, Oxford University Press for the Institute of Race Relations, in collaboration with the American Geographical Society, 1972.

MATHEWS, T. G., et al., *Politics and Economics in the Caribbean* (Special Study No. 3), Río Piedras, Institute of Caribbean Studies and the University of Puerto Rico, 1966 (2nd rev. ed., Special Study No. 8, 1971).

MATTHEWS, DOM BASIL, *Crisis of the West Indian Family: A Sample Study,* Jamaica, Extra-Mural Department, University College of the West Indies, 1953.

MCINTYRE, A., and Watson, B., *Studies in Foreign Investment in the Commonwealth Caribbean: No. 1 Trinidad and Tobago,* Jamaica, Institute of Social and Economic Research, University of the West Indies, 1970.

MINTZ, SIDNEY W., and Davenport, William, editors, *Working Papers in Caribbean Social Organization,* Special issue of *Social and Economic Studies,* Vol. 10, No. 4, Jamaica, 1961.

MORAL, PAUL, *Le paysan haïtien: étude sur la vie rurale en Haïti,* Paris, G. P. Maisonneuve and Larose, 1961.

O'LOUGHLIN, CARLEEN, *Economic and Political Change in the Leeward and Windward Islands,* New Haven, Yale University Press, 1968.

OTTERBEIN, KEITH F., *The Andros Islanders: A Study of Family Organization in the Bahamas,* Lawrence, University of Kansas Press, 1966.

PEACH, CERI, *West Indian Migration to Britain: A Social Geography*, London, Oxford University Press for the Institute of Race Relations, 1968.

RIVIÈRE, P. G., *Marriage Among the Trio: A Principle of Social Organisation,* Oxford, Clarendon Press, 1969.

RODMAN, HYMAN, *Lower-Class Families: The Culture of Poverty in Negro Trinidad,* New York, Oxford University Press, 1971.

RUBIN, VERA, editor, *Caribbean Studies: A Symposium,* Jamaica, Institute of Social and Economic Research, University College of the West Indies and Program for the Study of Man in the Tropics, Columbia University, New York, 1957.

SEGAL, AARON, *The Politics of Caribbean Economic Integration* (Special Study No. 6), Río Piedras, Institute of Caribbean Studies, University of Puerto Rico, 1968.

SIMEY, THOMAS S., *Welfare and Planning in the West Indies,* Oxford, Clarendon Press, 1946.

SMITH, M. G., *Kinship and Community in Carriacou,* New Haven, Yale University Press, 1962.

——, *West Indian Family Structure,* Seattle, University of Washington Press, 1962.

SMITH, RAYMOND T., *The Negro Family in British Guiana,* London, Routledge and Kegan Paul, 1956; New York, Humanities Press, 1956.

SPECKMANN, JOHAN D., *Marriage and Kinship Among the Indians in Surinam,* Assen, Netherlands, Van Gorcum, 1965; New York, Humanities Press, 1965.

STYCOS, J. MAYONE, and Back, Kurt W., *The Control of Human Fertility in Jamaica,* Ithaca, N.Y., Cornell University Press, 1964.

THOMAS, CLIVE Y., *Monetary and Financial Arrangements in a Dependent Monetary Economy: A Study of British Guiana, 1945–1962,* Supplement to *Social and Economic Studies,* Vol. 14, No. 4, December 1965.

THOMPSON, EDGAR T., *The Plantation: A Bibliography* (Social Science Monographs, IV), Washington, D.C., Pan American Union, 1957.

Tourism in the Caribbean: Essays on Problems in Connection with Its Promotion, Assen, Netherlands, Van Gorcum, 1964.

WEST INDIAN PERIODICALS

Cahiers d'Outre-Mer. L'Institut de la France d'Outre-Mer de Bordeaux. Bordeaux, France. Quarterly.

Cahiers du C.E.R.A.G. (Centre d'Études Régionales Antilles-Guyane). Fort-de-France, Martinique. Irregular (about three a year).

Caribbean Quarterly. University of the West Indies, Extra-Mural Department. Kingston, Jamaica, and Port-of-Spain, Trinidad. Quarterly.

Caribbean Studies. Institute of Caribbean Studies, University of Puerto Rico, Río Piedras, Puerto Rico. Quarterly.

New World Quarterly. Georgetown, Guyana, and Kingston, Jamaica. Irregular.

Nieuwe West-Indische Gids. The Hague. Three per year.

Social and Economic Studies. University of the West Indies. Institute of Social and Economic Research. Kingston, Jamaica. Quarterly.

INDEX